This Torrent of Indians ———

PART of NOR

0 60 120
English Miles

North CARO.

od Pasture Ground

AM

ERICA

Cuttambas

Waterees R. Waxsaws

NORTH CARO.

Watries

Iron
Mine

Charakeys
30 vill.

Charakeys
10 villages

Saluda Desert

Congeres

An English
Corp.

Charakey's Mt

Savana R.

Apalatchas

Edistow

Colleto

pala che Mountains

AZILIA

Tohogaleas

Apa

Granv

Co

SOUTH

Pollachuchlaw

Flint R.

Ockfaskes

Westras

Cowetas

Addasles

Oconery's

Howgeche

Golde

Islands

Ta llabutes

Chattahuces

Baskegas

Sowagles

Collames

Cheh

Eurches

ams

Counelias

Allatamatha R.

Yellow R.

CARO

Gowalega

LINA

King Charles y II Granted to y
Carolina

Present Proprietors of
in 1663

St.Iohans I.

St M

St Fo

St. Maria de Pal
axy D st in 1705

Appalata

FLO

St. Pedro

R.St Pedro

Alachua

Attuchuco

Assilla

St. Francisco

St Au
gustin
Mona's
tery

Fort St.
to Spa

R.de Vasti

St. Martin

RIDA

Nughella

of the GULF

MEXICO

The South Bounds of Carolina

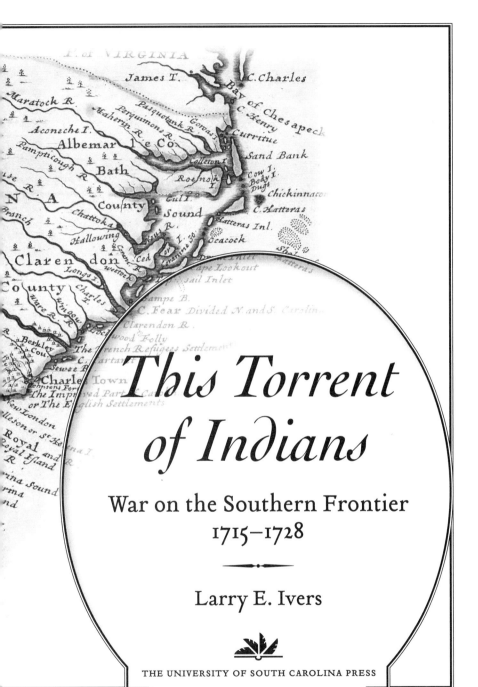

This Torrent
of Indians

War on the Southern Frontier
1715–1728

Larry E. Ivers

THE UNIVERSITY OF SOUTH CAROLINA PRESS

© 2016 University of South Carolina

Published by the University of South Carolina Press
Columbia, South Carolina 29208

www.sc.edu/uscpress

Manufactured in the United States of America

25 24 23 22 21 20 19 18 17 16
10 9 8 7 6 5 4 3 2 1

Library of Congress Cataloging-in-Publication Data
can be found at http://catalog.loc.gov/.

ISBN: 978-1-61117-605-6 (hardcover)
ISBN: 978-1-61117-606-3 (paperback)
ISBN: 978-1-61117-607-0 (ebook)

This book was printed on recycled paper with
30 percent postconsumer waste content.

Contents ───

List of Illustrations and Maps ⸺

Illustrations

Maps

Preface ——

This is a study of the frontier war waged by the Yamasees, Creeks, Catawbas, and several other Indian groups of southeastern North America
against the British colony of South Carolina during 1715–28. The conflict is
commonly known as the Yamasee War. The purpose of this work is to fill
a void that exists in the history of the war. The intent is to provide a detailed narrative and an analysis of military operations, introduce the an-
tagonists' principal characters, and discuss the organization, equipment,
and tactics of South Carolinians and Indians. Such a study was beyond the
scope and intent of the excellent studies of the war that have been previously published.

The mainstays of research for this study were original documents, letters, and maps. I am grateful to all of the libraries and archives that have
been so helpful to me during the past forty years. During service with the
United States Army, I spent many weekends and vacations in South Carolina at the Department of Archives in Columbia and in the South Carolina Historical Society Library in Charleston. I also spent some time at
the Georgia Department of Archives and the Georgia Surveyor General
Department mining their resources. Many trips were made by my family
and me on the back roads of South Carolina, Georgia, and Florida visiting
old forts and battle sites. Over the ensuing years, I have continued to visit
the Southeast to conduct research and explore the terrain involved in the
war. I have often used the resources of the University of Iowa and Iowa
Historical Society libraries. Libraries across the United States provided
rare works via the interlibrary loan service through the Public Library
of Eagle Grove, Iowa. John E. Worth, an expert regarding the Yamasees
and certain other southeastern Indians, generously gave me critical items
of his research from Spanish archives. Nathan Gordon, a graduate student at the University of Colorado, kindly helped me by translating early

eighteenth-century Spanish letters. My wife, Kristin, deserves special thanks for being tolerant of my research and terrain explorations and for giving me constructive criticism of this work. Lynne Parker used her graphic-design skills to prepare the maps. I am especially indebted to my editor, Alexander Moore, a historian in his own right, who made timely and astute suggestions and patiently instructed me in twenty-first-century publication techniques and requirements.

While evaluating research materials and studying the relevant terrain, I relied a great deal on my own experience. For more than a decade I trained as an infantry soldier, served as an instructor in the Army Ranger School, and fought alongside South Vietnamese provincial troops during primitive combat in the Mekong Delta. Those experiences provided insights into the tactics, techniques, and psychological effects of combat actions like those that occurred in South Carolina, Florida, and present-day Georgia three centuries ago.

The text of this work locates forts, plantations, battles sites, and Indian towns in relation to present-day counties, towns, highways, and streams. Therefore events in the text can be followed by referring to detailed present-day maps of South Carolina, Georgia, and Florida.

During the early eighteenth century, Spain and much of Europe used the modern Gregorian calendar. Great Britain and its colonies used the old Julian calendar. To avoid confusion, dates in the text and notes are cited according to the Julian calendar. Under the Julian calendar, the new year began on March 25 rather than January 1 and was eleven days behind the Gregorian calendar.

For consistency I refer to European Americans as white, African Americans as black, and Native Americans as Indians. I believe that using the term *group* is more accurate than the term *tribe* when classifying southeastern Indians. I apologize to anyone whom these characterizations may offend. It has been my goal to avoid showing favoritism or allegiance to any culture. That is obviously a difficult task, especially when interpreting three-hundred-year-old records. I have given it my best effort based on my education and my experience as a farm boy, soldier, and country lawyer.

—— CHAPTER I ——

Warnings of War,
April 10–14, 1715

On Sunday, April 10, 1715, two South Carolinians, Samuel Warner and William Bray, saddled their horses in preparation for a long, difficult ride to Charles Town, present-day Charleston. They were in the Upper Yamasee Indian town of Pocotaligo on the mainland of southwestern South Carolina. The town was located about 13.5 miles northwest of the present-day city of Beaufort. Both men were in a hurry. Their lives and the lives of their fellow South Carolinians were in danger. Several prominent Yamasees and men from other Indian groups had recently conferred in Pocotaligo and debated whether to declare war on South Carolina. The Yamasees had already completed their war-making ritual. Warner and Bray crossed the adjacent Pocotaligo River to the east, probably in a dugout canoe, while their horses swam behind or alongside. They rode north and then east for about a dozen miles, across the head of swamps and through savannahs. Their route lay along an unimproved dirt path, through the Yamasee reservation, commonly known as the Indian Land. They crossed the Combahee River on Joseph Bryan's Ferry and rode east into Colleton County.[1]

Samuel Warner was an Indian trader. He sold British guns, ammunition, iron tools, and cloth to the Yamasees and to the nearby Lower Creek Indians of Palachacola. Warner seems to have been an honest man; there are no records of any Indian complaints against his trading practices. While he was in Palachacola during early April, some warriors informed him that they were distressed because of the abuse and threats meted out by their white traders. They were angry with the government of South Carolina for its refusal to discipline the traders. They vowed that they and other Lower Creeks would kill the traders and go to war the next time a trader offended them.[2]

William Bray was an Indian trader to the Yamasees. He sometimes served as an interpreter for the South Carolina Indian commissioners. The Indians had made several complaints against him. One complaint involved his sale of a free Indian woman and her child into slavery, probably to collect payment for debts owed by her husband. Nevertheless an Indian, called Cuffy by South Carolinians, was his friend. Cuffy resided in the Yamasee town of Euhaw. During the first week in April, Cuffy visited his wife, Phillis, and daughter, Hannah, who were Indian slaves owned by Landgrave Edmund Bellinger. They may have resided on Bellinger's Ashepoo Barony, located west of the conflux of the Ashepoo River and Horseshoe Creek in Colleton County. Either before or after his visit, Cuffy took a side trip to Bray's plantation. He met with Bray's wife and informed her that the Lower Creek Indians, most of whose towns were located to the west in present-day Butts County, Georgia, were planning to kill their traders and attack South Carolina's plantations. When Bray returned home, his wife warned him of the threat.[3]

Warner and Bray may have initially questioned the seriousness of the information. However, on April 10, several angry and troubled Yamasee headmen and warriors approached them. The Indians complained regarding the conduct of the white traders who served their towns. Some traders were threatening to seize all of the Yamasees' families and sell them into slavery as payment for the warriors' trading debts. Their debts had grown so great as to be unpayable. Based on the traders' past conduct, the threats seemed credible to the Yamasees. They demanded that the South Carolina governor meet with them and redress their grievances. Otherwise, they warned, they would kill the traders and attack the colony. Bray and Warner took the warning seriously and pleaded for time to inform the governor.[4]

The straight-line distance from Pocotaligo to Charles Town is about fifty-five miles. The dirt path that skirted the worst of the cypress swamps, marshes, and boggy savannahs caused the actual distance to increase by several miles. In their haste Bray and Warner would have taken less than two days to reach Charles Town.[5]

After crossing the Combahee River, Warner and Bray went east-northeast over the Combahee Marsh causeway. They passed John Jackson's plantation and entered the widespread frontier cowpens of Colleton County on South Carolina's southwestern frontier. About 120 families resided in two principal locations: on the western side of the county near the head of Chehaw River, now known as the Old Chehaw River, and on the eastern side close to the Edisto River, near present-day Jacksonboro. The riders continued generally east, through the forest of longleaf pine to a bridge over the Ashepoo River south of Horseshoe Creek. They were near the center of Colleton County.[6]

Warner and Bray rode fast, day and night, and would have exhausted their horses. The riders would have exchanged horses, more than once, with the owners or overseers of plantations known as cowpens, most of which were situated near large grass savannahs along the route. They would also have eaten some food, probably at the homes of cowpen owners. The two men may have warned the people living near the path of the impending danger, but there is no indication that anyone took effective precautions. It would have taken more than an unsubstantiated warning of a possible Indian attack to convince people to leave their homes and property.

After crossing the Ashepoo River, Warner and Bray rode north and east to the Edisto River. Much of the land along that portion of the path was cypress swamp. They likely crossed the Edisto on the newly constructed Pon Pon Bridge, close to another of John Jackson's plantations, near present-day Jacksonboro. They left Colleton County and continued east in Berkeley County, present-day Charleston County, on the Charles Town Road. That part of the colony was more thickly settled. The land was mostly oak and hickory forest, and some savannah. Some land had been cleared and was planted in corn and beans. Rice was making its appearance as a cash crop.[7]

The riders crossed two branches of the upper reaches of the Stono River, probably using the bridges near the plantations of James LaRoche and Thomas Elliott. They continued eastward to the Ashley River Ferry. After crossing the Ashley River, they turned south and rode down the Broad Path on the "Neck," or peninsula, toward Charles Town. They probably went directly to the recently constructed governor's home. It was located about 3.75 miles north of the southern tip of present-day Charleston, and about half a mile west of the Cooper River.[8]

Werner and Bray arrived on April 12, 1715, and reported to Gov. Charles Craven (1712–16). The governor called together members of his council and some members of the Board of Commissioners of the Indian Trade. They listened to the reports of the two traders and realized the gravity of the situation. They decided that the governor should meet with the headmen of the Yamasees and Lower Creeks, as soon as possible, and hear their complaints. Letters from the governor were quickly prepared for the

Yamasees in Pocotaligo and the Lower Creek towns of Palachacola and Coweta. The letters informed the headmen that the governor and a military escort were on the way to Savannah Town, also known as Savano Town, on the upper Savannah River. They would meet there and confer with the Indians' representatives. Warner, who was apparently considered the more reliable of the two traders, was given the task of delivering the letters. He was directed to return to Pocotaligo, continue westward to Palachacola, and then ride on to Coweta on Ochese Creek, the present-day Ocmulgee River.[9]

The governor would have provided Warner and Bray with food and replacement horses during their short stay in Charles Town. They began their return ride late Tuesday, April 12, or early the next morning. They arrived, undoubtedly exhausted, in Pocotaligo on Thursday, April 14, and delivered the letters to Thomas Nairne, South Carolina's Indian agent. Nairne read the letters and informed the Yamasees that the governor was en route to Savannah Town with a military escort. They, and the Lower Creeks, were to meet with the governor at that location and present their grievances. The Yamasees seemed content.[10]

—— CHAPTER 2 ——

South Carolinians, April 1715

In 1715 the British colony of South Carolina was forty-five years old. It was a proprietary colony. In theory it was owned and administered by a group of politically influential Englishmen who had received royal charters from King Charles II giving them the authority to organize settlements between Virginia in the north and Florida in the south. They planned to form colonies whose settlers would include a landed gentry and freemen from Great Britain. The colony of Carolina, soon divided into South Carolina and North Carolina, was the result. Few Lords Proprietors of Carolina ever left England to visit their colonies. They occasionally invested funds in the enterprise with the hope of ample profits; however the financial returns were minimal. Over time their relationship with South Carolinians became difficult. South Carolinians were independent, sometimes quarrelsome, and entrepreneurial, which often caused them to be less than cooperative with their absentee landlords. By 1715 the original proprietors were dead, and the second-generation owners had largely lost interest in the enterprise. The governor, his council, and the Commons House of Assembly governed South Carolina with only occasional interference from the proprietors. The proprietors continued to exercise some control, though, especially in regard to the ownership and conveyance of South Carolina real estate.[1]

During early 1715 South Carolina's population was composed of four small groups of people. There are no precise population figures, but the white, mostly Protestant Christian, population totaled approximately six thousand people. Many people, or their parents or grandparents, had immigrated principally from the British Isles and the British colonies in the West Indies. Some commonly referred to their place of origin, rather than

South Carolina, as their home. About 20 percent of the white people were French Huguenot Protestants who had originally fled religious persecution in France. Most of the white people were free persons of various social classes, but some, perhaps two hundred, were indentured servants. They were orphans, convicts, and financially poor of both sexes who agreed to work for South Carolina merchants and planters for an established term of service. Black slaves were owned by free white planters and merchants, and they may have numbered as many as eight thousand people. There were also approximately two thousand Indian slaves, mostly women and children, who had been captured by Indian war parties allied to South Carolina and sold into slavery. Several groups of free Indians, or Settlement Indians, lived in the vicinity of the colony's plantations. Their total population was probably less than one thousand. Thus the entire population of South Carolina in April 1715 was probably about seventeen thousand, less than several present-day South Carolina cities.[2]

South Carolinians were governed by English common law, by several English statutes, and by laws passed by the colonial government. The provincial courts dealt with disputes between individuals and with criminal prosecutions. The only courts in the rural areas were the magistrates' slave courts that dealt with crimes under the slave code. All other courts were in Charles Town. Plaintiffs and defendants had to travel to Charles Town and spend time there while their cases were being considered. The provincial courts included vice-admiralty, common pleas, assize, and general sessions. All of the courts were under the domination of the powerful, but unpopular, Chief Justice Nicholas Trott.[3]

The culture of South Carolinians was patriarchal; inheritance of property and family name passed through the father. Free white men had control of the colony. Most of them could vote, and many could hold public office. Women could do neither. Men were the farmers, merchants, Indian traders, artisans, and militia soldiers. When men married, they normally received ownership of the property owned by their wives. Women gave birth and raised children. They were in charge of their households and did the cooking, food preservation, tailoring and mending, washing, and house cleaning. In prosperous families women had the assistance of household slaves and indentured servants. Women whose families were lower on the economic rung often did their chores and then assisted their husbands' labors. However single women and widows could own property in their own right. Married women could retain any property they owned, if they and their fiancés signed prenuptial agreements prior to marriage. It was possible for a woman whose husband refused to support her to be awarded alimony. A man could bequeath and devise unlimited property to his wife by executing a last will and testament. If he died without leaving a will, and he and his widow had no children, she would receive one-half of his property, and his heirs would receive one-half. If he and his widow had children, she would receive a life estate in one-third of his real estate and would receive ownership of one-third of his personal property. The children received the remainder. Several older widows maintained investments, especially in the business of money lending. Many women exercised the ability to influence their husbands' political and business decisions, either purposefully or inadvertently.[4]

Many planters, merchants, and their families could read and write. Charles Town had a public library. There were several schools that were staffed by male schoolmasters. Many other free whites could probably read and write; however it is doubtful that many indentured servants could, and most of the slaves could not. The manners and decorum of South Carolinians imitated people of similar social and economic classes in Great Britain. Some of the colony's Anglican pastors were impressed with South Carolina polite society, but others believed the people were becoming morally depraved.[5] Rev. Gideon Johnston, an Anglican Church cleric and the Bishop of London's representative in South Carolina, wrote in 1708 that "the People here, generally speaking, are the Vilest race of Men upon the Earth they have neither honour, nor honesty nor Religion enough to entitle them to any tolerable Character, being a perfect Medley or Hotch potch made up of Bank[r]upts, pirates, decayed Libertines, Sectaries and Enthusiasts of all sorts . . . and are the most factious and Seditious people in the whole World."[6] Reverend Johnston was not respected by some South Carolinians. For example, the Commons House refused to grant his application to serve as a commissioner of the Indian trade. Thomas Nairne, an educated, well-traveled soldier, statesman, and planter, disagreed with Johnston in a pamphlet that was published for prospective immigrants. Nairne praised his fellow South Carolinians for being sober, hard-working, intelligent, hospitable, generous, and increasingly religious.[7]

The style of the South Carolinians' clothing was typically British, although the warmer climate probably dictated that lighter garments were preferable. Housing and furniture also adhered to the styles that were found in the British Isles, but locally available building materials were often used. The South Carolinians were reliant largely on many items of British manufacture, including tools, weapons, and cloth, but local industries were beginning to produce many of the colonists' necessities.[8]

The colony was divided into counties, each of which was supposed to have contained roughly 480,000 acres. From north to south, they were located as follows: Craven County occupied both sides of the Santee River; Berkeley County, which contained Charles Town, was the most populous; Colleton County was on the western frontier; and Granville County was a recent designation for an area of coastal islands in the southwest that was commonly known as Port Royal. South Carolinians began a rapid settlement of the frontiers during the period 1700–1715. Plantations were established in each county. It appears that a plantation was established as far south as Saint Catherines Island, on the present-day Georgia coast at a place then called Paycomb's Wells, perhaps on an old Spanish mission site.[9]

During the early eighteenth century, the Society for the Propagation of the Gospel began sending clergy as missionaries to South Carolina. To anticipate their arrival, the colony was divided into nine parishes for religious purposes. The colony's official religion was the Protestant Anglican Church of England. However perhaps one-fifth of the population was French Huguenot, and sizable numbers were dissenters, Protestants of other denominations such as Presbyterian, Congregationalist, and Anabaptist. Tradesmen often served as the dissenters' part-time preachers. Reverend Johnston described the Anabaptist ministers as "Mechanicks." For several years the dissident Protestants suffered political discrimination; however by 1715 they were tolerated. The dissenter congregations, especially the Presbyterian, included several prominent families. About one-fourth of the people on the frontier in Colleton County were dissenters. The Society's missionaries and dissenter pastors spread their religious messages by traveling from one plantation or cowpen to another, but they accomplished little work with Indians and slaves.[10]

Each Anglican Church parish was responsible for the administration of the colony's "Relief of the Poor" law. No welfare would be provided for a person who needed financial assistance if he or she had a close family member who was financially able to assist. Parents, children, grandparents, or grandchildren could be ordered to provide a weekly sustenance to their poor relative. If no suitable relatives were available, the needy person was given a weekly allowance from the parish fund that was maintained through the levy of taxes on real estate and personal property. Poor children were apprenticed to a tradesman until they were of legal age, eighteen years for girls and twenty-one for boys. During Easter week of each year, a public meeting was held in each parish, and the recipients of welfare could be required to attend and explain why they needed assistance.[11] Many refugees would rely on the law during the coming war.

The only urban center in the colony was Charles Town. It was situated on the peninsula between the Cooper and Ashley Rivers where their waters emptied into the Atlantic Ocean. It served as the colony's capital and principal seaport. South Carolina's government also acted as Charles Town's city government. In the early spring of 1715, Charles Town was little more than a village. Its permanent population may have been about two thousand people, including slaves and indentured servants, although there were times—when the Commons House was in session, ships were in port, or the governor held conferences with Indian headmen—that the population considerably increased. Several merchants and prominent planters maintained houses and businesses in or near the town. Some of them illegally increased the size of their lots by encroaching on nearby streets. Although small, Charles Town was a seaport where visiting seamen had access to taverns, called punch houses, and prostitutes. Sidewalks, and perhaps streets, were paved with broken oyster shells. Fire was a constant fear, and preventive measures were taken. Chimneys were required to be made of brick rather than wood, and hay and straw were forbidden to be stored in buildings. There was an ongoing problem with putrid odors from human feces. Householders were directed to maintain tubs in their privy houses and to empty them each week, probably into the harbor, where the tide carried the waste away. Charles Town's drinking water was described as "brackish" by Reverend Johnston, but he said it could be made potable by mixing it with liquor. The town was surrounded by an earthen wall and had batteries of cannons, but a hurricane had battered the town two years earlier, and the fortifications and the cannons' carriages were in disrepair. Each family was required to provide a man to serve periodically on the night watch. Watchmen maintained the peace, were on the lookout for fires, and were prepared to give warning of the approach of an enemy. There had been no serious invasion threat to the town since a failed Spanish-French attempt nine years earlier.[12]

The "lowcountry" was the most heavily settled area of South Carolina. It was the coastal plain, located within a forty-mile radius of Charles Town, where most of the population resided. The lowcountry bordered on the Atlantic Ocean to the southeast. Islands on the coast were separated from the mainland by rivers, creeks, and sounds. Tides rose in height from five to seven feet. The tidal flats had a mud bottom, and oyster beds often covered the muddy banks at the mouth of the rivers. Salty water extended a short distance upstream, producing salt marshes. Fresh tidewater flowed fifteen to thirty miles inland. A dozen rivers that were navigable by shallow-draft boats penetrated the lowcountry. Marshes and cypress

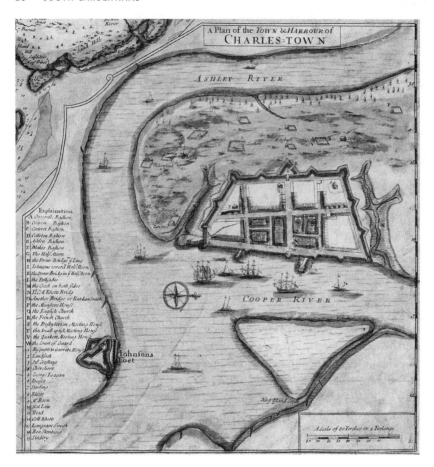

A plan of the Town and Harbor of Charles Town, ca. 1711–28. Inset of Charles Town and vicinity in John Harris, *A Compleat Description of the Province of Carolina in 3 Parts*. London: Edward Crisp, 1711. The fortifications of Charles Town and Fort Johnson are depicted. Courtesy of the South Caroliniana Library, University of South Carolina, Columbia.

swamps bordered the rivers and streams. Pine forest began near the fresh tidewater and extended inland. Grass savannahs occasionally broke up the forests.[13]

The weather in the lowcountry portion of South Carolina was semi-tropical, but it varied with the seasons. The average annual temperature was about 68 degrees Fahrenheit. During December and January, the days were warm, but the nights were cold, with northwest winds sometimes

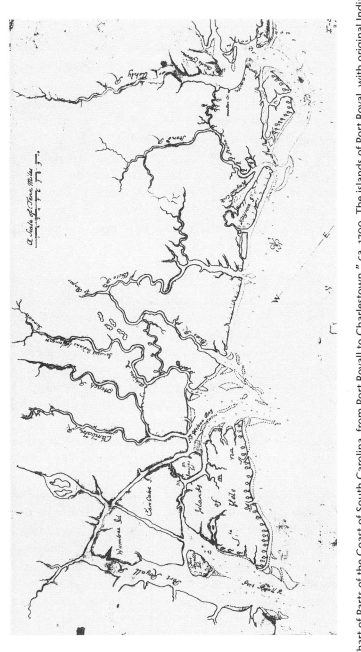

"Chart of Parts of the Coast of South Carolina, from Port Royall to Charlestown," ca. 1700. The islands of Port Royal, with original Indian names, are shown on the left (southwest) portion of the map, and Charles Town is shown on the right (northeast). The location of Yamasee settlements for the period 1685–1700 is shown on the upper Ashepoo River. In *Crown Collection of Photographs of American Maps*, edited by Archer Butler Hulbert (Cleveland: Clark, 1907), series 1, volume 5, plate 31.}

producing frost. Periods of cold weather seldom lasted longer than a few days. The average annual rainfall totaled about forty-eight to fifty-three inches. During winter rain showers that blew in from the south were common. Spring began with frequent showers in April. There were thunderstorms and heavy rains during May through June. Rain also occurred during late July and August, and the summer heat and humidity became oppressive. By then the marshes were overflowing. The fall months were normally pleasant; however the hurricane season lasted from July through November, and South Carolina was often a target.[14]

Promotional pamphlets, which were published to encourage British citizens to settle in South Carolina, depicted the colony as an idyllic place where people lived long and happy lives. Actually at that time the lowcountry was one of the unhealthiest areas in British North America. During those early years, South Carolinians had not yet developed any immunity to subtropical diseases, of which malaria and yellow fever were probably the most dangerous. Those infectious diseases were spread through bites from mosquitoes that lived in the humid swamps. Late summer and fall were the most debilitating times of the year for their victims. Most people seem to have been affected to some degree. Pregnant women and children were particularly susceptible. Other diseases such as dysentery, smallpox, scarlet fever, typhus, and typhoid also took a toll of lives. South Carolina became notorious for its high mortality rate. Few people survived to reach the age of sixty years.[15]

Land routes within the colony were grandiosely styled as roads or highways. They were constructed and maintained by local landowners and were supposed to be at least sixteen feet wide to enable two farm carts to pass one another. Roads seldom measured up to expectations. They were dirt or sand, without a surface of gravel or other material. Roads were often in disrepair and choked with fallen timbers, saplings, and underbrush. The government later acknowledged that the "want of convenient roads" was detrimental to the colony's defense. All roads and paths twisted and turned in an attempt to avoid deep stream crossings, wet marshes, and dense swamps. Streams that were not easily forded were sometimes crossed on ferries, infrequently on wooden bridges, and often in a canoe while the travelers' horses crossed by swimming. Some marshes and swamps were made passable by the construction of earthen and timber causeways. Bridges and ferry boats were built by contractors, and the expense was paid by taxing landowners. Managers were appointed to operate ferries. Passengers were charged fees, which were doubled when the passenger was on horseback. Fees were waived during alarms.[16]

Farmers resided on widely separated farms, called plantations, with their families, employees, and slaves. Plantations were located on tracts of tillable land that had been cleared of forest, and varied in size from large agricultural enterprises to small family farms. The ideal location for a plantation's farmstead, where the buildings were located, was close to a navigable creek or river so that boats could be used for transportation. A typical plantation house was one and one-half stories in height. Construction was usually post and beam on a masonry foundation, with external chimneys of brick. It was sided with wooded clapboards, which were also known as weatherboards. Wood shingles covered a roof of a type that was either peaked (gable) or Dutch (gambrel). A modest plantation house was small, but additions were added as the family grew. Nearby buildings included a kitchen; cabins for employees, servants, and slaves; toilets; a workshop; barn; corn crib; granary; and stable. Thomas Nairne, a prominent South Carolinian, advised new immigrants who intended to become farmers, commonly known as planters, to seek a grant of two hundred acres. He recommended that they furnish the land with two slaves, a few livestock, a small house, necessary hand tools and implements, and provisions to last a year, all of which would cost £100 sterling. To clear land the trees and underbrush were cut, placed in piles, and burned. The tree trunks were left in place to decay, and grain and vegetables were planted between them. Planters were often isolated from their neighbors by uncleared forests, heavily timbered swamps, and grass savannahs. The plantations in the most settled areas of the colony tended to become larger, while small planters often moved to the frontiers and established cattle plantations known as cowpens.[17]

Rice had become the most valuable cash crop, but the grain was also eaten by South Carolinians and the straw fed to livestock. It was raised in the more densely settled portions of the colony. There were two methods of cultivation: open-field planting without irrigation, and planting in swampy fields, or paddies, using fresh water for irrigation. Rice yields varied from thirty to sixty bushels per acre. Harvested rice was cleaned by horse- and ox-drawn mills. Black slaves furnished most of the labor for rice production. They were considered best suited for the hard work required. Rice appears to have been responsible for the growth of the slave population. Perhaps half of South Carolina's black slaves were involved in rice production.[18]

Corn, or maize, was a principal crop. The planter's corn tool was a hoe. During April each year, five or six grains of corn and two or three beans were dropped into a hole in a small earthen mound called a hill.

South Carolina plantation house. A prerenovation depiction of Hanover Plantation House constructed during 1714–16 by French Huguenot Paul de St. Julien, north of Charles Town in Berkeley County. Gun slits in the north foundation indicate the house was prepared to serve as a small fortress. It was probably similar to several South Carolina homes during 1715–28. Such a home could receive additional protection by constructing a log stockade or a wall of boards around the house and nearby outbuildings and placing flankers, or towers, at the corners. The renovated Hanover House is now located on the South Carolina Botanical Garden, Clemson University, Clemson, South Carolina. Photograph by Frances Benjamin Johnston, 1938. Prints and Photographs Division, Library of Congress, Washington, D.C.

Hills were located three to four feet apart and were planted in a straight line. An earthen covering was placed over the hills. After the corn began growing, all except three stalks were pulled out and discarded. The beans grew up, clinging to the remaining cornstalks. Weeds were killed by cutting them out of the ground. During the month of June, excess corn leaves were "suckered," or stripped off. During August the tops of the stalks and the leaves were cut and tied into bundles for use as winter livestock fodder. The corn ears were bent down to prevent water from entering the shuck.

The corn was harvested during October by cutting or pulling the ear, with the shuck attached, from the stalk. The ears were shucked just prior to use. The corn yield averaged eighteen to thirty bushels per acre, and the beans averaged six bushels.[19]

Corn was one of the South Carolinians' standard foods. Cornmeal was baked into small round loaves of bread. Mush was also made from cornmeal. In order to make hominy, kernels of corn were boiled with beans for up to ten hours. Hominy was eaten with milk or butter. South Carolinians, like Indians, also ate roasted green ears of corn during early summer.[20]

Meat from livestock and from wild game was eaten whenever available. Because of the warm climate, excess meat was preserved by smoking, drying, or salting. Various English breeds of sheep were kept. Hogs were small and were usually a rusty color. Many of them ran wild, but bacon hogs were held in pens and fed corn and peaches to fatten them. Pork was considered a delicacy.[21]

The principal agricultural pursuit on the frontiers was cattle. Most plantations in Craven, Colleton, and Granville Counties were isolated cowpens. Cattle were domesticated for meat, milk, and hides. Cattle multiplied fast; even a small planter might own two hundred or more head. A planter's cowpen usually consisted of a farmstead that contained a house, a few outbuildings, and small fields enclosed by rail fences. The remaining asset of a cowpen was several hundred acres of common, or unowned, woods and savannah surrounding the buildings and fenced fields, or pens. Cattle were allowed to run wild in the woods and savannahs, where they grazed on grass and plants. During winter the dead vegetation was burned so that a better crop of grass would grow in the spring. When cows fed on salt marsh grass, the milk and butter had a bitter flavor.[22]

The cowpen planter and his family were assisted by a few slaves or white indentured servants mounted on horseback, who worked as "cattle hunters." A planter's cattle mingled with other peoples' livestock while free ranging, so each spring cattle hunters rounded up their cows and newborn calves and confined them in a pen. The yearlings and calves were branded, either by use of a branding iron or by cutting patterns in the ears. The cows were allowed to range free during the day and graze, while the calves remained in the pens. During fall both cows and calves were released to run free. The pens were used during subsequent years as vegetable plots to take advantage of the fertilizer produced by the cattle manure, and the rail fences protected the crops from grazing cattle. Each fall the cattle hunters rounded up most of the bulls and the wild cattle that had not been branded. Those cattle were butchered, and the beef was salted, placed in barrels, and sold to Charles Town merchants, who shipped it to the West Indies.[23]

South Carolina was a major supplier of naval stores. Tar, pitch, and turpentine were manufactured from longleaf pine trees that grew in the sandy lowcountry and were shipped to Great Britain for use by its navy and merchant fleet. Naval stores became a major industry in 1705, when the British government awarded bounties to producers. Tar was made by burning sap-soaked wood from pine trees and collecting the resulting liquid. Pitch was prepared by boiling tar to concentrate it. Distilling sap from live pine trees produced turpentine. Much of the manufacturing was accomplished between March and November of each year.[24]

Slaves provided much of the agricultural labor. There were four categories of slaves. First were Negro, or black African, slaves. They were considered good workers who were well suited to hard work in the semi-tropical climate. Some were born into slavery in South Carolina or on Britain's Caribbean islands. Other blacks were first-generation slaves, mostly men who had been captured in Africa and shipped to America. During their first year in South Carolina, they had to be closely watched to prevent escapes and suicides. The second category of slaves was the offspring of black mothers and white fathers. They were called mulatoe or mulatto. Third were Indians, most of whom were Indian women and their children who had been captured by Yamasee and Creek war parties. Fourth were Mustizoe, or Mestizo, slaves, usually the offspring of black men and Indian women. Most slaves were field hands, but others were household servants, and some became skilled artisans. Legally slaves were chattel, or personal property, of the owner. Potatoes were the principal food of slaves, and they also ate corn mush mixed with cider, hog lard, or molasses.[25]

Most South Carolinians believed that slaves were "of barbarous, wild, savage natures."[26] The colony adopted slave statutes in order to "restrain the disorders, rapines and inhumanity, to which they are naturally prone and inclined."[27] Slave statutes codified the criminal law for slaves and mandated severe punishments that included whipping, branding, maiming, and execution, depending upon the crime. The slave statutes also established several rules designed to control the slaves' conduct, such as forbidding slaves to leave their plantation or place of work without a written ticket issued by their owners. Owners were given the responsibility of controlling their slaves. For example owners were required to inspect their slave quarters at least once every fourteen days for weapons and contraband. Fines were supposed to be levied on owners if they failed to enforce the rules. Owners were also required to inflict most of the mandated punishments such as whipping; however they could pay a constable to perform that duty. As the number of slaves in the colony increased, the free white population began to worry about the possibility of a slave insurrection. Successive slave statutes increased the severity of the criminal law and added more rules designed to retain control of the slaves' conduct.[28]

Although most white people disapproved of the raucous conduct of some slaves and the crimes committed by others, the slave statutes indicate that some owners tended to deny or trivialize such conduct by their own slaves, either out of affection or trust or because of a protective attitude toward their property. They appear to have adopted a quasi-parental attitude toward their slaves. Many owners allowed their slaves to spend Sundays working on small plots of land where they cultivated vegetables and grain, maintained a few livestock, and used the produce to supplement their diet and earn money. A section of the 1714 slave statute ordered the practice to cease. However enforcement of the ban on private farming by slaves was sporadic at best, for it was a source of slave pride and was materially beneficial to both the slaves and their owners. Some owners had such faith in their slaves that they allowed them to use firearms, probably for hunting wild game or protecting livestock from predators. Consequently many owners either ignored their duties under the slave statutes or were careless in their performance of their policing responsibilities, despite the fines that could be levied against them.[29]

The failure of some owners to enforce the slave statutes, and their slaves' flouting of established rules, may have been a reason for the development of a governmental control mechanism. A 1704 statute established mounted constabularies, known as patrols, in each militia company's district. Each patrol was manned by a captain and ten white militia soldiers. The introduction to the statute stated that patrols were necessary because of the danger of a slave insurrection during a foreign invasion when slaves would be congregated together in refugee centers. However the statute was much broader. It also directed the patrols to ride from plantation to plantation, at the patrol captain's discretion, to police the slaves' conduct and to prevent them from congregating.[30]

Some slaves took the ultimate risk and attempted to escape. Their usual destination was Spanish Florida, a long, difficult, and dangerous journey on foot along forest paths or in a stolen canoe via the Inland Passage, now known as the Intercoastal Waterway. Those slaves who reached Florida were welcomed and given their freedom if they adopted the Catholic faith.

A few slaves hid in the South Carolina forests and swamps and survived for a time as highwaymen. Militia company commanders were taxed with the responsibility for apprehending fugitive slaves, and fellow slaves and Indians received rewards for capturing escapees. Many runaways were captured and received severe punishment that varied from whipping to execution.[31]

The Indian trade was also a major economic interest. It was originally based on the exchange of deerskins and occasional furs by the Indians to the traders for guns, tools, cloth, and rum. By the first decade of the eighteenth century, Indians also began using captive enemy Indian women and children as barter for trade goods. South Carolina traders sold the captives into slavery. Slaving soon became an important aspect of the trade. Few planters and merchants who were engaged in the Indian trade went to the Indian towns. They hired employees as field traders to accomplish the actual buying and selling and function as their storekeepers. They also lent money to those traders who were self-employed. The Indian trade offered a method of economic and social advancement for South Carolinians. Several prominent men started as traders or assistants. During 1715 there were at least two hundred traders in the towns of the various Southeastern Indian groups. Each trader maintained one or more employees, indentured servants, and slaves at their stores.[32]

South Carolinians preferred to ride horseback when traveling on paths and roads. Most of their horses were a small, hardy Spanish stock. Some planters imported English stallions to improve the stock by breeding them to local mares. Horses were required to be branded in order to discourage thievery. Farmers often transported produce and supplies within the settled areas of the colony by two-wheeled carts pulled by oxen. However most heavy cargo was shipped by boat along the numerous rivers and creeks. In the coastal areas, boats were the primary means of transportation. The Inland Passage was a series of inlets, rivers, creeks, cuts or small canals, bays, and sounds that ran between the coast and the offshore islands. Boats could travel along the Inland Passage from the Savannah River in the south to the Cape Fear River in the north and not venture into the open sea. There were two principal types of boats: canoes and piraguas. Both were locally constructed from large cypress and cedar logs, but the piraguas were larger and relied more on sails than oars.[33]

South Carolinians participated in several sports and leisure activities. Horse racing, bearbaiting, bullbaiting, football, and card games were popular. All were forbidden on Sundays. People often congregated around bonfires to visit and play games. Music was important. The ballads, dance numbers, folk songs, and psalms had English, Scottish, Irish, French, and African roots. Musical instruments included violins, flutes, fifes, and drums. Couples participated in the repetitive steps and progressive forms of popular English country dances. Many people frequented the licensed, and unlicensed, taverns and punch houses throughout the colony, which served wine, cider, beer, brandy, and rum.[34]

At the beginning of 1715, South Carolina appeared to be the principal military power in southeastern North America. Except for the failed invasion of Florida in 1702, its campaigns during Queen Anne's War (1702–13) depopulated and laid waste to much of northern and western Spanish Florida and prevented the expansion of French Louisiana. During the Tuscarora War (1712–13), two South Carolina campaigns were successfully waged on behalf of North Carolina against its Indian enemies. Several South Carolina militia officers and Indian traders gained extensive combat and leadership experience during those wars. Their bravery, skill, and tenacity proved to be South Carolina's strength during the ensuing years. However large allied Indian contingents accomplished most of the fighting during Queen Anne's War and the Tuscarora War. As a result allied Indian warriors received considerable combat experience. Most of South Carolina's junior officers and lower ranks of the militia were seldom involved in those wars and received minimal combat experience.[35] Those developments proved to be early detriments to South Carolina's combat readiness.

The colony's ability to conduct offensive military operations was based primarily on alliances with groups of Indians, such as the Yamasees, Lower and Upper Creeks, Cherokees, Chickasaws, and Catawbas, who normally provided war parties for South Carolina's campaigns. South Carolina's defense against raids and invasions by the Spanish in Florida and French in Louisiana was provided by allied Indian towns that were located astride the major land invasion routes into the colony. The southwestern entrance into the colony at Port Royal was guarded by the Yamasees. They had migrated to South Carolina to escape domination by the Spaniards in Florida and to be nearer to the source of British trade goods. The northwestern entrance into the colony was guarded by Apalachees. They had been captured in Florida by South Carolinian and allied Indian armies during Queen Anne's War and moved to strategic sites on the upper Savannah River. The Catawbas and several small Indian groups guarded the northern and northeastern entrances. Those Indians remained in South Carolina's sphere of influence largely because of the Indian trade, which satisfied their desire for British manufactured goods.[36]

Most of South Carolina's men were enrolled in two militia regiments and three independent militia companies. The Northward Regiment of Foot included ten militia companies, manned by men who lived in Craven and Berkeley Counties. The Southward Regiment of Foot included six militia companies, whose men had settled in Colleton and Granville Counties. The independent units of the militia included the Governor's Troop of Horse Guards, the French Independent Company near the Santee River, and a small independent company at Winyah on the northern frontier.[37]

White males, both freed and indentured, and male slaves between sixteen and sixty years of age were required by law to serve as militia soldiers. The slave population was considered a reservoir of military manpower. During 1703, 1704, and 1708, the South Carolina government passed statutes that authorized trustworthy male slaves to be drafted into the militia companies during war. The government was required to purchase the freedom of those slaves who killed or captured an enemy or who were disabled while in service. Owners were reimbursed for those slaves who were killed or disabled.[38] During the next year, South Carolina's slaves rendered valuable military service.

During war each company of the militia was to include a captain, a lieutenant, an ensign, a sergeant, a corporal, a drummer, fifty white privates, and fifty black and Indian slave privates. Ideally the colony could field about seventeen hundred armed and able-bodied men, but that was probably never possible. When farm work was in progress, planters were reluctant to allow many of their employees, indentured servants, or slaves to serve as soldiers. Planters could exempt their men from military duty by paying a small fine. The continuing ravage of disease was also a major detriment to the maintenance of an adequate number of able-bodied militia soldiers. Malaria, yellow fever, and other ailments rendered men, both white and black, physically unable to bear arms during sporadic bouts of sickness.[39]

The required arms and equipment of each white militia soldier was a flintlock musket with a leather cover for the lock; a ramrod; a leather box filled with twenty paper cartridges, each of which contained gunpowder, ball, and two or three turkey shot; a ball of wax to wipe the metal parts of the musket and protect it from rust; a steel worm for withdrawing a ball in case of a misfire; a wire to pick the touch hole clean; and four spare flints. Military muskets were supposed to be loaded and fired by following several steps in an established and practiced method. The procedure began by first holding the musket parallel with the ground and pulling the cock, or hammer, back to the half-cock position. The cock would have been secured in that position with a "dog," if the musket was fitted with an obsolete dog lock. A paper cartridge was removed from the leather box with the right hand, the gunpowder end of the cartridge was torn off with the teeth, a small amount of gunpowder was poured into the pan, and its cover, the frizzen, was closed on the pan. The butt of the musket was then placed on the ground, and the remaining powder was poured down the barrel. The ramrod was removed from its housing on the underside of the stock. It was used to force the paper, turkey shot, and ball down on top of the powder, to the lower depths of the barrel. The ramrod was then returned to its housing. To fire the musket, the butt of the stock was pressed into the right shoulder with the right hand, the left hand was positioned forward on the stock to aim the musket toward the target, the cock was pulled all the way to the rear with the right hand, and the trigger was pressed with the right index finger. The flint in the jaws of the cock struck the steel frizzen, throwing it forward and producing sparks, which fired the gunpowder in the pan and drove fire into the adjacent touch hole. The gunpowder in the barrel exploded, driving the large lead ball and turkey shot toward the target. Companies of well-trained British infantrymen were expected to load and fire their muskets three or four times per minute. Although individual smoothbore muskets were inaccurate beyond a distance of about fifty yards, the rapid, massed volley fire by an entire company could be deadly. The rate of fire of South Carolina militia soldiers, who had minimal time for rapid-fire training, may not have exceeded two shots per minute. However during the ensuing years there would be few opportunities for volley fire by platoons and companies. Most shooting would involve individual militiamen firing at individual Indians. The addition of turkey shot to cartridges increased their odds of hitting targeted warriors.[40]

A good leather belt and a sword, bayonet, or hatchet were required to be carried by militia soldiers. There were few swords and bayonets in the colony; most men would have carried hatchets, a common agricultural and wilderness tool that served as an excellent close-quarter weapon. Powder horns were sometimes carried to provide additional ammunition during extended operations. Slave militia soldiers were also armed with muskets, if enough were available; otherwise they carried handcrafted lances, lightweight spears that could be thrown. Each company's drummer had a snare drum, used to produce standard patterns of drumbeats that transmitted the commander's orders to his men. Officers carried swords and were supposed to be armed with half pikes, a type of spear. It is doubtful whether half pikes were carried on combat operations. Officers owned red uniform coats. Enlisted militia soldiers would have worn workingmen's clothing that included shoes, stockings, knee breeches, shirts, jackets, and hats or caps. The most popular types of head covers were probably the wide-brimmed hat, cocked or not, for protection from the sun and rain and the Monmouth cap, a knitted wool cap similar to the modern watch cap, for use during cold weather. Each company had colors, a distinctive flag that was similar to the modern guidon. Drums, colors, and half pikes were purchased from London suppliers.[41]

South Carolina's militia served under the colony's militia statute that prescribed the personal and unit "military discipline" that was to be followed while on active duty. Companies and regiments mustered for one or more days at least every other month. During musters they practiced the "manual of arms" with their muskets, conducted parade formations, and engaged in battle drills. Battle drills would have included loading and firing muskets, volley fire by platoons, and assault tactics.[42]

In addition to the militia, there were small, regular provincial military units on full-time duty guarding the coastal areas of the colony. The garrison of Fort Johnson was authorized a captain, a lieutenant, and twelve men to guard the entrance to Charles Town harbor. The Stono scout boat crew included two white men and two Settlement Indians. Two white men and three Settlement Indians manned the Port Royal scout boat. Scout boatmen reconnoitered the Inland Passage between Charles Town and the Savannah River. Lookouts, usually composed of a couple of white men and one or more Settlement Indians, watched for invaders from stations on the coastal islands.[43]

The use of Settlement Indian warriors was a necessity when conducting military operations. Unlike South Carolinians, Indians developed the skills, taught from childhood and honed by hunting, to survive and prosper in the wilderness. The most efficient South Carolina officers recruited Indians, usually warriors of the Etiwan, Kiawah, or Winyaw groups, to serve with their units. Settlement Indians served as scouts who screened the movement of military units and hunted deer to feed the soldiers. They also conducted long-range patrols, on the lookout for marauding war parties. Some South Carolinians criticized their martial ability and their loyalty; most of them provided a valuable service, however.[44] While serving as soldiers, the Settlement Indians probably retained much of their native dress and would have been armed with flintlock trade muskets. It is unknown whether they adorned themselves with the standard Southeastern Indian war paint of red and black, but that is likely.

The homes of the Etiwans were scattered among the South Carolina plantations. During the summer they resided near the lower part of Cooper River and on Daniels Island, formerly Etiwan Island, near Charles Town. During the winter they moved inland. They could muster about eighty warriors. The Kiawahs was a smaller group, perhaps having less than twenty warriors. During summer months they lived on Kiawah Island, but during the winter they moved inland. The native language of those groups is unknown, but many of them, especially the young, spoke English. The Winyaws had about thirty-six warriors, who lived with their families in one town located north of present-day Georgetown. They probably spoke Siouan.[45]

Alarm cannons were used to warn the colonists when an invasion was imminent. Cannons were placed at the Yamasee Indian town of Altamaha, about 12 miles southwest of present-day Beaufort; at Thomas Nairne's plantation on Saint Helena Island, approximately 9 miles east-southeast of present-day Beaufort; at John Cochran's plantation at present-day Seabrook Point, on the north end of Port Royal Island; and on William Livingston's plantation, about 3.75 miles southwest of present-day Adams Run, and 1 mile east of the Edisto River. During February 1715 the government ordered the cannons to be moved from Nairne's plantation to Coosa Island, from Cochran's plantation to the planned site of Beaufort, and from Livingston's plantation to the tiny village of Willtown, on the east bank of the Edisto River, one mile to the west. The ensuing war prevented the moves from being completed.[46]

By the early spring of 1715, South Carolinians had become a confident people. Religious differences, which had previously caused political rifts among the population, had almost ceased. The colony was doing well economically; plantations were being enlarged; the frontiers were extending south, west, and north; and the Indian trade appeared to be thriving. Militarily South Carolinians had proved themselves capable, and several men had developed skills in leadership and frontier warfare. However South Carolina's government was somewhat complacent regarding its defensive capabilities. Charles Town's earth and timber walls were storm damaged. There were no frontier fortifications. Only minimal stores of small arms and ammunition were maintained. The Indian alliances had provided adequate offensive and defensive capabilities for several years, but the system was about to collapse. South Carolinians would soon discover that they were unprepared to wage war, especially a total war. They would need superior military skill and great confidence to survive.

— CHAPTER 3 —

Southeastern Indians, April 1715

The southeastern portion of the North America continent is immense. From the Mississippi River eastward to the Atlantic Ocean, is more than 560 miles at the narrowest point. From the Ohio River at its conflux with the Mississippi River in the north to the Gulf of Mexico in the south is about 480 miles. The Florida peninsula extends the eastern portion of the land more than 330 miles farther south. At the beginning of 1715, the principal inhabitants of that huge land mass were more than thirty-two thousand Indians. Most of their towns were found deep in the interior. People of many Indian towns had loosely banded with other towns to create confederations or groups. Some towns merged because the people had a common language or heritage, while the people of other towns became allies for mutual protection. They had waxed and waned in population, power, and prestige over the years. The people of most of those groups were trading customers of South Carolina.[1]

The Cherokees spoke Iroquoian. They had at least four thousand fighting men. Their towns were in the foothills and mountains, 215 to 300 miles northwest of Charles Town. South Carolinians divided the Cherokee into three groups. Lower Settlement Cherokees included eleven towns with about six hundred warriors, in the foothills of northwestern South Carolina and present-day northeastern Georgia. Middle Settlement Cherokees lived in thirty towns, most of which were in the mountains of North Carolina, and included about twenty-five hundred warriors. The Upper Settlement included nineteen towns with about nine hundred warriors. The Upper Settlement was actually two groups: Valley towns were in present-day northeastern Georgia and southwestern North Carolina, and Overhills towns were in present-day southeastern Tennessee.[2]

The Catawbas spoke Siouan. They resided in seven towns about 150 miles north-northwest of Charles Town, on the South Carolina–North Carolina border, near present-day Fort Mill. The Catawbas' total fighting strength was approximately 570 warriors.[3]

Several independent towns of Siouan-speaking Indians were located to the north and northeast of Charles Town. Their towns could call on nearly six hundred warriors. They included Cape Fears, Cheraws, Congarees, Pedees, Santees, Seewees, Waccamaws, Waterees, and Waxhaws.[4]

The Apalachees resided in four towns, which may have been consolidated to some extent. Their towns were on the east bank of the upper Savannah River, between present-day North Augusta and Beech Island. They spoke Muskogean. The Apalachees were a former Spanish ally who had resided in several mission towns in northwestern Florida. During Queen Anne's War, large raiding parties of South Carolinians, Yamasees, and Creeks devastated their mission towns. They killed the adult men of the towns that mustered a strong defense and sold their women and children into slavery. The Apalachees, who surrendered, were marched to the upper Savannah River, where they built towns and guarded the entrance to South Carolina's northwestern frontier. Many other Apalachees willingly migrated to the upper Savannah River, probably to escape the labor draft, enforced cultural changes, and other mandates of the Spanish mission system. In early 1715 the four towns could field about 275 fighting men.[5]

The Savannahs, or Savanos, were three small towns of Shawnee Indians who spoke Algonquian. Their towns may have been consolidated. They had resided on or near the site of present-day Augusta, Georgia, since about 1681, but many of them had recently migrated to other areas. Only about sixty-seven warriors and their families remained.[6]

The Yuchis was a group that included several towns scattered over the Southeast. The Yuchi language was unrelated to any other language of that area. Two of their towns were on the west bank of the Savannah River, about fifteen miles northwest of present-day Augusta near Uchee Creek in Columbia County, Georgia. Those two towns, which may have been consolidated, could field about 130 warriors.[7]

The Chickasaws maintained six towns in northern present-day Mississippi. Their language was Muskogean. They had about seven hundred warriors who had the reputation of being ferocious. They held sway over parts of present-day Alabama, Kentucky, Mississippi, and Tennessee. Most Chickasaws were enemies of the French and their allies, the Choctaws.[8]

The Creeks clustered their towns into two major groups, the Lower Creek and the Upper Creek. During the late seventeenth century, several towns of Muskogean-speaking Indians and towns of allied people of other linguistic affiliations were living near the Chattahoochee River on the present-day Georgia-Alabama border. Other towns were near the Alabama, Coosa, and Tallapoosa Rivers in south central Alabama. About the year 1691, Spanish soldiers burned some major Chattahoochee River towns as punishment for the townspeople's refusal to stop dealing with South Carolina traders and their failure to welcome Christian missionaries. Those Indians moved their towns northeastward to the area of Ochese Creek, now known as the Ocmulgee River, in present-day Butts County, Georgia. Other Chattahoochee River towns were moved farther eastward to the Oconee and Savannah Rivers. South Carolinians began referring to all of those migrant people as Ochese Creeks. Their migration proved profitable for South Carolina's traders. The people of those towns became important customers. Their new locations made the traders' overland trip from Charles Town considerably shorter, and boats could deliver heavy and bulky goods via the Inland Passage, the Altamaha River, and Ochese Creek. By 1712 those people on Ochese Creek, Oconee River, and Savannah River had formed a loose confederacy and were often known by South Carolinians as Lower Creeks. In early 1715 the Lower Creeks had ten towns and could field about 731 fighting men.[9]

The Lower Creeks developed a political alliance with the Upper Creeks who were in present-day Central Alabama. The Upper Creeks were loosely divided into three groups: Alabama, Abikha, and Tallapoosa. The four Alabama towns were near the confluence of the Alabama, Coosa, and Tallapoosa Rivers. The Abikhas and Tallapoosas maintained approximately twenty-eight towns on the Coosa and Tallapoosa Rivers. The Upper Creeks had approximately 1,352 warriors.[10]

Yamasees were more closely associated with South Carolina, both commercially and militarily, than the other groups. Some of their towns had been in the southwestern part of the colony for thirty years. They were two separate groups: Yamasee and Guale, the latter of which they pronounced as *Wally*. Both groups probably spoke Muskogean. The Yamasee and Guale people resided in several segregated towns. The identity and location of their towns were often in flux, and sorting out the changes is often a puzzle. They often moved towns from one location to another, and they were occasionally consolidated with other towns. Sometimes people withdrew from one town and joined another, and at other times they dropped old town names and adopted new ones.[11]

Previously, during the sixteenth and seventeenth centuries, Guale towns were in the Spanish mission province of Guale, along the coast of present-day Georgia. Many Guales became Catholic Christians and adopted Spanish names. They were under the protection and supervision of the Spanish colonial government of Florida, which maintained small detachments of soldiers near the missions. Their relationship with the Spanish was sometimes turbulent.[12]

During the late seventeenth century, the Guales began suffering from slave raids by Westo Indians. The Westos, also known as the Richahecrians, had previously lived to the north near Lake Erie. In 1656 the Iroquois defeated them, forcing them to flee south to Virginia. With the encouragement of Virginia traders, who armed them with muskets, the Westos raided Guale and other Indian towns in southeastern North America. They captured women and children and bartered them to the traders who sold them as slaves. Pirates also began raiding the Guale mission towns. By 1684 it became obvious to some Guales that the Spanish could not adequately protect them. More important the Spanish refused to supply them with adequate firearms for self-defense. The Guales also had other grievances. Spaniards drafted Indians as laborers to work in the mission corn fields and as soldiers for the Indian militia. Guales were encouraged to adjust their culture to comport with Spanish standards. The Spanish sometimes meddled in the political affairs of the Indian towns and occasionally punished the people of a town for the misdeeds of a few warriors.[13]

Westo gunmen also raided the Yamasee towns that were in the central and eastern portions of present-day Georgia. By 1662 the people of several Yamasee towns moved southeast to the vicinity of present-day Savannah, Georgia. Not long afterward the Westo raiders again attacked. Many Yamasees then moved south and settled near the Guale missions under the protection of small Spanish garrisons. Spaniards regarded most of the Yamasees as pagan, although a few became Christians.[14]

The Westo Indians were finally defeated and driven away by South Carolina with the aid of Savannah, or Shawnee, Indians during 1680–81. However pirates continued to prey on the Guale and Yamasee towns along the present-day Georgia coast. During 1683–85 many Yamasees and Guales fled north to South Carolina. They established two major towns in present-day Beaufort County, then commonly known as Port Royal. Altamaha was settled on Port Royal Island and Pocotaligo on Saint Helena Island. During 1685 a Yamasee war party, armed with British firearms received from Scottish traders at nearby Stuarts Town, raided a Spanish Timucua Indian mission west of Saint Augustine. The Yamasees killed eighteen people and captured twenty-five women and children, brought them back to Port Royal, and traded them to the Scots, who sold them as slaves. The

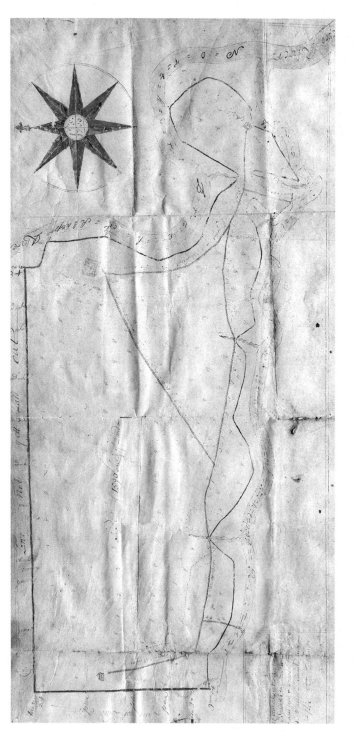

Location of Yamasee towns near the Ashepoo River, ca. 1685–1700. "Colored Plat of 1590 Acres Located between Two Branches of the Ashepoo River, Purchased by John Stanyarne," 1701. Tuscagy Old Town (Tuskegee) is shown in the upper left (northwest) of the tract, fortified Cheachese Old Town (Chechessee) is in the upper right (northeast), and an Indian house is in the lower right (southeast).

Courtesy of the South Carolina Historical Society, Pringle-Garden Family Papers (0275.00), Charleston.

Spanish retaliated by conducting two raids. They killed and captured several Yamasees and burned Stuarts Town. The Yamasees quickly sought safety from future Spanish attacks. They moved inland to the northeast and reestablished their towns on more defensible sites in the vicinity of the Ashepoo and Combahee Rivers. A thirty-year period of mutual hostility between the Yamasees and the Spanish began. After about a decade, the Yamasees began moving to more permanent town sites on the mainland, northwest of Port Royal. They were probably encouraged to move by the establishment of new South Carolina cowpens near the Ashepoo and Combahee Rivers.[15]

South Carolinians began referring to all of the inhabitants of the Yamasee and Guale towns as Yamasees, perhaps not realizing that they were two distinct groups.[16] However the ethnic distinction between Yamasees and Guales may have started to blur. Considerable interaction between the towns of the two groups probably occurred, to include visitations between friends, courtships, and marriages.

During Queen Anne's War, a strong military alliance developed between South Carolina and the Yamasees, Lower and Upper Creeks, Cherokees, Chickasaws, and Catawbas. The Yamasees were exceptionally loyal to South Carolina. Several Yamasee warriors accompanied the South Carolina expedition on the ill-fated invasion of Saint Augustine, Florida, during 1702. During the siege of Castillo de San Marcos, the principal Spanish fort, a Yamasee warrior, Juan Lorenzo, and his immediate family appeared at the *castillo*'s gate and asked for asylum. His secret mission was to blow up the fort's powder magazine. The Spanish soon made him a prisoner after he attempted to persuade the Spanish Indian allies inside the fort to mutiny. Under torture he refused to give any information regarding South Carolina. During the invasion of Florida, South Carolina destroyed the remaining missions on the coast north of Saint Augustine. Soon afterward some Guales that had remained in Florida moved north to Port Royal and settled with their kinfolk. Other Guales remained in Florida and moved closer to Saint Augustine. During 1712 South Carolina dispatched a military expedition to assist North Carolina during that colony's initial Tuscarora Indian uprising. The expedition included Indian allies, among whom were Yamasee warriors. They were the bravest, most skillful, and most tenacious of South Carolina's Indian allies.[17]

By the beginning of the eighteenth century, several Yamasee towns were located on the mainland northwest of the islands of Port Royal. Their location helped guard South Carolina's southern frontier, so it was in South Carolina's interest to retain them there. In 1707 the South Carolina government set aside a large tract of land that was used as a reservation for the Yamasee. It was known long afterward as the Indian Land. It was bound on the west by the Savannah River, on the south by the islands of Port Royal, on the east by the Combahee River, and on the north by an invisible border drawn from the head of Savannah River to the head of Combahee River. By April 1715 all ten towns had been relocated to the Indian Land.[18]

The approximate Yamasee population in 1715 was 413 men, 345 women, 234 boys, and 223 girls, for a total of 1,215 people. They resided in ten towns divided into two divisions, Lower Yamasee and Upper Yamasee. Altamaha was the principal, or head, town of the Lower Yamasee, and Pocotaligo was the head town of the Upper Yamasee. It is unknown whether the Yamasees or the South Carolinians established that hierarchy, but it is likely that the Yamasees were responsible. Little is known about the political and economic relationship between those two principal towns and the other towns in their divisions. Controversy exists regarding which towns were Lower and which were Upper.[19] Yamasees placed their towns on sites that were close to navigable streams and safe from floods in all but the worst hurricanes. A study of period maps, the designations of rivers and landmarks used during the eighteenth century, a search for suitable terrain, and recent archaeological discoveries suggest that the towns would have been located as follows.

By early 1715 the Lower Yamasees had four towns in the southwestern portion of the Indian Land. Ethnic Yamasees occupied three towns. Altamaha, the head town, was on the north side of the conflux of the Okatie River, Chechessee Creek, and the Colleton River, formerly the Altamaha River, in present-day Beaufort County. It was a large town, having about forty households, spread over about 125 acres. The South Carolina government had placed an alarm cannon in the town. Its purpose was to warn the other towns, and the people at Port Royal, of the approach of an invasion force. The principal mico, or chief, of Altamaha was Don Antonio de Ayala. Chechessee was situated about 2 miles northeast of Altamaha on the west side of Chechessee Creek. Its mico is unknown. Okatee was situated about 1.75 miles northwest of Altamaha, on the west side of the Okatie River. Its principal mico was Alonso. Euhaw, a fourth town, was a Guale community. Its headman was commonly known as the Euhaw King. The Euhaws were the last of that group to immigrate to South Carolina. They had been part of a Spanish mission on Amelia Island in Florida. During early 1703 they settled on Euhaw Creek in present-day Jasper County.[20]

The Upper Yamasees resided in six towns. People of the Yamasee group inhabited Pocotaligo, the head town. It was on Pocotaligo Neck on the west side of the Pocotaligo River in present-day Jasper County. During 1713 the principal mico of the town was a man known to South Carolinians as Lewis. Four years later the mico was a man named Don Francisco Yaquisca. The micos of most other Upper Yamasee towns are unknown. The town of Pocasabo may also have contained Yamasee people. It was situated on the eastern bank of Haulover Creek, formerly Pocosaba Creek, also in present-day Beaufort County. Guales inhabited four towns. Tulafina was on the west side of the Tullifinny River, in present-day Jasper County. Huspaw was likely on the east side of Huspah Creek at Bull Point on a tract of land formerly known as Huspah Neck. It was about 2.25 miles north of the conflux of Huspah Creek and the Broad River in present-day Beaufort County. Huspaw King was the principal mico. Tomotly may have been on the east side of the Pocotaligo River, near present-day Oak Grove Plantation, due west of Sheldon, in Beaufort County. Its people may not have moved to South Carolina until after 1697. Sadkeche was the northernmost town. Its exact location is a mystery. The Salkehatchie River is the upper portion of the Combahee River, suggesting that it derived its name from the nearby town of Sadkeche. However the Salkehatchie and Combahee Rivers meander through swamp and marsh and have few locations suitable for a town site. One of the few likely sites is on the west side of the upper Combahee River, east-southeast of present-day Yemassee in Beaufort County, which provided higher ground and canoe access via a small bayou, or creek, to the river.[21]

There were at least two other Yamasee towns during early 1715, but they were not located on the Indian Land. The first, Chiaha, was initially near Old Chehaw River in Colleton County, circa 1686–95, but was moved to the Lower Creek towns in present-day Georgia, sometime before 1712. The second, Tuskegee, had been on the Ashepoo River in Colleton County near Chechessee Town ca. 1687–95, but its people moved to be with the Lower Creeks before the year 1700.[22]

The following descriptions of Indian culture would apply to most Southeastern Indians, especially groups such as the Yamasees and Lower and Upper Creeks. Their frequent moves, the joining of two or more towns, the division of towns, and their relationships with South Carolinians would have contributed to some changes in their culture. Nevertheless they held on to many of their traditional practices. Fortunately archeology is beginning to uncover valuable information about the Southeastern Indians.

Maintaining an orderly town required everyone to follow traditional religious and social rules to remain pure and unpolluted. The religious worldview of Southeastern Indians is difficult to understand and probably appeared as alien to the South Carolinians as Christianity did to the Indians. Stated simply without elaboration, the Southeastern Indians' universe consisted of three worlds: the upper world, the underworld, and this world. The upper world was perfectly ordered. It included the sun, which was a principal deity, along with the moon and thunder. Fire was the sun's earthly representative. The underworld was all madness and disorder and was inhabited by witches and monsters. Water represented the underworld on earth. This world, the earth, was conceived as an island, having several levels, and included elements of purity and elements of pollution. The Indians strived through adherence to established social rules to balance this world between the upper and lower worlds and achieve order. As an example they could not extinguish fire with water. Contemporary Christians may have interpreted the Indian beliefs as God, heaven, and hell and good versus evil, but there was little relation to Christian beliefs. The Indians did believe in a form of afterlife.[23]

Southeastern Indians were individualists in regard to town politics and warfare. They had to be persuaded, rather than ordered, to follow the directions of their town headmen. Town government, which consisted of the headmen and the council, seldom sat in judgment over disputes or crimes. Every Indian was a member of a clan, such as Wind, Tiger, Bear, or Eagle. The clans maintained cultural discipline. They were the arbiters of disputes and could invoke punishment or sanctions. Withdrawal of public approval, isolation, and ridicule sanctioned minor crimes and violations of town rules. Serious crimes were prosecuted and punished through retaliation that was administered by victims' clans. Indians maintained a degree of personal freedom that was unimaginable in early eighteenth-century British and European cultures and especially in most present-day cultures. However there was no anarchy in the towns. Traditional beliefs, clan rules, and respect for the opinions of others, particularly the elders, restrained individual conduct.[24]

Kinship among most Southeastern Indian groups was matrilineal; descent passed through the mother. The mother was head of the household. She owned all of the household property. Her brothers acted as the father figures for her children, while her husband acted as the father figure for his sisters' children. The husband lived in his wife's house, which was in her town near other members of her clan.[25]

The Muskogean title for their headmen was *mico.* Cherokees called their headmen *uku.* A consolidated town could have a headman for each of the formerly separate towns, but only one man would be the town's principal headman. South Carolinians often assumed that a headman exercised considerable power over his townspeople, and they called him by the name of his town, as with the Altamaha King. However headmen had few powers normally claimed by European kings. Their influence was limited to the democratic acceptance of their decisions by the townspeople. They had few privileges. Each headman had a deputy, or speaker, who informed the people of his wishes. Before a headman attempted to make an important policy decision, he consulted the town council, which included the most revered men in the town, usually the elders. Often the headman was succeeded by a nephew. Towns had war captains, men who were respected warriors and leaders. They exercised limited authority during preparations for war and during combat operations.[26]

Towns were normally situated on elevated terrain near freshwater rivers or creeks. The dugout canoe was a major form of transportation. Some towns were dispersed over an area of more than one hundred acres. Agricultural fields were nearby. A town's ceremonial center included a public square reserved for ceremonies, government activities, and the men's leisure time. Men had little contact with their women outside the family homestead. Each morning that a man was in the town, he joined the other men in the square and fasted, smoked tobacco, and participated in the social ceremony of drinking *cassina,* or black drink, made from the leaves of the yaupon holly. The leaves were boiled, strained, and the resulting tea was drunk while it was hot. The purpose of black drink was to purify the men from sin and bind them closely to their fellow warriors. After drinking copious amounts of the tea, the drinker temporarily left the gathering, hugged himself, and regurgitated to complete the purifying process.[27]

A large public townhouse was near the square. It was used during bad weather and during winter. Some townhouses may have been constructed on raised earthen platforms. A summer council house, consisting of four open sheds, was situated near the square for use during warm weather. The men's favorite gambling sport, *chunkey,* was played in a large yard nearby. A small stone wheel was thrown, and players threw spears at the spot where they believed the wheel would stop. The closest spear designated the winner. Dances were also held on the chunkey yard. Captured warriors were often tethered to upright posts in the chunkey yard and tortured to death. Family homesteads surrounded the public areas. Each homestead was composed of a house and storage buildings and could be separated by 50 to 120 meters from neighboring homesteads. Those buildings were well constructed of wattle and daub, which consisted of wooden poles, sticks, cane, bark, mud, and grass. Some Yamasee houses were large round structures and had humans buried under the earthen floors. The houses of most other Indian groups may have been rectangular. It is doubtful that any towns were fortified with wooden walls before the spring of 1715.[28]

The men were hunters. Their principal task was to provide meat and skins during the winter hunting season. Hunting grounds were sometimes more than a hundred miles from the towns. Some families accompanied the men to the winter hunting camp. Before beginning a hunt, the men used special medicines and charms to bring them success. They skinned and butchered the game animals they killed. Women maintained the hunting camp and processed the skins. The skins of animals, especially deer, were sold to the South Carolina traders in exchange for guns, tools, cloth, and rum. Men also constructed the buildings in the town, made canoes, fashioned tools, and cleared land used for growing grain and vegetables. Men of some groups helped their women plant and harvest late corn, beans, and squash on their family plot in the large fields. They had to be tough. Men worked hard and often underwent privation on hunts and during war. Nevertheless they enjoyed leisure time while in town, participating in games, town politics, and social ceremonies.[29]

Women were in charge of their households. They were farmers. Corn, beans, and squash were their primary crops. Early corn, or maize, was planted in garden plots near their houses during March and April. It was harvested ten to twelve weeks later and was roasted and eaten before it fully developed. Late corn, beans, and squash were planted during April and May in large fields near the towns. They harvested those crops in the fall. They kept chickens and hogs, a practice they learned from the Spanish and South Carolinians. Dogs were common pets. Cats were a rarity, although the Indians acquired a few from South Carolinians. Women prepared the meals. They broiled or boiled their favorite meat, venison or bear, but they also prepared small game animals, birds, and fish. Several types of corn were used in a variety of dishes. The staple food was hominy corn. Indians commonly ate vegetables, beans, nuts, roots, fruit, berries, honey, and squash. Women cultivated the crops; tended the livestock; harvested fruit, nuts, and herbs; gathered firewood; processed and tanned animal skins for the family's use and for barter with the South Carolina traders; made clothing from skins and English cloth; and raised their children. They worked hard and had scant leisure time.[30]

Many Southeastern Indian men were tall and athletic in appearance. They plucked facial hair before it developed into beards. Some rubbed red-pigmented and scented bear grease and herbs on their bodies to make their skin a dark copper color. Hairstyles varied. Warriors of some groups wore their hair plucked or shaved on one side and long and braided on the other. Warriors of other groups wore their hair long and rolled up on top or over their temples. The favorite hairstyle for many warriors involved shaving or plucking the hair from the sides of the head and leaving a thick, standing roach on the top of the head. A longer and wider shock of hair was left in the back in which feathers, beads, or quills were fixed and ended in a tightly bound tail. Many men wore bluish tattoos on their bodies. During warm weather they wore only a breechclout made of leather and went barefoot when in town. During cold weather men wore moccasins, leggings, a breechclout, and a cloth shirt. A "matchcoat" made from a trade blanket or leather robe was worn over both shoulders like a poncho.[31]

Most European men agreed that Indian women, especially the Muskogeans, were attractive. The women were much smaller than the men, and their skin was a lighter color, perhaps because they did not rub bear grease and herbs on their bodies. They oiled their long hair, formed it into a topknot, and decorated it with ribbons. Women sometimes used face and body paint, and some had tattoos. They commonly wore earrings, necklaces, and bracelets. They sometimes made gowns and petticoats from tree moss. Women normally wore skirts that covered them from their knees to their waists and left the upper body exposed. The skirts were made of cloth whenever available, preferably in red or blue. During cold weather women wore matchcoats over the left shoulder and under the right arm, so they could work with their hands. Their right breast was exposed. Young children often went naked.[32]

Games were a popular form of recreation. Women played a dice game with pieces of cane. Besides chunkey the men engaged in team sports such as the "ball game," a rough-and-tumble sport similar to modern lacrosse. Men and women also enjoyed songs and dances. Some dances were performed during traditional ceremonies such as the busk, the green corn feast, an important cleansing and purification rite that lasted several days during midsummer. They performed some dances solely for social enjoyment. There were separate dances for men and women, but there were also mixed dances. People normally danced clockwise around a fire to the accompaniment of singing supported by drums, rattles, and rasps. Songs often involved a lead singer and responses from a chorus. Flutes made of cane or bone were popular wind instruments. A debilitating pastime was drinking rum, liquor that was provided, often illegally, by South Carolina traders. Drinking to excess was common, and drunkenness brought grief to many Indian families.[33]

Indian men had superbly developed hunting and woodcraft skills. They used the same skills to great advantage when conducting forest warfare. Indians maintained a warrior society. During spring, summer, and early fall, they waged limited wars of raids and ambushes. They took revenge on other Indian groups who had killed or captured some of their women and children or tortured some of their men to death. Only occasionally did they make forays with economic or subjection goals. A significant part of the lives of Indian men was centered on war. Indian warriors were brave, skillful, tenacious, and brutal. They largely based a man's prestige and his ranking in his town on his ability and bravery in battle. Taking a scalp or a captive or accomplishing another success in battle entitled a young man to a war name. If a warrior was exceptionally brave, his people could award him with a war title, such as "Cherokeekiller." Before battle warriors painted their upper body in red and black. Their purpose was to terrify the enemy with their appearance and their actions. Their favored military tactic was to surprise the enemy with sudden raids and ambushes. Warriors were reluctant to assault fortified positions. The only times they stood their ground and fought to the death was when trapped by the enemy or the terrain or when defending their town from an attack. Manpower was limited; they could not afford to lose men who were the town's hunters and defenders. They tried to carry off their wounded to prevent them from being captured and tortured. Indians also removed their dead after a battle, whenever possible, to prohibit them from being dismembered and defiled. A captured warrior was considered dead by his family, because they knew his captors would probably torture him to death. Although Indian warriors were skilled fighting men, their individualism could adversely affect their military performance. All members of war parties were volunteers; no one was coerced into joining. War captains had to persuade rather than command. The warriors' belief in taboos and magic was also a hindrance. Those men who had bad dreams or witnessed events they considered to be sinister signs could refuse to join a war party or abandon it without censure.[34]

They wore a pouch at their belt or across one shoulder, which contained personal items such as pipe, tobacco, flint, and steel. When traveling or on the warpath, they wore a breechclout, leggings, and moccasins. War parties were organized into files, or squads, of not more than seven or eight warriors, a practice that was similar to that of the South Carolina militia. Squads traveled, ate, camped, and fought together. Traditional weapons were bows and arrows, war clubs, and spears. Bows were four to five feet in length and made of hardwood. Bowstrings were fabricated from twisted animal gut or deer rawhide. Arrow and spear shafts were made of a hardwood or cane reed with added bone or flaked stone points. After the South Carolinians initiated trade with the Southeastern Indians, they began selling them iron hatchets, knives, arrow and spear points, and English-made flintlock muskets. Only those men who were successful hunters could afford expensive muskets. Trade muskets were lightweight, smooth-bored, fully stocked, and mounted in brass. Many warriors were probably skilled marksmen. They carried gunpowder, ball, and shot in a leather bag. Warriors sometimes also purchased cutlasses and flintlock pistols. Traditional weapons were not completely abandoned. Several warriors, especially young men who could not yet afford guns, were armed with bows and arrows. All warriors carried an iron hatchet and knife.[35]

Just before battle warriors placed amulet bags around their necks for perceived protection. During battle they cut off and preserved the scalps of the men, women, and children they killed. Captured enemy warriors were taken to the captors' town and usually tortured to death in the chunkey yard. It was a ritualistic form of taking revenge against the victims' group. Warriors expected to suffer the same fate if they were captured. A warrior being subjected to a slow, painful death attempted to pretend that he was not suffering pain. He was expected to taunt his captors and brag about his reputation as a warrior. Traditionally Indians kept some women and children they captured as slaves or adopted them into their families to replace casualties from war and disease. During Queen Anne's War, the Yamasees and Creeks began conducting war as a business. They became slavers hunting people. They ranged throughout Florida in search of Indian women and children to capture and barter to South Carolina traders, who sold them into slavery.[36]

CHAPTER 4

Path to War,
1712–15

The close, long-term economic and military ties between South Carolina and its Indian allies began to unravel in 1712. Indians began to dread and hate South Carolinians. Three years later Yamasees and Lower Creeks began seriously debating whether to kill their traders and attack South Carolina's plantations. The situation became so volatile that a random spark would ignite a war. What had caused the rift between trading partners and comrades in arms?

Most of the South Carolinians with whom the Southeastern Indians were acquainted were field traders who worked during the spring and fall of each year in the Indian towns. Some traders had intimate relations with Indian women, who became their wives or concubines and gave birth to their mixed-race children. Traders who respected the Indians would have attempted to follow their culture. They learned some of their hosts' language, bathed in a nearby stream early every morning, never extinguished a fire with water, did not spend too much time with their Indian women, socialized with the towns' warriors, and obeyed many other social rules for men.[1]

However many traders felt no compulsion to respect the culture of their Indian customers and hosts. Some were dishonest, immoral, and violent in their lifestyle and business practices. They physically abused the Indians and insulted their customs and traditions. Traders, who spent considerable time in the Indian towns, were removed from the restraints provided by the presence and social judgment of their South Carolina peers. Many shook off the laws and social rules of their British culture. It might be said that they went native, but that would be incorrect. Some of them abandoned elements of their British culture, but they failed to adopt the Indian culture. For example unmarried women of some Indian groups had considerable sexual freedom, and traders took advantage of them, not recognizing that it was the unmarried women who had the freedom of choice and not them. Indian wives were not free to associate with other men; adultery was punished. However there were instances in which traders propositioned married women and, in some reported incidents, raped them.[2]

Several traders sold rum to the Indians, violating South Carolina law. Alcohol was popular. Some Indians sold their deerskins or captives for rum and often went into debt over it rather than purchasing items that their families needed for farming and hunting. Traders sometimes kidnaped women and children as payment for their warrior customers' debts. Occasionally traders physically assaulted warriors and even micos. Indian women were also physically beaten, and one trader beat his Yamasee wife to death.[3]

The commissioners of the Indian trade attempted to enforce trading laws by restraining and punishing abusive traders, but their efforts were ineffective. By the summer of 1714, most traders were ignoring the requirement to secure trading licenses. The system was broken. The crimes of some traders and the perceived indifference of the South Carolina government were frustrating and frightening to the warriors and their families. Traders were the only white people that most Indians personally observed; therefore they could assume that most South Carolinians were impure and polluted and were causing Indian lives to become unbalanced. Indians may have blamed bad weather, sickness, and general misfortune on South Carolinians. The micos were unable to convince the South Carolina government to control the traders and restore harmony to the towns.[4] Their limited authority over the townspeople may have begun to erode as a result. Warriors' pride and prestige would also have been affected. A man who was physically beaten, who was cheated in a trade, whose property was seized, whose wife was solicited for sex, or who was incapable of paying his debts would have appeared weak to his family and his peers.

Traders were not the only abusers. Until 1710 Yamasee warriors served alongside South Carolina soldiers in the colony's coastal lookouts and in the scout boat crews. However during that year the Yamasees complained that the soldiers were abusing them, and they refused to serve any longer. A few South Carolinians who illegally established cowpens in the Indian Land caused an additional irritant. The presence of their free-ranging cattle damaged the Yamasee crops and discouraged the range of the deer that were the Indians' supply of food and skins for trade.[5]

The Indians suffered the traders' abuse for several years. They were not impetuous; they had good reasons to wait and see if the abuses would cease. From time to time, the Indian agent and commissioners assured them that the government would make reforms to protect them from the abuse of the traders. The commissioners took judicial action against a few offending traders in South Carolina courts. Some warriors had developed friendships with traders and other South Carolinians, especially those soldiers with whom they had served during Queen Anne's War and the Tuscarora War. They probably hoped that their white friends could eventually help them. Trade was undoubtedly a factor in their procrastination as well. Indians had become somewhat reliant on certain British trade goods.[6] They tolerated considerable ill-treatment while they could receive sufficient credit to enable them to buy all of the items they needed and wanted.

The traditional Indian trade included the Indians' barter of animal skins, principally deer, to South Carolina traders for British guns, tools, cloth, and rum. Sadly an additional, dark side to the trade had developed: the barter of captive Indian families for British goods. In the late seventeenth century and especially the early eighteenth century, South Carolina Indian traders sold flintlock muskets to the Yamasees and Creeks. They encouraged them to use the muskets to capture enemy Indians. Firearms gave the Yamasees and Creeks a tremendous advantage in battle. War parties captured whole families of Timucuans, Apalachees, Mocamas, and other Florida Indians, most of whom did not have firearms and were poorly protected by the Spanish. They put most captive men to death. The captive women and children were bartered to South Carolina Indian traders. The traders sold them into slavery in South Carolina and the other British colonies. Slaving was a profitable arrangement for South Carolina's Indian allies. For a time it became the primary occupation of many warriors. Captured women and children were more valuable than deerskins. A successful military campaign of a few weeks allowed a warrior to expend less effort than was required for a long winter deer hunt. In addition it saved his wife the labor of processing deerskins. He could trade his captives for a wealth of arms, ammunition, and miscellaneous trade goods. An additional reward was the experience of combat. He was fulfilling his destiny as a warrior.[7]

The practice of slaving had been so successful, and so thorough, during Queen Anne's War that by 1712 Florida was largely depopulated of Indians. The Indian slave trade temporarily ended in 1713 following the Tuscarora War. A deepening financial crisis for both Indians and traders resulted.

Dealing in Indian slaves had been financially beneficial for the traders and their financial backers. They apparently did not fully appreciate that their quarry of Spanish allied Indians was nearly extinct, so they continued to sell the same goods in the same quantities to their Indian clients. The Indians had no slaves to barter; deerskins again became their primary trade item. However they could not harvest and process enough deerskins to continue the standard of living to which they had become accustomed, unless they could buy on credit. The traders exacerbated the Indians' fiscal difficulties by extending liberal amounts of credit, a practice that was illegal under South Carolina law. In the past Indians had been diligent about paying their debts; however by the spring of 1715, the debts of many Indians were so immense that payment in full was impossible.[8]

Some traders, especially those who operated as sole proprietors, were deeply in debt, facing foreclosure and financial ruin. Likewise their financial backers and the planters and merchants who owned trading companies were in debt to their English creditors. By late 1713 traders were becoming desperate. Over the next two years, some traders began haranguing their warrior customers in an attempt to collect payment. They warned the warriors that their families would be taken, enslaved, and transported out of the colony on ships. During early 1715 the traders apparently informed them that a ship was anchored nearby at Port Royal Island, prepared to take them aboard. The traders lied. The ship was a suspected smuggler's vessel that had been seized and impounded at anchor in the present-day Beaufort River. Although South Carolina's government did not sanction enslavement of Indian debtors and traders' threats had no basis in fact, the Indians had good reason to believe their families were in danger. For years they had been slavers, and traders previously had seized and temporarily held warriors' women and children as security for their debts. Several free Indian women and children had already been sold into slavery.[9]

Adding to the Indians' concern was the census of the Indian towns that Thomas Nairne, the Indian agent, made during early 1715 with the help of several traders. The Spanish later believed that the census was a critical factor in convincing some Indians that the South Carolinians were counting their numbers in preparation for enslaving them.[10]

Therefore the concern of the Indians that began to outweigh all others was having their families enslaved by the South Carolina traders to pay their indebtedness. To the Indians the traders would have seemed representative of the South Carolina government. It was reasonable for them to be concerned that South Carolina would muster the militia to help the traders enslave their families. Headmen and warriors—especially the

Yamasees, who received the brunt of the threats—became fearful, frustrated, and malevolently angered. The people of some Yamasee towns began seriously considering a declaration of war on South Carolina. War would prevent them from being enslaved and would cancel their oppressive trading debts. They believed they would continue to have access to European trade goods from the Spanish at Saint Augustine. South Carolinians later became convinced that the Spaniards encouraged the Yamasees to destroy South Carolina. Alexander Hewett, writing sixty-four years after the event, related that some Yamasee warriors had been visiting Saint Augustine since early 1714. That is undoubtedly true, and they may have requested Spanish troops and supplies to help them in a war against South Carolina. Francisco de Corcoles y Martinez, the governor of Spanish Florida from 1706 to 1716, probably gave the visitors presents and treated them well. He presumably agreed to initiate trade with them if they broke with South Carolina. However he would not have given or promised direct military aid, for Spain and Great Britain had been at peace since 1713. Governor Corcoles later provided Yamasees with sanctuary, limited arms, and supplies, but he did not help them with troops.[11]

William Rhett, a prominent South Carolinian, believed that the Huspaw King, the principal mico of the town of Huspaw, was heavily involved in promoting war. The Huspaw King was about forty-one years old. He may have been born on Cumberland Island on the present-day Georgia coast and was about ten years old when he moved to South Carolina with some of his townspeople. He may have been the nephew of the former mico of the town or he may have achieved his position through superior leadership ability. By 1715 South Carolinians began to consider Huspaw as an important town; however the Guale people of Huspaw continued to be subservient, in some degree, to the Yamasee people of the town of Pocotaligo. The Huspaw King probably chafed under Pocotaligo's dominance. Evidence indicates that he was politically ambitious. Guale leaders had long included politically ambitious men. Subsequent events showed that the Huspaw King may have been a major player in the decision to declare war on South Carolina, as part of a campaign to gain personal power and prestige.[12]

Deciding to go to war against an old ally such as South Carolina was a laborious and lengthy process for Indians. A traditional story repeated by Hewett in his account of the war stated that for about a year the Yamasees had been involved in war discussions with the Lower Creeks. The people of each town considered themselves independent. No town mico or war captain had enough authority to declare war without going through their customary political decision-making procedure. Spontaneous war occurred only defensively when an enemy attacked a town without warning. Advance planning was necessary for offensive action, because their primary principle of war was surprise. Indians shunned attacks without the benefit of surprise; too many warriors might be lost, placing a future burden on the town's defenses and food procurement.[13]

Traditionally Southeastern Indians prepared for offensive war by following an elaborate procedure. The headmen, war captains, and warriors of each town met and debated whether to go to war. They usually held such conferences in the town's square or the townhouse, depending on the weather. The youngest warriors would have agitated for war. They craved an opportunity to take scalps, capture prisoners, earn reputations, and receive war names. After the decision was made to go to war, the warriors began preparing for battle. Over a period of several days, those who were going to take part in the war drank a special herb concoction, fasted, avoided the company of women, listened to inspiring war stories from old warriors to give them courage, smoked a pipe together, prepared weapons, participated in a war dance, and ate a feast. They commonly displayed banners of red cloth in the towns, and red and black war paint was prepared. During early April 1715, the Yamasees initiated their war-making ritual. It is unknown whether the inhabitants of all of the Yamasee towns participated. The only clear evidence for a concerted decision for war is the fact that most of the traders who were present in the various towns were later assassinated. Several people at Port Royal heard a rumor, probably information initiated by traders, that the Yamasees at Pocotaligo were making preparations for war.[14]

Lower Creek Indians were also deeply in debt to South Carolina traders, but they suffered the South Carolina traders' abuses with few official complaints. However in late 1714 or early 1715, a South Carolina trader to Coweta killed the oldest nephew and designated heir of Yslachamuque, the mico of Coweta. South Carolinians knew him as Emperor Brims. He was a respected civil and war leader who was probably between forty and fifty years of age. Brims had more authority and influence than most Southeastern Indian headmen. His nephew had surely been killed during a quarrel regarding payment of trading debts. Brims quickly became actively engaged in solving the indebtedness problem and halting the traders' abuse. He sent agents to the towns of the eight principal Indian groups in the Southeast: the Catawbas; the Lower, Middle, and Upper Cherokees; the Chickasaws; the Lower and Upper Creeks; and the Yamasees. His agents asked whether the headmen and warriors of the various

groups would support the Lower Creeks in a confrontation with South
Carolina concerning their common indebtedness problem. The headmen
of 161 towns, who represented more than eight thousand warriors, agreed
to support Brims. Brims then scheduled a meeting with representatives
of the principal groups. They were to meet during early April 1715 in the
Upper Yamasee town of Pocotaligo to discuss their options in dealing with
South Carolina.[15]

During the early spring of 1715, the traders to the Yamasee towns arrived to collect deerskins from Indian families who were returning from
their winter hunt. John Cochran, William Bray, and others were accompanied by their wives, children, and employees. Some traders rejoined
their Indian wives, concubines, and children. Several traders, particularly
John Wright, took the reckless and dangerous tactic of increasing their
threats to enslave the warriors' families and transport them out of the
colony unless they paid their debts. Wright, a man about fifty years old,
arrived in South Carolina as a young indentured servant and improved
his social position over the years. He was a former Indian agent. During
early 1715 he was a trader to the town of Pocotaligo and perhaps Huspaw.
Wright was said by other traders to be arrogant, especially among the
Indians of Pocotaligo. He and his wife, Eleana, resided in Goose Creek,
north of Charles Town, where he owned land and slaves. He had heavily
mortgaged his property to borrow money to subsidize his Indian trading.
Eleana did not accompany him on his trading excursions.[16]

At the beginning of April 1715, representatives from several Indian
groups arrived in Pocotaligo to attend the meeting that Brims had called.
The Indians secretly discussed their options in dealing with their indebtedness. Brims did not personally attend, but a Lower Creek war captain
named Yfallaquisca represented him. The Spanish knew him as Perro
Bravo, or Brave Dog. He may have had skills as a linguist. Brave Dog was
from Chalaquilicha, or Satiquicha, a Spanish designation for one of two
closely related towns on the lower Savannah River. South Carolinians often referred to both towns as Palachacola. Brave Dog represented Chisla-
casliche, who was probably the mico or war captain of one of the towns.
South Carolinians knew him as Cherokeeleechee, or Cherokeekiller. He
apparently was respected among the Lower Creeks for his ability as a successful war leader. Cherokeekiller appears to have previously consulted
with Brims regarding their possible courses of action. Thus Brave Dog had
the prestige of representing two respected Lower Creek headmen at the
Pocotaligo meeting. Brims had carefully weighed the options for reducing
the Indians' indebtedness and then instructed Brave Dog regarding how

he should guide the deliberations. War was not his first option. Through Brave Dog he recommended to the Indian representatives that they compromise by requesting the South Carolina governor to restructure their debts. Brave Dog explained to the representatives that Brims believed they should offer to pay the South Carolina traders over an extended period. They would pay with deerskins, furs, and additional items such as livestock and agricultural produce. He may also have suggested that the warriors and their wives should develop less opulent lifestyles. Brave Dog informed the representatives that Brims recognized that if the South Carolinians did not accept the extended payment option, the Indians would have to adopt the second option, war. About April 10, after extensive deliberations, the representatives adopted Brims's plan and agreed to attempt a compromise with South Carolina's governor. The Yamasees may have reluctantly agreed; they had already completed their war rituals and were fortifying a remote site in the Upper Yamasee. An archeological discovery suggests that work may also have begun on a palisade at Altamaha Town in the Lower Yamasee.[17]

By the first week of April 1715, Indians began leaking information regarding their plans. Traders Samuel Warner and William Bray were warned by Lower Creek and Yamasee informants that the Lower Creeks were threatening war. They seem not to have taken the warnings seriously. Hewett stated that about April 6 John Fraser, a trader to the Yamasee town of Tomotly, learned from his Yamasee friend Sanute that the Indians were going to attack the South Carolinians. Sanute had visited Saint Augustine about a year before with a war captain named Ishiagaska. He was determined to take part in the coming attack against South Carolina, but he advised his white friend to flee to Charles Town. Fraser wisely placed his wife, their child, and their most precious personal property in a canoe and fled northeast to Charles Town by way of the Inland Passage. For some unknown reason, they seem not to have alerted their white neighbors before they left. The story may have some basis in fact; Fraser was a trader among the Yamasees before the war, and he was a trader who remained alive.[18]

During Sunday, April 10, 1715, some Yamasee headmen and warriors confronted Warner and Bray. They threatened to kill the traders and attack the colony unless the South Carolina governor met with them and solved their indebtedness problem. April was "Big Spring" month, the time of the year when warriors went to war. Warner and Bray realized that the secretive conferences and ceremonies that they had observed during the past few days must have been serious preparations for war. They quickly saddled their horses and rode for Charles Town to warn the governor. The following day rumor circulated among Port Royal residents that the Indians at Pocotaligo were preparing to go to war. The information was passed on to Nairne, the Indian agent. By Tuesday the war rumor began to subside. The representatives that were meeting in Pocotaligo had reached a consensus. They were prepared to present Brims's extended payment proposal to South Carolina's governor.[19]

The Yamasees did not know if their debts would be restructured. They had probably considered strategic objectives in the event they had to resort to war. Their priority would have been to kill the traders who had polluted their world. Beyond that they had two likely objectives. The first was to inflict many South Carolina casualties, cause as much destruction as possible, and then flee to the protection of the Spanish. If they followed tradition, they would have chosen that course of action: a limited revenge war. The second objective was to destroy or cripple South Carolina. To accomplish that difficult task, they would need the assistance of the Creeks, Cherokees, Chickasaws, and Catawbas. The Huspaw King soon issued a malevolent warning that the Southeastern Indians would conquer South Carolina. The Yamasees' plans and preparations during the early spring confirm his threat as their chosen military objective. They did not plan to evacuate the Indian Land. Women planted the early corn crop in March and early April. If they had failed to plant corn, the traders and local planters would have taken note and been alarmed. The Yamasees intended to harvest the corn and celebrate the busk, the traditional green corn ceremony, in midsummer. The busk was very important and would not have been voluntarily canceled. Their recent work in fortifying two defensive locations also indicates the Yamasees' intention to remain in the Indian Land. In addition they had not removed the previous fall's corn harvest from their towns and cached it.[20]

The Yamasees' wars traditionally consisted of limited raids and ambushes; however their experiences during the campaigns of Queen Anne's War and the Tuscarora War had expanded their concept of warfare. A few South Carolina officers and large war parties of Yamasees and Creeks had destroyed entire Indian towns. Yamasees apparently gave short shrift to the leadership and administrative contributions of South Carolina's officers during those campaigns. Under the circumstances that may have been a reasonable deduction. They had observed South Carolina conduct its military campaigns with only a few white men and large contingents of Indian allies. The only time they had seen a large South Carolina army in action was during the 1702 invasion of Saint Augustine, and that failed enterprise was an unimpressive demonstration.[21] Thus the Yamasees underestimated South Carolina's military capability.

Thomas Nairne arranged to go to the Upper Yamasee town of Pocotaligo. He planned to talk with the Yamasee micos and the representatives from other Indian groups. Nairne had probably been made aware of the meeting of various Indians in Pocotaligo. He also would have received information regarding the Yamasees' apparent preparations for war. The Indians may have requested his presence so that he could be presented with Brims's solution for the payment of their indebtedness. Nairne was familiar with the headmen and principal warriors of Pocotaligo, Altamaha, and Huspaw. He had visited those towns during the past three years. He probably arranged to be transported to Pocotaligo by the small crew of Port Royal scout boatmen. They were the only military unit in the area. The presence of the scouts would provide some protection to the South Carolinians in the town and would present a show of arms to the Yamasees, though the scouts totaled only about half a dozen white men and Settlement Indian warriors. Capt. Seymour Burrows was apparently their commander. They were stationed at or near Henry Quintyne's plantation on the northeast side of Lady's Island, near the junction of the Coosaw River and Saint Helena Creek, present-day Lucy Point Creek. On Wednesday, April 13, 1715, Burrows and his crew rowed their scout boat to Nairne's Saint Helena Island plantation. His house was probably on the south side of Nairne's Creek, present-day Eddings Point Creek. They took Nairne aboard and rowed north and west through present-day Morgan River, Parrot Creek, Coosaw River, Whale Branch, and Broad River. They continued north on the Pocotaligo River to the town of Pocotaligo. The trip would have taken most of the day.[22]

Nairne was Scottish by birth. He had been in South Carolina for at least twenty years and had owned a plantation on Saint Helena Island since about 1698. Nairne was more than fifty years old. He was well educated and was a former member of the South Carolina Commons House. He was an experienced soldier, having commanded a company during the 1702 invasion of Saint Augustine and later during the 1704 devastation of the Apalachee towns in northwestern Florida. Nairne had also accompanied Yamasee war parties on slaving raids deep into southern Florida. He had traveled to England and had written extensively regarding South Carolina and the Indians of southeastern North America. He had drawn maps of the region. As Indian agent he had spent part of each year since 1712 visiting the Yamasee, Creek, Chickasaw, and Cherokee towns in an attempt to control the conduct of the traders. He was one of South Carolina's most experienced men in political, military, and Indian affairs. Nairne was an imperialist, advocating the use of Indian allies to conquer and colonize all of southeastern North America for Great Britain. He was an advocate for Indian slaving to thin the ranks of the Spanish and French Indian allies. His wife, Elizabeth, the widow of Richard Quintyne, was also a native of Scotland. She was fifty-seven years of age. She had four adult Quintyne children and one teenage son, Thomas Nairne Jr.[23]

Warner and Bray returned to Pocotaligo from Charles Town on Thursday, April 14, carrying the governor's letters to the Indians. Nairne, Wright, Cochran, and several traders had been meeting with Yamasee micos, war captains, and principal warriors, probably in the town square. Brave Dog and other Lower Creek warriors were also present. Nairne and Wright were old political and business enemies, but what occurred between them at Pocotaligo is unknown. The Indian representatives that were present for the meeting presented Nairne with Brims's proposed solution to pay their indebtedness. They asked for additional time to discharge their debts and for creditors to be willing to accept additional commodities as payment. Nairne read Governor Craven's letter to the Yamasees. They were informed that the governor and his military escort were on their way to Savannah Town, across the river from present-day Augusta, Georgia, where he would meet with them. Nairne promised that the governor would restructure the Indians' indebtedness and would consider removing the most abusive traders from their towns. The Yamasees had heard similar promises before. They probably suspected that the governor was in collusion with the traders. Nevertheless they and the other Indian representatives agreed to travel to Savannah Town and listen to the governor. The warriors and white men shook hands and drank *cassina*, or black drink. Both white men and Indians may have drunk some of the traders' rum. Unknown to Nairne, the Yamasees had already decided to go to war before Bray and Warner had set out for Charles Town. They were restrained only because Brims was attempting to solve the indebtedness problem through compromise.[24]

That evening the Pocotaligo traders withdrew to their houses in the town. Some of them invited visiting traders to spend the night in their homes. The Indians provided the remaining white men with supper and beds in the townhouse. That structure was a large, round wattle-and-daub building with a central hearth and platforms around the wall for sitting and sleeping. That evening a trader's Yamasee wife listened intently to a conversation that Wright had with other traders. Later that night she met with three men: the Yamasee mico of Pocotaligo; the Guale mico of Sadkeche; and Brave Dog. She reported that Wright had revealed that South Carolina planned to attack the Yamasee and capture them. They would hang four of the Yamasee micos, and they would enslave and ship the remaining people out of South Carolina. She said that Wright had boasted that South Carolina would overcome the Yamasees, because their warriors were no more of a threat than women. Wright may have been intoxicated on liquor and not fully aware that the loitering Yamasee woman was conversant in English and was listening to him rant. However he was known for treating Indians with disdain, and he probably held them in such low esteem that he was not concerned with their reaction. Of course she may have misunderstood Wright, and she could have embellished his comments. Nevertheless some Yamasees would have recalled his previous threats and remembered that he had recently helped Nairne take a head count of their people.[25]

The Indians had previously warned Warner and Bray that the South Carolina traders would be killed after the next provocation. The Yamasees were provoked by Wright's comments. The headmen and warriors assumed that he had inadvertently disclosed South Carolina's plan for their destruction. Fear and dread for their families and themselves seem to have suddenly overwhelmed the Yamasee headmen and warriors. The letter that Nairne had read to them stated that the governor was en route to Savannah Town, accompanied by a military force. They jumped to the conclusion that the governor was bound for Pocotaligo. Their deduction was confirmed to their satisfaction less than five days later when their scouts discovered the governor and his South Carolina soldiers at John Woodward's plantation not far from the Indian Land. That night they rashly assumed that the governor's letter directed Nairne and the other traders to get the Indians intoxicated on rum. Thus after the governor's arrival, the soldiers could easily kill the micos and warriors who resisted capture. Why else, they probably reasoned, would Wright have bragged that they would fight like women? Yamasee men were renowned as great warriors. They believed that soldiers would invade their towns, kill or capture the drunken headmen and warriors, and seize their women and children. Captive Yamasees would be loaded onto the ship that was anchored nearby at Port Royal Island. They would be transported out of the colony and sold into slavery. The Yamasees became convinced that they had to act quickly for their self-preservation. Despite any reservations that Brims's Lower Creek emissary, Brave Dog, may have voiced, the Yamasees determined to attack before the governor and his soldiers arrived. The next morning, Good Friday, was designated as the time to make a preemptive strike, whether ready or not. Runners alerted the headmen of the other Yamasee towns. Wright's caustic remarks were the spark that ignited a war. The warriors applied red and black war paint.[26]

--- CHAPTER 5 ---

Easter Weekend,
April 15–17, 1715

At first light on Good Friday, April 15, 1715, several white men were sleeping on raised bed platforms around the walls of the round townhouse in Pocotaligo. They were suddenly awakened by screaming warriors painted in red and black and carrying hatchets. As they burst through the doorway, they captured Indian agent Thomas Nairne and most of the others and bound them. However Seymour Burrows, the scout-boat captain, battered his way through the milling warriors, gained the doorway, and ran from the town. He was hotly pursued. Captain Burrows should be classified as one of the toughest, most athletic men of his time. A warrior shot him in the neck, and the ball exited through his mouth. Another Indian shot him in the back, and the ball lodged permanently in his chest. He nevertheless outdistanced his Yamasee pursuers. Burrows swam east across the Pocotaligo River. He then ran and swam south across more than five miles of marsh islands and creeks to the Coosaw River, the present-day Whale Branch. He swam downstream to Port Royal Island, ran to John Barnwell's nearby plantation on the northwest part of the island, and raised the alarm. It is unknown whether the crew of Burrows's scout boat had returned to Port Royal before Good Friday or whether they had remained in Pocotaligo. Burrows was later evacuated to Charles Town and provided the first accurate information regarding the Good Friday massacre. A few weeks afterward, he was again commanding a scout boat, leading assaults on Yamasee war parties.[1]

Other warriors broke into the local traders' houses and began killing and capturing the traders and their white guests. When the South Carolinians went to bed the night before, some of them suspected that their lives might be in danger. Those men slept with loaded pistols. Some of them put up a defense and fired on their assailants. The traders who resisted were the fortunate ones; warriors would have quickly killed most of them and spared them a lingering, torturous death.[2]

The Huspaws, east of Pocotaligo, heard the distant sound of the gunfire. The Huspaw King, the town's principal mico, was host to a visiting Yamasee who lived near the white plantations with his family. When the visiting Indian asked why so many guns had been fired, the Huspaw King replied that the white traders were being killed. He invited his guest to join him in utterly destroying the white plantations. The visiting Indian slipped out of Huspaw, ran northeast to the Combahee River, and swam across to Colleton County. He reported the news of the massacre at Pocotaligo to nearby planters, and they passed the alarm to neighboring cowpens.[3]

Another man, a trader whose identity is unknown, also escaped during the massacre. When the killing began, he crawled undetected into a nearby marsh and hid in the tall grass. All day long, during at least twelve hours of daylight, he saw and heard some white men being tortured and killed. They also tortured and killed some white women who were in the town. The trader distinctly heard their cries of terror and pain, but he later refused to divulge any details regarding their ordeal. That night he disguised himself as a Yamasee by taking his clothes off. He walked naked through the town, swam across rivers, and made his way through marshes and swamps. He eventually arrived in Charles Town.[4]

During the melee a young white boy, probably an indentured servant or the son of a trader, ran unnoticed into a nearby marsh and hid himself when the killing began. When he had an opportunity, he headed eastward, swam rivers, including the Combahee, and walked through forests, evading Yamasee war parties. Nine days later, on April 24, he appeared, starving and exhausted, at the newly erected fort on Woodward's plantation, about seventeen miles northeast of Pocotaligo.[5]

Some of the white captives were tortured to death on April 15. The Yamasees may have taken some of them to other towns, so that their populations could participate in the torture ceremonies. When each captive's turn came, he was stripped naked, his hands were tied, and he was tethered to a stake in the town's chunkey yard. The warriors and women chased him around the stake and beat him with clubs. They impaled him with fire brands, which were large wooden splinters, and set them alight. They prolonged his pain, reviving him when he fell. The purpose of the ritual torture was not to punish the victims personally, although that was probably a factor regarding the traders. Like most Indians, Yamasees tortured captured men to death as a demonstrable method of taking vengeance against their enemies. Nairne was a captive. As Indian agent he was South Carolina's official representative, a principal target of Yamasee revenge. He had fought alongside Yamasee war parties. He was a student of Indian culture. He knew that they expected him to stay on his feet, to show no pain, and to express verbal contempt for them during his long, terrible suffering. In the end, after he collapsed and they could no longer revive him, they scalped him, and he was left to die.[6]

John Cochran, his wife, and their four children and William Bray, his wife, and their two children were captured. They were temporarily spared because of their friends among the Yamasees. A few days later, they attempted to escape, but they were discovered. The Indians killed Cochran, Bray, and their wives. There is no information regarding the fate of their children or other white children that were captured during the following days. Many children probably became slaves or were adopted as Yamasees. It is unlikely that the traders' Yamasee wives, concubines, or children were harmed. Members of their clans would probably have protected them, unless they tried to defend their husbands and fathers.[7]

About thirty traders, not including their families, employees, indentured servants, and slaves, served the various Yamasee towns. All but about five traders were present in the towns. It is unknown how many of them had gathered in Pocotaligo. Several of them traded there and probably maintained houses and Indian families. News of the Pocotaligo massacre quickly spread to the other Yamasee towns, where warriors killed their traders. The total number of South Carolinians who were killed or captured in the Yamasee towns is unknown. It is clear that the Yamasees killed the men noted here. Most were traders. Two-thirds of them had been accused of, and in some cases prosecuted for, abusing their Indian customers. Shippy Allen, an interpreter, had purchased captives and failed to pay for them. Thomas Ayre had no complaints made against him. William Bray, a Pocotaligo trader who had made the recent trip to Charles Town, had previously established an illegal cowpen on the Indian Land. He had seized and sold two free Indians into slavery for payment of debts. John Cochran, who traded at Euhaw and Tomotly, had sold a free Indian into slavery and had threatened to take a Tomotly warrior's wife as payment for rum debts. John Cockett, a Pocotaligo trader and part-time interpreter for the Indian commissioners, had traded without making adequate payments for skins and captives. Nicholas Day was known for selling rum to the Indians. Edmund Ellis, a trader at Pocotaligo, also sold rum to the Indians. William Ford, who traded at Huspaw, sometimes sold rum to the Indians and had seized an Indian slave for payment of a warrior's debt. John Frazier, who traded at Palachacola, Tomotly, and Pocotaligo, had physically assaulted the Tomotly mico and seized a slave from a warrior for payment of a debt. Barnaby Gilbert, or Barnabas Gillard, had no record of complaints against him. Phillip Gilliard got a young Indian woman drunk and kidnaped her. Richard Hacher had no record of ill conduct. Samuel Hilden of Pocotaligo sold rum to the Indians. He had threatened to take one of the slaves of the principal mico of Pocotaligo as payment for debts. On at least one occasion, he had helped another trader physically assault two warriors. John Hogg had no complaints made against him. Evan Lewis previously had a complaint made against him, but the Indian commissioners dismissed it. Cornelius Meckarty, a Pocotaligo trader, occasionally served as interpreter for the Indian commissioners. He had helped Hilden assault two warriors and had seized a warrior's wife and child for payment of a debt. Alexander Nicholas traded at Altamaha. He had beaten a pregnant Indian woman to death and assaulted the Chechessee mico's wife and the sister of the mico of Altamaha. Indians had accused James Pattison of physically beating an Indian, but he apparently proved his innocence. Thomas Ruffly was a scout boatman or an employee of Nairne. Thomas Seebrook had no record of complaints against him. Samuel Warner, a Tomotly trader who had recently made the trip to Charles Town, appears to have had no complaints filed against him. George Wright, a trader in Tomotly, had taken a warrior's wife for payment of a debt. John Wright, a former Indian agent, was a trader in Pocotaligo. He had previously attempted to coerce the townspeople into building him a new house. He sold rum to the Indians and left a wife in financial ruin on his Goose Creek plantation.[8]

It appears that at least five traders escaped death: Daniel Callahan, a trader to Pocotaligo; John Fraser, of Pocotaligo and Tomotly, who had assaulted the Tomotly mico four years before and had left Port Royal with his family after being warned by a Yamasee friend; John Hillard, a trader to Huspaw; Alexander Mackay, who had an Indian complaint filed against him for failing to pay for a captive slave; and Edward Nichols, perhaps a trader to Altamaha. One of those men was the trader who escaped from Pocotaligo. The other four were not in any Yamasee towns at the time of the massacre.[9]

Torturing the captured traders and pillaging the trading houses occupied many Yamasee warriors during most of Good Friday. After the wounded Captain Burrows stumbled into Barnwell's plantation on Port Royal Island, people quickly spread the alarm from neighbor to neighbor. It is likely they fired the alarm cannons on Cochran's plantation on Port

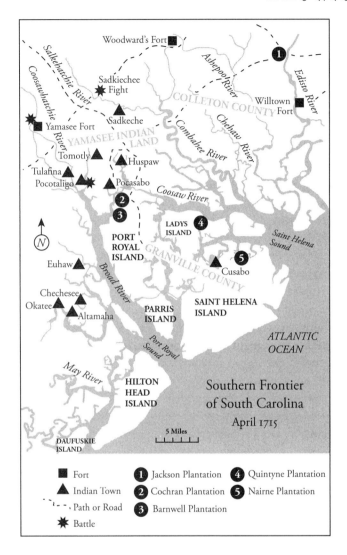

Royal Island and on Nairne's plantation on Saint Helena Island. Fortunately for the South Carolinians on the islands of Port Royal, Burrows's heroic warning gave many of them a large part of Friday to prepare for the Yamasees' assault. The total white and black population of Port Royal was probably less than five hundred people. They armed themselves, gathered all the personal property and supplies they could carry, and attempted to escape to Charles Town.[10]

Late in 1714 a ship commanded by Joseph Swaddale or Swaddell had been seized by South Carolina authorities for smuggling. Authorities impounded and anchored the ship near Port Royal Island, probably in the Beaufort River, formerly Port Royal Little River, near the present-day city of Beaufort. The ship had remained at anchor for several months while government officials considered its proper disposition. Yamasees apparently believed it was there to transport their enslaved women and children to other lands. Its existence was a lifesaver for many South Carolinians. Several families were aware of the presence of the smuggler ship and made their way to it. Before nightfall on Good Friday, about two hundred refugees were on board.[11]

That afternoon several Yamasee warriors beached their canoes on Port Royal Island and began searching the plantations for victims and plunder. About sundown the warriors discovered Swaddale's ship. It was packed with refugees. The Yamasees began shooting at the ship and attempted to board it. However the ship's cannons and the South Carolinians' muskets kept them at bay. South Carolinians reported three Indians were killed, and several more were wounded. Yamasee warriors kept shooting at the ship for most of the night, but the refugees did not suffer any casualties. Early the next morning, Saturday, April 16, Captain Swaddale weighed anchor and sailed down the river with the tide to the sea.[12]

Saturday and Easter Sunday were horror for those people who remained at Port Royal. Yamasee warriors roamed the islands. They operated without any tactical plan other than to burn plantation buildings, kill hogs and cattle, and kill or capture South Carolina families who had not been warned or who had foolishly delayed their departure. The makeup of the war parties would have varied from as few as two men to more than fifty. Some Cusabo warriors who resided on their Polawana Island reservation, which bordered Saint Helena Island, joined the Yemasee in their attacks. Their actions may have been voluntary, or the Yamasees may have coerced them. Two years later, forty-six Cusabos were settled in the town of Pocosapa, or Pocasabo, near Saint Augustine, where they were known as Casapuyas. Later the South Carolina government sometimes dealt harshly with those Cusabos who remained in the colony. Twenty-three years later, South Carolina granted Polawana Island to a group of Natchez Indians.[13]

South Carolinians could not escape by land, because the initial miles of the road to Charles Town lay across the eastern portion of the Yamasee Indian Land. Many families and their slaves, perhaps one hundred to two hundred people, boarded their canoes and piraguas and began fleeing up the Inland Passage to Charles Town. Rev. William Guy had lived on Port Royal Island for only a short time. He ministered to the inhabitants there, but he did not yet have a parsonage or a building to use as a church. Guy only had time to pack some clothing and a few books. A white man and three black slaves rescued him in their canoe. Guy and his companions avoided the Inland Passage and put out to sea, a dangerous choice of action when traveling by canoe. The refugees' terrified flight from Port Royal was remembered by some South Carolinians for more than two and a half centuries. As late as 1971, Jack Leland, then a newspaper journalist in Charleston with the *Evening Post*, recalled oral history handed down in his family concerning two young refugee boys. Their parents placed them in a canoe just before the Yamasees' attack on their homestead. The boys later appeared unharmed at a planter's house on James Island south of Charles Town, where they received shelter. The fate of the people at Paycomb's Wells on Saint Catherines Island, on the present-day Georgia coast, is unknown.[14]

The Yamasees were superb canoeists. They probably caught more than one family waiting for the tide to change. Mary Atkins's family may have been one of those. They killed her husband and two daughters. One daughter, twenty years old, was badly wounded and later died. Mary and three smaller children reached Charles Town. They were destitute, and for a time they had to rely on poor relief to survive.[15]

Northeast, between the Combahee River and the Edisto River in Colleton County, there were about 120 families, perhaps more than 800 people. They included free whites, white indentured servants, and black and Indian slaves. Many of their small plantations and cowpens were congregated around the upper reaches of Chehaw River, now known as the Old Chehaw River, in the western part of the county. A few plantations were situated near the middle of the county close to the Ashepoo River. Others plantations were located in the eastern part of the county west of the Edisto River. The Indian who slipped out of Huspaw on Friday morning warned some people of the impending attack. The alarm was passed from one cowpen to the next. Many planters and their slaves had less than a half day's warning before fleeing east along the primitive roads toward Charles Town. Rev. Nathaniel Osborne, who had lived near the Chehaw River for the past year, escaped with only the clothes on his back. He died of a "flux & feaver" four months later while a refugee in Charles Town. Several people did not escape.[16]

Apalachicola warriors joined the Yamasees in their raids. They resided in two small towns on the western border of the Indian Land near the Savannah River, about thirty-five miles north-northwest of present-day Savannah. The inhabitants spoke Muskogean and were part of the Lower Creek. They had migrated from the Chattahoochee River to the Savannah River about the year 1691 to escape Spanish domination and to be closer to the source of South Carolina trade goods. The two towns had a total population of about 214 people, of whom about 64 were warriors. A town was apparently located on each side of the Savannah River. South Carolinians generally referred to the geographical location of both towns as Palachacola; whereas the Spanish seemed to have identified the location as Cusa, or Coosa. South Carolinians apparently specifically designated one of the towns as Tukassa, or Tuckesaw, and the other as Palachacola. The Spanish identified them as Chalaquilicha, or Satiquicha, and Apalachicola. The town on the west side of the river was probably Tukassa, or Chalaquilicha. It was located in the northeastern part of present-day Effingham County, Georgia. On the east side of the river, Palachacola, or Apalachicola, was situated near the southwestern corner of present-day Hampton County, South Carolina.[17] Two decades later Cherokeekiller, then the mico of Apalachicola, bragged that before the war he was a wealthy headman with a good house, and his clothing and his horse were as fine as any owned by South Carolinians. However he said that once the war began, he "did the English all the harm [he] could."[18] Apalachicola warriors captured three young white girls. A Spanish officer ransomed two of them more than a year later. Cherokeekiller kept the third girl, and she remained his slave ten years later. Her eventual fate is unknown.[19]

Several old Yamasee men and young boys remained in their towns, guarding their white and black captives. Other warriors continued to raid the plantations of Port Royal and Colleton County. War parties apparently did not conduct their raids according to any detailed plan; they ranged at their whim. They continued to kill and capture people and loot their homes. The attacks continued throughout the weekend, and more than 10 percent of the South Carolinians in Port Royal and Colleton County became casualties. About sixty people were killed during the initial attacks on Port Royal and Colleton County. War parties captured more than fifty white people and several black slaves. They took the captives to Florida and to the Lower Creeks. Several adult men suffered a ritual death by torture. Most women and children were enslaved or adopted to replace Yamasee losses. South Carolina later ransomed some captives, but others were never heard from again. The Yamasees' assault on the traders and the nearby plantations was successful. Many South Carolinians became Yamasee prey before they had time to escape. By late in the day on Easter Sunday, April 17, 1715, many South Carolina homes at Port Royal and in Colleton County were burning. The countryside was largely deserted except for rampaging war parties.[20]

— CHAPTER 6 —

Counterattack,
April–May 1715

Late on April 12, 1715, Gov. Charles Craven began preparing for the journey to Savannah Town, where he intended to confer with the principal headmen of the Yamasees and Lower Creeks. Savannah Town was on the east side of the Savannah River near present-day Beech Island, south of North Augusta in Aiken County, South Carolina. He decided to use the Governor's Troop of Horse Guards as his escort. The Horse Guards was a militia cavalry unit, composed of about forty gentlemen who lived in and near Charles Town. The troop served as the governor's personal guard and was used to impress visiting dignitaries and Indian delegations. Troopers had to furnish their own horses and equipment. Each trooper was armed with a flintlock carbine, two flintlock pistols, and a sword. Each officer was to have an aide, a young man under the age of sixteen years, who could be a relative, a white indentured servant, or a slave. The troop had a standard, which was its distinctive flag. A kettle drum and two trumpets were used for signaling and parading.[1] The governor sent messengers into the countryside to notify the Horse Guards to muster. Troopers secured horses, arms, equipment, and supplies in preparation for the expedition. It was more than 125 miles to Savannah Town, so the officers had to insure that food and other supplies for more than two weeks were gathered. Packhorses were rounded up and loaded. The troop would soon become a combat team.

Thirty-three-year-old Governor Craven had arrived in South Carolina three years earlier. He was familiar with the colony, having served as the Lords Proprietors' secretary in England. Craven was a capable administrator. He settled the political and religious differences that for several years had sharply divided the colonists between the Protestant Church of England and the dissident Protestants such as the Presbyterians, French

Huguenots, and Anabaptists. However he could not quell the Indian traders' violations of law or their abuse of Indian customers. Nevertheless he
was a good soldier who provided timely military leadership to the colony.[2]

The governor and his troop, accompanied by several Settlement Indian
scouts, left Charles Town about April 15 or 16, 1715, and began their ride to
Savannah Town. They followed the Broad Path northwest from Charles
Town, paralleling the Ashley River. The horsemen may have progressed as
far as the head of the Ashley by nightfall on the first day. They would have
stopped at or near the Ponds plantation, eaten some supper, and allowed
the horses to graze. The next day they rode over Slann's Bridge and continued northwest along the Savannah Town path.[3]

Governor Craven and his escort crossed the Edisto River at James
Rawlings's Edisto Bluff Plantation, a distance of about eight miles from
the Ponds, and entered Colleton County. They continued riding northwest, parallel to the south side of the Edisto River. About April 16 or 17,
messengers caught up with Craven and informed him of the Yamasees'
attacks. They likely turned left and rode south on a primitive path that
skirted the west side of Round O Savannah. About 3 miles northwest of
present-day Jacksonboro, they turned to their right and followed a path
that took them northwest through the Horseshoe Savannah. When they
were about 6.5 miles southeast of present-day Walterboro, the path turned
south and led to the Ashepoo River. After crossing the river, about April
18, they arrived at the plantation of John Woodward. The plantation was
on the west side of the river near the head of Folly Creek, about 9 miles
south of Walterboro. Woodward and his wife of thirteen years, the former
Elizabeth Stanyarne, may not have been present. Craven and his troop
established a bivouac and began building a fort on the plantation as their
base of operations. They excavated a moat on the outer side of the fort's
perimeter. The dirt from the moat was used to construct an earthen wall
on the inside. The workers probably planted a wooden palisade of vertical
logs atop the earthen wall. The wall may have enclosed some of the buildings on Woodward's plantation. They would have built rough shelters inside the walls for the militiamen. The ruins of the fort were still visible
nineteen years later.[4]

Those families in western Colleton County who had received timely
warning of the Yamasees' attacks were fleeing eastward toward Charles
Town. Militia patrols directed some male refugees to Woodward's plantation, where they were assigned to militia companies and put to work
building the fort. One of the militiamen was underage (fifteen years old)
Thomas Heyward II, whose distraught mother was reported to have later

petitioned the governor for his discharge. Women and children would have been placed in the care of the Colleton County slave patrol. The patrol's normal function was to police the slaves' conduct; however during invasions it had the additional mission of gathering all women and children and escorting them to a safe place. The part-time patrol was authorized a captain and ten white freemen, who were armed and mounted in the same manner as the Troop of Horse Guards. En route to Charles Town, the refugees passed over the Ashley River via the ferry owned by Eliza Harvy and operated by Shem Butler. No fees were charged by the ferryman during alarms. Harvy later petitioned the Commons House, asking for the fees of three thousand refugees who she claimed had used the ferry. Her petition was rejected, probably because the Commons House believed the number of passengers was excessive, despite the fact that the law also defined passengers as horses, oxen, cattle, hogs, and sheep.[5]

Governor Craven declared martial law and sent messengers south and east to spread the warning. He ordered militia officers to fire the alarm cannons and muster their companies. The governor was aware by then that most Port Royal settlers had escaped the Yamasees and made their way by the Atlantic Ocean and the Inland Passage to Charles Town. He ordered Alexander Mackay and John Barnwell to muster an armed force from the Port Royal refugee men and proceed south in boats to the Indian Land. Both Barnwell and Mackay were experienced soldiers. During 1711–12 Barnwell had commanded a South Carolina expedition to relieve North Carolina during the Tuscarora War, and Mackay had been his executive officer. Craven had not approved of Barnwell's conduct of the 1712 campaign; therefore he placed Mackay in command of the waterborne force, and Barnwell assumed the position of executive officer. Craven ordered a coordinated attack on the Yamasee town of Pocotaligo to take place on April 22. He planned to assault the town by land from the north with his Horse Guards and those militiamen he could muster, while Mackay and Barnwell made an amphibious attack from the south. Unexpected developments would render Craven's part of the plan unworkable.[6]

Within a few days, Craven had mustered about two hundred armed militiamen in addition to his Horse Guards. Most of the militiamen were from Colleton County. Port Royal and Colleton County normally contributed six companies to the Southern Regiment of Foot, probably about four hundred white, black, and Indian men; however by then most of the militiamen of Port Royal and their families had escaped from the Yamasees and arrived in Charles Town. Mackay and Barnwell recruited many of them for their waterborne force.[7]

The Yamasees knew from the letter Thomas Nairne had read to them that Craven was marching with a military force. Their scouts went looking for him. Sometime before April 20, they discovered him and his men at Woodward's plantation. The Yamasees lingered around the encampment for a day or two, sniping at the militiamen, but they did not conduct an assault. They soon left and resumed their plundering of abandoned frontier cowpens. At about that time, the militia companies of Capt. Paul Lebas and Capt. Richard Harris, consisting of both white and black militiamen, arrived. They assumed garrison duties at Woodward's Fort. Both companies were units of the Northern Regiment of Foot from Berkeley County, north of Charles Town.[8]

Craven organized the other militiamen and the Horse Guards into a provisional battalion. After he conferred with his officers and received their approval, they set out on the path toward the Salkehatchie River, at the head of the Combahee River. Their goal was Pocotaligo. The path they followed led in the general direction of Sadkeche, the northernmost Yamasee town. Sadkeche was probably located on the west side of the head of the Combahee, east-southeast of present-day Yemassee in Beaufort County. Craven's force of about 240 militiamen moved slowly and cautiously westward on the path toward the river, with Settlement Indian scouts screening their front and flanks on the lookout for an ambush. The Yamasees were aware of Craven's advance. On the second or third evening of their march, perhaps April 21 or 22, the governor and his men bivouacked. They were probably a few hundred yards northeast of the Salkehatchie River, not far from the present-day Highway 21 bridge. He sent Indian scouts out to reconnoiter the surrounding countryside. The scouts returned and informed him that many Yamasee warriors were gathering in the nearby woods. That night the battalion was kept awake and on alert in shifts. The militiamen would have been apprehensive.[9]

At dawn the Yamasees, probably reinforced by Apalachicola warriors, were so confident that they prepared to engage the South Carolinians in open battle. They arranged themselves in a half circle, or crescent, facing the battalion. The maneuver was a double envelopment, a typical Southeastern Indian battle formation used to surround an enemy. Those warriors in the center of the crescent formation engaged Craven and his battalion in close combat, while the warriors on each wing attempted to outflank the South Carolinians and meet in their rear, effectively encircling them. For the better part of an hour, the Indians and South Carolinians fired at one another while the wings of the Yamasees' formation advanced and attempted to surround the battalion. Those militiamen who had bayonets would have fixed them to the barrels of their muskets. Some militiamen became fearful and attempted to flee, but they were restrained by their officers and sergeants. Finally Craven took the initiative before the Yamasees could completely encircle the battalion. He personally organized some of his men into a skirmish line. Despite their confusion and fear, they fired a deadly volley and then charged a section of the Indian's crescent formation with fixed bayonets, hatchets, and musket butts. The Yamasees were not willing to stand and fight. They retreated and left the battlefield to the South Carolinians. The governor later reported that they had killed and wounded several Yamasee leaders and warriors during the "Sadkiechee Fight," probably named after the nearby Sadkeche town. Rev. Francis Le Jau reported secondhand that about a dozen Indians were killed. The battle was costly for South Carolina. Craven's battalion suffered five white men and six Settlement Indians killed and twenty men wounded. Despite their losses the militiamen and the gentlemen who filled the ranks of the Horse Guards acquitted themselves well.[10]

One of the Yamasees' dead warriors was a man South Carolinians knew as Smith. He was probably the son of a sister of the Huspaw King and one of three South Carolina traders named Smith. The warrior was found in possession of a letter from the Huspaw King to the governor. It was surely written under threat by Hugh Bryan, a young man who had been taken prisoner the previous week near his father's ferry on the Combahee River. The letter was hate filled and full of invective. It was a warrior's bombast. The Huspaw King began by summarizing his understanding of the extemporaneous comments that John Wright had made about eight days previously in Pocotaligo. He reported that Wright revealed that South Carolinians would invade the Yamasee towns and capture all of their people. They would show no mercy. They would hang four of their principal micos, sell the remaining Yamasees into slavery, and transport them out of South Carolina. As a final insult to the Yamasees, the Huspaw King reported that Wright made the terrible mistake of piercing their warrior pride by saying they could do little to stop the enslavement because they fought like women.[11]

The remainder of the letter was the Huspaw King's boast regarding the future fate of South Carolina. He said the warriors had already killed forty or fifty white people. He was apparently unaware that war parties had actually killed more than thirty white people in Pocotaligo and perhaps another sixty in Port Royal and Colleton County. The Huspaw King warned that three hundred warriors would destroy Woodward's Fort and a fort that the militia was constructing at Willtown. He bragged that all of

A Dutch view of the Yamasee War. Peter Schenk, *The Gruesome Attack of the Indians on the English, April 19, 1715*. Amsterdam, 1716. This fanciful depiction of a battle between South Carolina soldiers and Indians reportedly depicts Gov. Charles Craven on horseback. Courtesy of the South Caroliniana Library, University of South Carolina, Columbia.

the Indian groups in the Southeast were joining with the Yamasees to destroy South Carolina. Craven, who they considered a friend, would not be harmed if he left the colony. White men would not be killed if they did not resist the Indians' attacks. He hinted that the white men who surrendered, and all of the women and children, would become captives, probably to be treated as slaves or adopted Yamasees.[12] The Huspaw King obviously intended to induce feelings of dread in South Carolinians. For most of South Carolina's militia and political leaders, the letter made it clear that they faced total war and the possible loss of their liberty or their lives. The letter gave them the determination to fight for their families and property.

Craven and his officers wisely decided not to cross the Combahee River and pursue the warriors into the Indian Land. None of them were familiar with that terrain. Men who knew the route to Pocotaligo had either been killed or were serving with Mackay and Barnwell. Craven knew that the Yamasees had a total strength of more than four hundred warriors. Because of the thickness of the forest and swamps, an ambush was a major concern. The wounded men needed to be removed from the field. They probably buried the dead at the battle site. Governor Craven turned the battalion around and marched toward Charles Town. He intended to protect South Carolinians by fortifying strategic locations against invasions and raids. Thus "Sadkiechee Fight," the first battle, was a draw.[13]

Meanwhile Mackay and Barnwell quickly collected a provisional battalion of perhaps two hundred militiamen, about three or four companies, and a few Settlement Indians. They left Charles Town in canoes and piraguas, rowing and sailing south down the Inland Passage. Several men were planters and boatmen with knowledge of the waters and terrain around Port Royal.[14]

Mackay, a Scot, was one of the few Yamasee traders who had not been in the Indian Land at the time of the Good Friday massacre. He and his wife, Helena, resided at Port Royal, where he owned land. He was an old soldier who had accompanied allied Indian war parties and was well aware of the Yamasees' fighting capabilities. Mackay had served in both the 1712 and the 1713 campaigns against the Tuscarora Indians in North Carolina.[15]

Barnwell, an Irishman, was about forty-four years old. He was born a Catholic but became a dissenter, probably a Presbyterian, for which his father disinherited him. He immigrated to South Carolina about 1701. Barnwell married Anne Bemers of Charles Town, and they had six living children by 1715. He and his family settled in Port Royal, where they accumulated several hundred acres of land on the northwestern part of Port Royal Island, across from the Yamasee reservation. Barnwell was active in South Carolina's military operations during Queen Anne's War. He distinguished himself while leading a South Carolina expedition against the Tuscarora Indians in 1712, during which he was wounded. He admired the Yamasees as warriors, having relied on their martial skills during that operation. People fondly called him "Tuscarora Jack."[16] Both Mackay and Barnwell were among several South Carolinians who were courageous, experienced, and proficient in battle.

The attack on Pocotaligo was late and uncoordinated. The Sadkiechee Fight prevented the governor's battalion from advancing into the Indian Land. The governor also failed to take into account the length of time required for Mackay and Barnwell to assemble the men, equipment, supplies, and boats for the waterborne force. A trip along the Inland Passage from

Charles Town to Port Royal by a convoy of boats required several days. The waterborne battalion under Mackay and Barnwell did not arrive at Port Royal until the last week of April 1715. On April 28 they rowed up the Port Royal and Pocotaligo Rivers and landed near Pocotaligo, which was unfortified. They quickly assaulted the town. The skirmish that was later known as the "Picotalava Fight" was brief. Many of the warriors were away pillaging the Port Royal and Colleton County cowpens and plantations. Most of the Yamasees' families fled, abandoning their supply of corn and booty. More than a year later, the government paid the militiamen for the corn they carried away.[17]

The battalion captured one warrior during the skirmish. Under interrogation he informed the officers that the Yamasees were building a fort where they planned to make a stand if necessary. Reverend Le Jau later reported that the Yamasee fort enclosed about two acres, that its construction was not complete, and that it was located at a distance of twenty miles "in the Middle of the way."[18] His general site description is more helpful than his mileage estimate. Although the exact location of the Yamasee fort is unknown, one of the most easily defended sites is a tract of elevated terrain about 9 miles northwest of Pocotaligo. It is a ridge line, 2.25 miles wide, that extends 3.5 miles south-southwest from present-day McPhersonville in Hampton County. The site lies about 6.75 miles southwest of present-day Yemassee. The southern end of the ridge butts against the conflux of the Coosawhatchie and Tullifinny Rivers. At that point the ridge rises sharply to a plateau seventy feet above the Coosawhatchie River and its swamp on the northwest and west sides and the Tullifinny River and swamp on the south side.[19]

The men of Mackay's battalion hastily fortified part of Pocotaligo with felled trees and wood taken from the Indian buildings and then spent the night on alert. The next morning a young, energetic militia officer named John Palmer was dispatched northward with a scouting party of 16 men. Two weeks earlier Palmer and his wife, Margaret, had fled from their home near the head of Chehaw River, present-day Old Chehaw River, in Colleton County. A few men of the battalion were detailed to load the Indians' corn and plunder in boats and then guard Pocotaligo. Mackay and Barnwell took the remainder of the battalion, a force of about 140 men, and advanced northward toward the new Yamasee fort. The battalion's Settlement Indian scouts soon discovered the site of the fort, probably by observing and following Yamasee families who were fleeing to the fort's protection. Mackay and Barnwell moved toward the fort by one of two routes. First they may have rowed up the Pocotaligo River for about five miles and passed the town of Tomotly, which was probably deserted. At some point, where the river became too shallow, they left their boats and marched overland. However it is also possible that the assault force approached the fort in their boats by moving north on the Coosawahatchie River. When the battalion arrived near the fort, they found several Yamasees defending a large site, part of which was protected by a palisade that was not yet completed. The men under Mackay and Barnwell took up positions near the entrances to the fort, perhaps on the northeastern side, and began firing into it.[20]

The Yamasees had probably initiated work on the fort about a month earlier, when they began planning for war. No detailed descriptions of the Yamasee fort exist. They had erected forts against the danger from Spanish raids during the period 1685–1700. Those forts appear to have been oblong in shape, and the main defenses were palisade walls made of logs. Their knowledge of fortification had improved since then. One hundred fifty-eight Yamasee warriors had accompanied John Barnwell to North Carolina in 1712 during the Tuscarora War. They closely observed and then assaulted at least two skillfully constructed Tuscarora forts. Construction of the Yamasee fort may have been similar. The eastern and northeastern portions of the ridge, the land side, may have had a moat filled with tree limbs and sharpened pieces of cane. An earthen wall could have been placed against the front of a palisade of logs. Several round bastions may have been constructed along the wall. Nevertheless the fort was vulnerable to attack, because the wall was not finished.[21]

Palmer's scouting party may have crossed the Pocotaligo River and patrolled north-northwest toward the towns of Tomotly and Sadkeche. They heard the sound of gunshots and quickly changed direction and marched to the site of the battle. When they arrived at the fort, Palmer decided to storm it. He and his men climbed over a section of the wall that probably appeared to be lightly defended. However the Yamasees counterattacked, and the scouts were forced to scramble back over the wall to safety. After catching their breath and renewing their courage, Palmer and his men again climbed the wall, probably at another location, and gained entry into the fort. This time they placed a heavy volume of musket fire on the Indian defenders, causing them to abandon the fort. The militiamen on the outside put the fleeing Indians under fire, killing several before they escaped into the surrounding swamps. Mackay, Barnwell, and their men took possession of the fort. The battalion would have taken an amount of stored corn that they could easily carry and then burned the buildings and palisade.[22]

Mackay and Barnwell moved the battalion downstream to Port Royal Island. Several members of the battalion spent the month of May constructing a wooden fort on Cochran's Point, at or near John Cochran's farmstead. The fort's location, across the present-day Whale Branch from the Indian Land, allowed the South Carolinians to keep an eye on a major waterway used by the Indians. The fortification soon became known as Port Royal Fort and was used as a scout-boat base throughout most of the war. Mackay and Barnwell's waterborne battalion apparently remained in Port Royal during most of May and had several more skirmishes with war parties.[23]

The appearance and bold attacks by the South Carolina militia in Colleton County and in the Indian Land may have forced the Yamasees to reconsider their strategic objective. If they had intended to force the evacuation of the colony or to drive South Carolinians permanently from Colleton County and Port Royal, they miscalculated. After their initial successes, during the first week of the war, they may have assumed that victory of some sort was attainable. However they had not reckoned with the leadership of Governor Craven or with the ability of the South Carolina militia to muster quickly and react. They had expected to receive help from the Lower Creek towns, but they had panicked and struck before those towns could prepare for war and march to South Carolina. However if their objective was to inflict as many casualties and cause as much destruction as possible and then flee, they were successful. After the Sadkiechee Fight, the Picotalava Fight, and the battle at the new Yamasee fort, they withdrew their families and their white and black captives southward down the Inland Passage. By the middle of May, many Yamasee families were camped near the mouth of the Altamaha River in present-day Georgia.[24]

The first phase of the thirteen-year war was complete. The Yamasees were temporarily restrained, and Mackay and Barnwell's waterborne battalion guarded the colony's southern frontier. However the western and northern frontiers lay open and vulnerable to attack by the very Indian groups that had provided South Carolina with protection against overland invasions for more than a decade.

—— CHAPTER 7 ——

Preparations for Survival, May–July 1715

During May 1715 Emperor Brims was in the Lower Creek town of Coweta, about 190 miles upriver from the Yamasees' temporary encampment. He was probably shocked and disappointed when he received Brave Dog's report. He probably believed the Yamasees had recklessly initiated the war without first consulting him. The Apalachicolas were the only Lower Creeks who had been available immediately to support the Yamasees. The other Lower Creeks had not completed their preparations for war. They would not send a large war party into South Carolina until July. Brims was undoubtedly dissatisfied with the Yamasee warriors' military performance; nevertheless their experience showed that fighting South Carolinians in open battle could lead to disaster. During future engagements with South Carolina, the Lower Creeks would avoid open battle and rely on their traditional tactics of raids and ambushes.

The Creeks, and many other Southeastern Indians, had killed the South Carolina traders in their towns. That action eliminated their primary source for guns and ammunition. Although the Creeks and Yamasees had been enemies of the Spanish in Florida for more than a generation, Saint Augustine was an obvious source of supplies. Brims prepared to render a degree of obedience to Spain, if necessary, to secure guns, ammunition, and other goods. Yamasee micos were seeking shelter for their families, but the Lower Creeks did not have the resources to feed several hundred additional people. Brims planned to ask the Spanish to house and feed them. He assembled a delegation to deliver his requests to Saint Augustine. He appointed two trusted Lower Creek men as his emissaries. The first was Ystopojole, probably the mico of Tukabahchee, a town near Coweta. The second was Brave Dog, the Lower Creek war captain who had represented

Brims a month earlier at the meeting of Indian headmen in Pocotaligo. Brims must have respected Brave Dog's skill as an ambassador. He dispatched the two men to Saint Augustine, Florida, to mend fences with the Spanish and seek their help.[1]

Ystopojole, Brave Dog, and their escort cruised down Ochese Creek, the present-day Ocmulgee River, to its junction with the Altamaha River. They continued southeast along the Altamaha River to the Yamasees' temporary encampments near the coast of the Atlantic Ocean. The two emissaries were probably following Brims's instructions when they stopped to recruit some Yamasee headmen to join them. They convinced two Yamasees to accompany them to Saint Augustine: Alonso, the mico of the town of Okatee, and Gabriel, a young warrior who may have been an inhabitant of the town of Tomotly.[2] The delegation then completed the long journey south on the Inland Passage to Florida. Approaching Saint Augustine was hazardous. During more than two decades, they and their fellow warriors had raided Florida, killing Spaniards and capturing and selling Spanish-allied Indian families into slavery.

They arrived in Saint Augustine during the night of May 16 and were taken before Gov. Francisco Corcoles y Martinez. He welcomed them and requested they return the following day. The next day the delegation met with the governor and members of his staff. Ystopojole was the ranking delegate, but Brave Dog was the spokesman. The interpreter was Antonio Perez Campana, a Guale who had remained in Florida when other Guales fled to South Carolina a generation earlier. Brave Dog explained that he was an emissary of Brims, the principal mico of the Lower Creek, and Cherokeekiller, a principal war leader. He informed Governor Corcoles that they came to give obedience to the king of Spain. Brave Dog claimed that the delegation represented the people of 161 towns in the eight largest Indian groups in the Southeast. To prove his claim, he produced eight long leather straps that contained a total of 161 knots, each of which represented an Indian town. He handed them to Ystopojole, who gave them to the governor.[3]

Corcoles asked why the Lower Creeks and Yamasees wanted to ally with Spain. Brave Dog admitted that they had been enemies of Spanish Florida. He informed the governor that Brims wanted to be pardoned and receive the governor's favor. Brave Dog went on to explain why they had broken with South Carolina. He said that they purchased muskets, pistols, swords, ammunition, liquor, and clothing from South Carolina traders. The traders preferred that they pay for those items with Spanish-allied Indians that they had captured in Florida. The traders then sold the captives into slavery. For the past two years, there had been no more Florida Indians available to be captured. The traders began threatening to enslave them and their families and ship them to other British colonies as payment for their mounting debts. He said that Brims realized the traders were not making idle threats when his heir, a nephew, was murdered by a trader who was attempting to collect the nephew's debts. Brave Dog told the governor about the conference of Indian representatives at Pocotaligo. He explained that the representatives met with three of the South Carolina governor's captains, probably referring to Thomas Nairne, John Wright, and John Cochran. The captains assured them that their indebtedness would be restructured. Shortly afterward, however, a trader's Yamasee wife informed them that she had overheard a trader reveal that the captains were in Pocotaligo as part of a military operation during which the Yamasees would be captured and enslaved.[4]

Brave Dog told Corcoles that the Yamasee warriors killed the captains and other white men in the town at dawn the next day. He boasted that they had later forced the South Carolina governor and two hundred of his soldiers to retreat. He requested that the Yamasees be given arms, ammunition, supplies, food, and land in Florida on which to settle. Governor Corcoles did not specifically pardon Brims. The reason may have been faulty translation rather than a slight, for he enthusiastically welcomed the delegation. He promised to provide some supplies. Corcoles authorized some Yamasees to settle at Pilijirba, a deserted Mocama Indian mission on the south bank of the Saint Johns River near its mouth, in present-day Jacksonville. He promised others town sites at San Mateo, a deserted Timucua Indian mission near present-day Covington, southeast of Tallahasee.[5]

Most of the Yamasees soon moved from the mouth of the Altamaha River to Florida. However the inhabitants of Tomotly canoed up the Altamaha River and temporarily settled among the Lower Creeks. Two years later most of the Tomotly joined their kinsmen near Saint Augustine. The Euhaw King and his people occupied an old Spanish mission on Amelia Island, and the Huspaw King and his people remained at the Altamaha River encampment for most of the summer before moving on to Florida. During June and most of July 1715, the Yamasees occupied their new town sites and built houses, storage buildings, and townhouses. They planted crops even though it was late in the growing season.[6]

For many refugee Yamasees, a period of suffering began that lasted throughout the remainder of 1715. They were not strangers to hardship. Over more than three generations, they had moved their towns several

times to avoid danger; families had lost men, women, and children to enemies and disease; and hurricanes had destroyed their houses and crops.
Nevertheless they had lived well during the past generation. The Yamasees had usually harvested adequate food from their fields, the forest, and
the rivers, and they had access to many material items from South Carolina traders. However their standard of living sharply deteriorated after
they were forced to flee the Indian Land and become refugees. Several of
their warriors, women, and children had become casualties. Small children were especially susceptible to the hardships of their flight from the
Indian Land.[7]

The sudden influx of several hundred Yamasee refugees into Florida
during the spring of 1715 strained the food supplies of the Spaniards and
the local Indians. Corcoles was unable to provide the large number of new
arrivals with sufficient corn, vegetables, and fruit. Over the years the governors had often had difficulty maintaining sufficient food supplies for the
permanent residents of Saint Augustine. Mackay and Barnwell's waterborne militia battalion had captured or destroyed much of the Yamasees'
surplus corn, and it was almost too late in the year to expect a good harvest
at their new town sites. It became necessary for the warriors to trek north
into South Carolina and forage for their hungry families.[8]

Governor Craven and his troops returned to Charles Town about May
1, 1715. He proceeded to secure the authority and assistance of the South
Carolina Commons House of Assembly to make and execute war plans.
The Commons House had ended its normal session three months earlier and was not scheduled to reconvene until June 14. However William
Rhett, the speaker, called the members back into a special session by proc-
lamation. When they met on Saturday, May 6, only sixteen of the thirty
members were present, but that was sufficient for a quorum. The missing
members were probably on duty with the militia. The Commons House
did not have a meetinghouse; they met in a private home in Charles Town.
Craven also called his council into a session, perhaps meeting at his home
north of town.[9]

The South Carolina government began taking the necessary steps to
survive. The Yamasees had been temporarily restrained. South Carolinians
became aware that other Indian groups were killing their white traders,
however. The large populations and military expertise of some of those
Indian groups was well known and dreaded. South Carolinians knew they
were outnumbered in fighting men by approximately five to one.[10]

The Creeks and several other groups killed their traders when they
received information regarding the Yamasees' initiation of the war. The

nearby Apalachicola Indians of Palachacola on the lower Savannah River had helped the Yamasees from the beginning. Some other Lower Creek Towns were about 170 miles west of the Indian Land. Those people would have known about the war less than four days after the Yamasees' uprising. They probably used their early awareness to surprise and kill their traders. A trader named John Smith managed to escape from one of the Lower Creek towns, perhaps with the aid of a concubine, and made his way south to the Spanish village of Pensacola, near the Gulf of Mexico. More than sixty years later, a story was told that twenty Lower Creek traders were warned by their Indian wives and concubines that they were to be killed. They congregated in one town at the house of a trader, ostensibly under the protection of the local headmen, to plan a course of action. Warriors laid siege to the house and set it afire, killing all of the traders. Many Indian groups within the South Carolina trading sphere became aware of the war within two weeks and killed their traders. Several other Indian groups followed suit within a month after the beginning of the war. Indians put at least ninety traders to death.[11] It is unknown how many of the traders' families, employees, and slaves they killed.

The actions of the Creeks did not surprise members of the South Carolina government; they had been aware of their threats since April 12. However they were disheartened by the news that the Catawbas, and most of the small northern and northeastern Indian groups, had also killed their traders. Although South Carolinians initially assumed the worst regarding the fate of their traders among the Chickasaws and Cherokees, they would later discover that only a few of those warriors gave vent to their feelings against the traders. The Chickasaws killed at least four of their traders but later blamed the act on Creek warriors. Likewise at least two traders were assassinated in a Lower Cherokee town, but the town's headman later claimed that the killers were two Creek warriors.[12]

Only a few traders were fortunate not to be in the Indian towns when the massacres occurred. Seven traders who survived later petitioned the South Carolina government to be placed on welfare. They were James Lucas and Henry Evans, traders to the Creeks; John Chester, Eleazer Wiggan, John Fancourt, and Robert Gilcrest, traders to the Cherokees; and Alexander Mackay, trader to the Yamasees and leader of the waterborne battalion. The government hired several of them during the following year to work in the Indian trade after the South Carolina government assumed its control.[13]

Governor Craven was well aware of the colony's plight. He warned the government that "if we do not, at this juncture, strenuously exert ourselves and animate one another with a courage superior to our enemies; if we do not make speedy and necessary preparations of Ammunition and provisions for our Men, and take requisite care of the Women and Children, we shall soon be sensible of the inactivity and uselessness of the one, and the burden of the other."[14]

The decision-making process of the Indian leadership was slow, but so was the decision-making process of the South Carolina government. The governor was well aware that the Commons House often approached problems slowly and hesitantly. In an attempt to hurry them, he said, "I hope there will be no need to incite you to dispatch. . . . We have but little time to deliberate. . . . I therefore again recommend it to you to avoid all occasions of unnecessary delay at a time when all that is near and dear to us is certainly at stake."[15] During the following days, the Commons House passed several resolutions. Some became law; others were impractical and were discarded.

The governor and the Commons House correctly assessed the strategic situation. Defensive measures had to be immediately instituted to protect people and property. However offensive actions against the warring Indian groups also had to be planned. Gaining the assistance of at least one of the large Indian groups was necessary before they could undertake a major offensive. The Lower and Upper Creeks had killed their traders and were in no mood to help the colony. Cherokee assistance might be forthcoming, but the headmen and principal warriors were waiting to see what course of action would be in their best interests. It is likely that some Cherokees were in or near the settlements, for on May 9 James Moore brought two of their warriors into Charles Town. The governor sent John Chester, a Cherokee trader, and the two warriors north to the Cherokee towns to assess the likelihood of securing their assistance.[16]

South Carolina's government was faced with a new problem regarding the type and extent of defensive measures to be taken. The colony had never had to contend with major raids and invasions by Indian war parties. Until then friendly Indian towns guarded the approaches into the colony, but those Indians were now the enemy. The Commons House and Governor Craven made decisions and took defensive actions that seemed reasonable at the time. Some measures worked well; some did not. They would revise the colony's defenses several times over the next twelve years. The Commons House began by resolving to construct a large, fenced cowpen in the Goose Creek area. Cattle were to be rounded up and placed in the cowpen to supply the colony with a source of food. There is no evidence that the cowpen was ever constructed. Stored grain and livestock were to

be collected from the deserted farms and cowpens at Port Royal and in
Colleton County, but that was probably not practical because of the war
parties that roamed at will in those areas. An inventory was taken of the
military weapons and equipment on hand. An inventory may have been
taken of all firearms on the ships in Charles Town's harbor. The colony
was short of muskets; therefore blacksmiths forged lances to arm some
black slave militiamen until more muskets could be obtained. A building
in Charles Town was designated as a hospital for the sick and wounded.[17]

Many women and children refugees from Port Royal and Colleton
County initially fled to Charles Town. Several families from Berkeley
County and Craven County also made their way to Charles Town. Others took refuge in nearby forts. Daniels Island, northeast of Charles Town
across the Cooper River, and James Island to the southwest across Charles
Town harbor were designated by the government as refugee centers, but
few refugees used them. The plantations owned by John Ballauglis, Steven
Watts, and Dr. Nathaniel Snow were to be fortified and receive women
and children who had fled their homes. Snow's Fort was north-northeast
of Charles Town. It was ideally placed for access by water on the west
bank of the Cooper River, about two miles south of the junction of Fosters Creek and the Back River in Berkeley County. Living conditions in
Charles Town and in the plantation forts were crowded and often unhealthy. Many refugees became physically miserable and psychologically
fearful.[18]

The colony already had a militia law that included punishment for
such offenses as desertion. Craven and his council wanted a more complete
articles of war developed, but the Commons House believed the existing
militia law was adequate. The governor and council continued to argue
for more severe punishment for offenses. They displayed letters from
Col. John Fenwick and Col. John Barnwell, who reported that militiamen
were deserting. The members of the Commons House began to relent and
suggested a compromise: severe discipline would only be exercised when
soldiers were in actual combat. They asked the council to prepare draft
articles of war for their perusal.[19]

Most of South Carolina's militia companies had previously been organized into two infantry regiments and three independent companies.
During its May session, however, the government temporarily reor-
ganized the militia companies into three elements: garrisons to defend
fortified plantations and cowpens, a mobile force to conduct offensive operations by land in the north, and a waterborne force to operate in the
southwest.[20]

The government ordered forts to be constructed and garrisoned with militiamen. Two plantations were already fortified and garrisoned. Craven's battalion had completed Woodard's Fort in western Colleton County, and the waterborne battalion under Mackay and Barnwell had constructed Port Royal Fort on Cochran's Point at Port Royal. Other plantation homes were already being fortified by their owners and garrisoned by their families, employees, and slaves. Initially the government planned to fortify and garrison six plantations and cowpens in Berkeley County to provide a close protective ring from east to west around Charles Town. However only three of those plantations were fortified and garrisoned: Schenkingh's cowpen, Izard's Wassamassaw cowpen, and Rawlings's Edisto Bluff plantation.[21]

Benjamin Schenkingh's cowpen was on the south bank of the Santee River, northwest of present-day Eadytown. Schenkingh and his wife, Margaret, the sister of James Moore, did not reside at the cowpen. They had a residence and land in the Goose Creek community and a house in Charles Town. The commander of Schenkingh's Fort was a man named Redwood. The site of that fort is now under Lake Marion.[22]

Walter Izard's Wassamassaw cowpen, named for the nearby swamp, was on the east side of the Cypress, now known as the Great Cypress Swamp, about six miles northwest of present-day Summerville in Dorchester County. Izard was a militia captain, but he may not have been stationed there. At one time the commander of the fort was Maj. John Herbert.[23]

James Rawlings's Edisto Bluff plantation was on the east bank of the major bend of the Edisto River. The site was on or near present-day Givhans Ferry State Park, due west of present-day Summerville. The fort was situated on the river crossing site of the Upper Savannah Path. Its commander was John Cantey.[24]

The South Carolina government's plan of forts changed several times during the war. In fact it was changing as the Commons House and governor's council were deliberating during May 1715.[25] Eleven additional plantations were hurriedly fortified from east to west around Charles Town and came under government control. Those forts received militia garrisons.

Robert Fenwick's fort was probably constructed on his plantation known as Data or Datah. Data was on the southeast side of the Wando River, northeast of Charles Town, near Wapacheconee Creek, present-day Holbeck Creek. Government troops were placed there during August 1715. They guarded the northeastern approaches to Charles Town and nearby settlements. Fenwick was a militia captain and a religious dissenter. He and his wife, Sarah Patey, probably resided at the fort site.[26]

Rev. Claude Philippe De Richbourg's parsonage was a short distance west of the Santee River, near present-day Jamestown. It became a government fort but was also used as a refugee center by Richbourg's family and members of his congregation of French Huguenots. During early May, at the beginning of the war, many people of his congregation left their homes in search of places to take refuge. However after a week they returned and fortified Richbourg's parsonage. Richbourg was about sixty-two years old. He and his wife, Anne, had married in 1700 in France. They had six children, the last of whom, Claudius, was born in 1715, at the beginning of the war.[27]

Wantoot plantation was the home of Pierre De St. Julian and his wife, Damaris Elizabeth. The site was situated north of Charles Town, on the east side of the west branch of the Cooper River, about four miles west of present-day Bonneau. Wooden walls were probably constructed around St. Julian's large house. The house was built of cypress timber and had a Dutch roof. By midsummer 1715 Wantoot was South Carolina's northernmost fortification. It became a major government fort that John Barnwell commanded at one time. The site is now under Lake Moultrie.[28]

The plantation of Peter Cattell was fortified and received a government garrison. It was on the west side of the Ashley River, north-northwest of Charles Town. The plantation was later known as Ashley Hill. Cattell, his wife, Catherine, and their family probably resided there.[29]

Thomas Elliott's plantation was west of Charles Town. The site was northwest of the conflux of the north and middle branches of Stono River, present-day Rantowles Creek and Wallace River. A government fort was constructed there during August 1715 to guard the nearby bridge over Rantowles Creek on the principal east-west road from Port Royal to Charles Town.[30]

James LaRoche's plantation was on the west side of the west branch of the Wallace River. The fort's militia garrison guarded the bridge that was traversed by the same Port Royal to Charles Town road that went to the bridge near Elliott's Fort a short distance to the northeast. James LaRoche and his wife, Christian, resided in Charles Town.[31]

John Beamor's plantation was on the north side of the Stono River, across from Johns Island between present-day New Cut and Log Bridge Creek. It was about two miles south of LaRoche's plantation. The fort and its garrison protected Stono Bridge, the major crossing site to Johns Island. Beamor's second wife, Judith, died in 1716, during the war.[32]

The plantation of Andrew Percival, a London lawyer, was known as the Ponds or Weston Hall. Edward Arden managed the plantation. The Ponds was southwest of present-day Summerville on the east side of the Cypress. The fort's garrison helped guard the northwestern frontier. Slann's Bridge, which crossed the Ashley River, was nearby to the southeast.[33]

Henry Nichols's plantation was northwest of Charles Town. The exact site of that fort is unknown. A likely location is north-northwest of present-day Ravenel, near Draytons Swamp and Horse Savannah, close to the crossroads of a north-south path and an east-west path. A garrisoned fort at that site would have defended two critical approaches to the heavily settled areas of the colony. One path extended from the Port Royal–Charles Town road north-northwest to the crossroads and then northeast to the upper Ashley River. The other path began at the Edisto River, about six miles north of Jackson's Fort. That path extended east to the crossroads and from there southeast, between present-day Rantowles Creek and the Wallace River. Nichols and his wife, Hannah, may have resided at the plantation.[34]

A militia detachment constructed a wall of wooden planks around John Bassett's house and outbuildings in the new village of Willtown. The tiny village, also known as New London, was on the east bank of the South Edisto River, south-southwest of Charles Town. Willtown Fort was one of the first constructed. Bassett was a house carpenter who resided in Charles Town. He had constructed a house in Willtown and applied for a grant to the lot. The grant was not finalized until 1716. A store of lumber and tools on his lot was used by the militiamen to construct the fort. Willtown Fort soon received a government garrison and became a scout-boat base for waterborne patrols on the Edisto River.[35]

Richard Bennett's Point plantation was on the southern tip of present-day Bennetts Island. The site was later called Gibbs Point. The plantation was probably fortified during May 1715 as a private fort, but it soon received a government garrison. It became a base for scout boats that patrolled the Inland Passage between Port Royal and Charles Town.[36]

At least six additional plantations were fortified, but they were not under government control and were not garrisoned with militia. They remained private places of refuge for the owners, their families, the people of their households, and their neighbors.

Robert Screven's fort was on the south side of the Sampit River, south of present-day Georgetown in an area known as Winyah. The location was on the sparsely populated frontier north of the Santee River. Winyah's independent militia company included only ten men.[37]

The parsonage home of Rev. Thomas Hasell and his wife, Elizabeth, was situated on a 140-acre tract of land northeast of Charles Town on the south bank of the east branch of the Cooper River. The plantation was later called Pompion Hill. It was occupied primarily by refugees who were members of Hasell's congregation.[38]

Rev. Robert Maule's parsonage was north-northeast of present-day Moncks Corner, east of the west branch of the Cooper River, now known as the Trail Race Canal. Maule and his family initially sought safety in Thomas Broughton's Mulberry Plantation fort during the spring and early summer of 1715. His parsonage was probably not fortified until late summer. It was a private fort, used by refugees, many of whom were members of his congregation. Reverend Maule became sick in early 1716, and he died on December 23 of that year.[39]

Broughton's Mulberry Plantation home was on a low bluff on the west bank of the west branch of the Cooper River, north of Charles Town. The central feature of his fort was probably the new brick "mansion house" constructed the previous year. It served as a principal refugee camp. He and his family resided there during the war. Broughton was heavily involved in the Indian trade.[40]

The plantation home of George Chicken and his wife, Catherine, was at the head of the Back River, about 5.5 miles north of the present-day city of Goose Creek. It became the main fort in the Goose Creek community; it seems never to have been a government fort, though, and was probably manned by Chicken's household and his neighbors.[41]

John Jackson's Pon Pon plantation was on the northwest side of the Edisto River, at or near the site of present-day Jacksonboro in Colleton County. Jackson and his wife, Jeane, may have been living there when the war began. The fort was near the new Pon Pon Bridge, which spanned the Edisto River. The plantation may have been fortified in late April 1715; it was abandoned less than a month later, however, because of the threat posed by Yamasee war parties who were roaming the area. It appears that the fort was not occupied again.[42]

By the end of the year 1715, at least twenty-two plantations and cowpens had been fortified. In Europe fortifications were planned and constructed under the guidance of military engineers and were designed to withstand long sieges and bombardment by cannons. Some of South Carolina's forts were constructed in a semi-European fashion. A moat was dug around the outer perimeter. The soil excavated from the moat was used to create an earthen wall. A stockade or a palisade was then set atop the earthen wall or in the bottom of the moat. The result was a better fort, but many man-hours were required to complete its construction.[43]

Southeastern Indians had no cannons and were not supplied with sufficient reserves of ammunition and food to conduct a long siege. Therefore during the spring and summer of 1715, a typical South Carolina plantation fort would have consisted of a wooden wall quickly constructed by neighbors, employees, and slaves around a plantation house and nearby outbuildings. The wall needed to have a thickness of at least four inches to stop arrows and musket balls. The terms *stockade* and *palisade* were often used interchangeably, but a stockade was normally a tight wall of upright logs reinforced with a row of horizontal boards. A walkway was sometimes constructed along the inside of a stockade wall so that defenders could observe and fire their muskets over the top. A palisade was also constructed of upright logs but was not as tight and was less rigid than a stockade. The construction of both types of wall was similar. First a narrow trench was dug along the line that the wall would follow. Straight trees were felled, stripped of limbs, cut to uniform lengths of about twelve to sixteen feet, and set upright, side by side, in the ditch. The finished wall was usually eight to twelve feet in height. Wooden walls were also sometimes constructed by nailing or pinning thick wooden boards horizontally or vertically to a framework of wooden posts and rails, as was the case with the wall surrounding Willtown Fort. Bastions, also called flankers or towers, made of logs or thick boards were usually constructed in two or more corners of the fort. The towers projected beyond the wall so the defenders could fire on attackers who attempted to scale the wall to the left and right of the towers. A fort also had a water well and one or more latrines. Stock enclosures inside and outside the walls contained horses, cattle, sheep, and hogs. Long-serving forts were provided with Great Britain's flag, which was displayed atop an upright pole. The area surrounding a fort was cleared, sometimes up to a distance of two hundred yards, of trees and anything else that could provide cover to Indians.[44]

About the middle of May, South Carolina temporarily abandoned Woodward's Fort in Colleton County. Supplying and reinforcing its garrison at that stage of the war was too difficult and too dangerous; it was at least twenty miles from the nearest fort. The militia companies of Capt. Paul Lebas and Capt. Richard Harris were withdrawn eastward to help defend the northern part of the colony. Mackay and Barnwell's mobile waterborne force continued to combat the Yamasees at Port Royal and in the Indian Land. The Commons House suggested to Governor Craven that

Col. James Moore be commissioned to lead the mobile force of white men, black and Indian slaves, and friendly Indians that were organizing to conduct operations in the northern part of the colony.[45]

Craven, his council, and members of the Commons House realized that South Carolina did not have enough men or weapons to combat the Indian groups surrounding the frontiers. They dispatched a message to North Carolina, asking its government to send military detachments, under Col. Theophilus Hastings and Maj. Maurice Moore, to South Carolina's assistance.[46] North Carolina prepared to return the assistance it had received from South Carolina during the Tuscarora War in 1712–13.

Hastings was a trader among the Creeks. He was an experienced soldier, having accompanied a Creek army that invaded the Choctaw towns in present-day Mississippi during 1711. He had also served as an officer under James Moore during the expedition to North Carolina in 1713. Hastings enlisted approximately thirty white volunteers from three North Carolina companies of militia. Each white soldier received five pounds to buy any needed clothing and equipment. Hastings received ten pounds, and each of his officers received seven pounds. A servant, probably a black slave, was provided for each file of ten men. The company was transported from Bath to Charles Town in a sloop captained by Thomas Raymow.[47]

Maj. Maurice Moore was a younger brother of Col. James Moore. He, like his brother, had been raised in the Goose Creek area of South Carolina. Maurice had served under James against the Tuscarora Indians. He liked North Carolina and established his home there shortly after the Tuscarora War. Moore married Elizabeth, the widow of Samuel Swann, a union that provided him with valuable business and political connections. He began enlisting white North Carolina volunteers and Tuscarora and Coree Indians. Each man and each officer received the same per diem funds as those in Hastings's company. Major Moore's company prepared to move overland via the coastal path to South Carolina.[48]

Governor Craven dispatched a prominent South Carolinian, Arthur Middleton, to Virginia to ask its acting governor, Alexander Spotswood, for troops, weapons, and supplies. Relations between South Carolina and Virginia had been cool for several years because of rivalry over the Cherokee and Catawba Indian trade. Nevertheless Spotswood and his government recognized the seriousness of the situation. They feared that their people would become insecure if the war became widespread. The Virginia government took the precaution of organizing several parties of rangers to patrol its frontiers. Spotswood made an offer to the planters of Port Royal and Colleton County to take in and protect their slaves. Some slaves were apparently sent there. Virginia agreed to provide South Carolina with some weapons and 300 soldiers; however the assistance was furnished at a steep price. South Carolina was to send a black slave woman to Virginia as a laborer for every soldier that Virginia furnished. The slaves were also to be held as collateral for South Carolina's compliance with all assistance requirements. The soldiers were to be transported at South Carolina's expense. South Carolina was to reimburse Virginia for their arms, equipment, and clothing. The Virginia soldiers were to be paid while in service and were to be employed as a unit under their own officers, rather than as replacements for South Carolina companies. Middleton, as South Carolina's agent, signed an agreement that included all of Virginia's requirements, although he had no authority from the South Carolina government to do so. The offer of 300 soldiers was never fulfilled. About half that number was raised from volunteers and draftees. Middleton traveled south with 118 Virginia soldiers. An additional 31 Virginians arrived in Charles Town aboard the sloop *William*. Most were in South Carolina by the end of July 1715. Virginia also shipped 160 serviceable muskets to South Carolina, along with some ammunition.[49]

The Commons House continued to work late into the evenings by candlelight. Francis Holmes was appointed as the government's agent to go to the New England colonies. He was to obtain a thousand firearms and pay for them with deerskins. He eventually purchased six hundred muskets in Boston. On Sunday, May 8, the members of the Commons House noted that a British Navy man-of-war was in Charles Town's harbor. Its commander, Capt. Samuel Meade, was requested to provide some gunpowder to the colony. He refused. Meade was then asked to make a voyage to England to procure arms and supplies. He refused. They asked Meade to sail to New England to obtain arms and gunpowder. This he agreed to and soon sailed for Boston. Meade returned to Charles Town in August with a store of arms and ammunition, probably those that Holmes had purchased. The Commons House provided Meade and his officers with a present of several tons of rice.[50]

Governor Craven grew impatient. On May 8 he asked the members of the Commons House to hurry and pass the necessary defense laws and then return to their homes to complete work on fortifications and begin spring planting. The Commons House members believed that Craven might be preparing to take to the field again as leader of an expedition. They feared he could be killed, so they asked him not to expose himself to personal combat again. Craven would ignore the request. On Tuesday, May 10, he sent a message to the Commons House, again exhorting the members to finish their work and return to their military assignments. He sent Chief Justice Nicholas Trott to hurry them along.[51]

The Commons House passed several acts. The following actions that Craven had previously taken during April 12 to May 10, 1715, were retroactively legalized: the appointment of Robert Daniel as deputy governor, the declaration of martial law, the embargo of all ships, the muster of the entire militia, and the seizure of arms, equipment, and stores for military use. In addition the governor was authorized to continue to impress private ships, boats, arms, ammunition, provisions, and medicine. The act ordered an inventory of those items in the colony. It approved the seizure of deerskins and other goods that could be used as payment for arms, equipment, and provisions purchased from other colonies. Elections for the Commons House had been scheduled for August, but its members were retained in office until November. Craven was authorized to carry on the war against the Indians. The members of the Commons House gave him the power to declare martial law again in extreme circumstances. Bills of credit, South Carolina's paper money, in the amount of thirty thousand pounds, were printed, and taxes were raised on real estate and personal property to pay for the defense measures. Ten percent interest was to be paid on all personal loans made to the colony. On Friday, May 13, the Commons House adjourned until August 2.[52]

The government had planned for the colony's survival in a mere eight days, a remarkable feat for any governor and legislature, then or now. Obviously desperation drove them, but their decisions were calculated and well considered. It is a testimony to the experience and courage of the members of the government that, under the circumstances, their actions should not be faulted. However some South Carolinians estimated that the measures taken would enable the colony to survive only until the end of the year.[53]

—— CHAPTER 8 ——

Northern Indians' Invasion, May–June 1715

During the May 1715 Commons House and council sessions, the members of the government correctly determined that the colony was in "more danger from the Northern than from the Southern parts."[1] They had received information that the Catawbas and several small towns of Siouan-speaking Indians whose towns were located to the north and northeast had declared war on South Carolina and killed their traders. They feared that the powerful Cherokees would follow suit. The governor commissioned James Moore, the son of a former governor, as colonel to command a mobile force to conduct operations in the northern part of the colony. Moore was directed to "follow after, take, and destroy all our Indian enemies."[2]

Colonel Moore was about thirty-three years old and was an experienced soldier. His most recent military service was his successful 1713 Tuscarora War campaign in North Carolina. He owned several hundred acres of land north of Charles Town and was involved in the Cherokee Indian trade. Moore, his wife, Elizabeth, and their young children resided on Boochawee plantation in the eastern part of the present-day city of Goose Creek.[3] He quickly began assembling the militia companies that would constitute his command.

Moore was directed to construct and garrison a fort on the northern edge of the frontier at the plantation of John Hearn. Hearn's plantation was north of Charles Town on the west bank of the Santee River, near the site of the present-day Interstate 95 bridge. Soldiers stationed there would be in a position to interdict the paths from the northern Indian towns of the Cherokees, the Catawbas, and other groups. Moore directed his brother-in-law and neighbor, Capt. Thomas Barker, to assemble a small, provisional battalion of Goose Creek militia, march north to Hearn's plantation, and secure the site. Moore planned to follow with more troops and construct a fort.[4]

Thomas Barker was about thirty years old. He had been a member of the Commons House for one year, and he had recently been commissioned as a captain of militia. He and his wife, Rebecca, resided on their plantation in the present-day city of Goose Creek, less than a mile west-northwest of Moore's plantation home. On Sunday, May 15, Barker and about ninety white and twelve black militiamen began marching north toward Hearn's. Most of the men were mounted on horseback. They would have had pack-horses to carry supplies and equipment. There is no indication that Barker or any of his men had combat experience. An Indian, who South Carolinians knew as Wateree Jack, was the battalion's scout and guide. He was an emancipated slave whom Moore's father had owned, and he had scouted for Craven in the Sadkiechee Fight three weeks earlier.[5]

The South Carolina government's movement to block the paths from the north was tardy. The northern Indians took the initiative. Unknown to Moore or Barker, some warriors were marching south, looking for victims and plunder. The invaders included Cherokees. However, only about seventy of their warriors were on the warpath. Like most Southeastern Indian groups, the residents of each town made their own political decisions, including whether to declare war. The majority of the Cherokees had not yet made that decision.[6]

Most of the remaining northern Indian groups that were on the war-path spoke Siouan. Their total fighting strength was nearly twelve hundred warriors, but not all of them were marching south. Several would have remained in their towns to defend against possible raids by their principal enemy, the Iroquois. Included were the Catawbas, whose seven towns were north-northwest of Charles Town on the present-day South Carolina–North Carolina border. Many of their warriors had gained extensive combat experience while fighting the Iroquois. Cheraws, or Saraws, resided in one town on the upper Pee Dee River near present-day Cheraw. Waxhaws lived in one town on the north side of the Wateree River near present-day Lancaster. Waterees inhabited a town near present-day Great Falls. Pedees were located in one town near present-day Peedee. Congarees resided in one town located near present-day Cayce. The Waccamaws were a large group that inhabited four towns near present-day Conway. The Santees were a small group in two towns in the southwestern part of present-day Clarendon County, near the Santee River. Seewees lived in one town a few miles northeast of Charles Town. Cape Fears had five towns near the south side of the lower Cape Fear River in present-day Brunswick County, North Carolina.[7]

The northern Indians traveled light, but their progress was not swift. Like most Southeastern Indians, they usually marched only during daylight. They lived off the land, which required their scouts to stop periodically and hunt deer and other animals for food. South Carolinians estimated that there was one large war party of three hundred to four hundred warriors; however each town would have had its own war party, only occasionally joining others for a concerted action. Their war paint, clothing, weapons, and accoutrements were similar in many respects to those of other Southeastern Indian warriors.[8]

On Saturday, May 14, the day before Barker began his march, northern Indians appeared at John Hearn's plantation on the west bank of the Santee River. He may have offered them food and drink. At some point the Indians fell on Hearn and killed him. The fate of the other people at the plantation is unknown. The Indians then marched southeast toward the heavily settled part of the colony.[9]

Barker's route from the Goose Creek settlements to Hearn's began as an improved dirt road. The road continued north to present-day Moncks Corner and then northwest parallel to the west branch of the Cooper River. At the head of the river, the road became a path and paralleled the west bank of the Santee River, northwest to Hearn's. From Hearn's a path continued northwest to the Cherokee towns, and an alternate path led north to the Catawba towns.[10]

Barker and his militiamen made good progress. On the evening of Monday, May 16, Wateree Jack left the battalion's camp, south of the Santee River, promising Barker he would return the following day. He did not. By noon the following day, the battalion had passed beyond the heavily settled area of the colony. Barker advanced without knowing what lay to his front, for it appears that no one was scouting ahead. He was unaware of the fate suffered by Hearn three days before, and he did not realize that northern Indians were nearby. The Indians were aware of the battalion's approach, however. Some South Carolinians later believed that the missing Wateree Jack betrayed Barker and warned the Indians; however the noise of a marching body of more than one hundred militiamen with horses would have been easy for the war party's scouts to detect. After learning of the South Carolinians' approach, the war captains skillfully selected a battleground.[11]

The battalion's route was northwest, along a path that paralleled the Santee River. About 1.5 miles northeast of present-day Eutawville, the path traversed a section of the forest that had suffered heavy wind damage from a hurricane or tornado. Warriors hid themselves in the maze of torn tree trunks, limbs, and roots near the narrow path. In order to negotiate the path that had been cut through the fallen timber, the battalion would have dispersed into a single file more than 150 yards in length. As Barker and his battalion were moving through the site, the Indians suddenly fired a volley of musket balls and arrows directly into them from short range. Several horses and riders went down, crashing onto the path and into the wall of twisted timber on each side. Barker and some of his men fell dead at the first volley. Fortunately for most of the militiamen, the Indians seem to have triggered the ambush too early. They probably attacked only the front of the long file instead of waiting for the entire battalion to enter their kill zone. Amid the gun smoke and the noise of yelling, screaming, and gunfire, the surviving militiamen reacted and returned fire. It appears that the Indians did not leave their hiding places and engage the South Carolinians in hand-to-hand combat. After exchanging fire for a few minutes, the Indians slipped away. It was a classic ambush, perhaps less than perfectly executed, but effective. The battalion lost twenty-five to twenty-seven men, one-fourth of its strength.[12]

The surviving seventy-five to seventy-seven militiamen did not attempt to negotiate the fallen timber and pursue the Indians. It was probably a wise decision. They retreated south, but in their haste they abandoned the dead and, unfortunately, some of their wounded comrades. One or more of the militiamen later reported that Wateree Jack had participated in the ambush and that he had fired the first shot that killed Captain Barker. The shock and confusion that affect many soldiers who are caught in an ambush render the report questionable. Nevertheless the reports and Wateree Jack's suspicious disappearance were sufficient evidence to prompt South Carolinians to treat him as an outlaw.[13]

Some planters to the north of Charles Town had remained in their homes after the beginning of the war. As word of Barker's defeat spread, most men quickly moved their families, employees, and slaves into the nearest fortified plantations. Some people would have gone to Dr. Nathaniel Snow's plantation, known as the Red Bank, north of Charles Town on the west side of the Cooper River, at the site of the present-day U.S. Naval Ammunition Depot. The plantation had been designated as a refugee camp for women and children. Other people, such as Rev. Francis Le Jau of Goose Creek and his family, left their homes in the middle of the night and fled to Charles Town.[14] Le Jau was despondent, believing that "in this Miserable Juncture of Affairs or [sic] sole hope is in God." He probably voiced

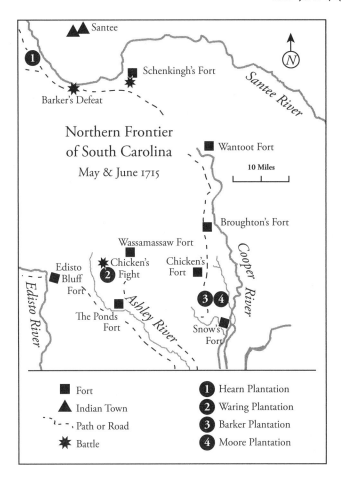

Northern Frontier
of South Carolina
May & June 1715

10 Miles

■ Fort
▲ Indian Town
┈ Path or Road
✸ Battle

① Hearn Plantation
② Waring Plantation
③ Barker Plantation
④ Moore Plantation

the concern of many South Carolinians when he wrote, "If this Torrent of Indians continue to fall Upon us there is no resisting ym [*sic*] as matters stand with us." He feared that the colony might be "forsaken," and if that came to pass, he intended to take refuge in Virginia.[15]

The planters' flight to safety was timely. Three days after defeating Barker's battalion, war parties of northern Indians penetrated the heavily settled portion of the colony. They progressed southward along the west branch of the Cooper River, looting abandoned plantations. They avoided three recently constructed forts. Wantoot, the fortified plantation home of Pierre De St. Julian and his wife, Damaris Elizabeth, was on the east side of the west branch, about four miles west of present-day Bonneau.

A wooden wall probably surrounded St. Julian's large house. The Indians continued their progress south past Mulberry, Thomas Broughton's forti-fied plantation home, on the west bank of the west branch of the Cooper, four miles southeast of present-day Moncks Corner. Broughton's brick house still stands as a private home. Broughton, his wife, Anne, and their children were at home, although their eldest son, Nathaniel, and at least one of their black slaves, Jemmy, were serving in the militia. By May 20 war parties had boldly advanced at least another six miles south to the vicinity of George Chicken's fortified home.[16]

Nearly three weeks after defeating Barker's battalion and after plun-dering several abandoned plantations and cowpens without opposition, some warriors were craving another fight. They had observed the strongly defended, fortified plantations and chose not to attack them. The Indi-ans turned their attention to the colony's northernmost fortification. The garrison consisted of about thirty white and black militiamen. They were in an exposed location; the nearest supporting troops were at Wantoot, more than fourteen miles to the southeast.[17]

On June 5 war parties of northern Indians, which included Cherokees and Catawbas, appeared outside Schenkingh's Fort and began firing at its defenders. The musket balls and arrows had little effect on the fort's timber walls. Conducting a successful attack on a frontier fort was not normally within the capability of most Indian groups. They avoided the risk of los-ing men while assaulting a fortified position. They also lacked artillery with which to breach the walls. However they were superb practitioners of unconventional guerrilla warfare. Indians relied on surprise and guile to accomplish their military objectives.[18]

The Indian war captains sent a message to Redwood, the commander of Schenkingh's Fort, probably by a white or black captive or a warrior who spoke English, asking him to meet with them and discuss peace. The fort's commander and the defenders were surely aware of the disaster suffered by Captain Barker's battalion almost three weeks earlier, and they appar-ently did not feel confident. Redwood relented and invited a delegation of unarmed Indians inside the stockade walls for a conference. As a show of trustworthiness, he ordered his men to lay down their weapons. The war captains accepted the invitation, and their representatives entered the fort. At some point during the subsequent negotiations, the warriors suddenly drew knives and hatchets that they had concealed about their persons and attacked the disarmed South Carolinians. During the chaos and terror that followed, a black slave militiaman named Wallace, who was owned by the merchant Benjamin Godin, fought his way through the Indians. He escaped from the fort, evaded his pursuers, and made his way through the swamps and forest to Wantoot. The South Carolina government later awarded Wallace a new hat and shirt for his heroism. Other militiamen were overcome by the warriors. Estimates as to the number of militiamen that the Indians killed vary from nineteen to twenty-two. The Indians captured about ten men. The war parties then renewed plundering the deserted plantations north of Charles Town.[19]

Capt. George Chicken commanded a small, provisional battalion of militia that was part of the northern mobile force. About the year 1707, after immigrating to South Carolina, Chicken married a land-owning widow, Catherine Bellamy, and became a planter in the Goose Creek community. He was a member of the Commons House, had at least four years' experience as a militia company commander, and was later reported to have been with Governor Craven as a member of the governor's Troop of Horse Guards at the Sadkiechee Fight. He and his wife had recently provided a refuge for neighbors by fortifying their home. By early June 1715, Chicken and some of his men were stationed at a fort on the Ponds, a plantation located about fourteen miles southwest of his home. His battalion included part of his company and perhaps elements of the companies commanded by Captain Lebas and Captain Harris. They had recently returned to reinforce the northern frontier after being withdrawn from the fort on John Woodward's plantation in Colleton County, nearly thirty miles southwest of the Ponds. Chicken's command totaled 110 to 120 men, of whom about two-thirds were white and one-third were black and Indian slaves.[20]

The Ponds, also known as Weston Hall, was owned by Andrew Percival, a London lawyer. It was about six miles southwest of present-day Summerville on the east side of the Cypress. The Ponds' garrison guarded the northwestern frontier, along with the garrisons of two other forts: Wassamassaw, named for the nearby swamp, northwest of Summerville, and James Rawlings's Edisto Bluff plantation on the east bank of the Edisto River.[21]

Early on June 13, Captain Chicken received information, probably from Settlement Indian scouts, that northern Indian warriors were looting the buildings of an abandoned plantation located about four miles to the north. The identification of that site is uncertain; however it may have been Benjamin Waring's plantation. His building site was on the east side of the Cypress, about four miles north of the Ponds. Chicken assembled his small battalion and began marching northward, probably on foot, with Settlement Indian scouts screening his advance. They would have used the path that meandered northward on the east side of the Cypress.

The assembly of the battalion and the march to contact took several hours.[22]

The northern Indians were confident. They had defeated Barker's battalion and the garrison of Schenkingh's Fort. They had spent a month ravaging the deserted plantations and cowpens north of Charles Town without being seriously challenged. They felt secure enough to have some of their women and children join them, probably to help carry their plunder. They may also have had thoughts of reestablishing their towns in or near the abandoned lowcountry plantations of a conquered South Carolina. Three runaway South Carolinians had joined the northern Indians. A white indentured servant, probably the man known as Young Kelly, was with the Waxhaws, and two black slaves, Pope and Pompey, accompanied the Catawbas.[23]

The Indian war captains obviously held the South Carolina militia in contempt, for they failed to post lookouts on the path between themselves and the Ponds. During mid-afternoon Chicken's battalion approached the plantation undetected. Chicken halted and briefed his officers on his planned attack, a double envelopment. He ordered one company to circle quietly to the left side of the plantation buildings, while another company circled to the right. They were directed to link up behind the Indians and create a blocking force to prevent the warriors from escaping into the swamps of the Cypress. Chicken, with his assault company, planned to hide in the forest a short distance from the buildings. When the two blocking companies were in position, they were to give the signal to attack, probably by using a gunshot or a whistle. Chicken would then lead his company in an assault into the plantation's farmstead and push the Indians against the blocking companies, where they could be killed or captured. Chicken probably did not know that the Indians were holding four surviving militiamen captured at Schenkingh's Fort.[24]

About four o'clock that afternoon, Chicken ordered his plan into motion. His two blocking companies began moving into position. He waited, hidden with his assault company. Suddenly two warriors left the plantation buildings and began walking directly toward the assault company's hiding place. The battalion's movements had probably caused suspicious noise. The two blocking companies were not yet in position, but Chicken was forced to trigger the assault prematurely. Both Indians were shot and killed when they came within musket range, probably not more than fifty yards distant. Chicken and his assault company immediately charged from their hiding place into the plantation's farmstead. The militiaman caught the Indians off guard. Both militiamen and warriors fired at one another with their muskets and then fought with clubbed muskets, hatchets, and knives. As in most close-quarter combat, the warriors and militiamen were excited, confused, and fearful. The warriors and their families soon began fleeing into the surrounding forest and swamp, through the gap that the blocking companies had not yet closed. The militia aggressively chased the fleeing Indians, forcing them to discard the plunder taken from abandoned plantations and concentrate on protecting their families. For several hours teams of South Carolinians pursued the northern Indians and brutally engaged them in independent skirmishes in the forest and swamps. Darkness finally ended the battle, and the Indians slipped away.[25]

A significant achievement of the militiamen was the liberation of four of their comrades who had been captured at Schenkingh's Fort. The rescued men reported that a fifth captive, Steven Ford's son, had been taken away the previous night by Cherokee war parties that had been recalled to their towns. The disposition of the other five or six captives is unknown, but a common fate of an adult male enemy taken captive by Southeastern Indians was death by ritual torture.[26]

Chicken lost two soldiers: one soldier was white, and one was black. The identity of the white man is unknown, but the black man was Jemmy, a slave owned by Thomas Broughton. A white soldier, John Carmichael, was severely wounded and invalided for six months. The militiamen reported that they killed forty to sixty Indian warriors, but those may be exaggerated figures. Two northern Indians were captured. One of them, a Catawba, was run down and subdued by Benjamin Waring's Indian slave, a drafted militiaman. Waring's slave had likely been a member of one of the Florida Indian groups and was captured when he was a young boy. The government later awarded Waring three pounds for his slave's bravery. After the interrogation of the two prisoners was complete, Chicken had them killed.[27]

The northern Indians and the South Carolinians had been armed in a similar manner; however that was their only commonality. Indian men were immersed in a warrior culture. They prepared from youth to excel in warfare and gain status through battle honors. Indian warriors were probably superior to most militiamen in individual combat; however the warrior culture had its imperfections when combating British colonial military units. Indian warriors were individualists. War captains had little coercive power over their warriors and had to depend upon their battle reputations and charisma to persuade men to follow their orders. War captains were also independent-minded. The invasion force consisted of war parties from various towns, each of which operated under its own war captain, who was not under any obligation to cooperate with the other war parties.[28]

Nevertheless the northern Indians displayed remarkable tactical skills prior to "Chicken's Fight." They defeated South Carolina's militia in two major battles, they forced people to abandon their homes, and they plundered deserted plantations without being seriously threatened. The shortcomings of their warrior culture did not hinder their actions until Chicken's Fight. By then their successes caused them to hold the South Carolinians in such low esteem that they became careless. Their war captains failed to employ scouts and outposts to warn of approaching militia. They also allowed some warriors to encumber themselves with the presence of their families, who became a burden when battle commenced.

Most South Carolina militiamen had minimal military training, and only a few officers had combat experience. Nevertheless they held an important advantage over the Indians. The colony's militia statute mandated punishment for any man who "doth forsake his colours, or be disobedient to his superior officers, or otherwise neglect his duty." A violator of the statute could "suffer such corporal punishment as the nature of his crime deserveth." The purpose of the statute was to encourage soldiers to function as a team rather than as individuals. The statue was also designed to make soldiers fear punishment and dread the disapproval of their peers.[29]

The efficiency of South Carolina's white, black, and Indian militiamen during Chicken's Fight was acceptable. The battalion's approach march was tolerably quiet and disciplined. A major concern during a clandestine approach to contact was the accidental discharge of a firearm that would alert the enemy. Perhaps Chicken ordered that the pans of the flintlocks were not to be primed with gunpowder until they were in position for an assault. They achieved surprise. The battalion's attempted, but incomplete, envelopment of the war parties at the plantation buildings worked as well as could be expected. The best battle plans often go awry when combat is initiated. Despite having spent the previous month being intimidated and frustrated by the Indians' successes, the men became aggressive during Chicken's Fight. The militiamen's disorganized pursuit was probably the result of the exhilaration they felt while finally routing a dreaded opponent; however it showed their need for better unit discipline. Had the Indians not been concerned with protecting their families, they may have counterattacked and overwhelmed small, scattered elements of the battalion.

Captain Chicken must be given considerable credit for the victory. He was the first South Carolina unit commander to attack the northern Indians after Barker's defeat. Even though he seemed to have had little previous combat experience, his tactical decisions were sound, and he functioned well under the stress of combat. Chicken knew the location of the war parties, but there is no indication that he knew how many warriors he was facing. He was undoubtedly wary of encountering Indian listening posts and a possible ambush, and events of the previous thirty days made him aware of the northern Indians' superb fighting ability. With all of that in mind, he could have taken more time to plan and prepare his march to contact and assault. He could also have sent a message to Colonel Moore requesting reinforcements and asking for permission to attack. Given more time, though, the Indians could have faded into the swamps and forest. Despite any misgivings he took swift action and aggressively led his battalion into the attack. Chicken's ability as an able military leader was recognized and rewarded; within two months he was promoted to lieutenant colonel.[30]

Chicken's Fight was a bright spot for South Carolina in an otherwise dismal spring. The battle proved beneficial for the colony in its conduct of the war. There was an immediate and lasting influence on the morale of both militiamen and Indian warriors. Militiamen understood that combat-experienced Indian warriors could be defeated, and they became more aggressive. Many Indian groups were taken aback; they were reminded that South Carolina soldiers could be dangerous opponents. Afterward Indian war parties usually avoided open battle with South Carolina military formations. Most of the northern Indians immediately returned to their towns and ceased combat operations. They later gave two reasons for attacking South Carolina. First they reported that a Waxhaw woman who had been a South Carolina slave escaped at the beginning of the war, returned to her people, and reported that South Carolinians had killed several northern Indians. Second they said the Yamasees threatened to destroy them after South Carolina was defeated unless they participated in the war. The second reason may have had some basis in fact, but the first was a fabrication that was probably designed to convince South Carolinians that the northern Indians had been led astray. The northern Indians failed to mention their fear of being enslaved, their desire to extinguish their immense indebtedness, and their assumption that victory was possible. Two years later most of the Siouan-speaking northern Indians agreed to a final peace settlement that required them to return all of the property they had plundered. They also "engaged to deliver up Wateree Jack," but there is no evidence that they did.[31]

During the days that followed Chicken's Fight, the government dispatched detachments of militia to Schenkingh's Fort and the site of Barker's defeat. They buried their dead comrades where they had fallen.[32]

CHAPTER 9

Western Indians' Raid, July 1715

During the midsummer of 1715, South Carolinians were frustrated and incensed over the destruction, hardship, and anxiety caused by the northern Indians' month-long invasion. Gov. Charles Craven planned to use the militia's mobile force for a punitive expedition against some of their towns. His first objective was the Cheraw town on the upper Pee Dee River, the home of the group considered the most troublesome. The governor planned to work in concert with Maj. Maurice Moore, who was en route from North Carolina with a force of about 110 men, including 50 white volunteer militiamen and about 60 Tuscarora and Coree Indian warriors.[1]

About July 10 Moore and his small battalion began marching south, probably from Bath, North Carolina, on a path that paralleled the coast of the Atlantic Ocean. Most of his soldiers were mounted on horseback. He planned to arrive at the Cape Fear River on July 17. He was to meet William Scriven, who was bringing piraguas from Winyah to ferry the battalion across the river. The government of South Carolina considered the Cape Fear River to be its northern boundary. When Moore and his unit approached the river, they came upon a North Carolina plantation. The owners, who may have been Thomas James and his family, were absent. About seventy to eighty Indian men, women, and children, perhaps some townspeople of the Cape Fear group, were camped there. Moore assumed, perhaps with some evidence, that the Indians had killed the owner of the plantation and his family. He had the Indians placed under guard. Two of the detained Indians were tortured for information, but they admitted nothing. However a third Indian avoided torture by confessing that they had murdered the people on the plantation. A few of the Indian men were probably killed. The remaining men, women, and children were transported to Charles Town in the Winyah piraguas and were sold into slavery.[2]

On July 18 Governor Craven and part of Col. James Moore's mobile force left the Ponds. They marched northeast for about 20 miles to the fort on Thomas Broughton's Mulberry Plantation, where they were joined by additional men. Craven left Broughton's with about two hundred white, black, and Indian soldiers and set out for the Santee River, twenty-two miles to the northeast. They crossed the Santee about a mile southeast of the present-day Highway 17A bridge. A ferry had been established in that area of the French Huguenot settlements, probably about 2.5 miles northwest of Rev. Claude Philippe De Richbourg's fortified parsonage. Craven intended to continue northeast to meet Maj. Maurice Moore's force above Winyah Bay. Shortly after they crossed the Santee River, however, a messenger arrived and reported that a large Indian force was pillaging and burning plantations west of Charles Town.[3]

Most of the Creeks and the Indians in the small towns on the upper Savannah River had watched and waited all during May and June. They were concerned about the South Carolina government's reaction to the assassination of their traders. They were aware that the Yamasees had devastated the southern and western frontier settlements and that South Carolina's frontier planters had fled eastward to Charles Town. They watched while the Yamasees easily enriched themselves with plunder taken from the abandoned southern frontier settlements. Perhaps more noteworthy, they watched while those warriors gained personal fame by taking white and black scalps and captives. However they were undoubtedly aware that the Yamasees had subsequently fled from the Indian Land and that the northern Indians had been defeated in Chicken's Fight. They waited for an opportunity to make a profitable raid on the South Carolina settlements near Charles Town without taking any undue risk. Their scouting parties quietly ranged through the abandoned plantations west and south of Charles Town. They gained intelligence of South Carolina's defenses and watched the movements of the militia. About the middle of July, when Craven and the mobile force began moving north, the Indians to the west and northwest of South Carolina saw an opportunity to seek vengeance against the colony and earn plunder and martial glory in the process.[4]

South Carolinians later reported that an Indian raiding force of five hundred to seven hundred men marched southeast into the settlements; however that was only an estimate with no basis in fact. The force included several independent war parties from the separate, unrelated groups of Indians whose towns were near the upper Savannah River: Apalachees from near present-day North Augusta, South Carolina; Savannahs who lived near present-day Augusta, Georgia; and Yuchis who were located northwest of Augusta. A few Apalachicola and Yamasee warriors may have also participated.[5]

Although South Carolinians apparently were unaware until later, Lower Creek warriors from the Ocmulgee River, north-northwest of present-day Macon, Georgia, were also part of the raiding force. Thirty years later Mary Bosomworth, an influential South Carolina woman of Lower Creek and British parentage, disclosed their participation in the raid. Her uncle Chigelly, Emperor Brims's younger brother and a principal war captain, led the largest contingent of the raiding force, made up of Lower Creeks.[6]

During late June or early July, John Pight, an Indian trader, sent three Settlement Indians on a long-range patrol to the northwest. They observed, and maybe even talked with, some Indians who were preparing to conduct a raid. The scouts returned to Pight and warned him. Pight sent messengers to warn the various garrisons in their forts and to inform Craven, who was marching eastward toward the Santee River with the major portion of the northern mobile force.[7]

The war parties probably rendezvoused on the east side of the upper Savannah River, near present-day North Augusta, South Carolina. Their intent was to raid South Carolina's western and southern settlements east of the Edisto River in search of scalps, prisoners, and plunder. Chigelly and the other war captains hoped to complete the raid before Craven's mobile force could react and engage them in battle. They traveled southeast on or near the Savannah Path, parallel with the southwest bank of the Edisto River. Scouts, who acted as navigators, preceded the main body of warriors and were prepared to give early warning of ambushes. The scouts also functioned as hunters, providing deer and cattle for the war parties. After marching for more than one hundred miles, they reached the vicinity of Edisto Bluff Fort, where the Edisto River bends to the south. They avoided the fort's garrison, turned south, and paralleled the west bank of the Edisto River. The warriors passed several plantations and cowpens that the Yamasees had previously plundered and burned. By about July 20, several war parties had reached the vicinity of John Jackson's Pon Pon plantation, near present-day Jacksonboro on the west side of the Edisto River in Colleton County. Jackson's plantation had been fortified; however about the middle of May, the men who garrisoned it abandoned the fort and retreated east over the Edisto River, using the nearby Pon Pon Bridge. The Indian scouts found the bridge unguarded.[8]

The war parties crossed the Edisto River on Pon Pon Bridge and broke out into the plantation country west and southwest of Charles Town. The war captains sometimes operated in concert. They were unhindered and perhaps initially undiscovered. The Indians continued south for about six miles, parallel with the east bank of the Edisto River. They soon arrived near the tiny village of Willtown. Willtown Fort may have been a major objective of the war parties. Three months earlier the Huspaw King had boasted that they would destroy the fort. The warriors burned a house on the plantation owned by William Livingston less than a mile east of Willtown. An alarm cannon was located on the plantation. Afterward they advanced to the edge of Willtown and set fire to another house. Militiamen had previously fortified a nearby village lot owned by John Bassett. They had constructed a thick board wall around his house and outbuildings. The garrison of at least three dozen men remained in the fort and fired their muskets at the advancing Indians. The men had no illusions about the Indians' intentions. They knew what had happened to the garrison of Schenkingh's Fort six weeks earlier. The warriors soon withdrew to attack targets that presented less danger.[9]

The war parties spread out. They moved south and then east but failed to discover Landgrave Joseph Morton's plantation near the head of Toogoodoo Creek, east of Willtown. During the next week, they ranged northeast along the north side of the Wadmalaw and Stono Rivers in present-day Charleston County, looting and burning plantation buildings. Among the larger farmsteads the Indians destroyed were those owned by Elizabeth Blake, Joseph Boone, George Evans, Abraham Eve, and Arthur Hall. They burned a ship that was under construction on land owned by Boone, which may have been the plantation located about 3.5 miles south of present-day Adams Run on the west bank of Toogoodoo Creek. Boone was absent, serving as South Carolina's agent in England.[10]

After burning the buildings on a plantation owned by a man named Farr, the war parties marched a couple of miles east and attempted to cross over the Stono River Bridge to Johns Island, a heavily settled area. However they clashed with the militia garrison of the fort on John Beamor's plantation near the bridge. Beamor's Fort was south of present-day Rantowles. It is unknown whether the garrison marched out of the fort, formed up, and fired volleys at the warriors or whether the fort was within musket range of the bridge. After an exchange of gunfire, the Indians backed off and continued burning and pillaging nearby plantations. They were operating less than fifteen miles west of Charles Town.[11]

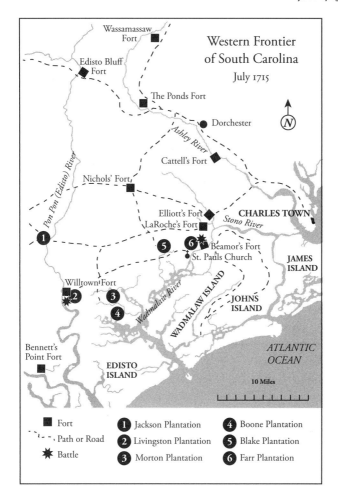

The garrisons of Willtown Fort and Beamor's Fort included several Virginia soldiers who had recently arrived and had been assigned to the various garrisons. An exaggerated report of their actions during the Indian raid reached Virginia's acting governor, Alexander Spotswood. The report led him to believe that his Virginians, operating as a unit, had met the war parties in open battle and defeated them. He opined that the Virginia soldiers' victory would be a major factor in ending the war.[12]

Most of the plantations were deserted; however four or five men had foolishly relaxed their security and ventured back to their homes. They were caught and killed. The Indians killed all the livestock they could find. They burned plantation buildings and destroyed the planters' household goods, farm tools, and stored grain. They burned the parsonage of Rev. William Bull, on the north side of the head of the Wadmalaw River about four miles southeast of present-day Hollywood. They did not burn the nearby Saint Pauls Church, but they vandalized the seven-year-old brick structure by breaking the windows and tearing the lining from the pews. The war parties destroyed or vandalized the buildings on about one-fifth of the plantations in the western part of present-day Charleston County.[13]

About fifty miles to the northeast, Governor Craven and his battalion were marching north toward the Cheraw town. Shortly after they completed the difficult and time-consuming crossing of the Santee River, a messenger sent by John Pight arrived. The messenger informed the governor that Indian war parties were burning and pillaging plantations a few miles west of Charles Town. Craven turned his battalion around, again crossed the Santee River, and hurriedly marched southwest.[14]

After a week of burning and pillaging a swath of countryside that was more than fifteen miles long and five miles wide, the war parties withdrew westward. They had successfully penetrated a heavily settled area of the colony, gathered a few scalps and much plunder, and withdrew without incurring many, if any, casualties. The war captains had not planned on becoming engaged in a major battle with Craven, who was fast approaching with his mobile force. They were intent on escaping with all the loot they could carry, without suffering casualties. The war parties again crossed the Edisto River via the Pon Pon Bridge without opposition. This time they burned the bridge behind them. Craven and his battalion arrived at the damaged bridge less than a day later. The war parties had disappeared.[15]

That fall, after the harvest, the Savannah River Indians packed and moved their families farther away from South Carolina to avoid reprisals. The Apalachicolas, Yuchis, Savannahs, and most of the Apalachees sought the protection of the Lower Creek towns near Ocheese Creek.[16] During the next several months, many of their warriors continued to organize small war parties and raid the countryside south and west of Charles Town, but the period of large-scale Indian invasions and raids was over.

South Carolina's defensive system of garrisoned forts and mobile battalions had failed twice to prevent war parties from penetrating the settlements. Nevertheless the system was a valid method of defending against such attacks. Garrisoned forts could protect critical areas, and mobile units could quickly move to engage war parties that were attempting to penetrate the screen of forts. To be more effective, however, the system had to be supplemented by accurate and timely intelligence concerning the Indians' movements. During the northern Indians' invasion in May and June, the militia commanders were unaware of the invaders' presence before Barker's defeat. During the western Indians' major raid in July, the militia had an accurate warning regarding the raid, but the information was gathered and disseminated too late. Conversely most of the intelligence collected and used by both the northern and western Indians regarding the militia's disposition and movements was accurate and timely.

—— CHAPTER 10 ——

Scout Boatmen,
July–October 1715

By the late spring of 1715, the Yamasee had deserted the Indian Land. After the battles during the last week of April and the first week of May, many of the men in the waterborne force under Alexander Mackay and John Barnwell were withdrawn from Port Royal. They were assigned to help garrison the fortified plantations around Charles Town. A garrison of about fifteen men and a scout-boat crew remained at Port Royal Fort. If the scout boatmen believed most of the action had bypassed them, they were mistaken.[1]

The scout-boat service was more than a decade old. As early as 1702, there were seven scout boats and crews stationed from Bull's Island in the north to the Savannah River in the south. In early 1715, before the Yamasee attack at Pocotaligo, South Carolina maintained two scout boats, each with a small, mixed crew of white men and Settlement Indians. One scout-boat crew of two white men and two Indians was stationed on Johns Island, probably on the west side of the Stono River at or near John Fenwick's plantation south of Penny's Creek. Its crew reconnoitered the Inland Passage between the Stono and Port Royal. The other crew of two white men and three Indians, known as the Port Royal Scout, was probably stationed at or near Henry Quintyne's plantation on the northwest part of Lady's Island. Its crew patrolled between Port Royal and Florida. Each scout boatman was armed with a musket, paper cartridges carried in a leather box, and a bayonet, cutlass, or hatchet. Some scouts may have adopted the innovation of carrying extra gunpowder in containers made from cow horns. Scouts could fight on land as marine infantry, and they could fight from their scout boats as sailors. They wore civilian boatmen's work clothing.[2]

Most scout boats were large dugout canoes. Indian canoes were propelled with paddles, but canoes used by South Carolinians were rigged to
row with oars. Construction of a canoe began with the felling of a large,
straight cypress or cedar tree that was four to six feet in diameter. The
resulting log was then cut to the desired length. A ten-oared canoe would
have been about thirty-five feet to forty feet in length. The log was flat-
tened on two opposite sides and was hewn into the shape of a double-ended
canoe. Holes about three inches deep were drilled at regular intervals
along the bottom of the log. The top, or inside, was then hollowed out
with axes and other tools until the holes at the bottom were exposed. The
sides of the canoe varied in width from about 3 inches at the bottom to
about 1.5 inches at the gunwales. Ribs, thwarts, and seats were fashioned
out of boards and fixed to the inside of the canoe's hull to provide strength
and reinforcement. The holes in the bottom were plugged. A plank about
2 to 4 inches thick and about 4 to 6 inches wide was fixed vertically to
the bottom of the canoe to act as a keel. A shaped plank known as a stem
continued the keel up the bow. Another plank was attached to the stern to
serve as a sternpost. A rudder was shaped from one or more boards and
was fixed to the sternpost with pintles and iron straps. Boards, about 1.5
inches in thickness and several inches in width, were fixed to the top of the
gunwales along the length of the canoe. The boards served as strakes, or
sideboards, to give the canoe more depth and protect it against waves. Most
canoes stepped two masts that supported a suit of simple leg-of-mutton or
Bermuda rig sails. Some canoes probably used shoulder-of-mutton sails
with gaffs. Sails were made of a heavy material known as duck. The last
step in the construction of a canoe was to paint the hull. Swivel guns were
mounted on posts that were fixed to the bow and sides of the canoe. They
were small cannons that fired turkey shot and a ball of about one pound.
Occasionally large blunderbuss muskets were used instead of, or to supplement, swivel guns. Each canoe carried oars, a grapnel for an anchor,
an ax, a water cask, and a pail. An ensign or flag, probably similar to ensigns on British warships and boats, was sometimes mounted on the stern.
Scout boats required periodic repairs, and equipment such as sails, keels,
oars, and other items were occasionally replaced.[3]

The terms *canoe* and *piragua* were often used interchangeably. However a piragua was larger than a canoe and was normally used to carry
cargo. Piraguas often exceeded forty feet in length and seven feet in width.
The construction of a piragua usually involved hewing out a large log,
cutting it in half lengthwise, fitting a plank with a keel between the two
halves, and closing the ends with wooden bow and stern pieces to create a

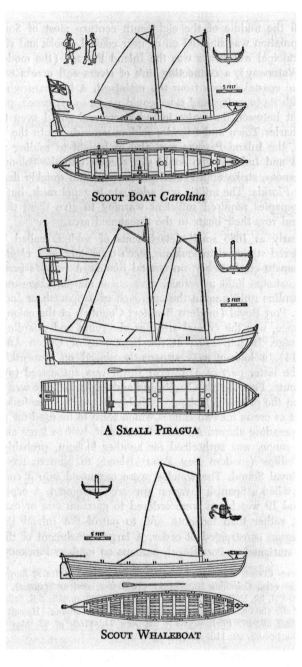

SCOUT BOAT *Carolina*

A SMALL PIRAGUA

SCOUT WHALEBOAT

South Carolina boats, 1715–28. In Larry E. Ivers, "Scouting the Inland Passage, 1685–1737," *South Carolina Historical Magazine* 73 (1972):117–29. Courtesy of the South Carolina Historical Society, Charleston.

wide boat. Some piraguas were constructed of cedar planks, similar to period longboats, pinnaces, and bateaux. A piragua often had partial decks at
bow and stern and a cabin, which was a term for sleeping bunks. It carried
two masts with leg-of-mutton or shoulder-of-mutton sails, which were
its principal source of power. During calm winds a piragua could be rowed
with a few oars. They were outfitted with additional oars when used to
transport soldiers.[4]

Navigating the Inland Passage required skill and experience. Movement was time-consuming and dangerous. The Inland Passage consisted
of rivers, creeks, cuts, and sounds along the tidewater. Boatmen rode the
current downstream with the ebb tide in their canoe or piragua. If the
flood tide began during their descent, they anchored the boat and waited
for the flood to recede. The crew then continued riding the ebb tide downstream. After arriving at the mouth of the stream, the boatmen moved
upstream on the next river or creek with the flood tide. At some places a
cut, or small canal, was excavated through a marsh to connect two rivers
or creeks. When a cut was available, they rowed or poled the boat through
it to the next stream during high tide. Then the crew went downstream
with the ebb tide. If the coxswains' timing was imprecise, his craft could
be temporarily stranded on mud banks in the sounds that lay at the mouths
of the rivers. They had to take care so that the ebb tide did not sweep the
boat out to sea, where it could be swamped by waves. The creeks and rivers of the Inland Passage had many turns and twists. The grass, reeds, and
other vegetation on the banks were often taller than a man standing in a
boat. If a navigator became confused, he had to have the crew land the
boat, and he climbed a tree to observe the terrain ahead. On one occasion
a black slave served as a pilot for a scout boat that was trying to find a par-
ticular plantation on one of South Carolina's many streams.[5]

During the war the scout-boat captains and their men developed into
a tough lot. One scout boat was commanded by Capt. Seymour Burrows,
the officer who escaped from Pocotaligo Town despite his severe wounds
and warned the people at Port Royal of the impending attack. He was in
overall command of both scout boats and crews that were in service. Burrows's scout boat was unusual; it was the type of coastal craft known as
a whaleboat. Whale boats of that period were similar in construction and
appearance to those used by New England whalers during the early nine-
teenth century. It would have been double-ended and built of planks that
were joined together in caravel (flush-laid) or clinker (lapped) fashion
or by a mixture of those techniques. Burrow's scout whaleboat probably
stepped one or two masts rigged with leg-of-mutton, shoulder-of-mutton,

or spritsails, but it was propelled primarily by several oars. The scout whaleboat had probably been impressed into service from a private owner and was retained in service until at least 1723. By July 1715 Burrows and his crew were apparently stationed at Bennett's Point Fort at the mouth of the Ashepoo River. Capt. John Palmer, the young officer who distinguished himself the previous April when he and his men scaled the walls of the Yamasee fort, commanded the other scout boat. Palmer and his crew were stationed at Port Royal Fort on the northern part of Port Royal Island. By April 1716 all scout-boat crews were stationed at Port Royal Fort.[6]

Beginning in late July and extending into the fall, Yamasee warriors from the towns that had relocated to northern Florida and present-day southern Georgia began trekking north on the Inland Passage in their canoes to the Indian Land. Their families were hungry. Florida's Spanish government did not have the resources to feed several hundred Yamasee refugees adequately. The warriors harvested the grain and vegetables that their women had planted in the Indian Land before the war began. They also continued to loot the deserted plantations on Port Royal and in Colleton County in search of food and supplies. Their desperate foraging placed them in harm's way. The Yamasees' reappearance on South Carolina's southern frontier resulted in several deadly clashes with South Carolina's scouts as they patrolled the Inland Passage and its connecting waterways.[7]

One of the first clashes between the Yamasees and the scouts occurred during late July 1715. Burrows and his crew were patrolling the waterways near Port Royal when they suddenly encountered six canoes that probably contained more than twenty Yamasee warriors. The Yamasees paddled toward the scout boat with the obvious intent of attacking it. Burrows and his crew were heavily outnumbered and were forced to bring their boat about and retreat.[8]

Shortly afterward Burrows sent a message to Governor Craven with information that Yamasee war parties were operating in the Port Royal area and reinforcements were needed. South Carolinians probably did not realize that the Yamasees were hungry and that their warriors were foraging for food and plunder rather than conducting raids and ambushes. Capt. William Stone was dispatched southward from Charles Town to support the scouts with one hundred men in six piraguas. Stone was an experienced sailor and marine, having commanded the *Country Galley* during Queen Anne's War. He owned land on the south side of Edisto River. Not long after arriving at Port Royal, Stone was leading some scout-boat crews on patrol when they confronted twenty-five to thirty Yamasees in six canoes descending a river near Port Royal Island. The scouts used their boats to block the Indians' escape. The warriors beached their canoes and fled into the nearby woods.[9]

One of the scouts' most successful battles, the "Daufuskie Fight," occurred about the last week of August 1715. The scouts at Port Royal became aware, probably from a Settlement Indian reconnaissance patrol, that Yamasees in several canoes were harvesting crops in the Indian Land and looting abandoned plantations in Port Royal and Colleton County. The crews of two boats, commanded by Palmer and Stone, rowed to Daufuskie Island, where the Indians would likely pass during their return to Florida. Palmer anchored his scout boat in Daufuskie Creek, a branch of the Inland Passage that flowed past the southern end of Daufuskie Island. Stone and his crew waited upstream, acting as lookouts. Both crews remained on alert for nearly two days. Finally Stone's boat appeared about 150 yards upstream from Palmer and landed on Daufuskie Island. Stone and most of his crew quickly disembarked and hid themselves in the nearby woods. Yamasees were approaching. Palmer's scouts primed their muskets and the scout boat's swivel guns and secured their oars.[10]

Stone and his men disappeared behind the trees near the shore, and their boat, with the remainder of the crew, moved on. About thirty Yamasees in eight canoes paddled around the island's southwest point and came into view. Palmer and his crew weighed anchor and began hurriedly rowing toward the heavily laden canoes. The Yamasees spied the scout boat bearing down on them and determined to flee to the safety of the island's woods. As the warriors paddled near the island, the pursuing scout boat drew within swivel-gun range and forced them to abandon their canoes and swim for the island. They reached the shore and were running to the cover of the woods when the trees erupted with blasts from the muskets of Stone's ambush party. The Yamasees were caught in a crossfire between the ambush party's muskets and the swivel guns and muskets of Palmer's scout-boat crew. All of the Yamasees in six of the canoes were casualties. Most of the occupants of the other two canoes escaped into the woods minus their weapons and cargo. When the Daufuskie Fight ended, the scouts had killed approximately twenty Yamasees. They captured two warriors. One young scout was killed.[11]

During the third week of September, another battle took place near Port Royal Island, when a scout-boat crew surprised a Yamasee foraging party. The warriors' canoes were loaded with corn and other crops that they had harvested from their fields near their deserted towns. The scouts raked the canoes with musket and swivel-gun fire. They killed about nine Yamasees and captured three. The scouts fought several additional skirmishes with the Yamasees. They claimed that during the summer and early fall of 1715, they killed thirty-seven Indian warriors, took seven prisoners, and captured fifteen piraguas loaded with provisions and plunder.[12]

An aged, white-haired warrior taken prisoner during the September battle reported, under torture, that a Yamasee town had settled on the present-day Georgia coast. The Indian died in captivity, perhaps from his wounds. He may have given information regarding the whereabouts of the Huspaw King. The Huspaw King and his people had spent the summer at the mouth of the Altamaha River at the site of present-day Darien, Georgia, planting and tending crops of corn and beans. Within a month Deputy Governor Robert Daniel led a large detachment of scouts down the Inland Passage. When the expedition arrived at the Altamaha River, they were disappointed; the Huspaws had harvested their crops and moved south to the mainland of Florida near Saint Augustine.[13]

Previously scouts had served South Carolina as a reconnaissance force. By the end of 1715, they had become efficient marine commandos. They made life precarious for Yamasee warriors who were harvesting grain, vegetables, and livestock from the Indian Land and the Port Royal and Colleton County plantations. Scouts provided excellent service to South Carolina, and later Georgia, for the next thirty years.

CHAPTER II

Reorganization, Late Summer 1715

During August 1715 some South Carolinians believed they had lost about two hundred people to Indian attacks. That estimate would grow. The surviving population had been suffering under refugee conditions for more than three months. Threat of Indian raids had forced families to leave their plantations in the countryside and move to Charles Town or to nearby plantation forts. Many people became sick and some died in the crowded, unsanitary living conditions. Those who had no means of financial support were placed on poor relief, or public welfare. Charles Town was considered the safest place in the province, but it became crowded. The more fortunate refugees had relatives or friends in town who gave them shelter. For a three-week period, the house of Rev. Gideon Johnston served as a refuge for 105 people. For others little shelter was available. A hospital was established and was manned by Dr. John Schuyle, a surgeon, but the facility lacked sufficient medicine, beds, and other necessary equipment. The town was fortified with an earthen and wooden wall, and Fort Johnson and its garrison protected the harbor. However a 1713 hurricane had badly damaged the fortifications of the town and fort. Portions of earthen walls had been washed away, bastions were demolished, and cannon carriages were broken. A new Saint Philip's Episcopal Church had been under construction, but the storm had severely damaged the brick structure. The north and south sides of the church had been blown down, all the windows were broken, and the roof was unfinished. The old Saint Philip's Church, a small wooden structure on the southeast corner of Broad and Meeting Streets, where Saint Michael's Church is now located, was used for another eight years.[1]

The plantations on which forts were placed suffered damage. Members of the garrisons and the refugees ate the owners' stored grain, vegetables from the gardens, fruit from the orchards, and livestock from the stock pens. The 1715 corn crop was bountiful, but harvesting was slow, difficult, and dangerous. Armed foraging parties visited the abandoned plantations and cowpens and gathered as much grain and other food supplies as possible under the circumstances.[2]

Finding shelter for the refugees was as great a problem as providing food. The forts usually consisted of a wooden wall surrounding a plantation house and the closest outbuildings. Young children may have found the experience exciting, but many of them became sick. Dozens of people lived shoulder to shoulder. Intimacy within families was lost. Many wives cared for their children and the people of their households without the assistance of their husbands, who were on militia duty. Many people had feelings of prejudice against a few men of the Quaker faith who refused to serve as soldiers. During the heat of July and August, living conditions were difficult. Smells from unwashed bodies, temporary latrines, and manure from the horses and livestock would have wafted through the fort and lingered. Under the best of circumstances, many areas of the South Carolina lowcountry provided an unhealthy environment during summer and early fall. Some plantation forts were near marshes and swamps, and mosquitoes were a constant harassment in their search for the blood of human victims. Some relief could be gained from the smoke from fires, but that preventive measure could have adverse effects on eyes and lungs. Those who were wealthy enough or fortunate enough to possess several yards of fine netting called catgut gauze could hope to sleep with less interference from the winged demons.[3]

More ominous were the diseases that sickened and killed many of the refugees. Malaria may have extracted the largest toll. It was introduced through frequent bites of mosquitoes. Malaria was a serious infectious disease caused by the introduction of the species of protozoa organism called plasmodium, which is parasitic in human red corpuscles. The bites of infected anopheles mosquitoes transferred the protozoa from one person to another. Unfortunately the connection between swamps, mosquitoes, and malaria was not fully understood in 1715, and quinine was yet unknown as a medicine for the illness. People infected with malaria suffered recurring attacks of chills and fever that were often debilitating. Malaria caused anemia and reduced a person's resistance to other diseases such as influenza and dysentery because of an enlarged spleen. Once contracted malaria usually lasted throughout a person's life, which was often shortened.

In early South Carolina, malaria caused many deaths, especially among pregnant women and young children. Malaria would also have adversely affected many soldiers in their duties, for a malaria bout of chills and fever could last for more than a week. Other diseases such as typhoid also extracted a toll. The period of August through November of each year was the dying time. In the closely packed frontier forts, many refugees died during that summer and fall.[4]

Simple cabins or lean-to shelters constructed in and around the forts served as homes for refugee families and soldiers. Poor sanitation affected the health of the refugees by serving as the source of some diseases. A knowledgeable and forceful garrison commander would have insisted that latrines and livestock pens be located downstream from the well or nearby stream, their source of drinking water.[5]

A few of the province's missionaries remained in the forts with their congregations. Rev. Robert Maule and some members of his congregation moved into the fort on Thomas Broughton's Mulberry Plantation, on the west bank of the west branch of Cooper River. It was a major refugee camp. Maule functioned as the fort's chaplain, baptizing children, helping care for the sick and wounded, officiating over the burial of the dead, preaching the Gospel, and saying prayers. During late 1715 his parsonage in Saint John's Parish was also fortified and sometimes used as a refuge by members of his congregation.[6]

Rev. Thomas Hasell's parsonage in Saint Thomas Parish became a fort where many of his neighbors took refuge. The home of Rev. Claude Phillip De Richbourg, in Saint James Santee Parish, was also converted into a fort. His parish was in an exposed position northeast of Charles Town, near the south bank of the Santee River. He and his French Huguenot congregation remained in the fort for more than eight months. Rev. William Tredwell Bull, of Saint Pauls Parish west of Charles Town, had found shelter in Charles Town. Many plantations in his parish had been destroyed during the western Indians' July raid. Despite the danger he traveled to one of the forts in his parish each weekend and conducted church services.[7]

Many refugees in the most secure portions of the province did not begin returning to their homes until late October. It would be many months, and in some cases years, before many people of Port Royal and Colleton County returned. By the late summer of 1715, some people were beginning to desert the colony.[8]

The Commons House went into session in Charles Town on Tuesday, August 2, 1715. It faced a mountain of work. It had been a frightening spring and summer. Indians had invaded the northern settlements during

May and June. Indians had raided the southwestern settlements during July. Yamasees were foraging in Port Royal and Colleton County. Strategic entrances into the colony to the north and west were open to invasions. The colony's economy had been severely disrupted. The Indian trade and the cattle industry had collapsed. South Carolina could not long continue to suffer the debilitating effects of war. It was short of soldiers and the muskets, ammunition, and shoes needed to supply them. The intentions of the powerful Indian groups of Creek and Cherokee were unknown. No traders were living in the Indian towns to give the government intelligence of Indian plans. Total war with either of those groups could possibly cause the evacuation of the colony. Many of the colony's best white, black, and Indian men were on full-time military duty rather than working in the fields. To allow most of the militiamen to return to work, it was essential that they be replaced by a small regular army. Governor Craven told the Commons House that the province was in a "miserable state." He asked the members of the Commons House to hurry their deliberations.[9]

By late June or early July 1715, letters from South Carolina detailing the calamity began arriving in London. Craven, members of the Commons House, and several private citizens addressed letters to Joseph Boone and Richard Berresford. Boone and Berresford were South Carolina's official agents in England. They had recently arrived in London, carrying some of the letters. The agents passed the correspondence on to the Lords Proprietors of Carolina. Copies of the letters were sent to the Lords Commissioners of the Council of Trade and Plantations, known simply as the Board of Trade. It was the office that administered most colonial matters for the British government. South Carolinians had little confidence of receiving much assistance from the Carolina proprietors, so some letters were addressed directly to King George I. South Carolinians made desperate pleas for arms, ammunition, supplies, and British soldiers. The Board of Trade estimated that South Carolinians would have to be supplied with food for an entire year, because the Indian raids prevented them from adequately planting, cultivating, and harvesting crops. The Board of Trade asked the proprietors how they intended to help South Carolina with their personal resources and how they would reimburse the British government for any support it would provide. The Board of Trade also asked the proprietors whether they would surrender their charter and allow South Carolina to become a royal colony in return for the British government's support.[10]

The proprietors replied to the Board of Trade by asking for assistance from the British government. They committed South Carolina to supplying ships and provisions, which could be used to transfer British soldiers from their garrisons in other American colonies to Charles Town. The offer was hollow; the South Carolina government did not own or have access to transport ships. The proprietors assured the Board of Trade that the colony would repay the British government with naval stores and other exports. However South Carolina was suffering and was unable to supply sufficient rice, naval stores, or other property for the purchase of arms and supplies. The proprietors did not offer to expend their own funds or to borrow funds by mortgaging their Carolina shares. They also refused to sell their ownership of South Carolina to Great Britain. The proprietors explained that some of their owners were minors and could not legally convey their shares in the colony. They informed the Board of Trade that they were selling some of their South Carolina rice that was stored in England and would use the proceeds to purchase arms and supplies for South Carolina. The proprietors probably could not conceive that Indians could pose a danger to the existence of a British colony. They also did not understand that dissatisfaction with their management was becoming widespread among South Carolina's population. The rental of the small ship that contained the proprietors' supplies and arms was paid for by South Carolina through its London agents. The ship arrived in Charles Town a year after the war began. Little additional support was forthcoming.[11]

It was obvious to members of the Board of Trade that the proprietors were "not able, or at least not inclined, at their own charges, either to send the necessary succours . . . or to support that province under the like for the future."[12] The British government remained reluctant to commit extensive funds to a privately owned colony without assurance of being reimbursed. It was difficult for the Board of Trade, and perhaps also for the proprietors, to analyze reports they received and assess the situation in South Carolina. They lacked accurate maps of South Carolina and Great Britain's other colonies in America. South Carolinians were essentially on their own, except for some assistance they received from other British colonies, most of which was purchased with scarce funds and trade items.[13]

A continuing quarrel had developed with Virginia. South Carolina had breached most of the agreement that its agent Arthur Middleton had signed with Virginia regarding its loan of soldiers and supplies. Craven urged the Commons House to reimburse Virginia for its expenditures and comply with the other provisions of the agreement. The Commons House refused. South Carolina was almost destitute in every respect and was in no position economically to comply with Virginia's requirements. No women slaves were sent to Virginia as worker replacements for the Virginia soldiers. South Carolina had little money with which to reimburse

Virginia transportation expenses or the cost of their soldiers' clothing. They paid Virginia soldiers the same low wages as South Carolina soldiers. South Carolinians complained that many Virginia soldiers were recent immigrants who were untrained in the use of firearms. They also pointed out that the Virginians' muskets were in disrepair. Colonel Evans, the commander of the Virginia troops, admitted that he had instructions not to participate in attacks on northern Indian groups. Those were Indians with whom the Virginia traders did business. More than half of the Virginians served ten months or less and returned home at their request. Nevertheless the Virginia soldiers bolstered the strengths of the garrisons when they were needed most.[14]

On Friday, August 5, the Commons House resolved to discharge the militia and raise a standing army to garrison the forts and serve as mobile units for offensive operations. The people were suffering, the economy was nearly defunct, the military situation was precarious, and the proprietors and Great Britain were providing little assistance. Nevertheless Craven, his council, and members of the Commons House made the strategic decision that after the crops were harvested, they would go on the offensive and attack the major Indian towns with whom they were at war. The decision demonstrates the high degree of courage and confidence that South Carolina leaders had in their ability to survive and prosper. The army was authorized six hundred white men, four hundred black and Indian slaves, one hundred Virginians, and one hundred Settlement Indians, for a total of twelve hundred men. That number did not include an additional eighty white men and sixty Indians from North Carolina. Militia company commanders were ordered to select the white soldiers to serve in the army. Previously slave militiamen had been selected by lot. Under the new procedure, commissioners were appointed to select the fittest of the black and Indian slaves to serve as soldiers. The owners of the slaves were to be paid for their service.[15] If the companies had been at full strength, the army would have included nearly fourteen hundred men. No muster returns have survived, but it is unlikely that the colony could field that many able-bodied soldiers.

The table of organization for the new South Carolina army authorized a staff consisting of a general, a colonel, a lieutenant colonel, and a major. James Moore was appointed general. John Fenwick was the colonel. Maurice Moore and Theophilus Hastings were also colonels; however, they carried North Carolina militia commissions. George Chicken was the lieutenant colonel, and John Herbert was the major. The army was to be organized into companies. The companies would be formed into provisional battalions and regiments as needed. Each company of white soldiers was to include a captain, a lieutenant, an ensign, and sixty men. White soldiers were each to be paid four pounds per month. Slave soldiers were to be segregated into separate companies, each of which was to include sixty men led by two white officers. Each slave's owner was to receive two pounds per month. Thus sixteen companies of white and slave South Carolina troops were supposed to be raised. One company of Settlement Indians was to be organized under white officers. Other Settlement Indians would be attached to the companies to serve as scouts. Indian soldiers were to receive a match coat and three pounds for every enemy scalp they collected. It is likely that the army's new companies mustered fewer than sixty men each. The government of Virginia later claimed, correctly, that its men were used as fillers for the South Carolina companies. The militia, severely depleted by the drafts of its men to the army, was nevertheless to remain in readiness and muster and train one day per month.[16]

Initially the army was stationed in and near the frontier forts that provided a screen around Charles Town and its nearby plantations. The army's mission was to protect the planters and their employees and slaves while they harvested the 1715 crops and rounded up cattle for butchering. The major forts were authorized a fixed number of men, but it is likely that most garrisons were under strength. The area east of Charles Town was the least-exposed portion of the province. It was supposed to be guarded by sixty men in Robert Fenwick's fort on the south side of the Wando River. Danger from the north continued to be anticipated. Peace with the Cherokee was being attempted but was not yet achieved. The Catawba would not enter into a formal peace for another year. A large force of four hundred soldiers was authorized for the northernmost fortification, Wantoot, at the head of the Cooper River.[17]

The part of the colony that the government believed to be most threatened was the area to the west and southwest, between Charles Town and the Edisto River. Less than a month before, large war parties from the upper Savannah River and Lower Creek towns had ravaged parts of the area almost unhindered. Small war parties continued to be sighted there. To protect the plantations, soldiers were stationed in and near seven forts located from the northwest to the southwest of Charles Town.[18]

Two hundred men were to be stationed in and near the Ponds Fort on the north side of the Cypress. One hundred men were authorized for Edisto Bluff Fort on the east bank at the major bend of the Edisto River. They were provided with three piraguas for transportation so that they could quickly move to a threatened area. One hundred men were ordered for Cattell's Fort, on the west side of the Ashley River. Two hundred men were designated for Elliott's Fort, on the east side of present-day Rantowles Creek, near a bridge. One hundred men were supposed to be stationed at LaRoche's Bridge Fort on the west side of the Wallace River, a short distance southwest of Elliott's. Two hundred men were authorized for Beamor's Stono Bridge Fort between present-day New Cut and Log Bridge Creek. Farther to the west, forty men were ordered for the scout-boat base at Willtown Fort on the east bank of South Edisto River.[19]

Several other existing forts remained in use and received detachments of soldiers intended for the garrisons of the major forts. Port Royal Fort continued to serve as a scout-boat base. Other forts that received army garrisons included Reverend De Richbourg's fort on the south side of Santee River northeast of Charles Town; Wassamassaw Fort, north-northwest of Charles Town near the head of the Ashley River; Bennett's Point Fort, a scout-boat base on the southern tip of present-day Bennett Island; and Nichols's Fort, northwest of Charles Town. Most of the other fortifications on major plantations continued in use as private forts for the protection of the landowners and their families, employees, slaves, and neighbors.[20]

The Commons House gave Craven the power to impress arms, ammunition, provisions, clothing, and other supplies to prosecute the war. They planned to set aside half of that year's harvest for the army and refugees. Provision was made to pay the owners of the impressed property. The army would take the offensive after the 1715 crops were secured. An expedition manned by part of the army was to invade the Creek towns, hopefully with the assistance of a Cherokee army.[21]

The Commons House took time to honor and reward several Settlement Indians who had exemplified themselves in South Carolina's service. Newly made coats were given to Robin, king of the Etiwan; Crowley, an Etiwan; John, king of the Winyaws; and John Pight's three Indian scouts who had warned of the western Indians' attack. Winyaw Will was paid three pounds for his service. Jack, a Winyaw who had captured a Yamasee warrior, was also awarded three pounds. Cuffy, a Euhaw Yamasee, was rewarded with ten pounds and a coat for giving the early warning of the Yamasees' attack the previous April. Two years and eight months later, Cuffy was dead of an unknown cause. The South Carolina government purchased his wife, Phillis, and daughter, Hannah, from Landgrave Edmund Bellinger and freed them.[22]

Despite the honors conferred on individual Settlement Indians, the alleged participation of Wateree Jack in the ambush of Captain Barker's battalion and the defection of some Cusabos caused several South Carolinians to be suspicious of their loyalty. To assure that the settlement warriors did not defect or give aid and comfort to enemy Indians, some members of the Commons House proposed that the warriors' women, and presumably their children, be assigned to garrisoned forts where they could be supervised. Each morning and each evening, the garrisons would conduct a roll call to insure that the Settlement Indian women and their children were not absent.[23] It is unknown whether that proposal was implemented to any extent.

Several Tuscarora warriors had come south with the North Carolina soldiers and were now fighting for South Carolina. Previously during the Tuscarora War of 1712–13, Indians allied with South Carolina had captured several Tuscarora women and children. The captives had been sold as slaves to South Carolinians. The Commons House recommended that some of those slaves be purchased from their owners and allowed the Tuscarora warriors to return them to their homes. Seven months later the government passed the recommendation into law. However the statute required that Tuscarora slaves could be freed only after they were exchanged for enemy Indians that Tuscarora warriors captured.[24]

Before the Commons House recessed, the members took measures to raise thirty thousand pounds, an amount considered necessary to continue prosecution of the war. Taxes were increased. Property assessors and tax collectors were appointed for all areas of the province to inventory and value all real and personal property. Persons whose property had a total value of less than two shillings and sixpence were exempt from tax. Also exempt were property owners who had been driven from their land because of the war.[25]

Small Indian war parties continued to prowl the countryside in search of scalps and plunder. Several men were ambushed and killed while on patrol. The warriors who moved through the settlements west of Charles Town were probably Yamasees, Creeks, and Indians from towns on the upper Savannah River. War parties that harassed the settlements north of Charles Town may have included Cheraws. South Carolina kept reconnaissance patrols moving between the forts, on the lookout for war parties. Friendly Settlement Indians conducted long-range patrols beyond the frontiers, sometimes as far west as the Combahee River. War parties, which hid beside the paths, sometimes ambushed army patrols. During November two soldiers from Goose Creek were killed near the Santee River.[26]

During the first week in August, Capt. John Cantey, a thirty-seven-year-old Goose Creek planter, an experienced soldier, and the commander of Edisto Bluff Fort northwest of Charles Town, warned the governor that a war party had been sighted in his vicinity. The Indians disappeared before they could be engaged in combat. During September Col. John Fenwick received information, probably from a Settlement Indian long-range patrol, that a Yamasee war party was harvesting crops and pillaging abandoned plantations in western Colleton County. Colonel Fenwick was on the army staff and also commanded the militia Southward Regiment of Foot. He was a plantation owner and a merchant. Previously, during 1706, Fenwick had been a militia company commander when a French and Spanish invasion force landed in South Carolina. Fenwick and his company defeated the invaders during two separate battles. Upon receiving information regarding the Yamasee war party, he assembled a detachment of soldiers from the western plantation forts.[27]

Most of Fenwick's soldiers were probably mounted on horseback. They marched to Pon Pon Bridge over the Edisto River. Fenwick and his men repaired the bridge, which had been burned by Indian war parties during the previous July. Afterward they marched southwest through the deserted countryside of Colleton County toward the Combahee River. Before the war many cowpens had been located in the western part of Colleton County; however during the war much of that area was abandoned.[28]

Settlement Indian scouts screened Fenwick's advance. A couple of miles east of the Combahee River, near the former site of Bryan's Ferry, the scouts spied sixteen Yamasee warriors camped at the abandoned plantation house of John Jackson. The Yamasees had paddled north on the Inland Passage from Florida in four canoes. They were harvesting crops from the fields in the Indian Land and plundering the abandoned farmsteads near the Combahee River in Colleton County. They had beached their canoes on the east bank of the river, walked over the causeway spanning the marsh, and camped in Jackson's house. Apparently the warriors did not post sentries. They probably did not expect that a South Carolina force would be so bold as to operate that far to the southwest. Fenwick halted his troops a mile or more east of Jackson's house, where they tethered their horses. Late that night the South Carolinians advanced on foot and quietly surrounded Jackson's plantation house. At dawn Fenwick gave the signal to attack. The soldiers caught the Indians unaware, and a sharp firefight resulted. During the battle, Fenwick's detachment killed nine of the surprised warriors. Two warriors were captured. Colonel Fenwick's men suffered two casualties: one white soldier was killed, and one black soldier was wounded. Five warriors ran to the river and escaped in three of their canoes. The following day Capt. John Palmer and his crew of scouts came upon the escaping warriors at the mouth of the Combahee River. They forced the warriors to abandon their canoes and swim for their lives. The war was only five months old, but many South Carolinians had become skillful soldiers.[29]

By late summer 1715, South Carolinians were suffering, physically and psychologically. They were "imprison'd between mud walls, stifled with excessive heats, oppress'd with famine, sickness, the desolation of their country, death of their friends, apprehension of their own fate, despairing of relief, and destitute of any hopes to escape."[30] The nightmares of South Carolinians would have involved falling into the Indians' hands. They knew that in such an event the men would be tortured to death and the women and children would be taken into the wilderness to live as slaves or as Indians. The Yamasees were also suffering. They were short of food; many of their people had been killed, wounded, or captured; and their future was uncertain. The recent successes of the scout boatmen and soldiers were probably causing the Yamasees to have nightmares of falling into the hands of the army. They knew that in such an event the men would be killed and the women and children would be sold into slavery and transported overseas.

— CHAPTER 12 —

Cherokee Expedition,
November 1715–February 1716

The most powerful Indian groups within striking distance of South Carolina were the Creeks and Cherokees. The governor and members of the Commons House realized that if those Indians acted in concert, they could probably defeat South Carolina's army and force the abandonment of the colony. Making peace with them was essential. However the prospect of making peace with the Creeks, especially the Lower Creeks, appeared remote during the summer and fall of 1715. Both Lower and Upper Creeks had killed their traders, and during July 1715 the Lower Creeks had participated in a large raid into the plantations southwest of Charles Town. Small Lower and Upper Creek war parties continued to raid the frontiers. By contrast the Cherokees apparently had not killed many traders. During the Commons House session, on May 9, James Moore had brought two warriors from the Lower Cherokee to Charles Town. The warriors claimed that their towns were not yet involved in the war. The governor dispatched John Chester, a trader, to the Cherokee towns with the two warriors. Shortly afterward, during May and June, a Cherokee war party participated in the invasion of the northern settlements, but Chester's diplomacy may have been instrumental in the war party's withdrawal prior to Chicken's Fight.[1]

Thus the best hopes of members of the South Carolina government rested on securing a peace treaty with the Cherokees. If the Cherokees could be enticed to become an ally, they might agree to accompany South Carolina troops on an invasion of the Creek towns. When the Commons House met in August, Indian traders Eleazer Wiggan and Robert Gilcrest offered to journey to the Cherokee towns and seek their assistance against the other Indian groups. They asked for a payment of fifty pounds to outfit them and purchase presents that were obligatory in Indian negotiations. They also asked for an additional three hundred pounds as their fee if they were successful. Their offer was accepted that summer, and they rode north to the Cherokee towns in the foothills and mountains northwest of Charles Town.[2]

Reaching a consensus among the Cherokee towns regarding any important subject, especially war, was time-consuming. Each town tended to be independent, and its headmen and warriors would have discussed the issue of assisting or assaulting South Carolina at great length. An agreement by all of the towns would have been difficult to achieve. During the summer and fall of 1715, some Cherokee headmen and warriors proposed war against South Carolina and were talking with emissaries from Creek towns. Others favored joining South Carolina in an attack on the Creek towns. Some argued for neutrality. Adding to the confusion was the false information that renegade South Carolinians gave to the Cherokees. Alexander Long, an outlaw trader, told the Cherokees that South Carolina was going to kill their war captains. Two of South Carolina's escaped black slaves informed the Cherokees that South Carolina intended to attack them.[3]

Finally, after about two months of negotiations, Wiggan and Gilcrest were partially successful. In October they returned to Charles Town with eight headmen, twelve war captains, and one hundred Cherokee warriors. Among the delegation was Caesar, of the Cherokee town of Chota or Echota. Until 1713 Caesar had been a slave owned by a Cherokee trader named John Stephens. During that year the South Carolina Indian commissioners purchased Caesar's freedom, hoping that he might someday prove useful. He spoke some English and was a friend of South Carolina; however he maintained his independence and on occasion proved troublesome. The Indian commissioners and army officers often dealt with Caesar as if he were a headman or a war captain. He was no headman and was a failure as a war leader, but he maintained some influence with both South Carolina and several Cherokees. The diplomatic ceremonies and discussions in Charles Town included a military parade, gun salutes, Indian dances, formal smoking, speeches, rum drinking, and most important, giving and receiving presents. The Cherokee headmen, the war captains, and Caesar promised Gov. Charles Craven they would assemble a force of warriors and join a South Carolina army at Savannah Town. Part of the combined force of South Carolinians and Cherokees would then invade the Upper Creek towns, and the other part would invade the Lower Creeks. That was good news for South Carolinians. At last they could take offensive action against the Lower Creeks, whom they believed had instigated the war. However—perhaps not understood by the governor—the delegation of headmen and warriors did not speak for all of the Cherokee towns.[4]

Preparations were immediately undertaken by the government to organize several companies of the army into a provisional regiment to serve as an expeditionary force against the Creeks. Part of the army remained in the settlements to garrison the frontier forts. The strength of the garrisons was severely reduced, and much of their security rested with the women and the young, old, and sick men. The regiment was to march to Savannah Town on the upper Savannah River, where a fortification was to be constructed. A large detachment of the regiment would then join with Cherokee warriors and invade the Lower Creek towns on the Ocmulgee and Oconee Rivers in present-day central Georgia. Another detachment would join other Cherokee warriors and invade the Upper Creek towns on the Alabama, Coosa, and Tallapoosa Rivers in present-day central Alabama. During the weekend of November 26 and 27, the regiment began assembling at the Ponds Fort. Gen. James Moore was in command. The regiment's field-grade officers were Col. John Fenwick, Col. Maurice Moore, Lt. Col. George Chicken, and Maj. John Herbert. The provisional regiment included ten companies. Companies commanded by captains Nathaniel Broughton, John Cantey, Robert Daniel Jr., and Thomas Smith were part of the army that had been drawn from the militia of the Northern Regiment of Foot. Captains William Bull and William Scott commanded companies of the army that had been drafted from the Southward Regiment of Foot. Captain John Pight commanded a company composed of Settlement Indians. Captains Stephen Ford and Charlesworth Glover commanded two companies of black and Indian slave soldiers. A small company of Virginia soldiers under Capt. William Gorham was included in the expedition. A few North Carolina soldiers later joined the regiment at Savannah Town. If all of the companies were at the authorized strength of officers and men, the expedition would have included more than six hundred soldiers; however it is unlikely that the regiment included many more than five hundred. Most of the soldiers were mounted on horseback. Several members of the regiment were combat-experienced veterans. Most of the officers and men were young, had the necessary physical stamina to undergo the hardships of a long winter campaign, and possessed remarkable courage. However like most South Carolinians, many would be dead of some pestilence before they were sixty years old. The exception was thirty-two-year-old Capt. William

Bull. He lived to the age of seventy-two. During his long life, he provided good service to South Carolina as a soldier, rice planter, member of the governor's council, acting governor, and adviser to the new colony of Georgia.[5]

By Monday, November 28, most of the companies had assembled near the Ponds Fort. Craven and several prominent citizens arrived from Charles Town to see the men off. The regiment was organized into three echelons. The Indian scouts and advance party were placed under the command of Col. Maurice Moore, Gen. James Moore led the main body, and Lieutenant Colonel Chicken commanded the rear guard. On Tuesday Colonel Moore moved the advance party about eight miles northwest, crossed the Edisto River, and encamped across from Edisto Bluff Fort. On Wednesday Craven returned to Charles Town, and the remainder of the regiment began its march. By nightfall the entire regiment was bivouacked on the west bank of the Edisto River. The march continued the next morning. On Friday Fenwick and the companies under Bull and Scott joined the expedition.[6]

The regiment traveled northwest along the Savannah Path, a march of more than 120 miles from Edisto Bluff Fort. The Savannah Path from Charles Town to Savannah Town was two trails, a northern route and a southern route. Both paralleled modern roads and highways. Half a century later, the southern route was the principal one. However period maps prepared by Thomas Nairne and John Barnwell show that during the early eighteenth century the northern route was the principal path. Then, as now, paths and roads followed the high ground to avoid as many swamps and river crossings as possible. The northern path extended west-northwest from present-day Givhans Ferry State Park along the west bank of Edisto River. It passed through the lower pine belt region of the colony and continued west-northwest through the upper pine belt region, avoiding the heads of the Edisto and Salkehatchie Rivers. The path then followed the "red hills" region northwest to Savannah Town. The terrain became rolling and then hilly during the last few miles.[7]

The regiment traveled as light as possible. Packhorses carried tools for use in building a fort, small cannons known as swivel guns, ammunition, and supplies. Probably the only food carried was salt and perhaps some cornmeal. The members of the expedition adopted the practice of Indian war parties of living off the land through which they passed. Indian scouts hunted deer, and soldiers hunted cattle that were running wild in and near abandoned cowpens. The kills were butchered and shared among the men. Typical military practice of the period was to divide each company into files or messes, similar to present-day squads, of half a dozen or more men each. Each file was responsible for preparing its own meals.[8]

The journey probably lasted about a week. Savannah Town was on the east bank of the Savannah River, about 3.5 miles downstream and across the river from present-day Augusta, Georgia, and a short distance northwest of Beech Island, South Carolina. Four Apalachee towns and three small Savannah towns in that general vicinity were deserted. The inhabitants had recently left the area, perhaps after they learned that the regiment was approaching. Indians had probably sacked and then destroyed the old palisaded trading post there.[9]

At Savannah Town the regiment prepared to begin its march into the Creek towns. They watched for the arrival of several hundred warriors that the Cherokee delegation to Charles Town had promised. While waiting for the Cherokees, General Moore set part of the army to work building a fortification to serve as a base camp and frontier fort. The fort, which the government would soon name Fort Moore, was constructed on the east side of the Savannah River atop what was long known as Fort Moore Bluff. The location was about 1.5 miles northwest of present-day Beech Island and about 6 miles south of the Savannah River fall line. The fall line, or rapids, was the northern limit of navigation on the river. Construction of the new fort began by felling trees with axes and saws. All lumber was fashioned on the site in two-man saw pits. The fort was square-shaped. Each side was approximately 150 feet in length. A typical palisade or stockade wall was not used. Instead thick planks were nailed or pinned horizontally to vertical fence posts, or puncheons, planted around the perimeter of the fort. The resulting wall was about four to five feet high. A projecting bastion also known as a flanker or tower was constructed at each corner of the fort. During an attack men stationed in a bastion could rake the wall on each side with gunfire. The bastions had shed roofs to protect sentries from the sun and foul weather. Swivel guns were mounted on platforms in the bastions. Clapboard houses and barracks were constructed for the officers and soldiers. A guardhouse, a corn crib, a gunpowder magazine, a well, and a latrine would also have been constructed inside the wall. A stable and livestock pens would have been placed outside the wall. The construction of the buildings was similar to present-day agricultural pole sheds or pole barns. Postholes were dug around the building's perimeter, long posts were planted in the holes, clapboards were nailed to the post framework as siding, clay was plastered in the cracks and holes, and a roof of rafters and shingles was placed atop the structure. Some floors would have been planked; others would have had bare earth. Some buildings used as houses and barracks would have had fireplaces and chimneys as soon as bricks could be made. Other buildings would have had a central hearth and a smoke hole in the roof. The fort's plank wall continued to be used when repairs and improvements were made over the subsequent decades. Frequent repairs were necessary because of the continual deterioration of wooden structures caused by termite infestation. Eight years later the guardhouse was rebuilt, and major repairs were made to the bastions, wall, corn crib, and houses. At some point, probably after 1760 and before the fort was abandoned in 1766, the wall was rebuilt as a stockade.[10]

After waiting for about ten days with no sign of the Cherokees, the South Carolinians were beginning to doubt the Indians' support.[11] It would have taken nearly two weeks to receive instructions from Craven in Charles Town regarding the unexpected change of events. Fortunately for South Carolina, the regiment included experienced officers who were efficient and confident. They were not reluctant to make decisions and take responsibility for their actions.

Gen. James Moore and his officers knew that both Cherokee and Creek scouts were probably watching their actions and were looking for any hesitation that would suggest weakness. The longer they waited, the more vulnerable they would become. They decided to take immediate action. Moore ordered Col. Maurice Moore to form parts of the companies into a provisional battalion, immediately march north into the Lower Cherokee towns, and attempt to secure their allegiance through a strong show of force tempered with diplomacy. That bold decision would be one of the most important actions of the war. Unknown to the South Carolinians, a few of the Lower Cherokee headmen were meeting with representatives of the Lower Creek towns and were contemplating a coordinated attack on the regiment.[12]

General Moore and Colonel Fenwick remained at Savannah Town with a garrison of perhaps two hundred soldiers. Some of those soldiers probably included those who were too sick to navigate the Cherokee hills. Men who possessed construction skills would also have been retained at the fort. The garrison had three tasks: prevent a Creek invasion of South Carolina via the Savannah Path, support Colonel Moore and cover his withdrawal if he got into trouble, and complete work on the fort.[13]

Colonel Moore's battalion staff included Lieutenant Colonel Chicken, Major Herbert, and the trader Eleazer Wiggan as interpreter. Captains Broughton, Bull, Cantey, Daniel, Ford, Glover, Pight, Scott, and Smith detached a few of their men to remain at Savannah Town and retained the remaining soldiers in their companies as part of Moore's battalion. A company of Virginians under Captain Gorham was also included. The battalion totaled approximately three hundred men. They began moving northwest toward the Lower Cherokee towns on December 18, 1715. The path they used initially followed the east bank of the Savannah River through the Piedmont region of South Carolina. On the second day, they passed close to the cowpen owned by John Stephens or Stevens. He was the previous owner of Caesar, the slave whom the government had freed and returned to the Cherokees. Stephens, a Cherokee trader, had probably operated the northernmost cowpen in South Carolina. The nearby Apalachees or the Savannahs probably killed him and his employees earlier that year and left the cowpen unattended. Members of the expedition killed a cow and a calf for rations near present-day Stevens Creek.[14]

The path to the Lower Cherokee towns became increasingly hilly as they moved north. They continued to live off the land. On the third day, Indian scouts killed a deer, and soldiers killed two more of Stephens's cattle. They averaged more than a dozen miles each day, despite the unimproved path and hilly terrain. On the seventh day, they crossed a large stream, perhaps Long Cane Creek, about fifty-five miles, by the path, northwest of Savannah Town. Several men fell off their horses while crossing the deep ravine through which the creek flowed. That same day they came upon a Cherokee hunting party that was cooking venison. The warriors shared the meat with the soldiers.[15] The Cherokees may have arranged the picnic to initiate a peaceful welcome.

On Christmas Day, a Sunday, Moore's force turned westward and crossed the Savannah River into present-day Georgia, probably near the present-day Hartwell Dam. The Savannah was broad and the current swift, and several men were swept off their feet. A soldier in Capt. Thomas Smith's company named Daues or Dawes drowned. The soldier had been a pipe maker and probably an indentured servant. It took two hours to get the entire battalion across.[16]

On Tuesday, December 27, two Cherokee Indians came to the battalion's night camp and gave the men some corn flour. The following day, as they neared the town of Tossee, several Indians met them with more corn flour and corn bread. Tossee was the southernmost Lower Cherokee town in 1715. It was on the west side of the Savannah River and south of Toccoa Creek. They spent the night nearby. That evening a Cherokee messenger arrived and invited Moore and his force to Tugaloo, a principal Lower Cherokee Town. The messenger requested that Moore and his men not take their horses into Tugaloo. The Cherokees had a few horses, but they probably kept them on the edge of town for safety and sanitation reasons.[17]

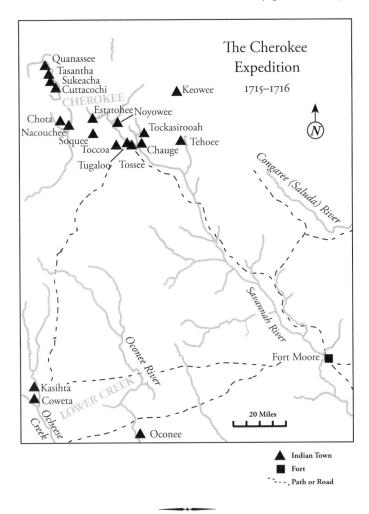

The Cherokee Expedition 1715–1716

Indian Town
Fort
Path or Road

On Thursday, December 29, Moore and a detachment of his men formed into ranks and marched on foot into Tugaloo. The town was on a point of land between the confluence of Savannah River and Toccoa Creek in present-day Stephens County, Georgia. Most men of the battalion would have remained with the horses, prepared to go to Moore's aid if necessary. When Moore and the delegation arrived, the warriors began welcoming them with a traditional ceremony. Some young warriors showed the town's peaceful intentions by performing a dance with eagle feather fans. Some older men presented the officers with black drink.[18]

The warriors then lined both sides of the path leading into the town and bid Moore and his delegation to follow the path to the townhouse.

The round townhouse would have been several yards in diameter, with wattle-and-daub walls, a bark roof covered with dirt, and a south entrance. On the inside it would have had a central hearth and wooden platforms around the wall. Chariety Hagey, the principal uku or headman; the war captains; and counselors sat in the townhouse waiting for Moore. South Carolinians called Chariety Hagey the Conjurer, probably because he was also a priest. Upon meeting they shook hands. Moore presented the Conjurer with two white flags. A white flag was a symbol of peace among Southeastern Indians. A warrior placed one of the flags on top of the townhouse. The officers and men of the delegation and the Cherokee headmen then ate a meal together.[19] Some members of the battalion probably spent the night in the town. They would have maintained a strong watch and slept with loaded weapons nearby; they were unsure of their status with Chariety Hagey and his warriors.

Moore and his officers wasted no time in their negotiations. On Friday they sat with Chariety Hagey and his council, and Moore bluntly asked if the Cherokees would join the regiment in a campaign against the Creek towns. Chariety Hagey chose his answer carefully. He said they would not fight against the Yamasees, giving the excuse that they were once related to that group. He probably knew better and hoped that the South Carolinians were ignorant regarding kinship connections between Indian groups. Moore and his officers then learned, for the first time, that the Cherokees were conducting serious negotiations with the Lower Creeks. Chariety Hagey informed them that a Lower Creek delegation planned to come to one of the Lower Cherokee towns and meet with both the Cherokees and Moore. The South Carolinians were unaware that several hundred warriors would accompany the Lower Creek delegation and that the Cherokee–Lower Creek negotiations might result in an attack on the regiment.[20]

When Chariety Hagey was asked whether his warriors would join South Carolina in a campaign against the Catawbas and other northern Indians, he initially avoided the subject and finally refused. He blamed the raids by northern Indians on the Waterees, a minor Siouan group, and claimed untruthfully that Catawba warriors had not been involved in the war. He finally admitted that the only Indian groups his warriors were willing to assault were the Savannahs, Yuchis, and Apalachees. As a diplomatic slap in the face, Chariety Hagey informed Moore that a delegation from his town had traveled to Virginia, received presents, and made peace with that colony. Moore and his officers probably suspected, correctly, that the headmen of the various towns were stalling while they attempted to reach some consensus regarding action they should take in the war. However the Lower Cherokees were undoubtedly aware of George Chicken's victory six months earlier. The presence of about three hundred well-armed and well-led South Carolina soldiers was beginning to dampen their ardor for war with South Carolina. Barely one-half of the Cherokee warriors owned guns, and they had no reserves of powder and shot.[21]

The next day Chariety Hagey informed Moore that he had sent a messenger to the Lower Creek towns, asking that they send a delegation to his town in fourteen days to discuss peace. He said he had asked the Lower Creeks to bring their white prisoners to be liberated. He indicated that a Savannah war party had recently captured a South Carolina woman near the Edisto River, and they had taken her to one of the Lower Creek towns.[22]

Moore temporarily quartered the companies of captains Smith and Broughton in Tugaloo and settled the remaining companies in nearby Lower Cherokee towns. The soldiers probably resided in the townhouse of each town until they constructed crude shelters. The townspeople provided them with rations of meat and grain. Moore decided that while he waited for the arrival of the Lower Creek delegation, he would travel to the nearby Cherokee towns and meet with their headmen in an attempt to sway them to aid South Carolina. Moore, Chicken, and Herbert set out from Tugaloo with a detachment of two dozen men at noon on Sunday, New Year's Day, 1716. Their destination was the town of Chota to the west-northwest. On the way the detachment passed through a newly established Cherokee town named Toccoa. They continued to the town of Soquee, near the Soque River, where they camped for the night. On Monday, January 2, they arrived at Nacouchee, a town in the Nacoochee Valley on the headwaters of the Chattahoochee River, where they prepared to present themselves to the people of nearby Chota.[23]

When Caesar and the headmen of Chota said they were ready, Moore and his detachment marched northwest a short distance to the town. The town was on the east side of the Chattahoochee River. The Chattahoochee in that area was known as the Chota River. Headmen and warriors from several towns were waiting for their arrival. Warriors conducted a welcome that involved firing their muskets into the air and dancing with eagle feathers. The warriors led the South Carolina officers to Chota's large, round townhouse. Moore presented the headmen with red and white flags that were placed on top of the townhouse. The white flag, the color of peace, was offered as a token of friendship, while the red flag, the color of war, was offered as an enticement to fight the Creeks. Inside the townhouse

Caesar gave a speech. He said that during his recent visit to Charles Town he had promised Governor Craven that he would go to war against the Lower and Upper Creeks. After he announced that he was ready to go to war, the younger warriors shouted their approval and prepared to conduct a war dance. However, the older warriors and the headmen cautioned the young men and explained the adverse consequences of such a war. They were aware of the depredations that had resulted from past wars. They may also have resented Caesar's grandstanding. Nevertheless the young warriors participated in a war dance during most of that night. It was clear to the South Carolinians that the Cherokees were not in agreement about what course of action to take in the war.[24]

The following day Moore became ill and returned to Tugaloo with Bull and Cantey and six soldiers. Lieutenant Colonel Chicken and Major Herbert stayed at Chota with the remaining soldiers and continued conferring with headmen and warriors from several towns. An Indian messenger gave Chicken letters that had been written by James Alford, a trader among the Chickasaws in present-day northern Mississippi. Alford reported that four traders to the Chickasaws had been killed. The other traders had been saved by Chickasaw headmen. However they were apparently being held captive, probably until the Chickasaws decided whether to join the Yamasees and Creeks against South Carolina. Meanwhile the Chickasaws blamed the deaths of the four traders on visiting Creek warriors. Ten years later Chicken learned that several young Chickasaw warriors from the town under the leadership of the Squirrel King had probably killed the four traders.[25]

The Cherokee headman of Tugaloo, Chariety Hagey, who was also present, admitted to Chicken that two traders in his town had been killed. He said two Creek warriors came to his town and killed the traders while he was away hunting.[26] So a few young Chickasaw and Cherokee warriors had taken personal revenge against the traders. Their headmen, who did not want to go to war without first considering all the possible consequences and reaching a consensus with the people of other towns, had restrained further killings. The Chickasaws and Cherokees did their best to cover up their people's involvement in the traders' deaths. South Carolinians accepted the explanations with little question. They were obviously relieved that the Chickasaws and Cherokees had not yet declared war.

On Wednesday, January 4, Chicken, Herbert, and their detachment escorted Chariety Hagey and Eleazer Wiggan back to Tugaloo. On the way it began snowing, so they spent the night at Soquee. The next day they passed through the town of Toccoa and rode on to Tugaloo. In Tugaloo they met a Cherokee warrior who had recently returned from the Lower Creek towns. He reported that the Lower Creek headmen favored making peace with South Carolina. The warrior also reported that most of the Yamasees had moved their towns to Florida, but the people of Tomotly had received refuge among the Lower Creeks. On January 7 Chicken sent the trader John Chester on a journey with a message to Alford in the Chickasaw towns. Chicken's message requested that Alford proceed to Tugaloo with delegations of Chickasaw, Upper Creek, and Choctaw headmen. It appeared to the South Carolina officers that diplomacy was going to be successful. They planned for the arrival of a delegation of the Lower Creeks and perhaps Upper Creeks, Chickasaws, and Choctaws. They intended to escort them to Charles Town, where a formal peace conference would be conducted.[27] Their assumptions and planning obviously did not take into account the intentions of those Cherokee warriors who were agitating to go to war with the Creeks.

The following three weeks were spent waiting for the arrival of the Lower Creek delegation. To keep the men occupied, Colonel had his officers conduct inspections and require their men to repair and maintain their arms and equipment. Some men were treated to watching the Cherokees play intertown ball games. Mostly they had to endure cold, wet weather that alternated between snow and rain. On January 12 Moore met with his staff and company commanders, and they discussed how they should negotiate with the Lower Creek delegation when it arrived.[28]

The following day Moore and a detachment rode to Chauge to inspect Pight's company of Indians and Ford's company of black and Indian slaves. Chauge was on the east side of the Savannah River, near the mouth of the Chauga River. Colonel Moore discovered that two Lower Creek warriors from Coweta were in the town. They had informed Pight's Indians that they and other scouts were spying on the regiment, both in the Cherokee towns and at Savannah Town. They were attempting to determine the number and location of the South Carolina soldiers. To alleviate any fears regarding their presence, they said that they had been directed, probably by Emperor Brims, not to attack the South Carolinians. They did not reveal that several hundred of their warriors were marching north toward the Lower Cherokee towns. Nor did they reveal that the probable goal of the Lower Creeks was to join the Lower Cherokees and attack the regiment. Moore must have become suspicious. Three days later he dispatched a mounted reconnaissance patrol of four white soldiers and two Indians commanded by Lt. Edward Catton or Keaton to determine if a body of Lower Creek warriors was approaching. The patrol spent five days scouting the paths to the south and west, but they did not encounter any Lower Creeks.[29]

A detachment of North Carolinians arrived at Savannah Town about the second week of January 1716. Among them were Col. Theophilus Hastings, three or four white soldiers, some Tuscarora warriors under war captain Blunt, and Lt. Martin Griffin, their white liaison officer. Hastings and a few soldiers continued on to the Cherokee towns and joined Moore on January 16.[30]

Another officers' conference was held on January 19. Some Upper Cherokees had requested that a South Carolina delegation visit them. Moore ordered Chicken and Herbert to meet with some of their headmen. They were directed to attempt to entice the Upper Cherokees to make war on the Catawbas and other northern Indians. The following day Chicken, Herbert, and a small detachment of soldiers began a journey to the Upper Cherokee. They traveled more than fifty miles northwest across increasingly steep and stony terrain that often forced them to dismount and walk. They spent the first night in the town of Soquee. The next day they rode to Chota. Late in the afternoon of January 22, they arrived at the town of Quanassee, located to the west of most of the Upper Cherokee towns. Caesar had recently arrived from Chota and was waiting for them. He informed Chicken that several Upper Cherokee headmen were on their way, but heavy snow in the mountains had delayed them.[31]

The next day, January 23, the Upper Cherokee headmen arrived and met with Chicken and Herbert. The headmen quickly came to the point; they were determined to join with South Carolina and immediately engage in a war against the Creeks. They emphasized that they were prepared to go to war without the assistance of South Carolina, but they needed ammunition. Chicken attempted to stall them, but they reasoned that Craven had asked them to fight the Creeks and that they were prepared to do so. They reminded Chicken that the Lower Creeks had been requested to send emissaries to the Cherokees within fourteen days or they would declare war on them. However the time had elapsed several days previously, and the Lower Creeks had not arrived. Nevertheless when Chicken went to bed in the townhouse that night, he assumed that he had convinced the headmen not to take action until he received instructions from Moore.[32]

Before Chicken and Herbert could depart Quanassee and return to Tugaloo the next morning, the Upper Cherokee headmen asked to speak with them again. The headmen stressed that they were going immediately to declare war against the Creeks, and Chicken again attempted to dissuade them. They disclosed one reason for their decision to go to war. The Chero-kees were afraid that if they made peace with other Indian groups, they would not have an opportunity to capture those Indians to sell as slaves to South Carolina. They intended to use the profits from slaving to purchase arms, ammunition, and cloth. Chicken noticed that the headmen were hurriedly attempting to convince him that war was necessary, but after additional persuasion he believed they would wait for Moore's instruc-tions.[33]

When they could diplomatically disengage themselves from the Upper Cherokee headmen, Chicken and Herbert struck out for Tugaloo. They traveled by an alternate route and spent the first night in the town of Cuttacochi. They remained there all the next day during a rainstorm, re-sumed travel the following day, and spent the night in Chota.[34]

As they prepared to leave Chota on the morning of Friday, January 27, a messenger arrived from Tugaloo with stunning news. A delegation of twelve Lower Creek warriors had arrived in Tugaloo, and the Cherokees had killed all of them during the night. Chicken and his detachment im-mediately set out for Tugaloo. They arrived late in the afternoon and con-firmed that the entire Lower Creek delegation had been assassinated. The Cherokees had effectively quashed South Carolina's prospects of an im-mediate peace with the Creeks. Chicken probably realized that the Chero-kees had decided to attack the Lower Creeks more than a week before. A dozen years later, some Cherokees claimed that they killed the Creek delegates to prevent them from taking the lives of Moore and his men. They also had other motives for the assassinations that would have been reasonable from the Cherokees' perspective. War could provide them with captive Creeks to sell to white traders. Perhaps just as important, they were warriors; they hoped to reap martial glory during raids upon the Creeks. They wanted more guns, a continual supply of ammunition, and the assistance of South Carolina's army to be sure of success.[35]

A Lower Creek warrior who had previously arrived in Tugaloo had been taken prisoner. He reported that between two hundred and three hundred warriors from Coweta, Kasihta, Oconee, and other Lower Creek towns had escorted the delegation. They were waiting nearby and were expected to retaliate. Most of the companies of Moore's battalion were recalled from their scattered locations and assembled at Tugaloo. Chero-kee reconnaissance patrols began searching for the Lower Creek warriors. On Saturday one of the patrols brought in a Lower Creek warrior who had been sent to see why the delegation of headmen had not returned. On Sunday a patrol captured another Lower Creek and a Yamasee. None of the captives had been aware of the assassination of the Lower Creek delegation.[36]

During that weekend some South Carolina soldiers and several Cherokee warriors prepared ambush positions south of Tugaloo, but without success. The Yamasee warrior who was captured on Sunday reported that a large body of Lower Creek warriors were camped about eight miles south of Tossee. A detachment from Moore's battalion spent the next two days in an attempt to find them, but the Lower Creek warriors had fled. They had obviously discovered that their delegation had been killed.[37]

On the last day of January, Moore and his officers met with Chariety Hagey and other Cherokee headmen to plan their next course of action. The Cherokees complained that the battalion was a severe drain on their food supplies. Moore proposed that Colonel Hastings and fifty men remain with the Lower Cherokees, while the remaining portion of the battalion returned to Savannah Town. He offered to send the Cherokees two hundred muskets and sufficient ammunition for use against the Creeks. The Cherokee headmen agreed. Two days later the Conjurer requested that the company of black soldiers also remain with the Cherokees. Moore agreed and ordered Captain Ford to stay with his company. Caesar complained in vain that more South Carolina soldiers should stay and accompany him on an expedition against the Creeks.[38]

On Sunday, February 5, Moore and some men of Captain Broughton's company set out for Charles Town via the Saluda River–Santee River path. The following day Lieutenant Colonel Chicken, who was then in the town of Noyowee on the east side of the Savannah River, gathered the remaining men of the battalion and set out for Savannah Town. They initially followed a path on the east side of the Savannah River and spent the first night in Chauge, where Ford and his company were quartered. During the next eight days, they marched through swollen creeks, cold rain, and frost. Deep creeks forced them to unload the packhorses and raft their burdens across. An unusual occurrence was the killing of a rare buffalo for their evening meal on Saturday, February 11. During their journey they received a message from Colonel Hastings that three of the soldiers who had been selected to remain in the Cherokee towns had deserted.[39]

Chicken's companies arrived at Savannah Town on Wednesday, February 15, and rejoined the regiment. The next day most of the regiment began a return journey to the lowcountry to assume garrison duties in the colony's screen of plantation forts. The officers assumed correctly that the Creeks would soon renew raids against the plantations. One hundred fifteen officers and men remained to garrison the new Savannah Fort.[40]

An invasion of the Creek towns did not occur. South Carolinians were naive to have hoped that the Cherokee would abandon their traditional hit-and-run warfare and organize an army to accompany the regiment in major invasions of the Creek towns. Gen. Maurice Moore and other officers who were familiar with the Cherokees' culture of war were probably not surprised. Nevertheless the expedition was successful. The Cherokees became an ally against the Creeks. The resulting Cherokee raids kept many Creek warriors occupied for more than a decade. Making peace with the Cherokees enabled South Carolina to begin reestablishing the Indian trade. The Cherokees' assassination of the Lower Creek headmen also gave South Carolina a strategic advantage: after harvesting their crops, the people of the Lower Creek towns packed and moved southwestward, farther into the interior. They established new homesteads at their previous locations, near the Chattahoochee River on the present-day Georgia-Alabama border.[41] They arrived in time for spring planting of corn and vegetables. The location of their new homes lengthened, and thus made more difficult, their war treks to and from the South Carolina's frontier plantations and cowpens. In addition the longer route made them more vulnerable to Cherokee ambushes.

The Cherokees reaped some gains from peace with South Carolina. They temporarily gained a favored place in the South Carolina Indian trade. They maintained a close association with South Carolina for many years. However the Cherokees became involved in a bitter war with both the Lower and Upper Creeks that lasted more than ten years. Raids and counterraids became common, and the Creeks held a grudge against the Cherokees for many years. Although Cherokee men fulfilled their destiny as warriors, they had to relocate several of their towns to more defensible locations and fortify them. Within a few years some Cherokees began to regret their rash action that provoked the war. They grieved the loss of those women and children who were killed and captured. They wanted peace.[42]

CHAPTER 13

Stalemate, 1716

At 7:30 A.M. on Wednesday, February 29, 1716, the bell in Saint Philip's Church in Charles Town began ringing, summoning the members of the South Carolina Commons House into the first of eight sessions of the Fifteenth Assembly. The year 1716 was an unusually busy one for members of the Commons House; they were in working sessions for 141 days. Fortune seemed to be slowly favoring South Carolina. The yield of the previous year's crops had been very good, so there was no food shortage yet. Indian war parties were wary of open battle with the army, especially after Chicken's Fight, Fenwick's Fight, the Daufuskie Fight and other scout boatmen's successes, and the regiment's march into the Cherokee towns. Nevertheless the colony was almost on its knees. Many cowpens and plantations in Port Royal and Colleton County had been destroyed. Those areas of the frontier remained sparsely settled for several years. Many plantations north of Charles Town had been sacked, and numerous plantations between the Edisto and Ashley Rivers, southwest of Charles Town, lay in ruins. Peace with the Cherokees had come at a high price, for a protracted war with the Creeks seemed likely. The treasury was nearly bankrupt. The Yamasees, Creeks, and a few other Indian groups had initiated hit-and-run warfare. Several soldiers had deserted their garrisons. Many refugees, especially those from Port Royal and Colleton County, remained in Charles Town and on the fortified plantations.[1]

The day began with the reading of Governor Craven's message to the Commons House. He was upbeat and suggested that the war was almost over. The members of the Commons House and their constituents did not agree. As it turned out, he was anxious to return to England and was probably putting the best possible face on the war. Craven informed the Commons House that the fighting should be concluded as swiftly as possible, "in order to put an end to that prodigious charge we are at for maintaining so expensive a war." To achieve that end, he recommended that the Indian trade law be reformed and reestablished. Craven had previously pushed the Commons House to ratify Colonel Middleton's agreement with Virginia regarding its assistance, but he admitted that the agreement contained "such terms as we did not expect (being very severe and almost impractical)." Nevertheless he recommended that they do everything possible to comply with the agreement. He praised the Carolina proprietors for the support they had sent, which had not yet arrived. He then reminded the Commons House that the enlistments of the army's soldiers would lapse in one month and should be continued.[2]

The priority of the Commons House was to reorganize the army and frontier defenses. Many of the colony's men were serving in the army, and they had to be retained on duty until reorganization was completed. However the expense of paying and maintaining them had become oppressive, and they were needed for spring farmwork that would begin in about two months. Reducing the number of garrisoned forts was necessary, but those forts that sat astride the entrances into the settlements had to be retained. In addition to the garrisons, two small mobile units were needed to continue offensive operations: a battalion for another expedition to help the Cherokees in operations against the Creeks, and a waterborne force to conduct a "Southern expedition" against the Yamasee towns that had relocated to Florida. Planning quickly began, and by March 7 the reorganization of the army was in draft form. The "Act for Raising Forces to Prosecute the War against Our Indian Enemies" was passed into law on March 24, the last day of the first session.[3]

The act severely reduced the size of the army from an authorized strength of almost 1,400 officers and men to a small force of about 267. A few additional, temporary men were recruited to fill out the ranks of the Creek and Southern expeditions. Volunteers were sought for the new army, but men were also pressed, or drafted, to fill out the ranks. John Bossard was appointed "pressmaster" for Charles Town. Men, other than the scout boatmen, who brought horses into service received additional pay. Horses were needed for patrol duties, but many of the colony's horses had perished in service or had been stolen by Indians. Planters were reluctant to allow their remaining horses to be pressed into service. Each soldier furnished his own equipment or reimbursed the government if such items were issued to him. Food rations supplied to the garrisons by the "commissary of the Garrisons" consisted of rice, black-eyed peas, bread flour, and pork. Most garrisons raised their own corn and kept some cattle. Clothing was obtained for the men by contracting with tailors and seamstresses such as Alexander Muckle, Martha Hart, Mary Heatly, and Darby McClarklin. Some recently discharged white soldiers, and probably some black soldiers, did not turn in their government-issued muskets, preferring to remain armed in case of renewed raids on their homes. Their company commanders were remiss in not collecting the weapons. The governor appointed officers for the new army, and they were given power to appoint their sergeants. An abbreviated "articles of war" was established for the maintenance of discipline. It provided punishment for offenses including mutiny, cowardice, and desertion. Nathaniel Partridge was appointed field marshal, or provost marshal, with powers to arrest and to enforce judgments and sentences entered under the articles. The colony's treasury was nearly empty. Additional bills of credit, paper money, was printed to pay the expenses of the army. During April 1716 a small ship carrying supplies and arms sent by the proprietors finally arrived in Charles Town.[4]

All of the soldiers in the new army were white men, except for some of the officers' personal servants. The army's black and Indian slave soldiers were discharged and returned to work for their owners. Their service in the militia continued, however. Several slave soldiers had been killed in action or died of disease or accident. Circumstantial evidence offered by South Carolina's postwar slave statutes indicates that white soldiers who had fought beside or commanded slave soldiers may have developed a grudging respect for them. For several years there was a continued tolerance by several owners toward their slaves' conduct. The 1722 slave statute shows that some slaves continued to congregate on Sundays, other slaves owned livestock and boats, some slaves carried firearms with their owner's permission, and some slaves openly frequented punch houses. The statute noted that constables were failing to carry out punishments handed down by slave courts.[5]

South Carolina's lax enforcement of the slave statutes appears to have continued for several years, until September 9, 1739, when a group of slaves initiated an insurrection in the lowcountry and killed several white people. A new, harsh slave statute was adopted, and enforcement became severe.[6] Nevertheless in 1747, after enforcement of slave laws had become very strict, members of the South Carolina government recalled the slave veterans' military service with appreciation by noting that "several negroes and other slaves have, in times of war, behaved themselves with great faithfulness and courage, in repelling attacks of his Majesty's enemies, in their descents on this Province."[7]

The new defense law reduced the number of forts garrisoned by the army from twelve to seven. One hundred seventeen men were to be recruited, or drafted if necessary, to garrison those forts. Monetary and strategic considerations played a prominent role regarding the final locations of the forts. The garrisons of the following forts were discharged: Richbourg's, Wassamassaw, the Ponds, Cattell's, Beamor's, Willtown, Bennett's Point, and Nichols's. Some of those forts continued to provide shelter for the owners' families and neighbors. The law gave the governor the authority to demobilize any fort's garrison if he and his council considered it unnecessary for the colony's defense, but that authority did not extend to Savannah Fort, or Fort Moore, the name it soon received.[8]

A new fort was supposed to have been placed on the plantation of Benjamin Clee or Clea, north of Charles Town, near the Santee River. A captain, a lieutenant, and twenty-eight men were to be its garrison. However the fort was never built or garrisoned. Wantoot Fort, located about four miles west of present-day Bonneau in Berkeley County, remained the northernmost garrisoned fort until a new fort at John Hearn's plantation was completed and garrisoned. In early 1716 John Barnwell was in command at Wantoot.[9]

By late summer the army had constructed and garrisoned a new fort at the plantation of the late Hearn, on the west bank of the Santee River near the present-day Interstate Highway 95 bridge in Orangeburg County. Its garrison guarded the northern approaches into the colony. Capt. Joseph Perkins commanded Hearn's Fort with a garrison of fifteen men. Some Commons House members wanted that fort to be replaced with a new fortification at the Congarees, about forty-five miles farther northwest, near present-day Cayce. The governor did not agree, and the plan for a fort at the Congarees was tabled. Peace had not been finalized with the Catawbas or the other Siouan Indian groups to the north, and a fort at that location was too far beyond the northern frontier to be supported in case it was attacked by those Indians.[10]

The fort on James Rawlings's Edisto Bluff plantation, on or near present-day Givhans Ferry State Park in Dorchester County, was retained. It was garrisoned by an officer and nine men. Capt. William Peters may have been the commander.[11]

An officer and nine men garrisoned a fort near Horseshoe Savannah at the head of Folly Creek, about 8.5 miles west-southwest of present-day

Walterboro in Colleton County. It was the newly repaired fort that Governor Craven had constructed there during April 1715 on John Woodward's plantation. Woodward's Fort was sometimes known as the Horseshoe Garrison. Captain Woodward may have been in command.[12]

A fort was planned for Rowland Evans's plantation on the east bank of the Salkehatchie River in Colleton County. Before construction began it was decided to place the fort farther south on the plantation of John Jackson, near the east bank of the Combahee River, close to Bryan's Ferry, about two miles east-northeast of the present-day Highway 17 bridge. It was the site of the August 1715 battle between soldiers under Col. John Fenwick and Yamasees who were camped in the plantation house. The new fort was known as Combahee Fort and was commanded by Capt. Rowland Evans. He was authorized a garrison of nineteen men. Evans had arrived in South Carolina four years before from Wales as an indentured servant.[13]

Fort Moore was authorized a captain, a lieutenant, two sergeants, a surgeon, and thirty-eight men. Men of the regiment on the Cherokee expedition had constructed the fortification during December 1715 and January 1716. The fort was on a high bluff on the east bank of the Savannah River, near the present-day Highway 28 bridge across the Savannah River, about five miles south of North Augusta, South Carolina. Maj. William Blakewey commanded the fort and its garrison and Capt. Charlesworth Glover was his executive officer. John Jones, a trader, served as interpreter. The garrison maintained a herd of more than sixty cattle. A piragua was assigned to the fort for resupply purposes. Fort Moore was in a precarious location, several days' travel beyond the nearest fort. Resupply and reinforcement was dangerous and time-consuming, whether overland by the Savannah Path or by water on the Inland Passage and the Savannah River. Nevertheless it was considered the colony's most important frontier fort.[14]

A captain, a lieutenant, and twenty-six men garrisoned Port Royal Fort on Cochran's Point, present-day Seabrook Point, on the northern part of Port Royal Island in Beaufort County. A few Tuscarora Indians under Indian Foster, their war captain, were members of the garrison. Port Royal Fort was initially commanded by Maj. Henry Quintyne, Thomas Nairne's stepson. In July 1716 a Yamasee war party ambushed and captured Quintyne and two of his men, Thomas Simmons and Thomas Parmenter or Palmenter. All were tortured to death. The same war party captured a man named Dr. Rose. He was wounded with a hatchet, scalped, and left to die. He survived, however. Capt. William Gray replaced Quintyne. Lt. Richard Reynolds was his executive officer. A piragua was assigned to the garrison for miscellaneous transportation duties. William Stone and Seymour

Burrows commanded South Carolina's scout boats stationed at the fort during 1716.[15]

The garrison of Port Royal Fort was in a position to overlook much of the abandoned Indian Land. The colony's government passed a law to appropriate the Indian Land, with the intent of granting tracts of three hundred to four hundred acres to white Protestant immigrants. New settlers were to be armed and had to reside on the land but were exempted from serving in the army. Irish Protestant immigrants began arriving in late June, expecting to receive grants of land. The settlement scheme was a defense measure that could have proved valuable, but the Lords Proprietors were angry because the South Carolina government had brushed aside their exclusive right to grant land. The proprietors repealed the act and granted baronies of twelve-thousand-acre tracts of the Indian Land to themselves and to Richard Shelton, their secretary.[16]

South Carolina's government authorized one hundred men, five officers, and a surgeon for a small mobile battalion. Its mission was to join the Cherokees in an invasion of the Lower Creek towns near the Chattahoochee River on the present-day Georgia-Alabama border. Eighty volunteers were recruited from the two militia regiments, and twenty of the men who were in the Cherokee towns were added to the battalion. The other soldiers in the Cherokee towns returned to Charles Town. The officers for the battalion were Lt. Gen. James Moore, Col. Theophilus Hastings, Col. Alexander Mackay, Maj. John Herbert, and Capt. Joseph Ford. Two hundred trade guns were supposed to be taken to the Cherokees for their use; however only 22 serviceable surplus muskets were available. Capt. Stephen Ford's company of black soldiers returned to Charles Town from the Lower Cherokee towns, and their muskets were turned in for distribution to the Cherokees. In addition 124 trade guns were purchased from Charles Town merchants. Little information is available about the battalion's expedition. Moore and his men marched to the Cherokee towns during April 1716. No invasion of the Lower Creek towns was initiated, probably because the Cherokees were reluctant to participate. While they were in the Cherokee towns, a soldier, Elias Thomas, deserted along with a Frenchman, probably a deserter from Louisiana. General Moore and his battalion returned to Charles Town during early June. The expedition had been a disappointment. Mackay and a few soldiers remained with the Cherokees to provide a South Carolina presence.[17]

Capt. William Stone was in command of the Southern expedition. Another party of Tuscarora warriors from North Carolina under Blunt, their war captain, and their liaison officer, Lt. Martin Griffin, joined the expedition. They had recently been part of the march to the Cherokee towns. At the request of the Tuscarora, five white North Carolina soldiers were recruited to accompany them.[18]

The Southern expedition involved one of the war's most poignant episodes. Previously, during early 1713, the Reverend Gideon Johnston of Charles Town had received permission from the Yamasee Euhaw King to take a seventeen-year-old warrior to England and educate him. South Carolinians assumed the young man was the son of the Euhaw King, but he was probably a nephew. He was a likely candidate to be the future mico of Euhaw. Until 1702 the people of Euhaw had been part of the Spanish mission system in Florida, and its people had received Catholic Christian instruction. When they immigrated to South Carolina, they became part of the Yamasees and were likely subordinated to Altamaha Town. The young man was soon known as Prince George, or the Yamasee Prince. During the summer of 1713, Johnston and Prince George arrived in London, where the English Society for the Propagation of the Gospel agreed to support the young man and sponsor his education. A tutor was hired to teach him to speak, read, and write English.[19]

Prince George had made little progress by the summer of 1714, and he was anxious to return to South Carolina. Johnston convinced him to remain in England a while longer. After a change of tutors, his education quickly improved. In January 1715 the Society for the Propagation of the Gospel decided to return Prince George to South Carolina. The Bishop of London baptized him in the Protestant Church of England during February or early March. He was then presented to the newly coronated King George I.[20]

Johnston and Prince George left England and sailed to South Carolina during the summer of 1715. Unknown to them a Yamasee warrior captured by scouts in the Indian Land in late April 1715 informed his captors that the Yamasees had killed the Euhaw King because he refused to join them in the war against South Carolina. The information was incorrect. By May 1715 the Euhaws were encamped near the mouth of the Altamaha River. During the late spring or early summer, the Euhaw King and his warriors loaded their families into six canoes and moved south on the Inland Passage to the safety of Spanish Florida. They established a town in Florida, probably near the site of the old Spanish mission on Amelia Island where they had resided before moving to South Carolina twelve years before.[21]

When Johnston and Prince George arrived in Charles Town on September 18, 1715, they found the colony in the midst of a terrible war with Prince George's people. The young man became Johnston's ward and lived in his Charles Town house. By December Prince George had become depressed but was apparently physically healthy.[22]

During February or March 1716, the scouts and Tuscarora warriors of the Southern expedition rowed south on the Inland Passage to Florida and raided the town of Euhaw. The Euhaw King, his family, and about thirty of his people were captured and transported to Charles Town. It appears that only two old men and four young warriors escaped. During late March the Euhaw King and his people, along with two Huspaws who had been captured, were shipped to the island of Barbados and sold into slavery. Prince George apparently continued to reside with Reverend Johnston; however Johnston drowned on April 23, 1716, when he was trapped in the hold of a sloop that was overturned by a heavy gust of wind in Charles Town harbor. The fate of nineteen-year-old Prince George is unknown. He disappeared from history after the death of Johnston.[23] Did he resume his old life as a warrior, make his way south to Saint Augustine, and join the Yamasee refugees?

On April 18, 1716, the Commons House was in its second session when Craven informed the Commons House that the war was over and that he had the proprietors' permission to return to England. Members of the Commons House were upset; war parties continued to penetrate the frontiers and kill and kidnap South Carolinians. The members believed the colony continued to need Craven's military leadership. Nevertheless the governor sailed to England at the end of April. Before leaving he appointed Deputy Governor Robert Daniel to be acting governor until the proprietors' new governor arrived in the colony. Daniel was an experienced soldier and sea captain, but he sometimes proved unable to exercise the quality of Craven's leadership.[24]

Most members of the Commons House apparently did not know that Governor Craven returned to England to face serious accusations of criminal conduct. The claim against him was based on an incident that had occurred almost a year earlier, during the darkest days of the war. John Lewis, the captain of an English brigantine, was transporting a Spanish nobleman, the Marquis de Navarres, from Jamaica to some of the Spanish island plantations that he was visiting. The marquis was the governor of the city of Popayan, in the southwestern part of present-day Colombia. The marquis disembarked at Santa Marta, Colombia, one of his destinations. Before Lewis delivered the marquis's baggage ashore, he helped himself to some of the marquis's valuables, which included a fortune in gold, emeralds, jewelry, and miscellaneous expensive personal property. He then sailed away. When Lewis later anchored in Charles Town's harbor,

James Cumberfort, a British passenger on the brigantine and a merchant of Jamaica, reported the theft to Craven. Craven seized Lewis and took the stolen property into his personal safekeeping. The Spanish government began making demands that the British government order Craven to return the marquis's valuables. The matter evolved into an international incident, and Craven was accused by the Spanish of misappropriating the marquis's property. Accusations against Craven increased after Lewis escaped from confinement in Charles Town. Craven's case dragged on for years, but by early 1728 he was exonerated. He was given his governor's pay that was in arrears, and he received a gift of one thousand pounds for his service during the war.[25]

The North Carolina soldiers and Indians performed good service. Some Indians and most of the soldiers returned home during the summer. The quarrel with Virginia continued. One aspect of the quarrel involved the sale of guns and ammunition by Virginia traders to the Cheraw Indians. South Carolina had not yet made peace with the Cheraws or other Siouan-speaking northern Indians. The principal basis of the quarrel involved the use of and payment for the Virginia soldiers. Virginia's acting governor, Alexander Spotswood, complained that South Carolina had badly used his soldiers. During the spring of 1716, about one hundred Virginia soldiers, those with debts and those who were married, were sent home in an attempt to mollify the Virginia government. During June the South Carolina Commons House informed Deputy Governor Daniel that the pay of the Virginia officers and men had been raised. They received an amount equal to the value of the work of the female slaves that Virginia had demanded. The Commons House also assured Daniel that South Carolina would reimburse Virginia for its expenses in equipping and transporting its soldiers. Deputy Governor Spotswood remained unsatisfied. By late fall most of the Virginians had returned home. A few Virginians, debtors and indentured servants, opted to remain in South Carolina.[26]

The Indian trade had been a major contributor to South Carolina's economy before the war. The trade had to be reestablished quickly to revive the economy and to help secure peace with the Creeks and other groups. The government understood that a major cause of the war was the failure of the commissioners of the Indian trade to control the traders' abuse of the Indians. Members of the Commons House completed and passed a new Indian trading act on June 30, 1716. Despite the objections of the Charles Town merchants, private trading was forbidden, and the trade was reestablished as a government monopoly. Commissioners were appointed to oversee the trade. Indians were required to trade at one of three "factories": the fort at Savannah Town for the Cherokees and later the Creeks; a new fort to be built at the Congarees for the Cherokees and Catawbas; and a northward factory close to Winyah Bay north of the Santee River for the coastal Indian groups. For a short time, there was also a small factory near the Santee River. Each site was to be operated by a factor or manager. The extension of credit to Indian customers was forbidden. The dark side of the Indian trade was retained; provisions were made for the legal purchasing and enslaving of captive enemy women, children, and men under the age of thirty years. Slaves were to be marked but not branded with a hot iron. Slave marks may have been tattoos made with gunpowder. Initially the largest customers for trade goods were the Cherokees. Over the next three years, they sold large quantities of deerskins and several dozen captives, probably Creeks, Yuchis, and others, to South Carolina. The government passed a supplementary trading law during December that mandated severe fines for the few traders who continued to conduct private trading. The system soon underwent additional changes resulting from complaints made by Indian customers and competition from Virginia. Changes included the establishment of factories in some towns for the Indians' convenience and the reduction of prices for British trade goods.[27]

In August 1716 Deputy Governor Daniel purchased thirty-two prisoners of war to serve South Carolina as indentured servants. They had been captured by the British army during the failed Jacobite rebellion of the previous year. Certain families and clans in northern England and Scotland had attempted to place James Francis Stuart, the "Old Pretender," on the British throne. Most of the newly purchased servants were combat-experienced Highland Scots. The South Carolina government drafted them as soldiers for the garrisons of Fort Moore and Port Royal Fort. Their terms of service were seven years, but if they displayed valor, bravery, and obedience, their term would be reduced to four years. A new, strict statute was passed regulating the conduct of all indentured servants. Several Scots servants later deserted to the Spanish at Saint Augustine.[28]

South Carolinians continued to be disappointed, even incensed, with the proprietors' minimal aid. The proprietor's lack of action was stirring feelings of rebellion in South Carolina. The Commons House became "fully convinced that the Lords Proprietors are neither able nor willing to afford that assistance to this province as is absolutely necessary to preserve it from ruin and desolation."[29] The members continued to push their agents in London to bypass the proprietors and lobby the British government for arms, ammunition, supplies, and British soldiers. The agents sent a letter directly to the king in March 1716, begging for the British government's military and financial assistance. The Commons House members apparently understood that the British government was reluctant to provide much support to a private colony. Therefore they addressed another letter directly to the king in late 1716 in which they argued that South Carolina had flourished before the war, suggesting that it could be profitable for the British government in the future if it were placed under the king's protection. It was a thinly disguised plea for South Carolina to be made a royal colony.[30]

When the Commons House met in its fifth session on November 13, 1716, it was obvious that the colony's system of defense had to be restructured again. Yamasees, Creeks, and other Indians were employing small hit-and-run raids, a tactic of forest warfare in which they were experts. They killed or captured men, women, and children who strayed too far from the fortified plantations. The discovery of bodies and the capture of acquaintances or relatives caused fear and despondency among South Carolinians. It was humiliating and discouraging to the soldiers of the army. During the summer a war party of Lower Creeks ambushed and killed a party of four horsemen, probably soldiers on patrol, and took their mounts. Some Lower Creek war parties probably came from Apalachicola, Cherokeekiller's town. He and his warriors continued to be a serious problem for South Carolina for more than a decade. While the Commons House was meeting, there was a skirmish at Daniel Donovan's cowpen on the northern frontier, near the path to the Cherokee towns. A war party, probably Creeks, attacked Donovan's cattle hunters and some Etiwan Settlement Indians. The war party withdrew after being attacked by a pack of dogs that Donovan had imported from Ireland. Deputy Governor Daniel recommended the adoption of a system of defense that would be used at various times by South Carolina during the next half century: rangers. Rangers, mounted soldiers who aggressively patrolled the frontiers on the lookout for Indian war parties, had been used by Maryland and Virginia since the mid-seventeenth century. While the Commons House was discussing Daniel's recommendation, Virginia and North Carolina were already employing small parties of rangers.[31] The deputy governor told the Commons House, "You see our Forts alone will not answer the ends they were designed for, because small parties of Indians will come between them undiscovered, and by that means they are more capable of doing mischief than a greater body. This was always my judgment, and I am sorry it is confirmed by fatal experience. To remedy this evil the best way in my opinion, is to have parties continually ranging in a body, or bodies of men under pay always attending this duty."[32] At that time a provisional company of rangers under the command of Capt. Cornelius Sullivant was patrolling near the Santee River, but he and his men resigned after about five weeks of service for unknown reasons.[33]

During the middle of December 1716, the South Carolina government continued the fortifications and garrisons of Port Royal Fort and Fort Moore. Port Royal Fort was authorized two officers and twenty-five men. Capt. William Grey had commanded the garrison since September, after Henry Quintyne was killed. Lt. Richard Reynolds continued as his executive officer. The garrison maintained and crewed the two scout boats. Fort Moore, commanded by Capt. Charlesworth Glover, who was also the Indian trading factor there, was authorized two officers and forty men. Lt. James How was Glover's executive officer.[34]

The government's defensive measures were supposed to include two companies of rangers, each with fifty men, a captain, and a lieutenant. It appears that there was some reluctance among South Carolina's men to enlist as rangers, probably because of the danger involved in leaving the security of a fort and spending long periods of time patrolling the forest paths, where death from ambush was always a possibility. Ships were restricted from leaving Charles Town until enlistments were complete. Impressment of militiamen for ranger duty was authorized and employed. Twenty "ranging dogs" were authorized to assist rangers in their patrols. The company commanders were given the responsibility of procuring and employing the dogs.[35] Dogs may have proved useful, for eight years later a small company of scouts was authorized, and each man was to have "a large mastiff or mungrel bred dog."[36]

Actually South Carolina fielded three companies of rangers. The Northward Rangers, or Northern Rangers, patrolled the northern frontier, probably from Hearn's Fort on the west bank of Santee River. Capt. Joseph Perkins assumed command. The Westward Rangers, or Western Rangers, under the command of Capt. John Jones, were stationed at Edisto Bluff Fort on the east bank of the Edisto River. The Southward Rangers, or Southern Rangers, perhaps commanded by Capt. John Woodward, operated from Woodward's Fort, also known as Horseshoe Fort, at the head of Folly Creek, west of the Ashepoo River and Horseshoe Savannah. Combahee Fort at Jackson's plantation on the east bank of Combahee River, near Bryan's Ferry, appears to have been abandoned. Indian raids continued, but at a lesser pace. Rangers apparently began attacking any Indians they contacted. The Cherokees were warned to make arrangements before entering the settlements, because of the danger from ranger patrols.[37]

During 1716, the second year of the war, South Carolinians were primarily concerned with improving defenses against Indians raids and ambushes. They had accomplished a few small, successful offensive operations, but they were unable to undertake large expeditions. South Carolina did not have sufficient manpower or material resources to invade the Lower Creek towns without the Cherokees' assistance. Cherokee promises of concerted action had gone unfulfilled. The Creeks were penetrating South Carolina's frontiers with small raiding parties, but they had not attempted another large-scale raid, probably because they were distracted by their hit-and-run war with the Cherokees. They were probably also hesitant to challenge a combined South Carolina–Cherokee army in a major battle. The war had become a stalemate.

CHAPTER 14

South Carolinians,
1717–20

By the spring of 1717, the plight of South Carolina and most of its people had scarcely abated. The government later estimated that the colony had suffered approximately four hundred deaths because of the war, about one in every forty people. Indians had killed many South Carolinians; others died of disease from their miserable living conditions. That spring a smallpox epidemic struck the people of Charles Town.[1]

War parties had captured and taken several black slaves to Florida. The Spaniards often ransomed captive black slaves from the Indians, but they refused to return them to South Carolina. The black captives, mostly men, were retained in Florida as free persons to serve as an incentive to encourage South Carolina's slaves to escape and achieve freedom. During the next thirty years, the Spanish policy was effective; several black slaves escaped and made the long trek down the Inland Passage or overland to Saint Augustine. Many failed in the attempt. Punishment for escaping slaves varied from sale to other colonies to execution. During the late spring of 1720, several slaves in Charles Town and vicinity, under a leader named Primus, planned an escape to Saint Augustine. The plot was discovered, and several slaves were arrested. However fourteen of the slaves made it as far as the vicinity of Fort Moore. The garrison found them half-starved. Creek Indians apparently captured them for the rewards that were offered. The runaways were escorted to Charles Town, where a firing squad executed them. Not all slaves were anxious to go to Saint Augustine. Buff Moore, a slave owned by Capt. John Woodward, was captured by Indians but escaped during 1716 and returned to South Carolina. The Commons House approved the purchase of his freedom. Harry, a slave owned by the Widow Perry, escaped from Saint Augustine in 1721 after being captured by

Indians. Upon his arrival in Charles Town, he gave intelligence regarding the Spaniards and their Indian allies. It is unknown whether Harry was freed, but he was awarded five pounds for "his said service and faithfulness." Coffee, a slave owned by a man named Jones, escaped Saint Augustine during early 1728 and was awarded ten pounds.[2]

Members of South Carolina's Commons House and their London agents continued to plea for assistance from the British government. The Commons House also continued to request that South Carolina be converted into a royal colony. Although the Board of Trade showed temporary interest in their request by securing information from South Carolina's London agents regarding the raw materials that were available from the colony, the British government took no immediate action.[3]

The war continued as a series of raids and ambushes, conducted primarily by small Yamasee and Creek war parties. Their objective was limited to securing captives and scalps. During December 1716 a war party fell upon the plantation of Thomas Summers, located close to Wassamassaw Swamp, northwest of present-day Summerville. Several of his children were killed, except a young daughter, whom the Indians captured and carried away. A few Santee warriors who were suspected of making the attack were arrested, taken to Charles Town, and interrogated. They confessed to the attack, but the severity of their interrogation is unknown. The government asked King Robin of the Etiwan Indian group if he and his warriors would "cut off" the Santee and frighten them by capturing some of their people, who would be sold into slavery. Robin agreed but made it clear that he would not capture the Santee who had intermarried with his people. The few Santees that were subsequently captured were placed in Robin's care until their final disposition was determined. In January 1717 the government decided to sell the Santee men into slavery, along with some Congarees. The captured women and children were given to the Etiwan as their slaves. The profit from the sale of the men was supposed to be used to pay the soldiers who had returned from the latest Cherokee expedition. Nearly two years later, the commissioners of the Indian trade learned that the Lower Creeks had conducted the raid and that Summers's daughter was being held in one of their towns.[4]

During December 1716 the Fort Moore garrison had a skirmish with Creek warriors, and Alexander Muckle, a soldier, was wounded. A more serious incident occurred about the middle of March 1717. The garrison of Fort Moore was normally supplied by piraguas via the Savannah River. Boatmen using the river were warned not to spend nights camped on the riverbank but to anchor and sleep in midstream. The Indian trade's

employees, Joseph Thompson and six white indentured servants, perhaps some Highland rebels, were transporting supplies up the river in a
piragua. A war party, probably Creeks, surprised them when they were
about halfway to Fort Moore. Thompson and his men were killed, and
their bodies were dumped into the river. Also in March a war party killed
William Stead at his Colleton County cowpen, about six miles from Edisto Bluff Fort. Two other men were killed a short distance away, probably by the same war party. About the same time, William Saunders and
his wife were killed. During May Col. Alexander Mackay and his soldiers
were ambushed by a Creek war party several miles southeast of the Cherokee town of Tugaloo. One soldier, a man named Willson, and a Cherokee
Indian were killed, and three horses were taken. That same month four
black slaves, three men and one woman, were captured by a war party.[5]

During the fall of 1716, the Indian commissioners established the Winyah trading factory at a place known as Your Enee, or the Great Bluff.
The site was on the west bank of the Pee Dee River, probably not far from
present-day Yauhannah in Georgetown County. By the end of 1716, Mer-
edith Hughes was the factor of Your Enee factory. The warlike Cheraws
resided about eighty miles farther north, on the upper Pee Dee River. Virginia traders supplied them, so they had no need to maintain good terms
with Hughes. Some of their warriors occasionally traveled to the area
where the factory was located and harassed Hughes and his employees.
One Cheraw warrior threatened to shoot him. By August 1717 threats from
Cheraw warriors forced Hughes to move the factory a few miles south
to Andrew Collins's plantation on the Black River. However the Cheraws
continued to harass him there. They remained an irritant to South Carolinians for several years.[6]

In October 1717 several Cherokee men were serving as burdeners
for South Carolina, carrying dressed deerskins from the Lower Cherokee town of Keowee to Charles Town. They were ambushed by a Creek
war party near the Saluda River. The Creeks killed a few Cherokee men,
wounded others, and plundered the deerskins. The Indian commissioners
were obviously upset about losing the skins, but they may have had little
pity for the Cherokee men. They knew that Cherokee burdeners had been
stealing deerskins from the convoys. Creek war parties were also prey-
ing on Catawba trade convoys and killing Catawba warriors who were
serving as burdeners. Indians had never liked transporting cargo for the
traders. It was not considered suitable work for warriors, and it made
them vulnerable to ambushes. Recruiting warriors to serve as burdeners
became difficult, and the system was inefficient. By the summer of 1718,

Indian burdeners were being replaced by packhorse trains throughout the Indian trade.[7]

Much of South Carolina's economy was in ruins. Food, especially corn, was scarce during the first half of 1717, and inflation was causing prices to rise. The government raised taxes, printed paper money, and added hefty duties on many imported items. None of those actions brought quick relief in reducing the government's huge indebtedness. Two important components of the economy, the Indian trade and cattle ranching, had collapsed. The continuing raids by the Yamasees and Creeks discouraged people from returning to the frontiers. Personal debts owed by planters and Indian traders to merchants and lenders in Charles Town and London had soared. Business indebtedness for the period 1714–19 was more than eight times larger than for a previous period, 1704–9. Some indebtedness was secured by real-estate mortgages, but the bulk of the indebtedness was based on promissory notes with personal property, such as slaves, as collateral. Many planters and the widows of assassinated Indian traders had little hope of paying their debts in full. Creditors sued their debtors in the court of common pleas to gain payment for the promissory notes that were in arrears. At the successful completion of the legal actions, the creditors were awarded possession of their debtors' collateral.[8]

South Carolina had adopted a new Indian trading statute in June 1716 that nationalized the Indian trade, but during the year following its passage, the number of deerskins traded was less than one-tenth of the prewar amount. Initially the only reliable customers were the Cherokees, but they also did business with traders from Virginia. Charles Town merchants and their suppliers and creditors in England complained to the proprietors that the public monopoly over the Indian trade was not in their economic interests. They wanted to conduct the Indian trade as part of their private businesses. The proprietors agreed and repealed the 1716 statute in the summer of 1718.[9]

Before the war a rich cattle industry had developed in Colleton County. Thousands of cattle were maintained by cowpen planters from the Edisto River westward to the Combahee River. Cattle provided hides for leather and salted meat for export. Many cowpens and plantations at Port Royal and Colleton County had been destroyed. The danger from Indian raids discouraged many people from resettling the western part of Colleton County. Consequently the cattle industry did not recover until the 1730s.[10]

The naval stores industry continued as a profitable enterprise. Workers ventured into the lowcountry woods to tap and harvest longleaf pine trees for the manufacture of tar, pitch, and turpentine. It was a laborious process that required the workers to remain in the woods for several days at a time. During the war it was a dangerous occupation while Indian war parties were afield, but work continued and production increased.[11]

Many families of Berkeley County, the present-day Berkeley, Dorchester, and Charleston Counties, returned to their homes and began rebuilding their lives. Some of them quickly provided a bright spot for the economy: they continued and expanded the cultivation of rice. For several years some plantation owners east of the Edisto River had been raising rice, mostly for export to Europe. Many of their plantations had escaped total ruin from Indian raids. Prewar levels of production were regained by 1718, and rice production soared. However rice farming required intensive labor. The work was backbreaking and placed workers in unhealthy areas of the colony. The result was lost man-hours from disease, especially among white employees. Black slave labor was considered more suited for rice farming, so the importation of African slaves began to increase.[12]

In June 1717 the defense act of the previous year, which provided garrisons for Port Royal Fort and Fort Moore and for companies of rangers, was continued in effect. However six months later the government passed a new defense act that provided for a reduced military force of 140 white officers and men. The new force was to be manned by volunteers, but militia company commanders were authorized to select men from their companies to fill the ranks when necessary. Indentured servants could be drafted, and their wages as soldiers were divided between them and their masters.[13]

The new defense act directed that Hearn's Fort should be replaced with a new fort at the Congarees, about forty-four miles to the northwest. Lt. James How, the executive officer of Fort Moore, was promoted to captain and received command of the new fort and its garrison of twelve soldiers. His replacement at Fort Moore was Lt. William Johnson. How began recruiting men and gathering equipment, arms, and supplies for Congaree Fort. A carpenter was hired to construct the buildings, and a piragua was purchased and repaired for the garrison's use. In May 1718 some new recruits took the piragua and the fort's arms, equipment, and supplies and deserted. As a result construction of the fort was delayed until late that year. When completed Congaree Fort was on the east bank of Congaree Creek. The site was a short distance west of the Congaree River, about 1.5 miles north of the conflux of those two streams and about 2.5 miles southeast of present-day Cayce in Lexington County. The fort was a semi-European design. It was a rectangular structure with a moat and earthen wall on the north, east, and south sides and a stockade on the west side

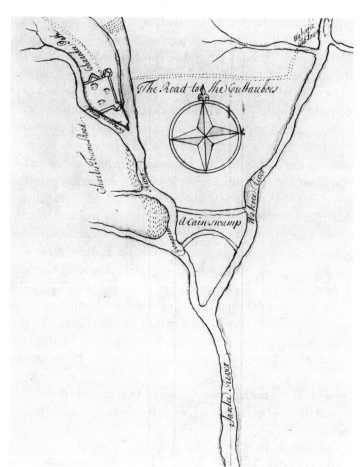

Congaree Fort, 1718–22. "A Sketch Map of the Rivers Santee, Congaree,
Wateree, Saludee, etc., with the Road to the Cuttauboes," ca. 1750. Congaree Fort
is shown in the upper left (northwest) portion of the map. In *Crown Collection
of Photographs of American Maps*, edited by Archer Butler Hulbert
(Cleveland: Clark, 1915), 3rd series, plate 25.

facing the creek. A stockade may also have been planted atop the earthen
wall. The northeast and southeast corners on the land side had protruding
bastions, and a ravelin protected the gate in the north wall. Three buildings were constructed inside the walls. It was South Carolina's northernmost fortification, situated near the trade paths to the Cherokee and
Catawba towns.[14]

South Carolina's new defense act reduced Fort Moore's garrison to a captain, a lieutenant, and fifteen soldiers under the command of Charlesworth Glover. They farmed a tract of land near the fort, and the government paid them for their harvested corn. A captain and six scouts manned the Port Royal Fort and its scout boat. An additional base for scouts was constructed at the "water passage" on the Inland Passage at the northern point of Pinckney Island. It was called Passage Fort and became the headquarters for a scout boat, the crew of which consisted of a captain and six scouts. Both scout-boat crews were reinforced by the addition of the eight Tuscarora Indians and the Highland indentured servants at Port Royal Fort. Two years later the surviving Highlanders, after serving only four of their seven years of bondage, were freed. They became South Carolinians and continued to serve as soldiers.[15]

The Southern Rangers, the largest ranger company, was authorized a captain, lieutenant, and twenty-eight rangers. The company was intended to have constructed and garrisoned a new fort near the deserted town of Palachacola on the east side of the Savannah River, where Yamasee and Creek war parties often crossed into South Carolina. However the construction of a Palachacola fort was not yet undertaken, and the Southern Rangers remained headquartered at Woodward's Fort. The company of Western Rangers, with a captain and five rangers, continued patrolling from Edisto Bluff Fort on Rawlings plantation on the east bank of the Edisto River. The company of Northern Rangers had a captain and nine rangers. They were probably located at Hearn's Fort, the northernmost fortified plantation. The December 1717 defense act established a new incentive: a bounty was paid for enemy Indian scalps.[16]

By 1717 South Carolinians were returning to the islands of Port Royal. As encouragement to settle on that frontier, they received free grants of town lots in the new village of Beaufort. Beaufort had been surveyed in 1711 but was not occupied to any extent. The planters were apprehensive about the continuing Yamasee raids. They were concerned with the conduct of Indian Foster and his seven Tuscarora Indians, who were part of the garrison of Port Royal Fort at Cochran's Point. The Indians were apparently hunting, fishing, and lounging. They were not scouting the countryside on the lookout for Yamasee war parties, nor were they serving as the garrison's messengers to warn people of approaching danger. Port Royal Fort was about eight miles to the northwest of Beaufort, too far away for people to reach in an emergency unless they had adequate warning. The local planters offered to construct a fort in Beaufort at their own expense, to provide a place for their refuge. They requested the government to supply twenty small arms with powder and ball, twenty grenades, four small cannons, and four or five soldiers to help them garrison the fort. They also requested that the large alarm cannons at the deserted Altamaha Town and Thomas Nairne's plantation be moved to the new Beaufort Fort. Much of their request was approved. The new fort was probably completed in late 1717 or 1718 on the west bank of Beaufort River. By 1720 the fort had twelve cannons, and thirty militiamen were available to garrison it when necessary.[17]

In 1717 the Commons House discovered that some rangers were not regularly patrolling their assigned areas. Ranging exposed soldiers to the hardships of life in the savannahs, forests, and swamps, and it was dangerous duty. The Commons House asked Gov. Robert Johnson to order the ranger company commanders to be diligent in maintaining patrols in order to prevent war parties from penetrating the frontiers. Despite the unceasing Indian raids, the excessive cost of maintaining an army forced the government to continue experimenting with ways to reduce expenditures yet maintain an adequate frontier defense. In July 1718 the army was again pared down, and the ranger companies were disbanded. However a provision was made for the governor to organize a large ranger company to be manned by a captain, lieutenant, and forty-eight privates. The government had received intelligence that a French and Choctaw expedition was being prepared to invade the Upper and Lower Cherokee towns. If French soldiers were involved in such an invasion, the rangers would support the Cherokees. The governor could also use the company for any other military purpose. The intelligence proved to be faulty. The invasion never materialized, and the company was never raised. Despite the military reduction in force, small garrisons were maintained at Fort Moore, Port Royal Fort, Water Passage Fort, Congaree Fort, and Fort Johnson.[18]

During March 1719 the South Carolina Commons House passed a new Indian trading statute that included a mixed scheme of public and private trading. The new statute also combined the garrisons and the principal trading factories of Fort Moore, Congaree Fort, and Palachacola. Usually the captain commanding each of those garrisons became the principal trading factor, his lieutenant became his chief assistant factor, and some soldiers became assistant factors. During the previous August, Capt. Charles Russell had been appointed commander of the garrison for the newly constructed Congaree Fort. He was also appointed as the principal trading factor for that location. The construction of the proposed fort and trading factory for Palachacola continued to be delayed, and Woodward's, also known as Horseshoe, Fort was used instead. The 1719 Indian trading statute did not entirely pacify the merchants or their suppliers and creditors. By 1721 the Commons House, under pressure, had abandoned all forms of public monopoly, and private trading was reestablished. By then the economic importance of the Indian trade had already begun to recover.[19]

In late 1719 the South Carolinians' dissatisfaction with the Carolina proprietors' rule became acute. Since at least 1695, there had been advocates in Great Britain who wanted to bring proprietary colonies such as South Carolina under the control of the British government. There were allegations, backed by evidence, of corruption by colonial officials and of their failure to follow British laws. Some officials ignored the Navigation Acts. Those acts were designed to restrict the colonies' trade with other European countries and bolster the profits of English manufacturers and shippers. The proprietors and the South Carolina Commons House had quarreled over several issues for years, but displeasure with the proprietors increased dramatically during the war. The proprietors gave their colonists a minimum of assistance. They were apparently unwilling to spend money on a colony whose near-bankrupt condition offered little hope of profit. They repealed the South Carolina government's recovery measures, including the issuance of additional paper money, making the Indian trade public rather than private, and settling the Indian land with small farmer-militiamen. The proprietors never realized how destructive the war was to life and property, and they failed to understand that South Carolinians remained in danger. The proprietors could not protect their colonists. Raids by Yamasees and Creeks continued. A planned Spanish invasion of South Carolina was narrowly averted, by pure fortune, during the spring of 1719. Robert Johnson, the proprietors' appointed governor from 1717 to 1719, chastised the members of the Commons House for their appeals to the British government for aid. In December 1719 the members of the Commons House, with the cooperation of the militia, rebelled against the proprietors and removed Johnson from office. The Commons House appointed the soldier, planter, and Indian trader James Moore as governor. (He served until 1721.) The proprietors lost political control of the colony, but they continued to be the legal owners of the land. Ten years passed before the British government convinced the proprietors to sell their interests in the land and allow South Carolina to become an official royal colony.[20]

In 1720 the severely downsized South Carolina army was posted to the following assignments: a captain and twenty men were garrisoned at Congaree Fort, a captain and twenty men were assigned to Fort Moore, ten scouts were stationed at Port Royal Fort, ten scouts operated from Passage Fort, and a captain, lieutenant, and twelve men were garrisoned at Fort Johnson, which commanded Charles Town harbor.[21]

The war continued. All of the northern Indians had made peace with South Carolina except the Cheraws and Waccamaws. Previously, during the middle of 1716, the Catawbas had attacked the Waccamaws. The Catawbas feared that the Waccamaws might place their own attempts to secure a peace settlement with South Carolina in jeopardy. The Waccamaws temporarily fled northwest to the protection of the Cheraws. By early 1720 they had returned to their homeland in present-day Georgetown County. During the first half of that year, South Carolina decided to force the Waccamaws into submission and conducted a short campaign against them. One South Carolina Settlement Indian warrior, a Winyaw, was killed. Sixty Waccamaws were killed and captured before they sued for peace.[22]

Colleton County remained sparsely populated. In 1721 only about 150 white people and 144 slaves resided in that part of the county, west of the Edisto River, apparently a little more than a third of the prewar population. Probably less than 200 people resided at Port Royal.[23] Much of South Carolina's economy was temporarily ruined. Many of its people mourned the loss of relatives and friends. They were distressed over the destruction of their property and suffered from miserable living conditions. The war continued. The killing was far from finished.

CHAPTER 15

Southeastern Indians, 1717–20

The lives of most Southeastern Indians had been severely disrupted. Their condition in the spring of 1717 varied from group to group. Some had been driven from their homes. Others had migrated to more secure areas. Several had lost warriors, women, and children in battles and raids. Some of those people had been killed; others had been captured and enslaved.

The Etiwans, Kiawahs, and Winyaws, South Carolina's Settlement Indians, continued to serve South Carolina. Several of their warriors had been killed in battle. At the beginning of the war, South Carolinians had mixed feelings regarding the Settlement Indians. The Commons House praised and rewarded some of their warriors. Some South Carolinians initially questioned the allegiance of the Settlement Indians and probably had not changed their minds during the past two years. However the Commons House was correct: most Settlement Indian warriors gave South Carolina excellent service. Several small groups of Indians still live in South Carolina today.[1]

The Catawbas and most of the Siouan-speaking northern Indians had ceased combat operations against South Carolina in the summer of 1715 and initiated peace discussions under pressure from the Cherokees. The colony of Virginia acted as mediator, and peace with the Catawbas was formally achieved by April 1717. However skirmishes with elements of the Waccamaws, Santees, and Cheraws continued for at least three more years.[2]

Most of the Cherokees had not taken part in the war against South Carolina. They became South Carolina's allies in January 1716 when they assassinated some Lower Creek headmen at Tugaloo. Most Cherokee leaders had probably envisioned that South Carolina would join them in raids against the Creeks. South Carolina did assist with arms and ammunition and supplied a small battalion of soldiers more than once in attempts to convince the Cherokees to conduct major attacks on the Creek towns. Total war was not the Cherokees' strategic objective, nor was it part of their warrior culture. During their war with the Creeks, they avoided major battles and resorted to a traditional limited war of raids and ambushes. The resulting war lasted more than ten years. As in most Southeastern Indian wars, the Cherokees gained few tangible benefits. Cherokee warriors raided Creek towns, took scalps, captured women and children, and achieved fame. However they also lost warriors, women, and children to Creek raids. By 1717 some Cherokee towns had been moved eastward, and several towns became fortified refuge centers.[3]

By early 1717 the Lower Creeks had been settled on their new Chattahoochee River town sites for a year. Coweta was on the west side of the river, near present-day Fort Mitchell in Russell County, Alabama. The people of Kasihta were on the other side of the river, on the site of present-day Fort Benning, Georgia. Many Savannah River Apalaches, Yuchis, and Shawnees had joined the Lower Creek towns near the Chattahoochee River. Creeks were incensed with South Carolina. They assumed that South Carolina had been directly involved with the Cherokees in the assassination of several Creek headmen during January 1716. In addition they were aware that South Carolina was providing arms and ammunition to the Cherokees and was purchasing and enslaving Creek families that had been captured by Cherokee raiders. Small Creek war parties were penetrating South Carolina's frontiers, inflicting casualties, and destroying property, but their greatest effect was spreading fear among the occupants of the plantations and cowpens. However the Creeks avoided pitched battles with South Carolina's army and limited their combat actions primarily to raids against civilian objectives. Their warriors' combat prowess was well known by South Carolinians, who had served with them during Queen Anne's War a decade earlier. It was essential that South Carolina achieve peace with the people of the major Creek towns before the war escalated.[4]

No South Carolinian had access to any of the Creek towns, so the government had no intelligence concerning their activities and intentions. Perhaps not fully appreciated by South Carolinians was the fact that for the past eighteen months micos and principal warriors of the Creeks had been visiting the Spanish in Saint Augustine and Pensacola and the French in Louisiana. Their visits were made to secure presents, to seek protection in case of a South Carolina invasion, and to establish trade for badly needed items such as arms, ammunition, cloth, iron tools, and liquor. The Creek micos had difficulty establishing a common foreign policy, because their people were divided into political factions. Some Lower Creek micos and the Upper Creek micos of the Abikha and Tallapoosa developed a close relationship with the Spanish in Florida. Brims and other Lower Creek micos wanted the Spanish to construct a fort in the deserted province of Apalachee in northwest Florida, near present-day Saint Marks. A fort could serve as a trading storehouse, and a Spanish garrison could provide some protection from South Carolina. The Alabama Upper Creeks grew close to the French in present-day Mobile, Alabama. They and the nearby Tallapoosas allowed the French to construct a fort near the four Alabama towns. Fort Toulouse was a short distance east of the confluence of the Alabama, Coosa, and Tallapoosa Rivers, about fifteen miles north of present-day Montgomery. Although many Creeks hated South Carolina, some towns, including Coweta, contained people, especially women, who were pro–South Carolina. They wanted peace, because only South Carolina could provide the quality and quantity of trade goods that they required. Despite their disagreement regarding whether or not to make peace with South Carolina, all factions of the Creeks continued to support raids against the Cherokees.[5]

The pro–South Carolina faction of Coweta and some other towns gained the attention of the micos. In March 1717 some Lower Creek headmen, who probably included Emperor Brims, took the initiative and made informal overtures to South Carolina, suggesting that a peace settlement could be negotiated. Deputy Governor Robert Daniel responded by sending Capt. John Jones and another man to the Lower Creek towns. They carried an invitation for the Creeks to send a delegation to Charles Town during the following June. Making peace with the Creeks was a delicate matter. The Cherokees, who had become the first Indian group to reestablish an allied relationship with South Carolina, were disturbed to see their ally attempting to make peace with their enemy.[6]

In May, Jones informed Deputy Governor Daniel that Emperor Brims had kindly received him. He reported that the crafty Lower Creeks were blaming the Yamasees for enticing them into making war on South Carolina. Jones told Daniel that a Lower Creek delegation would soon arrive in Charles Town. However during June only a headman named Bocatchee appeared instead of the expected delegation. The excuse that he gave for their failure to appear was that they could not make peace before their corn was harvested. That may have been a legitimate reason; it was nearly time for their important green corn celebration, the busk. The Creeks were angry, however, because South Carolina was providing arms and ammunition to the Cherokees, and they may have reconsidered whether to enter into peace negotiations.[7]

South Carolinians became discouraged. They gained an additional worry when Captain Jones reported that a delegation of Seneca Indians from the powerful Iroquois Confederacy in New York had arrived in the Lower Creek towns. The Senecas offered to assist the Creeks against their common enemies, the Cherokees and Catawbas. South Carolinians feared that a combined army of Creeks and Iroquois might defeat the Cherokees and Catawbas and then attack South Carolina.[8]

In July 1717 Daniel took bold action and sent Col. Theophilus Hastings, who was the factor of the Cherokee trade, to the Lower Creeks. He was instructed to secure a treaty of peace with the people of Coweta and Kasihta. Hastings was accompanied by Col. John Musgrove and a mounted detachment of eleven soldiers, a black slave, and about a dozen packhorses loaded with trade goods for use as presents. The journey from Charles Town to the Lower Creeks would have taken more than two weeks. When Hastings arrived at Kasihta, he and his delegation were refused entry. They went on to Coweta, where their presence was tolerated by Emperor Brims. Musgrove was related to the Creeks through his marriage to a Creek woman and through his mixed-race son, Johnny. Hastings left two men in Coweta to guard the packhorses and presents while he and the remainder of his detachment traveled westward to the Upper Creek towns, in present-day south-central Alabama. The French, who were then building Fort Toulouse, threatened Hastings, but he was protected by some people of the populous Upper Creek factions of Abikha and Tallapoosa, who were anxious to resume trade with South Carolina.[9]

The Spanish were also engrossed in making an attempt to gain exclusive influence over the Lower Creeks. Beginning in 1715 and continuing annually, delegations of a few Creek micos, war captains, and principal warriors made the overland pilgrimage to Saint Augustine. One of the most frequent of the pro-Spanish visitors was Brims's nephew Chipacasi, or Seepeycoffee, as he was known by South Carolinians. Another was Cherokeekiller, who was now mico of Apalachicola, or Palachacola. He magnified himself as the most important leader of the Lower Creeks. A visit by an Indian delegation involved an elaborate pageant, during which the Spanish received the Indians with the pomp and ceremony accorded very important persons. Infantry companies paraded and accompanied them into town. The warriors danced along the route behind their stoic micos. The Indians were saluted with cannons, and Florida's governor and staff greeted them at the door of his home. Speeches were made, presents were exchanged, feasts were held, and liquor was drunk.[10]

The Florida governor's ambassador to the Lower Creeks was retired lieutenant Diego Pena. Pena had made his first long and difficult journey to the Chattahoochee River during the summer of 1716, during which he convinced several micos and warriors to ally themselves with Spanish Florida. He discovered that Emperor Brims of Coweta, rather than Cherokeekiller of Apalachicola, was the most respected and influential leader of the Lower Creeks. Previously during May 1715, at the beginning of the war, Brims had dispatched two trusted emissaries, Ystopojole and Brave Dog, to Saint Augustine. They transmitted Brims's request to be pardoned for past military raids against Spanish Florida but Governor Corcoles did not reply. Brims personally journeyed to Saint Augustine late that summer, but after a brief visit, he may have believed that he had not been accorded sufficient respect. It appears to have been a problem of language translation in both instances, for the Spanish assumed that Brims was their close ally. However by late 1716 Brims's loyalty was uncertain, and it was clear to the Spanish that his support had to be secured before all of the Lower Creeks could be counted on as firm allies. What the Spanish failed to understand was that Brims and some other Lower Creeks were willing to live in friendship with Florida, but they did not want to become Spanish subjects. They remembered their move from the Chattahoochee River, northeastward to the Ocmulgee River, about the year 1691. They migrated to escape the domineering Spanish, who had burned some of their towns as punishment for trading with South Carolina and for refusing to accept Christian missionaries. Intermittent war between the Lower Creek towns and Spanish Florida had followed and continued for several years.[11]

During the summer of 1717, Pena was again dispatched overland to the Lower Creeks. His instructions were to secure the allegiance of Emperor Brims and prevent the Lower Creeks from making peace with South Carolina. He was directed to entice them to move their towns to Apalachee, in northwest Florida, where a new fort with a Spanish garrison would protect them. It took nearly a month for Pena, his escort of eight mounted soldiers, and a party of friendly Indians to reach Cherokeekiller's village on the Chattahoochee River. A week later he set out for Coweta. On his way to the town, he met a warrior who informed him that Colonel Hastings and his delegation had previously arrived at Coweta. The people of the Lower Creek towns were divided regarding whether to welcome the South Carolinians or to kill them. However there was a large pro–South Carolina faction among the people of Coweta, especially among women such as Qua, the wife of a mico or war captain and perhaps a relative of Brims. Before reaching Coweta Pena was detained at an Apalachee town to await the outcome of a conference being conducted by several Lower Creek headmen, including Cherokeekiller. The principal headmen of Coweta and Kasihta were not present. After nearly a week of drinking Pena's liquor and discussing what to do about the presence of the South Carolina delegation, the conference ended. The headmen decided to capture the South Carolinians and send them to Saint Augustine.[12] Of course their decision was subject to Brims's approval.

Two days later Seepeycoffee escorted Pena into Coweta. Colonel Hastings and his men had not yet returned from the Upper Creeks. Pena gave Brims a plumed hat, a dress coat, and stockings, but he was met with a chilly reception. Both men apparently formed an instant dislike of each other. At Pena's insistence Brims scheduled a conference for the following day so that Pena could confer with other micos of the Lower Creeks. Before the conference began, Pena privately scolded Brims for being hospitable to the South Carolina delegation. When Brims blamed some of his people for inviting the South Carolinians, Pena chided him for not punishing the pro–South Carolina people in his town. When the conference began, Pena presented the micos and principal warriors with presents, and they drank the remainder of Pena's liquor. The conference ended without a decision. Seepeycoffee and another mico remained behind and attempted to convince Brims to kill the South Carolina delegation and confiscate their property. Brims refused, and he remained noncommittal to Pena's attempt to secure his allegiance to Spain and to continue raiding South Carolina. Pena did not make a favorable impression with some of Brims's townspeople. He was soon informed by his Lower Creek supporters that he had become persona non grata to the pro–South Carolina faction of Coweta and that his life might be in danger. He left Coweta the following morning and rode to the protection of Cherokeekiller's village. Soon afterward he returned to Saint Augustine.[13]

Hastings and Musgrove returned to Coweta shortly afterward and exchanged presents with Brims. They negotiated with Brims to arrange a marriage. The bride was Brims's niece, a mixed-race woman about seventeen years of age named Cowsaponakeesa. As Mary Musgrove, and Mary Bosomworth, she would later exercise much influence with the British. The groom was Johnny Musgrove, who was probably not much older than his bride. The couple had been married in South Carolina a few months earlier by a Christian minister. Their Creek marriage in Coweta served to add pageantry to the peacemaking ceremony.[14] Brims made a peace of sorts with South Carolina, but he was not going to become a British subject.

In late 1717 Brims dispatched his nephew, Seepeycoffee, to the French and Spanish to assure them of the Creeks' friendship. Brims knew that only South Carolina could supply the Creeks with an adequate amount of trade goods. Therefore during November 1717 he sent Ouletta, his oldest nephew and heir, and a delegation of eleven headmen and several warriors with Musgrove to Charles Town to establish a formal peace treaty. Hastings and three or four men remained with the Lower Creeks as collateral for the Indian delegation's safety. South Carolina received important Indian delegations with pomp and pageantry that rivaled Florida's. A militia company saluted Ouletta and his entourage outside Charles Town. The Governor's Troop of Horse Guards escorted them into town, and they were saluted again in the town by volleys from militia company muskets and batteries of cannons. Speeches were made, presents were exchanged, food was eaten, and rum was served. Presents to the Indians sometimes included coats, hats, leggings, shirts, breechclouts, blankets, guns, and swords. South Carolina's new governor, Robert Johnson, had recently arrived and took charge of the negotiations. A treaty was outlined and agreed to by the delegation but was not yet ratified by the people of the various Creek towns. The key elements of the treaty were South Carolina's agreement to renew trade with the Creeks and the Creeks' agreement to cease raiding South Carolina. Initially only tools, cloth, and similar items could be sold to the Creeks, but within a month the sale of guns and ammunition was authorized, despite the Cherokees' anger.[15]

Shortly after the start of 1718, the government of South Carolina appointed Hastings as factor to the Creeks. Musgrove was ordered back to the Lower Creeks during the last week of February, with a bodyguard of thirty soldiers, a packhorse train loaded with trade goods, and a few Creeks who had been captives of the Cherokees. The allegiance of the Lower Creek towns remained divided between South Carolina and the Spanish. The allegiance of the Upper Creeks was divided between South Carolina, the Spanish, and the French. Nevertheless after a shaky welcome, Musgrove took part in a ceremony during which a knife and two arrows were broken to ratify the peace treaty between South Carolina and the Creeks. Several white captives who were held in the Lower Creek towns, such as Martha Hart and Hugh Banks, were released. A white indentured servant who had escaped his service and taken refuge with the Upper Creeks was returned to South Carolina. South Carolina's economic relationship with many Creek towns was reestablished; however the colony's political status with them remained tarnished for a decade because it provided arms and ammunition to the Cherokees.[16]

Afterward, during the latter part of March 1718, Brims held a conference with several Creek micos. They decided not to support the South Carolinians, the Spanish, or the French when they fought each other. Before long it became obvious to the South Carolinians, the Spanish, and the French that most of the people of the principal Creek towns would resist becoming the sole ally of any white government. Emperor Brims's reputation as a skilled politician was well established, and the Creeks followed his pattern of diplomacy for half a century. They would exchange presents with various governments and do business with white traders, but they would not be subservient.[17]

By the year 1717, the Yamasees had been badly mauled by South Carolina. They had lost many warriors in combat, and several families had been taken captive by South Carolina and sold into slavery. Just before the beginning of the war, in early April 1715, the South Carolina census of the Yamasees noted that there were 413 men, 345 women, and 462 children, for a total of 1,220 people residing in ten towns. Although several Yamasees initially sought safety among the Lower Creeks, most of them became refugees in northeast Florida. During 1717 a Spanish census found approximately 232 men, 191 women, and 174 children, for a total of 597 Yamasees and Guales residing in six towns in northeast Florida. The figures represent a 52 percent reduction in population. They had lost 44 percent of their men, 45 percent of their women, and 63 percent of their children. The hardships and dangers of war were obviously devastating for their children. The loss in population was probably even more severe than the census indicates, since some of those identified as Guale had never left Florida and had not been recorded in South Carolina's 1715 census.[18]

South Carolinians had always assumed that the Yamasees and Guales were members of one group, which they called Yamasee. However in Florida the Spanish usually identified them separately as Yamasee and Guale. A town named Santa Catharina de Guale harbored 125 Guale people. The 163 people in the town of Our Lady of Candelaria de la Tamaja, or Altamaha, included both Yamasee and Guale survivors from the towns of Altamaha, Huspaw, and Okatee. The people of the town of Pocosapa, or Pocasabo, included 126 Yamasees. Pocotalaca, or Pocotaligo, included 98 Yamasees and 6 Guale men. The latter were probably survivors of the town of Euhaw. The town of Tolomato, or Tomotly, contained 64 people, all of whom were Guales. San Buena Bentura de Palica was composed principally of Timucua and Mocama Indians; however 34 of the people were identified as Chachise, probably the remnants of the Lower Yamasee town of Chechessee. The Yamasees and Guales, who had been part of the Yamasee group in South Carolina, slowly began integrating with Timucuas, Apalachees, Mocamas, and those Guales who had never left Florida.[19]

The principal Yamasee-Guale towns in Florida were Pocotalaca, Tamaja, Pocosapa, and Tolomato. Pocotalaca, the former head town of the Upper Yamasees, was about 3 miles north of Saint Augustine. Tamaja, the former head town of the Lower Yamasees, had a palisade fort with a small Spanish army garrison and was served by a Franciscan friar, Marcos de Ita Salazar. The town was probably within a few miles of Saint Augustine. Pocosapa was about 4 miles from Saint Augustine, but exactly where is unknown. It also had a wooden fort with a small Spanish garrison. Tolomato was probably situated about 1.3 miles north of Saint Augustine, on the east bank of the San Sebastian River. Tolomato had a chapel served by a friar named Pedro de las Lastras. During the next dozen years, raids by pro–South Carolina Creek and Chickasaw Indians forced the Yamasee to move some towns from one location to another, sometimes to consolidate with other towns, and to adopt new town names. The Florida governor and the Franciscan missionaries were probably involved with those changes.[20]

The saga concerning the Huspaw King, the mico of the former Guale town of Huspaw, continued. A contemporary South Carolinian, Col. William Rhett, suspected that the Huspaw King had a major hand in instigating the war. Perhaps he aspired to achieve more authority and prestige and rise above his status as the mico of a small town that was subservient to the Yamasee mico of Pocotaligo. The Huspaw King and his people spent most of the spring and summer of 1715 near present-day Darien, Georgia, probably raising crops of corn, beans, and vegetables. After the harvest they moved on to Florida.[21]

A year later, in May 1716, the Huspaw King released Hugh Bryan, a young man about seventeen years old, whom his warriors had captured in the first days of the war. Hugh's father, Joseph Bryan, had operated the Combahee River ferry near the present-day Highway 17 bridge on the border of Hampton and Colleton Counties. It was the major crossing site between the Indian Land and Colleton County. After a few months, the Huspaw King took Hugh to the Lower Creek towns, where they spent several weeks before returning to Saint Augustine. Only fifteen of the Huspaw King's original warriors had survived, but he would soon recruit additional followers. When Hugh was released, he carried a message to Deputy Governor Daniel in which the Huspaw King claimed that he did not kill any South Carolinians and expressed a desire to return to South Carolina in peace. South Carolinians did not trust him. They would have remembered the letter he had written to Governor Craven in April 1715, in which he boasted that the Yamasees and their allies would conquer South Carolina. They would also have remembered his attempt to recruit a visiting Indian to join in the killing of South Carolinians. Nevertheless during December 1716 the government hired an emissary—Maria Charlton, the wife of John Charlton—to negotiate peace with him. John, an Englishman, was a wine merchant and apparently resided part-time in Florida. Maria, perhaps Spanish or Indian, was from Saint Augustine. She accepted the task but was unable to contact the Huspaw King. It was the first of several failed attempts over the next eleven years to make peace with the Yamasees.[22]

In early 1717 the Huspaws were quartered in the Yamasee town of Tamaja. The Huspaw King, the man the Spanish knew as Cacique Jospo, was the leader of twenty-three warriors, twenty-three women, and fourteen children. He was subordinate to Don Antonio de Ayala, the principal mico of the town. Two years later the Huspaw King had apparently become dissatisfied with his status in Florida and sent another message to South Carolina with some Creek Indians that stated he wanted to return to South Carolina with his people. During late March or early April 1719, Governor Johnson sent John Barnwell to negotiate with him. Barnwell took the two scout boat crews and a delegation of three Creek Indian warriors down the Inland Passage to Florida. The three warriors were probably acquainted with the Huspaw King or some of his people. A few Lower Creek men married Florida Indian women and traveled back and forth between their towns and their wives' towns. Other Creek men occasionally visited Saint Augustine to trade and receive presents. For several years those Creek men were a source of information for South Carolina regarding the whereabouts and activities of the Yamasees and other Florida Indians. When Barnwell's party arrived in Florida, he and the scouts hid on Saint Mary's Island, while the three warriors continued south on the Saint Johns River. They landed on the east bank of the river and walked southeast toward Saint Augustine. They arrived in the Huspaw King's town, probably Tamaja on the peninsula about three miles north of Saint Augustine. They were shocked to discover that he and his intoxicated followers were organizing and arming in preparation for a large-scale raid on South Carolina's southern frontier. The Huspaw King, who was probably about forty-five years old, had struck the bargain he probably had been trying for some time to make; the Spaniards had appointed him as the principal mico of the Yamasees. To commemorate the occasion, the Spanish awarded him with a triumphal parade. The three Creek men found the Huspaw King in a belligerent mood. At some point during the festivities, he grew suspicious of them and questioned whether they might be spies. They fled.[23]

Barnwell retrieved the warriors and began a hurried return to Port Royal. He and the scouts spread the alarm. Several South Carolina militia companies mustered in preparation for the expected raids. They were dismissed two weeks later after no war parties appeared. Later the South Carolina government learned that the Yamasee raids had been designed to coincide with a Spanish invasion of South Carolina. Fortunately for South Carolina, the French had recently captured Spanish Pensacola. The Spanish invasion fleet was diverted and used to assault and retake temporarily that settlement.[24]

The Yamasees and Creeks from pro-Spanish Creek towns, such as Cherokeekiller's Apalachicola, began a series of raids into Port Royal and Colleton County. The Huspaw King led a small raiding party against Port Royal during the late summer of 1719. He and his warriors attacked two homesteads. At the first plantation they killed a married couple named Cord. Their second objective was the plantation of Seymour Burrows, the former scout-boat captain and Pocotaligo hero. Captain Burrows was not at his Hilton Head Island home, but the war party captured his wife, their child, and two slaves, a black man and an Indian woman. At some point, either at the time of the raid or during their retreat, the Yamasees killed the child and the two slaves and carried Burrows's wife to Florida. When Burrows returned to his home and realized what had happened, he immediately gathered a few men and sailed for Florida. He arrived in Saint Augustine ahead of the war party. At first the Spanish accused him of being a spy, but when the Huspaw King arrived in Florida with Mrs. Burrows, they secured her release from captivity.[25]

Not long afterward Governor Johnson ordered a reprisal raid. John Barnwell was given the responsibility of planning an operation to be executed by allied Indians. After prodding from South Carolina's traders and the Indian agent, a few Settlement warriors and pro–South Carolina Lower and Upper Creek warriors were willing to raid the Yamasee and other Florida Indians. They planned to gather scalps and captives for profit, to gain war honors and trophies, and probably to retain a good trading relationship with South Carolina. Barnwell recruited a war party of fifty warriors. They included a mixed band of Creeks; a few Cusabos who had remained allies of South Carolina under their mico, Gilbert; and the Tuscaroras, who were attached to the scout-boat crews. Barnwell appointed a Lower Creek named Oweeka as war captain of the raiders and another Lower Creek named Whitle Mico, or Wettly, as his deputy. Barnwell included three South Carolinians in the war party. One was a white man named Melvin. The other two, Johnny Musgrove and Joseph Griffin, were brothers-in-law. Musgrove's wife, Mary, was Griffin's sister. All three were mixed-race children of Creek mothers and Indian trader fathers, John Musgrove and Edward Griffin. Their home was in Colleton County, west of the Edisto River. They were acquainted with Oweeka and several of the war party's Creek warriors. Wettly Mico was Musgrove's uncle.[26]

Oweeka's large war party assembled on Pinckney Island at Water Passage Fort. On September 28, 1719, they began cruising south on the Inland Passage in seven large canoes that Barnwell had probably leased from Port Royal planters. Twelve days later the raiders landed near the mouth of the Saint Johns River, where they hid the canoes. For two days they stealthily marched nearly fifty miles through the forest, south toward Saint Augustine. They arrived near the Indian towns during darkness in the early morning hours of October 12. Oweeka dispatched scouts to make a night reconnaissance of the Indian towns. One scout, probably a Lower Creek, had a Yamasee wife and family in the town of Pocotalaca, about three miles north of Saint Augustine. Oweeka had promised the scout that his family would not be harmed. Nevertheless the scout entered the town and extracted them. It was a mistake. His family alerted their friends, and their friends warned most of the townspeople. By the time the scouts returned to the waiting war party, all of the Indian towns had been forewarned, and the garrison of Castillo de San Marcos was placed on alert.[27]

Oweeka divided the war party into three detachments. At dawn they simultaneously attacked Pototalaca, Tolomato, and Pocosapa. Even though the Yamasees and other Indians had been warned, the Lower Creek war party captured twenty-four people and killed five or six others before most of the people reached safety behind Saint Augustine's walls. A Spaniard who had been in one of the towns, perhaps living with his Indian wife or lover, was taken prisoner. The warriors of the detachment that was assigned to assault Pocosapa, about 4 miles north of Saint Augustine, had been informed to expect the people of that town to welcome them. However they found the town deserted; its population had fled. The Lower Creeks burned the homes, storehouses, and townhouse of each town. The chapel at Tolomato, about 1.3 miles north of Saint Augustine, was sacked and burned, but the Franciscan friar, Lastras, escaped. By midmorning the Spanish garrison of San Marcos had organized a counterattack. A company of soldiers left the fort and marched north toward the war party. Oweeka had the Spanish prisoner stripped naked and sent him to the approaching Spanish under a flag of truce. The Spanish soldiers became incensed when they observed that their comrade had been shamefully treated. Although the company was out of musket range of the war party, they fired upon the Indians and began advancing. The war party moved toward the Spanish company and employed their favorite tactic: a crescent formation. They quickly enveloped both of the Spanish company's flanks. During the resulting battle, the Spanish were badly beaten and lost about fourteen men killed and ten taken prisoner, probably more than half the company. The war party stripped seven of the Spanish captives naked and sent them to Saint Augustine. The other three were carried to South Carolina.[28]

Yamasees retaliated. In June 1720 they raided a Lower Creek town, killed seven warriors, and took several people captive. A short time later, a Yamasee war party raided a plantation on Saint Helena Island. They captured a leather tanner named Inns, killed his white indentured servant, and captured twelve black slaves. Gov. James Moore, newly appointed by the rebellious House of Commons, took bold action and sent a delegation to Saint Augustine with a flag of truce in an attempt to negotiate a halt to the raids. The delegation was surprisingly successful. The Spanish governor was probably smarting from the drubbing the Lower Creeks had given one of his garrison companies, and the Yamasees were ready for a needed respite to relocate and rebuild their towns. The Florida governor helped the South Carolinians ransom Inns and fifty white captives, some of whom had been prisoners for five years and had been given up for dead. The delegation returned to South Carolina with the liberated captives. The families of those captives who returned were probably surprised and overjoyed. The families of those who did not return were probably bitter for the rest of their lives. A few of the captives, like two little girls who were ransomed from the Apalachicola in 1716, were retained and raised by the Spaniards. Others continued to be held by Indians, like the young woman whom Cherokeekiller kept.[29]

It may have appeared to some South Carolinians that the war with the Yamasees was over, but it was only a cease-fire. By 1720, after half a dozen battles and dozens of small skirmishes, both Yamasees and South Carolinians needed a rest.

— CHAPTER 16 —

Raids and Counterraids, 1721–27

Many South Carolinians believed there would be no permanent peace until the British drove the Spanish out of Florida. Their concerns were justified. Spain had planned and nearly executed a 1719 invasion of South Carolina. Nevertheless South Carolinians held a dangerous degree of contempt for Spain and had confidence that they could always defeat any Spanish assault. South Carolinians did not have the same level of confidence regarding any threatening actions taken by Great Britain's traditional enemy, France. As South Carolina's war with the Southeastern Indians progressed, the governor of Louisiana, Jean-Baptiste Le Moyne de Bienville, took advantage of the situation and initiated a series of aggressive actions. He built and garrisoned Fort Toulouse among the Alabama towns of the Upper Creeks during 1717. A new Louisiana settlement was established at New Orleans during 1718. That same year Bienville attempted to establish Fort de Crevecoeur near the mouth of the Apalachicola River; however the project was canceled amid Spanish complaints. During 1719 Spain and France fought each other for control of the northern coast of the Gulf of Mexico. France wrested the small settlement and fort of Pensacola from Spain, Spain took it back, and France once again recovered it. During 1720 Spain and France settled their differences, and Spain recovered Pensacola. Spanish Florida and French Louisiana, then, separately attempted to exert control over the larger Indian groups of the Southeast to the detriment of South Carolina.[1]

France initiated attempts to establish hegemony among the Indian groups that had long been trading customers of South Carolina. Several South Carolinians, and prominent persons from Pennsylvania, Virginia, and North Carolina, feared that the French planned to restrict the British colonies to the Atlantic coast and deny them access to the interior. Their fears were realistic. Before long France began establishing trading posts, forts, and small settlements around the Great Lakes, near the Mississippi River and its tributaries, and as far south as New Orleans.[2]

South Carolinians began considering strategic defensive measures to prevent their encirclement by French forts and to forestall French efforts to gain the allegiance of the Cherokees, Chickasaws, and Creeks. During 1720 the South Carolina government dispatched John Barnwell to England. Barnwell and the colony's agent, Joseph Boone, initiated a campaign to convince the British government to construct and garrison a fort at each of several strategic sites on South Carolina's frontiers. They recommended that each military base be bolstered with emigrant farm families from Great Britain and Europe.[3]

Barnwell and Boone were an efficient team. Barnwell was a respected combat veteran, planter, and businessman. He had extensive knowledge of the southern frontier. Boone had served South Carolina as its agent since the beginning of the war and had become experienced in dealing with the British government bureaucracy. The two men quickly convinced the government that South Carolinians' rebellion against the proprietors was justified. During late summer South Carolina was brought under the protection of the king, and Francis Nicholson was appointed as provisional royal governor from 1721 to 1725. Sixty-six-year-old Nicholson possessed an explosive temper, but he was a capable soldier with considerable colonial experience, having previously served as lieutenant governor of New York and governor of Maryland, Virginia, and Nova Scotia.[4]

The members of the Board of Trade were enthusiastic regarding Barnwell's suggestion of placing forts on South Carolina's frontiers and garrisoning them with battalions of infantry. However the king's Privy Council determined the proposal was too complicated and too expensive. Barnwell presented an alternate plan to the Board of Trade. He believed the French planned to occupy the mouth of the Altamaha River on the coast of present-day Georgia, although the intelligence upon which his concern was based appears to have been tenuous. He advocated the establishment of a British garrisoned fort at that location. The Board of Trade, and then the Privy Council, approved the revised plan. The Privy Council agreed to provide a company of regular infantry to serve as a garrison; an engineer to design the fort and supervise its construction; skilled craftsmen, such as brick makers, masons, and carpenters; and sufficient construction tools. Barnwell soon discovered that the only support the British government would provide was an Independent Company of Foot consisting of about one hundred officers and men, all of whom were in-valids. They had physical profiles that rendered them unfit for offensive combat and construction work. Barnwell had hoped to receive a coveted regular army commission as an officer of the company and commander of the fort. He was disappointed. The British government commissioned Governor Nicholson as captain and commander.[5]

Nicholson, Barnwell, four army officers, and ninety-four soldiers of the Independent Company of Foot arrived in Charles Town on May 22, 1721, aboard a British warship. The soldiers were sick with scurvy and were unable to continue to Port Royal. Barnwell was adamant that the project proceed without delay. During the first week of June, he petitioned Governor Nicholson to commission him to construct a temporary fort at the mouth of the Altamaha River until a permanent structure could be built. He wanted to use the Port Royal scout boatmen as laborers, to em-ploy local craftsmen, to hire a sloop to use as needed, and to receive per-sonal payment to accomplish the task. By June 9 he had official directions to undertake the mission and to obtain everything he had requested, in-cluding rations, supplies, four cannons, and the sloop *Jonathan and Sarah*.[6]

Three weeks later Barnwell wrote to Nicholson from Port Royal Is-land. It had been raining daily, and several scouts were sick. Those scouts who were physically able were killing and butchering wild cattle for ra-tions. He wrote to the governor again on July 21. He warned that the scouts were lazy, and some were alcoholics. Nevertheless Barnwell assured the governor that he knew from experience that they were skilled with boats and weapons and that under proper leadership they functioned well as marines. The Port Royal Scouts at Beaufort crewed the old scout whale-boat that had taken part in several battles and skirmishes since 1715. They also served as the garrison of Beaufort Fort. Another crew of scouts, an officer and seven men, garrisoned Passage Fort to the southwest. At Beau-fort, Barnwell selected twenty-six men, a few of whom were scouts and the others apparently hired laborers, to accompany him to the Altamaha River. He left seven scouts under the command of Capt. Jacob Wright to garrison Beaufort Fort. He ordered two of his black slaves to join the ex-pedition as laborers. He hired David Duvall and two of his black slaves who were skilled sawyers. Two Indian warriors, a Tuscarora and a Creek, agreed to serve as hunters. Supplies and tools were loaded on the sloop, which put out to sea, and the men sailed south on the Inland Passage in the scout whaleboat and Barnwell's personal piragua.[7]

Upon their arrival at Passage Fort, on the northeast point of Pinck-ney Island, Barnwell left seven sick scout boatmen there to recover. He added Capt. Joseph Palmenter or Parmenter, his scouts, and their scout boat, which was a large dugout canoe, to the expedition. Barnwell and the scouts had difficulty finding their way south along more than sixty miles of unmarked channels of the Inland Passage. They reached the area of the Altamaha River after a five-day journey. Barnwell made a reconnaissance of that area of the coast and became convinced that the best location for a later, permanent fort would be on the south end of Saint Simons Island. However he dared not build there with the troops and armament available at that time. A small wooden and earthen fort and an understrength garrison could not survive bombardment from French or Spanish warships in the nearby sound. For the site of the temporary fort, he selected a bluff on the Inland Passage near the mouth of the Altamaha River at present-day Darien, Georgia, where a replica of the fort stands today.[8]

On Thursday, July 13, 1721, Barnwell's expedition rendezvoused at the site. That night he held a small ceremony, during which they drank rum toasts to King George and Governor Nicholson. They began work on the fort the following morning. During the remainder of the summer, Barnwell and his men worked under the miserable conditions of heat, mosquitoes, and bad drinking water. They spent long hours felling cypress trees and floating them about three miles to the site. Construction of the fort and its buildings was hard and difficult work. The men often suffered periods of dysentery and malarial fever. By late summer one-third of the scouts were too sick to work, and one scout had died. Though Barnwell was about fifty years old and was sometimes not in the best of health, he labored alongside his men. He was dead three years later.[9]

Barnwell designed a triangular fort to cover the Inland Passage with its cannons and to provide protection from an attack. It had a bastion on the land, or northwest, side, which consisted of a moat with a palisade and an earthen wall. The east side overlooked a marsh and was protected by a palisade. On the south side a rampart, constructed of earth with a wooden retaining wall, stood on a bluff above the Inland Passage. Inside the fort's wall was an officer's house, a barracks for the men, miscellaneous huts, and a large blockhouse. The barracks building was constructed at Beaufort, dismantled, and shipped to the fort. The blockhouse was a three-storied structure, with cannons mounted on the second floor. It was uniquely constructed of four-inch-thick cypress planks fitted into wooden frames, rather than being nailed. Barnwell planned for the blockhouse to be dismantled later and reassembled as part of a permanent fortification on the south end of Saint Simons Island.[10]

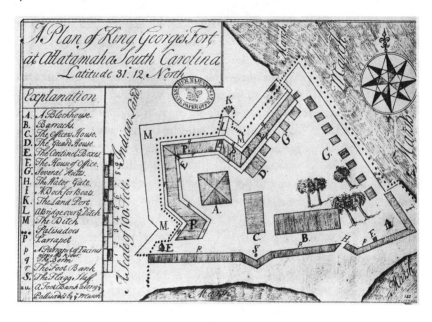

Fort King George, 1721–28. "A Plan of King George's Fort at Allatamaha, South Carolina, 1722." In *Crown Collection of Photographs of American Maps*, edited by Archer Butler Hulbert. Cleveland: Clark, 1915, third series, vol. 3, plate 132.

During early August 1721, the members of the Commons House worriedly asked Nicholson if South Carolina was expected to pay for the expense of the fort's construction. Nicholson urged them to provide the necessary labor, equipment, and supplies. The Commons House offered to pay, if Great Britain reimbursed the colony. The governor agreed to ask the king for reimbursement, and the Commons House agreed to advance the necessary funds. Some workers and suppliers did not receive payment until a year and a half later.[11]

The men of the Independent Company recuperated at Beaufort Fort on Port Royal Island. Nicholson did not expect them to be fit for duty before March 1722. In August 1721 he recommended to the Commons House that the soldiers of the Independent Company should become the garrisons of Beaufort Fort and Passage Fort while they were recovering their health. The scouts at those forts should move to and garrison the Altamaha Fort. Members of the Commons House knew that a mutinous situation would result. The scouts had families and maintained "little plantations" that they farmed near Beaufort Fort and Passage Fort, and they would refuse to transfer to the Altamaha Fort. However the Commons House was agreeable to have part of the Independent Company garrison Fort Moore, while its garrison transferred to the Altamaha Fort. Fort Moore's garrison was also unwilling to transfer, and negotiations continued without resolution for six months.[12]

When the Altamaha fort was completed early that fall, Captain Parmenter and a few scouts remained as a temporary garrison. In late September 1721, the new fort was named Fort King George. Less than a month later, two officers, two sergeants, two corporals, a drummer, and forty-five soldiers of the Independent Company of Foot arrived at Fort King George and relieved the scouts. The remainder of the company remained at Beaufort Fort and then followed in early 1722.[13]

Indian hunters soon informed the Spanish of Fort King George's existence. Spain considered the fort and its garrison to be an occupation of Spanish land. Official Spanish protests were made by delegations both in Charles Town and London. The fort was located in Florida's former mission province of Guale, an area that Spain had claimed during the previous century and a half. However Spain had not occupied that province for more than thirty years. During the next four years, the governments of South Carolina and Great Britain received Spanish delegations and listened to their protests, but they never agreed that they were trespassing on land that belonged to Spain. By the end of 1725, the Spanish realized that diplomacy alone would not drive Fort King George and its garrison from the Altamaha River.[14]

The Spanish government had temporary success in another diplomatic endeavor. Its ambassador in England complained to the British government regarding raids by South Carolina's allied Creeks against Indian towns in Florida. During late 1721 Governor Nicholson received instructions from the British government to halt such activity. Nevertheless during the summer of 1722, the governor dispatched Col. Theophilus Hastings to the Creeks, where he was directed to seek their assistance in making peace with the Yamasees. The governor, and others in the South Carolina government, continued to believe the Yamasees could be enticed to return to their homes in the Indian Land. If that proved impossible, Hastings was directed to convince the Creeks to destroy the Yamasees. As a result the Creeks seem to have made a few more raids into Florida, and the Spanish again complained. Nicholson soon received the British government's renewed instruction to keep the Creeks in check. Despite the reluctance of the members of the Commons House, many of whom had fought the Yamasees for the better part of a decade, the governor obeyed.

By the beginning of 1723, the British and Spanish governments had enforced a temporary cease-fire.[15]

During the lull in the fighting, South Carolina took actions to improve frontier defense. On February 15, 1723, the government expanded the articles of war regarding the conduct of all provincial soldiers. Drunkenness, sleeping on guard duty, being disorderly, disobeying orders, and belonging to a factious clique could result in a court-martial. Corporal punishment, "not extended to life or limb," could be administered. Drunkenness among soldiers had become a problem. Owners of punch houses were prohibited from serving beer, wine, or liquor to soldiers unless permission was first granted by the soldiers' commanding officers.[16]

A new defense act was passed by the government in July 1723. Capt. Gerard Monger and Lieutenant Maxwell were the officers of Fort Moore. Monger also served as a justice of the peace for the Savannah Town area. His garrison included twenty men, one of whom was a sergeant. Seventeen members of the garrison resigned during January 1724, but additional men were recruited. Monger and Maxwell retired during the spring of 1725 and were replaced by Maj. David Durham and Lt. Arthur Forster. The structures in Fort Moore were in poor condition, but repairs were made that summer. Two scout boats were kept on duty at Port Royal under captains Joseph Parmenter and Jacob Wright. Their crews were reduced to six scouts for each boat. The old canoe and the scout whaleboat were supposed to be replaced by two new boats, but the only craft that was quickly replaced was the scout whaleboat. The scouts' principal post, Beaufort Fort, was ordered repaired, but the work was not completed for more than two years. Wright maintained an Indian prison at or near the fort for a time. It was used as a holding place for Indians whose presence in Port Royal was suspect. Two stationary lookouts were located at Port Royal. Two white men and two Settlement Indians were at the mouth of present-day Broad River, and four white men were at the old Port Royal Fort on Cochran's Point.[17]

Congaree Fort had been abandoned during the summer of 1722, and its garrison of an officer and twenty men were discharged. The colony used the savings to place a similar garrison at a more strategic location. The government had long recognized that a garrisoned fort was needed near the old Palachacola Town, where Yamasee raiding parties that approached South Carolina by land crossed the Savannah River. The 1723 act directed that a company of rangers be recruited to construct a palisade fort at Palachacola. The rangers were to patrol at least once every two weeks eastward across the Indian Land and northward to the Savannah Path. Capt.

William Bellinger was appointed as commander and was made a justice of the peace for Granville County. His company included a lieutenant, a sergeant, and nineteen rangers. During the late summer of 1723, Bellinger and his recruits were engaged in constructing Palachacola Fort, later known as Fort Prince George. His sergeant was seriously ill, and some men were sick. The heat, snakes, and lack of a skilled carpenter caused delays. The completed fort was probably a stockade structure; however it may have resembled the old Congaree Fort, a semi-European type with a moat and earthen wall. Rangers continued to garrison Palachacola Fort for nearly twenty years.[18]

Governor Nicholson sailed to England in May 1725. His absence was intended to be temporary, but he never returned to South Carolina. Arthur Middleton, a wealthy planter who was president of the governor's council, became acting governor from 1725 to 1730. At about the same time, South Carolina reignited the war with the Yamasees. During the fall of 1725, a large war party of Creeks was organized under Chipacasi, Emperor Brims's nephew, to conduct a raid against the Yamasees. Brims had designated Chipacasi as his heir, after his oldest nephew, Ouletta, was killed by Yamasees. Chipacasi was pro-Spanish. Nevertheless he may have been seeking South Carolina's approval of him as Brims's chosen successor. He knew, when he eventually became mico, that his people would need South Carolina trade goods. Another reason for his raid may have been to avenge the death of Ouletta. The warriors that he recruited would have wanted scalps and captives, but the principal objective of the war party was to penetrate Florida's defenses and capture or kill the Huspaw King. The South Carolina government may have instigated the raid through Tobias Fitch, its agent to the Creeks. It is likely that the Creeks were encouraged by some of their South Carolina traders, who may have promised a reward for the Huspaw King or his scalp. The traders probably expected to purchase any Florida Indians captured during the raid. In any event the South Carolina government did not attempt to prevent that or any future raids.[19]

By 1725 Florida governor Antonio de Benavides had apparently moved the Yamasee town of Pocotalaca about sixteen miles south of Saint Augustine near the east coast of Florida, between present-day Crescent City and Palm Coast. At least three other towns, including Tamaja, were relocated to the same general area. Two or more of the towns contained palisade forts. Additional protection was available from Saint Augustine's cavalry troop, which was within supporting distance. The towns were in an area that appeared to be safe from raids. There were three approaches from the north that raiders could use to reach the towns. A landing from the

Atlantic Ocean was possible. An approach could be made by canoes and piraguas via the Inland Passage through Matanzas Bay, past Castillo de San Marcos. Or men in canoes and piraguas could navigate down the Inland Passage to the Saint Johns River, paddle or row south up the river, then march overland eastward. None of the approaches were without hazard. Besides, South Carolina could not send its soldiers into Florida while Great Britain and Spain were at peace. A raid by South Carolina soldiers could have been considered an act of war. However some Creek warriors began conducting raids against the Yamasees as South Carolina's surrogates, with or without official sanction.[20] Most Creek warriors who took the warpath against the Yamasee towns used a fourth approach: overland, southeast along ancient paths.

In October 1725 Chipacasi's Lower Creek warriors, who hoped to capture or kill the Huspaw King, set out from Coweta. A few Upper Creek warriors joined them under the leadership of a war captain named Steyamasiechie, or Goggle Eyes, as he was known by South Carolinians. They were accompanied by a guide, an Indian who had previously visited the Huspaw King's Florida town.[21] They marched southeasterly for approximately three hundred miles, avoiding the deep swamps on the present-day Georgia-Florida border. During their journey, which would have taken up to two weeks, they passed close to the sites of the present-day Georgia towns of Columbus, Albany, and Valdosta and the Florida towns of Lake City, Starke, and Patatka.

They crossed the Saint Johns River near Patatka, using a ford in that locality. The war party marched eastward in darkness for about fifteen miles. Unknown to Chipacasi, the mico of the Lower Creek town of Okmulgee had sent runners to the Yamasees warning of the war party's approach. During the early morning hours of November 1, 1725, Chipacasi and his men unknowingly bypassed about ten sleeping warriors who were supposed to be acting as a listening post to give early warning of their approach. The guide led the war party to an Indian town that he apparently believed was occupied by the Huspaw King and his family. However he had designated the wrong town. When the Creek warriors attacked, the townspeople ran into a palisade fort they had constructed in the midst of their town. As the warriors prepared to assault the fort, they observed the warriors of the listening post, who had been shocked awake by the gunfire, making their way around the town and running eastward. Some members of the war party followed them and discovered another town located nearer to the sea. It was probably Tamaja, the Huspaw King's town. By that time it was dawn. The Creeks shifted their attention to that town and hurriedly conducted an assault. Despite having been warned by the warriors of the listening post, three members of the Huspaw King's family were slow to respond and were captured. Most of the townspeople, including the Huspaw King, who may have been wounded, escaped into a palisade fort in the town. Soon the Yamasees organized a counterattack and erupted from the fort. After a short skirmish, the Huspaw King's war captain was captured, and the Yamasees withdrew.[22]

During the following three days, Creek warriors ravaged the exposed houses, mission chapels, townhouses, and storage buildings of the nearby towns. By the third day, they realized they could not gain entry into any of the palisade forts without taking heavy casualties. They began withdrawing westward. During their withdrawal the Yamasees attacked. Close-quarter fighting resulted. The Creek warriors initially gained the upper hand and drove the Yamasees into a pond. As the Creeks organized a final assault, the Spanish cavalry troop arrived from Saint Augustine. The fighting briefly paused while a Spanish officer approached, under a white flag, with the intent to arrange a cease-fire. Chipacasi seems to have favored a cease-fire, during which they could safely withdraw. However Goggle Eyes and his men took the officer under fire, forcing the Spanish to take part in the battle. The war party had remained in Florida too long. The odds were in the Yamasees' favor, and the Creeks began to retreat. With the Spanish cavalry's help, the Yamasees displayed their skill and ferocity. During their fighting withdrawal, the Creeks were savaged. When they reached and crossed the Saint Johns River, the Yamasees and Spaniards apparently halted their pursuit. Several days later the war party returned to Coweta with eight scalps and nine captives, most of whom were Yamasees from the town of Tamaja. The warriors complained to Emperor Brims about the casualties they had suffered: five men killed and six wounded.[23] He chastised them: "Such things as them must hapen or you would Be noe Warriours for if Men Should always goe out To Warr against Enemies and never loose any men then old Women would be good Warriors."[24]

Other Lower Creek raids into Florida followed. Few were successful. Pro-Spanish Lower Creeks convinced some war parties to return home or warned the Florida Indians of the approach of the war parties. A few weeks after his Florida raid, Chipacasi traveled to Saint Augustine and renewed his friendship with the Spanish and Yamasees. During the ensuing year, he went on an alcoholic binge and drank copious quantities of rum. He died shortly afterward from acute alcohol poisoning. Most of the Yamasees moved their towns closer to Saint Augustine. War parties composed of Yamasees, Guales, Cusabos, Timucuas, and Apalachees prepared to conduct retaliatory raids against South Carolina.[25]

In January 1726 a sergeant's house at Fort King George caught fire. The fire spread to the other buildings and to the barracks, destroying the soldiers' personal property and leaving them without adequate shelter during winter. The soldiers refused to make the necessary repairs until their commander, Lt. James Watts, promised them additional pay. Afterward hasty repairs were made and paid for with funds lent by the government of South Carolina to the British government. Two months after the fire, an army officer in England named Edward Massey was promoted to captain of the Independent Company. He arrived in South Carolina during August and found harsh conditions at the fort. The rebuilt facilities were substandard, and the soldiers were disgruntled. They were isolated, five days from the nearest reinforcements. The only other people they saw were the scouts who patrolled the Inland Passage and the occasional boatmen who brought supplies. Sickness was common, and several men had died. Recruits were scarce, apparently because conditions at the fort were well known. They were in a dangerous location, rum and beer were probably seldom available, and no women were nearby. On one occasion twelve men deserted to Florida. Resignations and reassignments of lieutenants and ensigns were common.[26]

South Carolina had enjoyed a tenuous peace with the people of several Creek towns for almost six years when an incident deteriorated their relationship. During March 1726 a war party of Cherokee and Chickasaw warriors attacked the Lower Creek town of Kasihta. They probably did minimal damage to the town and inflicted few casualties; however the war party was observed carrying a British flag and drum. The Creeks had long disapproved of South Carolina's supplying weapons and ammunition to the Cherokees, but after that attack they became incensed. They suspected that South Carolina had instigated the raid. The Creeks ceased acting as South Carolina's proxy raiders against the Yamasee towns. South Carolina immediately took diplomatic steps to calm Creek tempers. Nevertheless relations remained seriously strained and nearly resulted in war until an uneasy peace between the Creeks and Cherokees was established in 1727.[27]

In 1726 Florida's Governor Benadives took advantage of the Creeks' spat with South Carolina. He resorted to using his Indian allies, especially the Yamasees, to harass the South Carolinians in retaliation for past raids and to keep the British from encroaching farther south beyond Fort King George into the old Guale province. Indian war parties from Florida began bypassing the fort on their way to raid South Carolina. Some of them penetrated South Carolina via the Inland Passage, while others followed ancient paths that paralleled the coast. A war party of Cusabo Indians, perhaps some former inhabitants of the reservation on Polawana Island at Port Royal, navigated the Inland Passage past Fort King George. They landed on Hilton Head Island during August 1726 and raided a cowpen. They killed the planter, Richard Dawson, and his wife. A month later a small Yamasee war party penetrated the southern frontier by land as far as the Combahee River, northeast of Port Royal Island. The war party raided the cowpen of John Edwards. They surprised and killed Edwards in his home. They captured four of Edwards's black slaves, plundered his buildings, and escaped to Florida.[28]

The people living in eastern Colleton County, near the Edisto River, petitioned for more rangers for their protection. Although there was no absolute system of frontier defense, rangers who constantly patrolled the frontier provided a good deterrent to raiding war parties. The Company of Southern Rangers was activated during October 1726. The company was commanded by Capt. William Peters and included Sgt. William McPherson and fourteen rangers. A war captain named Harry and ten of his Kiawah warriors were also part of the company during the first year. Initially the rangers were stationed at Pon Pon, the area around present-day Jacksonboro, and patrolled Colleton County. In June 1727 James McPherson became sergeant when his brother left the service. By March 1728 Peters had resigned, and James was commissioned as captain of the Southern Rangers. Captain McPherson was a forty-year-old veteran who continued to command rangers for several years. He had been born in South Carolina, and he lived to reach the unusually old age of eighty-three. During 1729 McPherson and his rangers were transferred to the Indian Land, where they built and garrisoned Saltcatchers Fort, also known as Rangers Fort, near present-day Yemassee. He received at least three grants of land in the area and settled near the fort.[29]

The Yamasees' raids prompted the South Carolina government to adjust frontier defense. People were directed to carry weapons, even when attending church. At the beginning of 1727, the two scout-boat crews commanded by captains Joseph Palmenter and Abraham Graham received new muskets, cartridge boxes, and a blunderbuss for each boat. Graham had replaced Jacob Wright as commander of the Port Royal Scouts during the previous year. Capt. David Durham and Lt. Arthur Foster had recently replaced Gerald Monger and Anthony Willy at Fort Moore. That garrison also included Sgt. Stephen Dyers, Cpl. William Sladders, and twenty-four soldiers, an increase of seven men. Capt. Rowland Evans assumed command of Palachacola Fort from William Bellinger. Phileman Parmenter was his lieutenant, and William Johnson was sergeant. A man named Watt replaced Johnson in 1727.[30]

Violence flared again in January 1727. A war party from Florida captured a soldier who ventured outside Fort King George and carried him to Saint Augustine. In June warriors from Florida raided a plantation on the west side of Port Royal Island and killed William Lavy and John Sparks. The war party spared their wives but plundered their homes. The Indians warned the women that other war parties were on their way.[31]

In April 1727 Captain Massey finished preparing a report regarding the condition of Fort King George and the Independent Company. He described the miserable and unhealthy living conditions. He noted that during the past six years, replacements had to be found for four officers and a surgeon. One hundred thirty enlisted men had died at the fort. Massey recommended that the South Carolina government transfer the company from Fort King George to Beaufort Fort. The people who were living at Port Royal agreed. They petitioned the government in June with the demand that the Independent Company be withdrawn to Beaufort Fort for their protection. It was obvious by then that a garrison at Fort King George could not prevent war parties from penetrating South Carolina. The Independent Company was withdrawn to Beaufort Fort in September. However the fort was not abandoned; the Spanish would surely have occupied it in order to solidify Spain's claim to the coast of present-day Georgia. Two South Carolina soldiers were stationed at the abandoned fort as lookouts to gather intelligence, to act as caretakers, and to keep the British flag flying over the mouth of the Altamaha River.[32]

Florida governor Benavides continued outfitting war parties with arms, ammunition, and supplies. During the summer of 1727, a large war party of forty-eight Indians, accompanied by two Spaniards, traveled overland and penetrated South Carolina defenses. The Spaniards may have been soldiers, but more likely they were of mixed-race parentage or had married Indian women and were living in their wives' towns. The war party raided a plantation in eastern Colleton County and killed Henry Mushoe, captured Hezekiah Wood and ten of Mushoe's and Wood's slaves, and plundered their farmstead. Mushoe, Wood, and their slaves must have initially resisted and fired on their attackers. A local planter and militia company commander, Capt. John Bull, was alerted. Bull had a special reason to hate Yamasees. Twelve years before, at the beginning of the war, one of their war parties had captured his young wife. He never saw her again.

The Yamasees' attack on Mushoe and Wood provided him with an opportunity to secure revenge. Bull gathered fifteen of his mounted militiamen from the countryside and pursued the war party. During the Indians' retreat, a Spaniard beat Wood to death with a stick of wood. Bull and his detachment caught up with the burdened, slower-moving war party the next day. During the resulting battle, Bull's party lost one man, but they killed six Indians and one Spaniard, rescued the slaves, and retrieved the plunder.[33]

Dozens of black men in Saint Augustine had either escaped from South Carolina or had been captured by Yamasee war parties. The Spanish trained them as soldiers. About the latter part of September 1727, a war party left Saint Augustine in two large canoes. The raiders included several Indian warriors and six black warriors. More than a week later, they landed on Hilton Head Island and raided the home of Alexander Dawson. The Indians intended to kill Dawson, four children, and four other adults who were on the plantation and earn the Spanish bounty for white scalps. The black warriors intervened and prevented the massacre. Dawson and his people were carried to Saint Augustine as captives. Not long afterward a small schooner manned by Spanish and black seamen raided the plantation of David Ferguson near the North Edisto River and captured seven slaves.[34]

It was a desperate time for those few people who lived in Colleton County and Port Royal. They congregated in several fortified homesteads, each of which contained four or five families. Acting governor Middleton complained that "we having already experienc's that Garrisons and Rangers have hitherto given little or no protection to the Outsettlements."[35] The governor and others were upset with the failure of frontier defenses to prevent the raids. However without the deterrence of garrisons and rangers, the raiders could have multiplied their incursions with catastrophic results. No method of frontier defense could have entirely halted the raids of the Yamasees, a warrior society highly skilled in irregular forest warfare. The governor and other South Carolina officials were rapidly coming to the conclusion that the people on the frontiers could be protected only through an aggressive offense.

CHAPTER 17

Florida Expedition, 1728

Previously, in 1724, Lower Creek Indian traders Matthew Smallwood and John Bee and several of their employees had bypassed Fort King George in their piraguas and continued northwest up the Altamaha River. They had built a fortified storehouse on the south side of the Ocmulgee River to serve as a trading factory. It was about 5.5 miles northwest of present-day Hazlehurst, Georgia, and about 7 miles southwest of the "Forks," the site where the Ocmulgee and Oconee Rivers join to form the Altamaha River. The trading factory was in a precarious defensive location, more than seventy miles upriver from Fort King George. The South Carolina government favored the establishment of the factory. Acting governor Arthur Middleton hoped that its location, not far north of Florida, would tempt the Yamasees to renew trade with South Carolina and entice them to enter peace negotiations. It was South Carolina's last attempt to make peace with the Yamasees.[1]

About August 1, 1727, Jack, an Indian slave owned by Smallwood, arrived in Charles Town and reported that the trading factory's storehouse had been sacked. Johnny Musgrove and James Welch traveled to the Forks to investigate the incident. They returned in late September and reported that Smallwood's storehouse had been burned. Some deerskins had been destroyed, and the only evidence of the traders' fate was a shirt that was hanging on a nearby bush. Later it was determined that about the middle of July, a large war party had ambushed the traders' piragua on the Altamaha River and killed Smallwood and his assistants, Joseph Abbot, John Annesley, John Hutchinson, and Charles Smith. The war party then went to Smallwood's storehouse, where they captured John and William Grey and a man named Beans. John Bee was apparently absent when the attack occurred. The warriors plundered the trading goods, took about three thousand deerskins, and burned the storehouse. The war party reportedly included thirty-four Indians. Twenty-six of the warriors were Yamasees and their allies, and eight of them were probably some of Cherokeekiller's Apalachicola warriors. One of the war party's captains was a Lower Creek known as "Tyger."[2]

By the beginning of 1727, the South Carolina government had reached the conclusion that the Yamasees could never be enticed to make peace. Although military action had been considered, none had been taken. Now, however, the massacre of Smallwood and his men prompted the government to prepare to take the offensive against the Yamasees. The issue was how to accomplish that task. The Creeks were no longer willing to make war on the Yamasees; in fact the Lower Creeks were threatening to make war on South Carolina. South Carolina immediately halted all trade with the Lower Creeks and evacuated the traders and their staffs to the Upper Creek towns. On September 30, 1727, the government passed a law that authorized two military expeditions. The first was a campaign to invade the Lower Creek towns and compel their allegiance. That campaign eventually proved unnecessary. The second was a campaign to raid the Yamasee towns in Florida and destroy their ability to conduct war. The latter, the Florida Expedition, was a courageous plan, but it was hazardous. Great Britain and Spain were at peace, and the plan called for an unauthorized penetration of the Spanish colony by South Carolina soldiers. Acting governor Middleton commissioned Col. John Palmer, the experienced scout and member of the Commons House, to organize and command a waterborne battalion to raid the Yamasee towns in Florida.[3]

While the Florida Expedition was in the planning stage, another Yamasee raid on the southern frontier received little if any publicizing. More than a dozen years later, the South Carolina Commons House disclosed an old report of one of its committees that dealt with an incident that had occurred in January or February 1728. The report briefly described the ambush of a scout-boat crew on the south point of Daufuskie Island. Indian warriors killed the scouts and captured the commander, Capt. Barnabas Gilbert. The site of the battle became known as Bloody Point. It is unlikely that Gilbert and his men were regular provincial scout boatmen. They were probably one of those detachments of militiamen whom the government mustered for short periods when dangerous circumstances required additional soldiers. They had probably been stationed temporarily on Daufuskie Island to serve as lookouts. In early April after his release from captivity, Gilbert received pay for his time on active duty, which apparently included his time in captivity. In 1731, after his death, his widow received an additional two hundred pounds. Until that incident recruitment for the Florida Expedition had been slow and difficult. The attack convinced South Carolinians that the mission was essential, even though it was dangerous. Conducting a military operation in Spanish Florida could be considered an act of war.[4]

The final impetus that set the Florida Expedition in motion occurred when Governor Benavides released several white men, women, and children that the Yamasees had captured during the past two years. Benavides was probably feeling triumphant; he would have known that Fort King George's garrison had been withdrawn, and assumed that it was the result of the raids made by his Indian allies. A letter from Benavides accompanied the released captives to Charles Town. Translation of the letter into English may have been faulty. Acting governor Middleton believed that Benavides's letter chided him for being asleep while South Carolinians were carried away as captives. Middleton immediately sent an order to Colonel Palmer at Port Royal to assemble his battalion and strike out for Florida.[5]

Half of Palmer's battalion included 107 South Carolina militiamen. They were mustered in two companies that were commanded by captains William Peters and John Hunt. Peters's company included 56 men, and Hunt commanded 52. The remainder of the battalion was a war party of about 100 Indians from several groups. Included were Oweeka, the experienced Creek war captain, and his warriors; King Gilbert and some Cusabo; and the mico of the Edisto group with his warriors. Some warriors from Squirrel King's Chickasaw town on the Savannah River may also have been included. Palmer and his battalion were given the hazardous mission of conducting a commando raid into Florida to destroy the power of the Yamasees and their allied Indians. They were to kill and capture as many Yamasees as possible and burn their homes, townhouses, and storage buildings. Palmer had no intention of assaulting Saint Augustine's defenses. His orders from Middleton were not to harm any Spaniards. Besides, the fort of Castillo de San Marcos was too formidable, and the town of Saint Augustine was protected by walls and batteries of cannons.[6]

The battalion rendezvoused at Port Royal during late February 1728 and descended the Inland Passage in piraguas and canoes. An advance guard of one or both scout boats and a party of Indians likely preceded the main body and acted as navigators. They passed by the two South Carolina soldiers who were on duty as lookouts at Fort King George. Palmer and his raiders boldly, but quietly, entered Spanish Florida. They rowed west and then south on the Saint Johns River. The raiders probably landed north of present-day Picolata, where the main east-west road from Saint Augustine westward to Apalachicola crossed the river. It would have been too dangerous to risk detection while bypassing that strategic site. The battalion probably landed on the east bank of the river, and the men hid their boats in a creek. A likely location is Julington Creek, just south of present-day Mandarin, on the southern edge of greater Jacksonville. They left a small detachment to guard the boats.[7]

The Spanish had made considerable improvements to the defenses of Saint Augustine. An earthen and wooden stockade wall, the Rosario Line, protected the northern, western, and southern sides of the town. The western approach also received protection from the marshes of the San Sebastian River during high tide. A similar wall, the Cubo Line, extended from the town's northwest bastion westward to the San Sebastian River. An earthen wall, the Hornwork, about a half mile north of the Cubo Line extended from Matanzas Bay westward to the San Sebastian River. The Spanish garrison included about three hundred regular soldiers, plus civilian and Indian militia. The cannons of San Marcos commanded the nearby countryside for a radius of a little more than half a mile, depending upon the caliber and type of cannons. Smaller cannons were placed on Saint Augustine's protective walls. The defenses were formidable.[8]

Lower Creek raids had earlier decimated the populations of two of the principal Yamasee towns. Pocosapa or Pocasabo ceased to be a separate town, and its survivors joined other towns. Tamaja or Altamaha, also called Tama, had lost several people during the raids. Its survivors were given a new town site about eight miles from Saint Augustine. However after less than a year, they joined some Apalachees and Timucuas in a town known as Moze. By the beginning of March 1728, Governor Benavides had moved most of the surviving Indian towns closer to Saint Augustine to protect them from raids. Two towns that were inside Saint Augustine's defenses, Pocotalaca and probably Palica, would have been difficult to attack. However four Indian towns were located outside Saint Augustine's defenses: Moze, Tolomoto, Nombre de Dios, and Chiquito.[9]

A map dated 1730, sometimes known as the Palmer Map, was prepared by an unidentified person who either accompanied the Florida Expedition or gained information from Colonel Palmer or one of his soldiers. The map shows Saint Augustine, its defenses, and its immediate surroundings as they appeared at the time of the Florida Expedition. The map was prepared for Adm. Sir Charles Wager, a British naval officer, so it also served as a navigation chart for the entrance to Matanzas Bay, Saint Augustine's harbor. The map is a valuable research tool, but it is totally unreliable when depicting the terrain on Saint Augustine's peninsula north of Nombre de Dios. The map shows the San Sebastian River flowing southeast and emptying into the Diego River a short distance north of Nombre de Dios, thus inaccurately placing Saint Augustine on an island rather than a peninsula. The map shows the general locations of the Indian towns near Saint Augustine as they existed during early 1728, but it does not identify them. The members of the Florida Expedition were obviously not familiar with the names of those towns. However a 1728 Spanish Indian census identifies the Indian towns and gives the general location of some.[10]

Many Indians living near Saint Augustine had become Catholics, and four towns had chapels and resident Franciscan friars as missionaries. Guales, Timucuas, Apalachees, and Costas had probably contributed young men to the Yamasee war parties that had been striking South Carolina. The principal Florida Indian town was, or would soon be, San Antonio de Pocotalaca, or Pocotaligo. It was populated with fifty-six people and was near the southwest corner of the Rosario Line, a location it occupied for several years. The Palmer Map shows a chapel near the center of Pocotalaca, and a simple wooden fort was surely located nearby. The fifty-four-year-old Huspaw King was probably the town's principal mico. Tamaja, the previous town to which he served as mico, no longer existed as a separate political entity. Finally after more than a dozen years, he was mico of the old head town of the Upper Yamasees, to which his original town of Huspaw had once been subservient. Another town, probably San Buenaventura de Palica, which included about sixty people, had been relocated to a new site east of Pocotaligo and not far south of Saint Augustine's wall. It was positioned between Maria Sanchez Creek to the west and Matanzas River to the east. Both Pocotalaca and Palica were situated south of the Cubo Line and the Hornwork, which gave them limited protection.[11]

The Palmer Map depicts a "Yamacy Town Taken by Col. Palmer from Charles Town" on the west bank of the San Sebastian River, not far north of the westernmost extension of the Cubo Line, near an east-west road to the Saint Johns River. It was Santa Catharina de Gualecita, also known as Nombre de Dios Chiquito but commonly called Chiquito. It had a mixed population of seventy-one Indians, including Guales and Yamasees. Chiquito was a large town, because it was consolidated with another town, perhaps San Antonio de la Costa. That secondary town was probably populated by about sixty-five Indians from southern Florida. A Franciscan friar served Chiquito. The Palmer Map shows a structure that resembles a chapel on the south side of the town. The town did not have a fort.

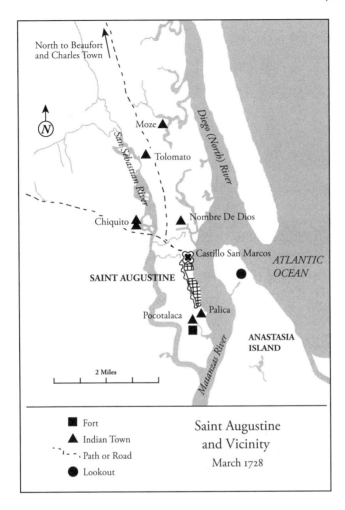

North to Beaufort
and Charles Town

Ⓝ

San Sebastian River

Diego (North) River

Moze ▲

▲ Tolomato

Chiquito ▲   ▲ Nombre De Dios

☒ Castillo San Marcos   *ATLANTIC*
                          OCEAN
SAINT AUGUSTINE   ●

Pocotalaca ▲ Palica
          ■

Matanzas River   **ANASTASIA**
                                ISLAND

2 Miles

■ Fort
▲ Indian Town
⌐- -, Path or Road
● Lookout

Saint Augustine
and Vicinity

March 1728

Chiquito was located about one mile northwest of San Marcos, beyond the maximum effective range of its cannons.[12]

A half mile north of San Marco, within the effective range of its cannons, on the north bank of Macaris Creek, present-day Hospital Creek, was the old mission town of Nombre de Dios Amacarisa. The town was commonly referred to as Nombre de Dios. A strong point of the Hornwork was located nearby, across the creek to the south. Nombre de Dios was served by a Franciscan friar who held services in a stone chapel. The town housed a mixed population of about fifty-eight Indians, including fifteen Timucuans. The informant to the maker of the Palmer Map believed the town was inhabited by Yamasees, for the Palmer Map shows "Yamacy Hutts" extending from Nombre de Dios westward almost to the San Sebastian River.[13]

The Palmer Map does not depict Tolomato, or Tomotly, apparently also known in 1728 as Nuestra Señora de Guadalupe. It was on the east bank of the San Sebastian River, about 1.3 miles northwest of Saint Augustine, with a population of about seventy-seven Guales. The map also does not show the town of Nuestra Señora del Rosario, also known as Moze, located about 2.25 miles north of San Marcos. Moze contained a mixed population of about ninety-two people, including Timucua, Apalachee, and about twenty-two Yamasees from Tamaja. Both towns may have had palisade forts, because they were situated far beyond Saint Augustine's defenses. The Palmer Map provides details of the defenses of Saint Augustine and San Marcos, but incomplete and inaccurate details are shown regarding the terrain to the north of those defenses. The map does not depict the area in which both Tolomato and Moze were located. The person who provided the information for the map had obviously never traveled very far north of Nombre de Dios.[14]

Palmer and his battalion marched quietly south-southeast on foot for about twenty miles toward Saint Augustine. They probably paralleled present-day Interstate Highway 95 and approached Saint Augustine from the west side of the San Sebastian River. If their route of march had been east of the river and paralleled Highway 1, they would have stumbled on the towns of Moze and Tolomato. Neither the period accounts nor the Palmer Map, mention those towns. The Indian defenses were lax. Apparently there were no listening posts on the northern approaches to Saint Augustine, so no one gave the alarm about the approach of about two hundred heavily armed men. However it was late winter, not the traditional time of the year to conduct, or to expect, raids. Neither the Spanish letters nor the Palmer Map provided details of the resulting combat actions. Period accounts confuse the towns of Nombre de Dios Chiquito and Nombre de Dios Amacarisa and interpret the battalion's actions at those towns as occurring at only one town. Most accounts give little information regarding a fortified Yamasee town that Palmer did not attack. Acting governor Middleton's account is an exception; he provided a few details. He heard Palmer's oral report and had access to Palmer's journal, which has apparently been lost. Middleton's report to the British government stated that the battalion first attacked an Indian town, probably Nombre de Dios Chiquito, and inflicted casualties. The battalion then burned another town, probably Nombre de Dios Amacarisa, and plundered its Indian chapel. Palmer then decided not to attack a third town, probably Pocotalaca.[15]

The action began about an hour before dawn on March 9, 1728. As the scouts of the battalion's advance guard approached Saint Augustine from the north-northwest, they discovered Chiquito, located across the San Sebastian River, west of the extension of the Hornwork. When Palmer received the scouts' report, he would have ordered his company commanders to prepare to assault. At first light they swept into the unsuspecting town. Palmer claimed that they killed thirty Indians, wounded fifteen, and captured fourteen before the survivors could escape across the San Sebastion River to the Hornwork. Five months later Dionisio Martinez de la Vega, the Cuban governor, prepared a letter to the Spanish government and reported the information he had received from Florida. He stated that the Franciscan friar, a Spanish lieutenant, and a sergeant had been wounded. He also reported that six Indians were killed, eight were wounded, and several were captured. He designated the site of the battle as the town of Nombre de Dios. He did not indicate which of the two Nombre de Dios towns he was referencing, but it is unlikely he knew there were two towns with similar names. The lieutenant and sergeant escaped capture despite their wounds. They had probably spent the previous night with Indian wives or girlfriends. Palmer and his men were apparently unaware of the soldiers' presence, but they knew that Chiquito's friar had been wounded, probably having briefly held him prisoner. South Carolinians were sorry for his wounds, but they noted that he was associating with bad company. Two of the Indians who were captured and later sold into slavery were the wife and daughter of Chiquito's mico, Francisco Iospogue. He was probably a Guale. The members of the battalion quickly plundered the town and burned the chapel, houses, outbuildings, and townhouse.[16]

Palmer set his sights on two other Indian towns. The first was the old Indian mission town of Nombre de Dios Amacarisa, situated a half mile north of San Marco's cannons. Elements of the battalion crossed the San Sebastian River that was "almost dry" and entered the town. Most of the townspeople had probably received sufficient warning from the attack on nearby Chiquito to enable them to escape behind the wall of the nearby Hornwork, just south of Hospital Creek. The South Carolinian soldiers initially occupied the stone chapel in Nombre de Dios and used it as a bunker to shoot at the defenders of the Hornwork. The garrison of San Marco answered with cannon shells. The soldiers and Indians plundered the mission's chapel and withdrew out of range of the cannons. After the raid

Governor Benavides had the stone chapel destroyed to prevent its future use as a fortification.[17]

The second targeted town was probably the Huspaw King's Pocotalaca, near the southwest corner of Saint Augustine's wall. A small wooden fort was surely located in the town. Pocotalaca received additional protection from the Hornwork and the Cubo Line to the north; the Rosario Line to the east; and the marshes of the San Sebastian River to the west. However the Palmer Map shows that Palmer's scouts crossed the shallow San Sebastian River and found the "Marsh passable at low Water for Man and Horse." Pocotalaca was a tempting target, even though its inhabitants had the protection of a palisade fort. Before Palmer could organize an assault, a small company of Spanish infantry was observed marching from a gate in Saint Augustine's Rosario Line to Pocotalaca's fort. Palmer then wisely decided against attacking Pocotalaca. The town and its fort were within effective range of cannons on the nearby Rosario Line. Palmer had no cannons of his own with which to breach the palisade, and he was probably not prepared for the heavy casualties that would have resulted from an assault on the fort. In addition his instructions were clear: he was not to attack any Spaniards.[18] Palmer had become more deliberate since the spring of 1715, when he had scaled the walls of the Yamasee fort. He was a dozen years older, and considerable combat experience had tempered his rashness.

Palmer's raiders roamed the countryside close to Saint Augustine. They burned Indian houses and outbuildings, but they did not attempt an attack on any Spanish defensive positions, except for some sniping with muskets. The townspeople of Tolomato and Moze apparently escaped injury. It is likely that a few white men and Indians of the battalion discovered the two towns, but they probably avoided them after observing that they were defended by palisade forts. The Spanish and their Indian allies fired cannons and muskets at Palmer's battalion from the protection of their walls, but they never left the protection of their defenses to conduct a counterattack. On the first or second day of the raid, Benavides wrote a letter to Palmer, undoubtedly reminding him that Spain and Great Britain were at peace and, therefore, his raid was an act of war. Palmer replied telling the governor that he was only punishing the Yamasees for their depredations in South Carolina. He offered to withdraw from Florida if the governor would provide six mounted cattle hunters to help corral cattle to feed his men. The governor complied. Spanish horsemen rounded up cattle for Palmer's hungry battalion.[19]

After three days the raiding force left a decimated and deserted countryside near the Spanish defenses. The battalion's only casualties were two wounded Indian warriors. The raiders marched unchallenged northwest to the Saint Johns River, boarded their piraguas and canoes, and returned unhindered to South Carolina.[20]

Although South Carolinians probably had hoped that Palmer's battalion would snare the Huspaw King, he survived. Later, in 1734, the Yamasee town of Pocotalaca retained its location a short distance southwest of the southwest corner of Saint Augustine's wall. The Huspaw King, whom the Spanish knew as Clospo, was sixty years old and continued to serve as the town's principal mico. His deputy was a twenty-year-old warrior named Antonio. The town included twenty-one men and boys. All except the Huspaw King had Spanish names and were probably Catholic converts. Three of them were sixty-year-old veterans who had been warriors at the beginning of the war, nineteen years earlier. The Huspaw King was dominant over the micos of eight satellite Indian towns. Four years later he was probably dead, for a man named Antonio Tospa was the principal mico of Pocotalaca.[21]

Palmer's battalion returned to Port Royal during the latter half of March 1728. Palmer dispatched two of his officers, Capt. Hunt and Lt. William Harden, to Charles Town, where they reported the expedition's success to the Commons House. Twelve days later Palmer appeared before the Commons House and read aloud his journal of the expedition. He received the members' thanks, and a committee was appointed to study his journal. Some members thought the physical results of the raid appeared inadequate. They were unhappy that the Yamasees had not been exterminated. Two days later Palmer was questioned about why he had not destroyed the Yamasee fort in the town of Pocotalaca. He explained that he did not have enough men. The Commons House asked acting governor Middleton to reinforce Palmer's battalion with fifty men and order him to return to Florida and destroy the Yamasee fort. When that request was refused, the Commons House asked the governor to retain at least part of Palmer's battalion on the southern frontier to repel expected war parties. The governor then revealed that he had ordered Palmer to disband his battalion. The militiamen and the Indian warriors had dispersed to their homes to prepare for spring planting. The governor reminded the Commons House that Great Britain and Spain were at peace and that the Yamasee fort contained "the Subjects of The Crown of Spain." He may have known that, as a result of Palmer's raid, the Spanish had recently moved all of the Indian towns within Saint Augustine's defenses. Any future raiding force would have to attack and penetrate Spanish defenses in order to reach the Yamasees. That would have been an obvious act of war.[22]

In June 1728 acting governor Middleton reported the results of the Florida Expedition to the British government. He detailed the deadly Indian raids of 1726 and 1727 against South Carolina's southern frontier, which he believed mandated retaliation. He explained that the entire South Carolina government agreed with the action and that no attacks were directed against the Spaniards. He insisted that only a hundred white men and a hundred Indians were involved in the expedition, despite the Florida governor's claim that Saint Augustine had been attacked by thousands of soldiers and Indians. He requested that the British government give him instructions regarding how to deal with similar provocations in the future. In September the British government replied that South Carolina could not declare war on its own volition, but it could retaliate against enemy Indian raiders.[23]

The long war ended with no formal peace treaty, no parades, and no triumphant speeches. A cautious peace settled on southeastern North America. Palmer's raid had frightened the Spanish, and they expected more attacks by South Carolina soldiers and Indians. However no South Carolinians landed in Florida. South Carolina expected Yamasee counterraids, but no Yamasee war parties penetrated the frontier. Palmer's battalion had left behind ruined Indian towns and a sheepish Spanish Florida government. The Yamasees had been shown that South Carolina's militia was capable of vengeful action. Several Yamasees were casualties, and some of their towns were destroyed again. Emperor Brims, of Coweta in the Lower Creek, had been angry with South Carolina and had sought increased trade with the Spanish. However he reconsidered his position after hearing reports of Palmer's defeat of the Yamasees and learning that Spain's garrison had not dared leave their defensive positions to counterattack Palmer's rampaging battalion. He and other Creek headmen were reminded that although South Carolinians appeared to be cumbersome and lack the boldness and gallantry of warriors, they could be very dangerous when provoked. Most people of the Lower Creek towns had suffered from South Carolina's trade embargo, and many were upset with the few young warriors who had killed Smallwood and his employees. South Carolina restored trade with the Lower Creeks during April 1728. In return several Creek towns sent war parties into Florida to kill or capture those Yamasees who dared venture outside of Saint Augustine's protective walls.[24]

South Carolina's quest for a perfect frontier defense had lasted more than a dozen years. Beginning in May 1715, the South Carolina government made continual, often annual, changes in its system of frontier defense.

Experiments were made using garrisoned forts, scout boatmen, and rangers. The locations and composition of those military units were often changed. Some alterations were made to reduce expenditures, but changes were also made in an attempt to repel war parties totally. South Carolina's frontier defenses worked well and often prevented Indian raids from succeeding. The system worked even better when the army had accurate and timely intelligence concerning the Indians' movements. However it was impossible to prevent all Indian war parties from penetrating the frontiers. Palmer and his battalion demonstrated that South Carolina's system of defense sometimes had to be supplemented with a bold commando raid into the Indians' homeland.

Conclusion

South Carolina had been unprepared for total war. Most men were enrolled in the militia, but they mustered and trained for only a short time every other month. There was an insufficient supply of serviceable muskets and ammunition available to equip all the militiamen. South Carolina had placed too much reliance on Indian allies for its security. For a decade the warriors of several towns of allied Indians had guarded the principal northern, northwestern, and southwestern paths into the colony. South Carolina's government had not constructed and garrisoned any frontier fortifications. A few soldiers stationed on the frontiers could have bolstered the allied Indians and helped maintain their allegiance. Rather the colony depended on the military capability of those Indians for its defense and relied on the Indian trade to retain their loyalty. During the spring and summer of 1715, the allied Indians revolted and raided the plantations they were supposed to protect. The entrances into South Carolina were left open.

South Carolina had been close to disaster. The Indians' initial attacks severely wounded the colony. There were days when people, for example Rev. Francis Le Jau, accepted that the colony might have to be evacuated. However some Indians, such as Emperor Brims, soon learned that they probably could not destroy South Carolina. By the fall of 1715, South Carolina's part-time soldiers had become battle-hardened and confident. The Indians dared not risk the series of major battles that would have been required to annihilate South Carolina's army. Fortune also smiled on the South Carolinians. The Indians' assaults had been uncoordinated and unsustained, and the Spanish canceled the planned 1719 invasion of South Carolina.

If the Indians had realized how unprepared South Carolina was for a preemptive strike, they might have exerted more effort to coordinate and sustain their attacks during the spring and summer of 1715. South Carolina could have fallen. A total Indian victory would have altered the course of the history of southeastern North America. Surviving South Carolinians would have become refugees in other British colonies. Great Britain's southern frontier would have receded from the Savannah River northeastward more than 240 miles to the Cape Fear River. Spain and France could have extended their political influence among the Southeastern Indian groups. However if they did not improve the efficiency of their Indian trading systems and the quantity of their trade goods, their newly gained influence with the Indians would surely have waned. Victorious Indian groups would not have kowtowed to any European government. Spain could have placed garrisoned forts in deserted South Carolina, with the Indians' permission, but the forts might have been undermanned and poorly supplied. The government of Spain had not been generous in supporting its Florida colony. The British government might have attempted to prevent the expansion of Florida and Louisiana by reestablishing the colony of South Carolina. In order to do so, a British army would probably have had to invade southeastern North America. That would have required a major undertaking. War with some Indian groups, and perhaps Spain and France, could have resulted. The British government would first have questioned whether sufficient benefits could have been derived from a new South Carolina. As John Barnwell had discovered, Great Britain was reluctant to spend large amounts of money on projects that would produce little or no profit. More dangerous was the possibility that Indian groups in and near the middle and northern British colonies might have become emboldened and threatened the existence of those settlements. Such an event would have absorbed much of Great Britain's resources.

South Carolina's Church of England pastors, and probably many of their parishioners, believed that the war was God's vengeance upon South Carolinians for their wickedness.[1] Perhaps they were correct. The Indian traders' bigotry, cruelty, and greed; the South Carolina government's failure to control the traders' conduct; and the people's acceptance of enslaving Indian families had caused the Indians to fear for their freedom. War was the only protective course of action the Yamasee, and some other groups, could envision. As a result South Carolinians suffered terribly. South Carolina averted disaster because it had combat-experienced leaders and was populated with white, black, and Indian people who possessed the physical and mental toughness that enabled them to weather the most terrifying and discouraging days. Most survived and prospered in an unforgiving wilderness during a dangerous period of history. Their toughness was likely passed on to future South Carolinians and enabled them to endure many terrible days during the Revolutionary War and the Civil War.

Within weeks after Palmer and his raider battalion returned from Florida, the South Carolinians' attention shifted to politics. During the late spring of 1728, the government partially collapsed under the administration of acting governor Arthur Middleton. A complicated economic issue had become political and had festered for years. The problem was directly related to the enormous military expenditures that the colony made during Queen Anne's War, the Tuscarora War, and especially the recent Indian war. In order to fund its offensive campaigns and its frontier defenses, the government had issued bills of credit, a type of bond that was used to pay the colony's creditors. Each issue of bills was redeemable on a specific date. Redemption was often made possible by printing more bills of credit. Since little silver and gold was available in the colony, people used bills of credit as paper money. As the issues of bills of credit increased, the value of that money, as compared with British pounds, declined. For several years one faction, usually planters and tradesmen, favored issuing more paper money, some of which they could use to pay their debts. Another faction, often merchant creditors of the planters and tradesmen, wanted the medium of exchange to be mostly British pounds, which they used to pay their creditors in England. The indebtedness of South Carolina's government grew with each issue of bills of credit. Finally the paper money quarrel became so heated in the Commons House and in the governor's council that the members refused to compromise regarding the issuance of more bills of credit. As a result the South Carolina government malfunctioned and remained mostly dormant for three years. Finally in 1729 the British government purchased most of the Lords Proprietors' interest in the colony, and South Carolina formally became a royal province. A new royal governor was appointed. Gov. Robert Johnson was the former proprietors' governor whom the Commons House had removed from office in 1719. He arrived in South Carolina in 1731 and skillfully managed compromises dealing with the issuance and use of bills of credit. Johnson restored the government's functions.[2]

Despite the South Carolina government's malfunction, the army establishment of 1727 was kept intact with few changes into the 1730s. Soldiers probably received little pay prior to 1731, because the government failed to collect taxes. They survived by farming small tracts of land and maintaining a few livestock. The soldiers were finally paid after Governor Johnson arrived. Johnson quickly began improving the colony's defenses by implementing his township plan. His townships were intended to be miniature military colonies that were established on the strategic paths leading into the settled areas of South Carolina. The first was the Swiss township of Purrysburg, established on the east side of the Savannah River in 1732. It was located south of Palachacola Fort in present-day Jasper County near Hardeeville. Other townships were eventually settled near the Congarees, Fort Moore, and other strategic locations. In 1733 a new British colony, Georgia, began the occupation of the old Guale province. Georgia acted as a buffer between South Carolina and Florida. South Carolina reciprocated by providing Georgia with military protection during its initial years. The scout boat *Carolina* and its crew, commanded by Capt. William Ferguson, and the Company of Southern Rangers, led by Capt. James McPherson, were loaned to the new colony.[3]

The war affected the status of the Indians with their British, Spanish, and French neighbors. Most groups initially avoided South Carolina's military and financial punishment by becoming its ally or by withdrawing into the interior, where some became allies of the Spanish or French. After realizing that South Carolina was capable of defending itself, most of the groups that had declared war made a wise strategic decision. They restricted their tactical actions against South Carolina to limited raids and ambushes. By doing so they preserved their warrior pride, allowed their young men to earn martial glory, and avoided heavy losses. When ammunition for their warriors' muskets and cloth and tools for their women became scarce, many of them negotiated for peace to regain the benefits of British trade goods. Some groups, such as the Creeks, learned to maintain diplomatic relationships with all three European colonies while refusing to side with one colony against another. Most Indian groups persevered for another century before they were expelled from the Southeast by the U.S. government.

The Yamasees were an exception. They were among the bravest and most resolute people of southeastern North America. They initiated the war, and they experienced horrible suffering as a result. They placed too much reliance on the assistance they hoped to receive from other Indian groups. By 1728 Yamasee ranks were thin. They seldom approached South Carolina's frontiers, perhaps restrained to some extent by Florida's governors. However during the War of Jenkins' Ear (1739–44) and King George's War (1744–48), Yamasees served as Spanish Florida's auxiliary light infantry. They dispatched war parties against the new colony of Georgia as late as 1744.[4]

The Yamasees never stopped viewing British colonists as their enemy. Their thirst for vengeance was never quenched. They never sought compromise, never bowed to the inevitable, never made peace. In 1763, when the Spanish left Florida at the end of the French and Indian War, some Yamasees chose to go to Cuba, others went to Veracruz, Mexico, and a few probably remained in the Southeast. Afterward the Creeks told tales of an elusive band of fugitive Yamasee warriors and their beautiful women who lived blissfully in a vast swamp at the headwaters of the Saint Marys River. The remnant of that vast swamp is the present-day Okefenokee National Wildlife Refuge on the Georgia-Florida border.[5]

Notes ──────

CHAPTER 1: Warnings of War, April 10–14, 1715

1. Pocotaligo Town was probably located in present-day Jasper County. A likely site is on the west side of the Pocotaligo River, on Pocotaligo Neck at MacKays Point at the southern end of Highway 33. The site is about 6 miles south of the Highway 17 bridge over the Pocotaligo River and about 13.5 miles northwest of the city of Beaufort. Green, DePratter, and Southerlin, "Yamasee in South Carolina," 14, 18; McKivergan, "Migration and Settlement," 181–90; *General Highway Maps*. When distances are referenced from cities or localities, measurement has been made from the legend symbol shown on South Carolina Department of Transportation county maps. Cooper and McCord, *Statutes*, "Act to Limit the Bounds of the Yamasee Settlement, to Prevent Persons from Disturbing Them, and to Remove Such as Are Settled within the Limitation Hereafter Mentioned," 2:317, 318; Cooper and McCord, *Statutes*, "Act for . . . Continuing the Road to Port Royal . . . ," June 12, 1714, 9:34; Cooper and McCord, *Statutes*, "Act for Mending and Keeping in Repair the Causway over the Marsh of Combee River," February 25, 1715, 9:37. Joseph Bryan's Ferry was located near the present-day Highway 17 bridge over the Combahee River. Salo, "Development of the Combahee Ferry," 5.
2. McDowell, *Journals of the Commissioners of the Indian Trade,* July 27, 1711, 10; March 14, 1712, 19; April 12, 1715, 65.
3. McDowell, *Journals of the Commissioners of the Indian Trade,* July 28, 1711, 12; August 15, 1711, 17; March 21, 1712, 20; May 16, 1712, 25; March 26, 1713, 42, 43; July 16, 1713, 47; April 12, 1715, 65. Cuffy was later given a reward by the South Carolina Commons House for his warning, but he was dead by late 1717 from an unknown cause. The Commons House purchased the freedom of his wife and child as a reward for his service; South Carolina Commons House Journals, manuscript, (hereafter cited as SCCHJ), August 12, 1715, 434; March 9, 1716, 33; March 17, 1716, 45; December 5, 1717, 392; receipt signed by Edmund Bellinger, June 29, 1717, Wills, Inventories and Miscellaneous Records, vol. 56. Cuffy was the name South Carolinians had given him, probably in derision,

for it was actually a name used by some Africans for a day of the week. Inscoe, "Carolina Slave Names," 533.

4. Governor Craven to Lord Townsend, May 23, 1715, in *CSP, AWI,* 1714–15, 227, 228; "Rodd to His employer in London," 167.

5. *State of South Carolina,* U.S. Department of the Interior, Geological Survey, Scale 1:500.000, 1970; De Brahm, *Map of South Carolina and a Part of Georgia.* For information concerning most-cited period maps, see Cummings, *Southeast in Early Maps.*

6. Nathaniel Osborne to the Secretary, March 1, 1715, 234, in Williams, ed., *Letters from the Clergy of the Anglican Church in South Carolina;* Cooper and McCord, *Statutes,* "Act for Establishing a Ferry . . . over Combahee River . . . ," September 22, 1733, 9:81, explains that in 1733 John Barton owned Jackson's old plantation. De Brahm, *Map of South Carolina and a Part of Georgia,* shows the site of Barton's plantation as "87," and Jackson's Creek is shown about seven miles to the south; Warner and Bray proceeded generally east along a path near present-day Highway 17. Cooper and McCord, *Statutes,* "Act . . . to Sell and Convey the Old Glebe Land at Chehaw . . . ," July 25, 1761, 4:152; *General Highway Maps.*

7. After crossing the Ashepoo River, they continued east, following the general trace of present-day Highway 17. *General Highway Maps.* The geographical area in which Jackson's Edisto River plantation was located was known as Pon Pon, which was the Indian name for that part of Edisto River. Moore and Simons, *Abstracts of the Wills of the State of South Carolina,* 102, and De Brahm, *Map of South Carolina and a Part of Georgia;* Cooper and McCord, Statutes, "Act for . . . Making a Bridge over South Edisto River," June 12, 1714, 9:33; "Historical Notes," *South Carolina Historical and Genealogical Magazine* 11 (1910): 190; H. A. M. Smith, "Radnor, Edmundsbury and Jacksonborough," 46; Meriwether, *Expansion of South Carolina,* 3, 4.

8. They continued east in present-day Charleston County along the Charles Town Road near present Highway 17; for Elliott's plantation see Moore and Simmons, *Abstracts of the Wills of the State of South Carolina,* 117, 168, 169, 247, 248; Cooper and McCord, *Statutes,* "Additional Act . . . for Cutting and Making a Path Out from the Road on the North Side of Ashley River to the Town of Wilton . . . ," November 10, 1711, 9:17–21; Cooper and McCord, *Statutes,* "Additional Act . . . for Making and Repairing of Highways," June 7, 1712, 9:27. Elliott owned a least two and perhaps more plantations on Stono River. The only one that can be pinpointed is the site that is shown on De Brahm, *Map of South Carolina and a Part of Georgia.* For LaRoche's plantation see Moore and Simons, *Abstracts of the Wills of the State of South Carolina,* 67; a 1701 plat of the area of LaRoche's plantation shows the bridge and house site and depicts Wallace River as the "Middle Branch of Stono." John McCrady Plats, No. 4. After passing LaRoche's and Elliott's plantations, they rode eastward along the trace of present-day Highway 57 to the Ashley River Ferry, near the site of the present-day railroad bridge over the Ashley River. After crossing the

river, they continued south on the Broad Path, which paralleled present-day Highway 642 and then Highway 52 on its way to the governor's house; SCCHJ, June 9, 1714, 276; H. A. M. Smith, "Charleston and Charleston Neck," 24, 25, and accompanying map.

9. McDowell, *Journals of the Commissioners of the Indian Trade*, April 12, 1715, 65; J. A. Barnwell, "Southeastern North America." Both sides of the upper Savannah River in the vicinity of present-day Augusta, Georgia, and Beech Island, South Carolina, were known as Savannah Town. The governor probably intended for the meeting to take place on the east side of the river about a mile northwest of Beech Island in Aiken County, where a trader had established a fortified storehouse. Savannah, Apalachee, and Yuchi Indian towns were located in that area. The towns of the Savannahs, or Shawnees, were located on the west side of the river, on or near present-day Augusta, Georgia. At least one fortified trader's storehouse was located there. The Savannahs had lived in the area for more than thirty-five years, and some of them may have earlier resided on the east side of the river before the arrival of the Apalachees. The Yuchis were located about fifteen miles northwest of Augusta on the west side of the river. Crane, *Southern Frontier*, 44, 132, 187; Swanton, *Early History of the Creek Indians*, 124, 288, 317; Corcoles, letter of January 25, 1716, which included copies of letters dated May 28 and May 29, 1715. This letter and letters of Corcoles dated July 5, 1715, and November 28, 1715, were kindly provided by Dr. John E. Worth from his research materials and were translated by Nathan Gordon.

10. Letter of Corcoles, January 25, 1716; McDowell, *Journals of the Commissioners of the Indian Trade*, April 12, 1715, 65; *CSP, AWI*, 1714–15, Governor Craven to Lord Townsend, May 23, 1715, 227, 228; "Rodd to His employer in London," 167.

CHAPTER 2: South Carolinians, April 1715

1. Sirmans, *Colonial South Carolina*, 6, 9–16, 40–43, 45–47, 51–54, 73, 105, 111, 122, 123.

2. Menard, "Slave Demography in the Lowcountry"; Clowse, *Economic Beginnings in Colonial South Carolina*, 160, 161; Van Ruymbeke, "Huguenots of Proprietary South Carolina," 38, 41; Friedlander, "Commissary Johnston's Report," 259; W. B. Smith, *White Servitude*, 38–41; Governor Johnson to the Council of Trade and Plantations, January 12, 1720, in *CSP, AWI*, 1719–20, January 302.

3. Nairne, *Letter from South Carolina*, 24–29; Sirmans, *Colonial South Carolina*, 38, 96; Cooper and McCord, *Statutes*, "Act for the Better Ordering and Holding the Court of General Sessions, Assize and Goal Delivery, and the Court of Common Pleas," June 7, 1712, 2:378; Cooper and McCord, *Statutes*, "Additional Act . . . for the Better Ordering and Governing Negroes and All Other Slaves," December 18, 1714, 7:365, 366. A Court of Chancery was formally established in 1721; Cooper and McCord, *Statutes*, "Act for Establishing a Court of Chancery," September 9, 1721, 3:132; Gregorie, *Records of the Court of Chancery*, 6, 69n, 70n.

4. Sirmans, *Colonial South Carolina,* 68; SCCHJ, August 11, 1721, 526; Winston, "Economic Power among Eighteenth-Century Women," 323; Pruden, "Investing Widows," 345, 346–51, 354.

5. Sirmans, *Colonial South Carolina,* 58–60, 77, 96; Benjamin Dennis to the Society, January 3, 1715, in G. W. Williams, *Letters from the Clergy,* 234; Gideon Johnston to the Society, in Klingberg, *Carolina Chronicle,* 39, 44 (July 5, 1710); 108–10 (May 28, 1712); 114 (June 17, 1712).

6. Johnston to the Bishop of London, September 20, 1708, in Klingberg, *Carolina Chronicle,* 22.

7. Johnston to the Society, January 27, 1711, in Klingberg, *Carolina Chronicle,* 83, 84, 87; Johnson's Explanation of Instructions by the Clergy of South Carolina, March 4, 1713, in Klingberg, *Carolina Chronicle,* 123, 126, 127, 129; Nairne, *Letter from South Carolina,* 41–43, 45.

8. Nairne, *Letter from South Carolina,* 15, 16; Sirmans, *Colonial South Carolina,* 58; Gregorie, *Records of the Court of Chancery of South Carolina,* 80; A. Moore, "Daniel Axtell's Account Book," 298.

9. Clowse, *Economic Beginnings in Colonial South Carolina,* map opposite 1, 158n48; Duff, "Creating a Plantation Province," 2, 6. Granville County included the following major islands: Port Royal, formerly known as Wambee Island; Parris Island, formerly Wambahee Island, Port Royal Island, and Archer's Island; Lady's Island, formerly Cambahe Island; and Saint Helena Island. Webber, "Colonel Alexander Parris," 137, 138; "Chart of Parts of the Coast of South Carolina, from Port Royall to Charlestown," ca. 1700; De Brahm, *Map of South Carolina and a Part of Georgia;* Representation of President William Bull to Council of Trade and Plantations, May 25, 1728 (citing an affidavit of Joseph Parmenter, February 16, 1727), in *CSP, AWI,* 1728–29, 104.

10. Johnson's Explanation of Instructions by the Clergy of South Carolina, March 4, 1713, in Klingberg, *Carolina Chronicle,* 122–27; Johnston to the Bishop of London, September 20, 1708, in Klingberg, *Carolina Chronicle,* 22, 23; Osborne to the Secretary, March 1, 1715, 243, in Williams, ed., *Letters from the Clergy of the Anglican Church in South Carolina;* Cooper and McCord, *Statutes,* "Act for the Establishment of Religious Worship . . . ," November 30, 1706, 2:282, 283; Cooper and McCord, *Statutes,* "Additional Act . . . for the Establishment of Religious Worship . . . ," December 18, 1708, 2:328; Sirmans, *Colonial South Carolina,* 36, 37, 61, 66, 76, 77, 96–100, the endpaper, or endleaf of Sirmans, is a map of the counties and the initial nine parishes. The South Carolina Anglican clergy were William Tredwell Bull, Claude Philippe de Richbourg, William Guy, Thomas Hasell, Gilbert Jones, Gideon Johnston, John La Pierre, Francis Le Jau, Robert Maule, Nathaniel Osborne, and Ebenezer Taylor; Van Ruymbeke, "Huguenots of Proprietary South Carolina," 38, 41.

11. Cooper and McCord, *Statutes,* "Act for the Better Relief of the Poor of This Province," December 12, 1712, 2:593–98; SCCHJ, August 5, 1715, 425.

12. Harris, *Compleat Description of the Province.* An overlay map of colonial Charles Town on present-day Charleston is in Halsey, *Historic Charleston on a Map;*

Coclanis, "Death in Early Charleston," 280–84; Sirmans, *Colonial South Carolina*, 77; Cooper and McCord, *Statutes*, "Act for Settling a Watch in Charlestown, and for Preventing of Fires and Nusances in the Same," August 28, 1701, 7:19–21; Cooper and McCord, *Statutes*, "Act for the Keeping and Maintaining a Watch and Good Orders in Charles Town," August 28, 1701, 7:23; Cooper and McCord, *Statutes*, "Act for Setting a Watch in Charles Town," May 7, 1709, 7:54, 55; Cooper and McCord, *Statutes*, "Additional Act . . . to Prevent and Suppress Fire in Charles Town," December 18, 1713, 7:58; Cooper and McCord, *Statutes*, "Act for the Good Government of Charlestown," June 23, 1722, 7:179; SCCHJ, November 19, 1713, 207; April 19, 1716, 181; June 15, 1722, 17, 21; Johnston to the Society, July 5, 1710, in Klingberg, *Carolina Chronicle*, 62; Governor Johnson to the Council of Trade and Plantations, January 12, 1720, in *CSP, AWI*, 1719–20, January 301, 306.

13. Nairne, *Letter from South Carolina*, 7; Clowse, *Economic Beginnings in Colonial South Carolina*, 28; Meriwether, *Expansion of South Carolina*, 2–4, 9; Catesby, *Natural History of Carolina*, 2: i, ii; Harris, *Complete Description of the Province of Carolina*.

14. Nairne, *Letter from South Carolina*, 14, 15; Catesby, *Natural History of Carolina*, 2: vi; Clowse, *Economic Beginnings in Colonial South Carolina*, 162; Waddell, *Indians of the South Carolina Lowcountry*, 36.

15. Waddell, *Indians of the South Carolina Lowcountry*, 33–35; Waring, "Colonial Medicine in Georgia and South Carolina," S143, S145; B. J. Wood, "'Constant Attendance on God's Alter,'" 206; Merrens and Terry, "Dying in Paradise," 534, 540–46, 549, 550.

16. Cooper and McCord, *Statutes*, "Additional Act . . . for Making and Mending Highways . . . ," July 19, 1707, 9:10, 11; Cooper and McCord, *Statutes*, "Act for Continuing the High Road from South Edisto River, to the Islands of Port Royal and Saint Helena, and Appointing Bridges and Ferries in the Said Road," November 10, 1711, 9:14, 15; Cooper and McCord, *Statutes*, "Additional Act . . . for the Cutting and Making a Path out from the Road on the North Side of Ashley River to the Town of Wilton, in Colleton County, and Appointing Ferries on the Said Road," November 10, 1711, 9:17; Cooper and McCord, *Statutes*, "Act for the Appointing a Ferry over the Eastern Branch of the T of Cooper River," June 7, 1712, 9:22; Cooper and McCord, *Statutes*, "Additional Act . . . for Making and Repairing of Highways," June 7, 1712, 9:27; Cooper and McCord, *Statutes*, "Additional Act . . . for Building and Erecting a Bridge and Causway over the River at the Landing of Mr. William Stanyarne and One Other Bridge or Causway, from the Landing of Mr. Thomas Seabrook to the Land of Madame Elizabeth Blake, over Wadmalaw River," December 18, 1713, 9:29–32; Cooper and McCord, *Statutes*, "Act for Continuing the Road to Edisto Island, and Making a Bridge over Dawhoe Creek, and Finishing the Road to Port Royal, and Making a Bridge over South Edisto River," June 12, 1714, 9:32–35; Cooper and McCord, *Statutes*, "Act for Making a High-Road out of Ashley River Road to the Plantation of Thomas Osgood, near Pon Pon

River," December 18, 1714, 36; Cooper and McCord, *Statutes,* "Act for Mending and Keeping in Repair the Causway over Combee River, in Colleton County," February 25, 1715, 9:37; Cooper and McCord, *Statutes,* "Act for the Making of a Road or Highway . . . ," February 12, 1719, 9:46–48; Cooper and McCord, *Statutes,* "Act for Continuing the Road on the South Side of Ashley River, from the Creek Commonly Called Jacob's or Wait's Creek to Westo Savana," February 12, 1719, 9:49. Several modern highways generally follow the courses of those old roads and paths.

17. Johnston's Explanation of Instructions by the Clergy of South Carolina, March 4, 1713, in Klingberg, *Carolina Chronicle,* 123; Menard, "Financing the Lowcountry Export Boom," 665; Catesby, *Natural History of Carolina,* 2:xvi; Hanover House, National Register Properties in South Carolina. Pickens County (Clemson University). The renvated Hanover Plantation house is a typical period South Carolina house. It was constructed during 1714–16 by French Huguenot Paul de St. Julien, north of Charles Town in Berkeley County and was moved to the South Carolina Botanical Garden, Clemson University, in 1941; Stoney, *Plantations of the South Carolina Low Country,* 43, 44, 47, 48, 51–53, 90–96, 106–14; Gregorie, *Records of the Court of Chancery of South Carolina,* 80; Tunis, *Colonial Living,* 28–33, 81, 82, 110; Nairne, *Letter from South Carolina,* 43, 51, 52.

18. Nairne, *Letter from South Carolina,* 11–13; Clowse, *Economic Beginnings in Colonial South Carolina,* 122–32, 167–70.

19. Catesby, *Natural History of Carolina,* 2:xvi, xvii; Nairne, *Letter from South Carolina,* 10.

20. Catesby, *Natural History of Carolina,* 2:xvii.

21. Ibid., 2:xxxi; Clowse, *Economic Beginnings in Colonial South Carolina,* 178, 179; Nairne, *Letter from South Carolina,* 9, 13.

22. Cooper and McCord, *Statutes,* "Act for Taking Up and Killing Wild, Unmarked and Out-Lying Cattle," September 17, 1703, 2:21–23; Cooper and McCord, *Statutes,* "Act to Prevent Stealing of Horses and Neat Cattle," February 17, 1705, 2:261, 262; Cooper and McCord, *Statutes,* "Act for Avoiding Receipts in Selling of Beef and Pork, Pitch and Tarr, Rosin and Terpentine . . . ," December 18, 1714, 2:615; Nairne, *Letter from South Carolina,* 13; Otto, "Origins of Cattle-Ranching," 117, 118, 122, 123; Catesby, *Natural History of Carolina,* 2:xxxi.

23. Otto, "Origins of Cattle-Ranching," 118, 122, 123.

24. Cooper and McCord, *Statutes,* "Act for Avoiding Receipts in Selling of Beef and Pork, Pitch and Tarr, Rosin and Terpentine . . . ," December 18, 1714, 2:615; J. Williams, "English Mercantilism and Carolina Naval Stores," 169–85; Clowse, *Economic Beginnings in Colonial South Carolina,* 132–35, 140, 170–79.

25. Cooper and McCord, *Statutes,* "Act for the Better Ordering and Governing of Negroes and Slaves," June 7, 1712, 7:352; Cooper and McCord, *Statutes,* "Act for the Better Ordering and Governing of Negroes and Slaves," February 7, 1691, 7:343, 344; Jones, Wilson, and Savelle, *Detailed Reports on the Salzburger Emigrants,* 104; Catesby, *Natural History of Carolina,* 2:xvii, xix.

26. Cooper and McCord, *Statutes,* "Act for the Better Ordering and Governing of Negroes and Slaves," June 7, 1712, 7:352.

27. Ibid.

28. Cooper and McCord, *Statutes,* "Act for the Better Ordering and Governing of Negroes and Slaves," June 7, 1712, 7:352–60; Cooper and McCord, *Statutes,* "Act for the Better Ordering of Slaves," February 7, 1691, 7:343–47; Cooper and McCord, *Statutes,* "Additional Act . . . for the Better Ordering and Governing Negroes and All Other Slaves," December 18, 1714, 7:365–68.

29. Johnston's Explanation of Instructions by the Clergy of South Carolina, March 4, 1713, in Klingberg, *Carolina Chronicle,* 123; Cooper and McCord, *Statutes,* "Act for the Better Ordering of Slaves," February 7, 1691, 7:343–47; Cooper and McCord, *Statutes,* "Act for the Better Ordering and Governing of Negroes and Slaves," June 7, 1712, 7:352–65; Cooper and McCord, *Statutes,* "Additional Act . . . to an Act for the Better Ordering and Governing Negroes and All Other Slaves," December 18, 1714, 7:365–68.

30. Cooper and McCord, *Statutes,* "Act to Settle a Patrol," November 4, 1704, 2:254, 255.

31. Cooper and McCord, *Statutes,* "Act for the Better Ordering and Governing of Negroes and Slaves," June 7, 1712, 7:357, 358, 362; Gallay, *Indian Slave Trade,* 87, 339; Chatelain, *Defenses of Spanish Florida,* 79, 160, 161; SCCHJ, June 20, 1711, 563.

32. Crane, *Southern Frontier,* 108–22, 123–27; Worth, "Razing Florida," 301–6; P. M. Brown, "Early Indian Trade," 125, 127, 128; Clowse, *Economic Beginnings in Colonial South Carolina,* 163, 164; McDowell, *Journals of the Commissioners of the Indian Trade,* July 27, 1711, 10; March 14, 1712, 19; Bossy, "Godin & Co.: Charleston Merchants and the Indian Trade," 97, 101, 113–19; Stern, "Economic Philosophies," 104–7.

33. Cooper and McCord, *Statutes,* "Act to Prevent Stealing of Horses and Neat Cattle," February 17, 1705, 2:263; Cooper and McCord, *Statutes,* "Act for Making a High-Road Out of Ashley River Road to the Plantation of Thomas Osgood, near Pon Pon River," December 18, 1714, 9:36; Catesby, *Natural History of Carolina,* 2:xxxi; Ivers, "Scouting the Inland Passage," 122, 123.

34. Cooper and McCord, *Statutes,* "Act for the Better Observation of the Lord's Day, Commonly Called Sunday," December 12, 1712, 2:397; Cooper and McCord, *Statutes,* "Act for Regulating Taverns and Punch Houses," June 28, 1711, 2:362–65; Sirmans, *Colonial South Carolina,* 229–31; Henning, *South Carolina Gazette,* 72, 73, 75, 79.

35. Crane, *Southern Frontier,* 79–86, 88–90, 95, 96, 158–61.

36. Ibid., 80, 82, 83, 87, 88, 91, 115, 187; Governor Johnson to the Council of Trade and Plantations, January 12, 1720, in *CSP, AWI,* 1719–20, January 301.

37. Governor and Council of Carolina to the Council of Trade and Plantations, September 17, 1709, in *CSP, AWI,* 1708–9, 466; Cooper and McCord, *Statutes,* "Act for the Better Settling and Regulating the Militia," July 19, 1707, 9:630. The composition of the militia had few changes between 1709 and 1721, except the Winyah Company became the Eleventh Company of the Northern

Regiment; Salley, *Journal of His Majesty's Council for South Carolina, May 29, 1721 –June 10, 1721,* June 1, 1721.

38. Cooper and McCord, *Statutes,* "Act for the Better Settling and Regulating the Militia," July 19, 1707, 9:625, 627, 628, 630; Cooper and McCord, *Statutes,* "Additional Act . . . to Appoint a Garrison to the Southward," December 23, 1703, 7:33; Cooper and McCord, *Statutes,* "Act for Enlisting Trusty Slaves as Shall Be Thought Serviceable to This Province in Time of Alarms," November 4, 1704, 7:347, 348; Cooper and McCord, *Statutes,* "Act for Enlisting Trusty Slaves as Shall Be Thought Serviceable to This Province in Time of Alarms," April 24, 1708, 7:249–51; Nairne, *Letter from South Carolina,* 31.

39. Cooper and McCord, *Statutes,* "Act for the Better Settling and Regulating the Militia," July 19, 1707, 9:625, 627; Governor and Council of Carolina to the Council of Trade and Plantations, September 17, 1709, in *CSP, AWI,* 1708–9, 466; Peterson, *Arms and Armor in Colonial America,* 160, 162; SCCHJ, May 7, 1715, 395; August 4, 1715, 419, 420; May 17, 1716, 109; B. J. Wood, "'Constant Attendance on God's Alter,'" 205–7, 210–12; Menard, "Slave Demography in the Low County," 282, 283.

40. Cooper and McCord, *Statutes,* "Act for the Better Settling and Regulating the Militia," July 19, 1707, 9:625, 626; Nairne, *Letter from South Carolina,* 32. Several of the muskets were probably equipped with the old dog-lock safety; Peterson, *Arms and Armor in Colonial America,* 28–32, 65, 96, 98, 99, 159, 160, 163, 164, 227, 229, 232, 233–35, 237, plates 26, 31, 36, 49–51, 165, 174, 221, 227; Public Treasurer, fol. 106; Luzader, *Saratoga,* 224, 225.

41. Cooper and McCord, *Statutes,* "Act for the Better Settling and Regulating the Militia," July 19, 1707, 9:625–27, 630; SCCHJ, June 4, 1712, 67, 68; May 7, 1715, 392; August 9, 1715, 430; November 20, 1720, 70, 72; Salley, South Carolina Commons House Journals, published (hereafter cited as *SCCHJ*), February 8, 1727, 100; Nairne, *Letter from South Carolina,* 32; Peterson, *Arms and Armor in Colonial America,* 268, 269, 290–92, plates 229, 299, 306; Public Treasurer, fol. 106; Lefler, *New Voyage to Carolina,* 10. Descriptions of workingmen's clothing are contained in notices regarding runaway, white indentured servants in the *South Carolina Gazette,* April 28, 1733, February 16, 1734, and June 29, 1734, and in Cooper and McCord, *Statutes,* "Act for the Better Governing and Regulating White Servants," December 11, 1717, 3:20; Buckland, "Monmouth Cap," 23–37.

42. Cooper and McCord, *Statutes,* "Act for the Better Settling and Regulating the Militia," July 19, 1707, 9:625–31; Peterson, *Arms and Armor in Colonial America,* 159, 160, 162.

43. SCCHJ, December 15, 1713, 219; Cooper and McCord, *Statutes,* "Act for Appointing Two Scout Canoes, and Providing Necessaries for the Same," December 18, 1713, 2:607–9; Cooper and McCord, *Statutes,* "Act to Settle a Guard in Johnson's Fort on Windmill Point," December 18, 1713, 2:613–15; Nairne, *Letter from South Carolina,* 32, 33; Mustard, "On the Building of Fort Johnson."

44. Normally only the Etiwans and Kiawahs are considered as Settlement Indians, but the Winyaws should also be considered as such because of their location

and their assistance to South Carolina during the war. Governor Johnson to the Council of Trade and Plantations, January 12, 1720, in *CSP, AWI*, 1719–20, January 302; Governor Craven to Lord Townsend, May 23, 1715, in *CSP, AWI*, 1714–15, 228; SCCHJ, August 9, 1715, 430, 431; August 10, 432; August 12, 434; August 20, 1715, 441; "Slavery in Province, Colony, and State," 527, 528.

45. D. E. H. Smith, "Broughton Letters," 173; Governor Johnson to the Council of Trade, January 12, 1720, in *CSP, AWI*, 1719–20, January 301, 302; Waddell, *Indians of the South Carolina Lowcountry*, 12.

46. SCCHJ, December 10, 1708, 391; February 19, 1715, 364. For the location of Altamaha Town, see the George Hunter plat, 1732, McGrady Plat Collection. Thomas Nairne was married to Elizabeth Quintyne, a widow; "Historical Notes," 117. For the location of Thomas Nairne's plantations, see the following: Records of the Secretary of the Province (Proprietary Grants), 38:434, 435; Records of the Secretary of the Province (Proprietary Grants), 39:4 #1, 17 #3, 156 #1 and #2, 438, 439, 442, 443, 494–96; Salley, *Warrants for Lands*, 582; Langley, *South Carolina Deed Abstracts*, 2:30; Auditor General Memorial Books, 4:320. For the location of John Cockran's plantation, see McDowell, *Journals of the Commissioners of the Indian Trade*, May 20, 1714, 58, and De Brahm, *Map of South Carolina and a Part of Georgia*. For the location of William Livingston's plantation, see H. A. M. Smith, "Willtown," 26; Zierden, Linder, and Anthony, *Willtown*, 127, fig. 61.

CHAPTER 3: Southeastern Indians, April 1715

1. Governor Johnson to the Council of Trade and Plantations, January 12, 1720, *CSP, AWI*, 1719–20, 301–4; Swanton, "Distribution of Indian Tribes."

2. Governor Johnson to the Council of Trade and Plantations, January 12, 1720, in *CSP, AWI*, 1719–20, 301, 302; "Part of the Purcell Map Compiled Not Later than 1770 in the Interest of British Indian Trade by John Stuart"; Swanton, "Locations of Indian Tribes"; Fogelson, "Cherokee in the East," 337–39; Bull, Southeastern North America; Hunter, "Cherokee Nation and the Traders' Path"; Woolley, "Cherokee Country prior to 1776"; Herbert, "New Mapp of His Majestys Flourishing Province"; Mouzon et al., *Accurate Map of North and South Carolina*.

3. Governor Johnson to the Council of Trade, January 12, 1720, in *CSP, AWI*, 1719–20, 301, 302; Merrell, *Indians' New World,* 92–94, 109; Rudes, Blumer, and May, "Catawba and Neighboring Groups," 308, 309; D. S. Brown, *Catawba Indians*, 98, 124; Swanton, "Locations of Indian Tribes"; Beck, *Chiefdoms, Collapse, and Coalescence*, 258–60.

4. Rudes, Blumer, and May, "Catawba and Neighboring Groups," 301, 302 (Fig. 1), 303, 308–10, 315–18; Urban and Jackson, "Social Organization," 704; Governor Johnson to the Council, January 12, 1720, in *CSP, AWI*, 1719–20, 301, 302; J. A. Barnwell, "Southeastern North America"; Milling, *Red Carolinians*, 203, 209, 212–16, 219, 222; Swanton, "Locations of Indian Tribes."

5. Governor Johnson to the Council of Trade and Plantations, January 12, 1720, in *CSP, AWI*, 1719–20, 302; Swanton, *Indians of the Southeastern United States*, 89–91; Swanton, *Early History of the Creek Indians*, 121–25; McEwan, "Apalachee and Neighboring Groups," 673, 674; Covington, "Apalachee Indians," 366, 374–77; J. A. Barnwell, "Southeastern North America"; Francis Le Jau to the Society, May 21, 1715, in Klingberg, *Chronicle of Le Jau*, 158; Swanton, "Locations of Indian Tribes."

6. Swanton, *Indians of the Southeastern United States*, 184; Swanton, *Early History of the Creek Indians*, 317; Governor Johnson to the Council of Trade and Plantations, January 12, 1720, in *CSP, AWI*, 1719–20, 302; Swanton, "Locations of Indian Tribes"; Swanton, "Territory of the States of Georgia and Alabama Illustrating the . . . Creek Confederacy" (endpaper map to *Early History of the Creek Indians*).

7. Governor Johnson to the Council of Trade and Plantations, January 12, 1720, in *CSP, AWI*, 1719–20, 302; Jackson, "Yuchi," 426. The Yuchi were also known as Uchee, Euchee, and Chiska. Swanton, *Early History of the Creek Indians*, 288, 289; Swanton, *Indians of the Southeastern United States*, 212, 213; J. A. Barnwell, "Southeastern North America"; Swanton, "Locations of Indian Tribes"; Swanton, "Territory of the States of Georgia and Alabama."

8. Governor Johnson to the Council of Trade and Plantations, January 12, 1720, in *CSP, AWI*, 1719–20, 302; Brightman and Wallace, "Chickasaw," 479, 490, 491; Swanton, "Locations of Indian Tribes"; Swanton, "Territory of the States of Georgia and Alabama."

9. Nairne, *Map of South Carolina;* Martin, "Languages," 72, 74; Swanton, *Early History of the Creek Indians*, 216, 225, 226, "Territory of the States of Georgia and Alabama"; Crane, *Southern Frontier*, 95, 96, 185, 258, 260, 261; Hahn, *Invention of the Creek Nation*, 10, 39, 40, 48–52, 71–73, 76; Governor Johnson to the Council of Trade and Plantations, January 12, 1720, in *CSP, AWI*, 1719–20, 301, 302; "Part of the Purcell Map Compiled Not Later than 1770 in the Interest of British Indian Trade by John Stuart"; Swanton, "Indian Tribes of the Southeastern United States"; Swanton, "Locations of Indian Tribes."

10. Nairne, *Map of South Carolina;* Swanton, "Territory of the States of Georgia and Alabama"; Governor Johnson to the Council of Trade and Plantations, January 12, 1720, in *CSP, AWI*, 1719–20, 302; Crane, *Southern Frontier*, 82, 83; Hahn, *Invention of the Creek Nation*, 51, 85, 86.

11. Worth, "Guale," 238, 239, 241; Worth, "Yamasee," 245–49; Bowne, "'Caryinge awaye Their Corne and Children,'" 107; Hudson, *Southeastern Indians*, 233.

12. Worth, *Struggle for the Georgia Coast*, 10–15; Worth, "Guale," 240, 242, 243;

13. Worth, "Guale," 243, 244; Worth, *Struggle for the Georgia Coast*, 15–18, 36, 37; Worth, "Razing Florida," 297–99; Beck, *Chiefdoms, Collapse, and Coalescence*, 99–134, 139, 140, 146–51.

14. Worth, "Yamasee," 245, 249–51; Worth, *Struggle for the Georgia Coast*, 18–22, 27, 30, 35; Green, DePratter, and Southerlin, "Yamasee in South Carolina," 14–17; Worth, "Razing Florida," 298.

15. Worth, *Struggle for the Georgia Coast*, 35–37, 42, 43, 45, 50; Worth, "Yamasee," 245, 249, 251; Beck, *Chiefdoms, Collapse, and Coalescence*, 148–50; Green, DePratter, and Southerlin, "Yamasee in South Carolina," 19–21, fig. 2.3; Salley, *Warrants for Lands*, 582; "Chart of Parts of the Coast of South Carolina from Port Royall to Charlestown," ca. 1700; Lord Cardross to [Governor Moreton?], January 10, 1685, in *CSP, AWI*, 1681–85, 760; Caleb Westbrooke to [Deputy Governor Godfrey?], February 21, 1681, in *CSP, AWI*, 1685–88, February 9; Information of Several Yamasee Indians, May 6, 1685, in *CSP, AWI*, 1685–88, 40; Gallay, *Indian Slave Trade*, 79.

16. The distinction between Yamasee and Guale was never addressed by the commissioners of the Indian trade. Both groups were referred to as Yamasee or by the names of their towns. McDowell, *Journals of the Commissioners of the Indian Trade*.

17. Crane, *Southern Frontier*, 81, 89, 163; Worth, "Yamasee," 252. Lorenzo had previously lived in Florida. He was probably a Guale who had been baptized a Catholic, had taken a Spanish name, and then moved with the people of his town to South Carolina during the 1680s or 1690s. Arnade, *Siege of St. Augustine*, 51, 52; John Barnwell to the Governor, February 4, 1712, in J. W. Barnwell, "Tuscarora Expedition," 30, 32–34, 36, 37, 39, 49, 50, 53.

18. Cooper and McCord, *Statutes*, "Act to Limit the Bounds of the Yamasee Settlement, to Prevent Persons from Disturbing Them with Their Stocks, and to Remove Such as Are Settled within the Limitations Hereafter Mentioned," November 28, 1707, 2:317, 318; "Chart of Parts of the Coast of South Carolina from Port Royall to Charlestown," ca. 1700; Green, DePratter, and Southerlin, "Yamasee in South Carolina," 21, 22, fig. 2.3.

19. The early 1715 census of the Indian groups was taken by Thomas Nairne, John Wright, Price Hughes, and John Barnwell. Governor Johnson to the Council of Trade and Plantations, January 12, 1720, in *CSP, AWI*, 1719–20, 301, 302; McDowell, *Journals of the Commissioners of the Indian Trade*, July 9, 1712, 30, 31; July 10, 1712, 35; July 17, 1713, 47. For differing opinions regarding the identity of the towns that made up the Upper and Lower Yamasee, see the following: Crane, *Southern Frontier*, 164; Green, "Search for Altamaha," 24; Green, DePratter, and Southerlin, "Yamasee in South Carolina," 15; Worth, "Yamasee," 253.

20. Altamaha (Aratomahaw, Altimahaw, Tamaja, Tama) was located about 11.5 miles southwest of present-day Ridgeland; Chechessee (Chasee, Chachise, Chachesee, Chechesy) was located on the west bank of Chechessee Creek, about 1.5 miles west of its junction with the Chechessee River, where Highway 27 ends at the creek in present-day Beaufort County; Okatee (Ocute, Okata) was located on the northwest bank of the Okatie River, about 1.75 miles northwest of the junction of Okatie River and Chechessee Creek, in present-day Beaufort County; Altamaha, Chechessee, and Okatee are shown on the George Hunter plat, 1732, McGrady Plat Collection. The location of the three towns is also detailed in Sweeney, *Archaeology of Indian Slavers*. Euhaw (Yewhaw, Youhau, Oapa, Yoa) was probably located on the west bank of Euhaw Creek,

about 8.5 miles southeast of present-day Ridgeland near Bolen Hall, in the vicinity of the eastern end of the unnumbered extension of Highway 387 in Jasper County. However it could also have been located about a mile to the northwest near the eastern end of the unnumbered extension of Highway 429. The town and its fields could have been scattered between the two locations. McDowell, *Journals of the Commissioners of the Indian Trade,* July 9, 1712, 30; July 10, 1712, 35; October 25, 1712, 37; Worth, "Yamasee," 248, 249, 253; McKivergan, "Migration and Settlement," 209; Worth, *Timucuan Chiefdoms of Spanish Florida,* 2:150, table 9-2; letter of Corcoles, January 25, 1716.

21. Pocotaligo (Polocotalaca, Ocotonico) was probably located at the site of present-day Mackay Boat Landing at the southern end of the unnumbered extension of Highway 33. The town probably extended north along the neck. The likely location of Pocasabo (Pocosapa) is about 1 mile northwest of the conflux of present-day Haulover Creek and Whale Branch in Beaufort County. Tulafina (Tullifinny) was probably about 2 miles northwest of the conflux of the Tullifinny and Coosawhatchie Rivers at the southeastern end of present-day Highway 172, in Jasper County There is a possibility that at some point Tulafina may have been consolidated, and located, with Sadkeche. There are three likely locations for Huspaw (Huspah Jospo, Tospe, Clospo). In the order of probability they are as follows: first at Bull Point between the junction of Huspah Creek and its eastern branch; second on the west bank of Huspah Creek near Huspah Plantation, 1 mile to the west-northwest; and third on the west bank of Huspah Creek, 1.75 miles south of Bull Point. Tomotly (Tolomato, Tamaxle, Tamasle) may have been located about 1.5 miles southwest of the junction of Highways 47 and 19 in Beaufort County. Sadkeche (Salchiches, Salkehatchie) may have been located in present-day Beaufort County, on the west bank of the Combahee River, about 4.25 miles east-southeast of Yemasee. At that site the land rises 20 feet above the river and swamp, and there is access to the river via a creek. The Salkehatchie River was known by South Carolinians at that time as the Saltcatchers. It is possible that a town named Sapelo, composed of Guale, was amalgamated with Sadkeche. McDowell, *Journals of the Commissioners of the Indian Trade,* May 30, 1711, 8; July 28, 1711, 11; August 25, 1711, 17; June 20, 1712, 27; July 9, 1712, 31; July 10, 1712, 35; March 19, 1713, 40; September 25, 1713, 50; Worth, "Yamasee," 245, 247–49; Worth, "Guale," 238, 239; Worth, *Timucuan Chiefdoms of Spanish Florida,* 2:150, table 9-2; McKivergan, "Migration and Settlement," 181–90, 209; H. A. M. Smith, "Tomotley Barony," 11, 12; De Brahm, *Map of South Carolina and a Part of Georgia.*

22. Green, *Search for Altamaha,* 24; Colored Plat of 1590 Acres Located between Two Branches of the Ashepoo River, Purchased by John Stanyarne, 1701. Also see the James Stanyarne Plat, 1700, Auditor General Memorial Books, 4:183; McDowell, *Journals of the Commissioners of the Indian Trade,* March 25, 1713, 42; Green, DePratter, and Southerlin, "Yamasee in South Carolina," 17.

23. Hudson, *Southeastern Indians,* 120–75, 317; A. Moore, *Nairne's Muskhogean Journals,* 48.

24. Chicken, "Colonel Chicken's Journal to the Cherokees"; Worth, "Yamasee," 250; A. Moore, *Nairne's Muskhogean Journals*, 32–35, 39–41, 63–65; Fogelson, "Cherokee in the East," 346, 347; Hudson, *Southeastern Indians*, 191–96, 202, 203, 224, 225, 229–32, 242; Swanton, *Indians of the Southeastern United States*, 691.

25. Hudson, *Southeastern Indians*, 185–91; Urban and Jackson, "Social Organization," 697, 698; Worth, "Guale," 241; Worth, "Yamasee," 250; A. Moore, *Nairne's Muskhogean Journals*, 61; Hudson, *Southeastern Indians*, 312, 313.

26. A. Moore, *Nairne's Muskhogean Journals*, 32–35, 39, 41, 42; Hudson, *Southeastern Indians*, 223–26, 233; Fogelson, "Cherokee in the East," 346.

27. Hudson, *Southeastern Indians*, 211, 213, 214, 218, 226–28, 260, 270, 292; Worth, "Guale," 241.

28. Worth, "Guale," 241; Hudson, *Southeastern Indians*, 214–22, 255–57, 421, 422; Swanton, *Indians of the Southeastern United States*, 386–93; Osborne to the Secretary, May 28, 1715, in Geiger, "St. Bartholomew's Parish," 176; Green, DePratter, and Southerlin, "Yamasee in South Carolina," 19; Sweeney, *Archaeology of Indian Slavers*. Houses found at Altamaha, ca. 1715, were round.

29. Hudson, *Southeastern Indians*, 226, 259, 267–69, 271; Braund, *Deerskins and Duffels*, 63, 66–68.

30. Hudson, *Southeastern Indians*, 259, 264–68, 292–95, 297–99, 300–307; A. Moore, *Nairne's Muskhogean Journals*, 51; David Crawley to Wm. Byrd, July 30, 1715, in *CSP, AWI*, 1714–15, 247.

31. Swanton, *Indians of the Southeastern United States*, 222–28, 456–65, 505, 506, 528; Hudson, *Southeastern Indians*, 260–62, 300, 301, 380; S. C. Williams, *Adair's History of the American Indians* 1–5, 7–9; Walker, "Creek Confederacy before Removal," 379, 380; Milling, *Red Carolinians*, 5–7, 26, 27, 216; Lefler, *New Voyage to Carolina*, 36, 39, 40, 197, 199, 201, 202; Bonnefoy, "Journal of Antoine Bonnefoy," 244; Gallay, *Indian Slave Trade*, 184, 185; A. Moore, *Nairne's Muskhogean Journals*, 51–53; Fogelson, "Cherokee in the East," 339 (fig. 2); Rudes, Blumer, and May, "Catawba and Neighboring Groups," 304, 305 (fig. 5); DeMallie, "Tutelo and Neighboring Groups," 295; D. S. Brown, *Catawba Indians*, 16; Le Jau to the Secretary, August 22, 1715, in Klingberg, *Chronicle of Le Jau*, 160, 161; Hudson, *Southeastern Indians*, 244, 245, 260–62, 380; Burke, "Eighteenth-Century English Trade Guns in the South," 6–11, 15; Bonar, "A Draught of the Creek Nation."

32. Burke, "Eighteenth-Century English Trade Guns in the South," 6–11, 15; S. C. Williams, *Adair's History of the American Indians*, 6, 8, 9, 447–48n260; Hudson, *Southeastern Indians*, 264, 380; Swanton, *Indians of the Southeastern United States*, 222–28, 470–72; Milling, *Red Carolinians*, 6, 10; Bonar, "A Draught of the Creek Nation."

33. Walker, "Creek Confederacy before Removal," 375, 378, 379, 387; Levine, "Music," 720–22, 724, 725; Hudson, *Southeastern Indians*, 400–403, 405, 406, 408–22; Swanton, *Indians of the Southeastern United States*, 775; Milling, *Red Carolinians*, 25, 26; S. C. Williams, *Adair's History of the American Indians*, 6, 122, 123, 326–28, 428–31.

34. S. C. Williams, *Adair's History of the American Indians*, 6, 158, 298, 406–28; Lefler, *New Voyage to Carolina*, 53, 207–9; SCCHJ, August 12, 1712, 98; Hudson, *Southeastern Indians*, 239–41, 243, 244, 247, 249, 251, 253–55, 258, 261, 270, 325, 326–28; Mahon, "Anglo-American Methods of Indian Warfare," 260, 261, 264; A. Moore, *Nairne's Muskhogean Journals*, 41–44; Swanton, *Indians of the Southeastern United States*, 528–31, 688–96.

35. Swanton, *Indians of the Southeastern United States*, 463–65, 694; Hudson, *Southeastern Indians*, 245–47, 261, 262, 273; A. Moore, *Nairne's Muskhogean Journals*, 55, 62; Lawson, *History of the Uniforms of the British Army*, 1:43; Milling, *Red Carolinians*, 27; Burke, "Eighteenth-Century English Trade Guns in the South," 6–11, 15; Beck, *Chiefdoms, Collapse, and Coalescence*, 109, 140; Mahon, "Anglo-American Methods of Indian Warfare," 255.

36. A. Moore, *Nairne's Muskhogean Journals*, 41; Swanton, *Indians of the Southeastern United States*, 689, 692, 693; Hudson, *Southeastern Indians*, 249, 251, 253–57.

CHAPTER 4: Path to War, 1712–15

1. A. Moore, *Nairne's Muskhogean Journals*, 60, 61; Hudson, *Southeastern Indians*, 226, 234, 260, 317, 324; Crane, *Southern Frontier*, 125.

2. P. M. Brown, "Early Indian Trade," 125–27; Hudson, *Southeastern Indians*, 200, 201; Swanton, *Indians of the Southeastern United States*, 703; SCCHJ, January 19, 1711, 505; David Crawley to Wm. Byrd, July 30, 1715, in *CSP, AWI*, 1714–15, 247, 248.

3. McDowell, *Journals of the Commissioners of the Indian Trade*, September 21, 1710, 3, 4; May 30, 1711, 8, 9; July 27, 1711, 10, 11; July 28, 1711, 11; August 1, 1711, 13; August 15, 1711, 16, 17; September 13, 1711, 18, 19; June 20, 1712, 27, 28; October 25, 1712, 37, 38; March 25, 1713, 41, 42; March 26, 1713, 42, 43; April 16, 1713, 44; September 12, 1713, 50; September 25, 1713, 50, 51; October 6, 1713, 51; November 24, 1713, 52; May 20, 1714, 57, 58; June 9, 1714, 58; August 31, 1714, 59; April 12, 1715, 65. See also Gallay, *Indian Slave Trade*, 312.

4. McDowell, *Journals of the Commissioners of the Indian Trade*, August 31, 1714, 59; Hudson, *Southeastern Indians*, 336, 337; Crane, *Southern Frontier*, 152, 153; Gallay, *Indian Slave Trade*, 317, 318, 322–27.

5. SCCHJ, October 23, 1710, 485; McDowell, *Journals of the Commissioners of the Indian Trade*, May 30, 1711, 9; July 27, 1711, 11; August 15, 1711, 16, 17; September 13, 1711, 18.

6. McDowell, *Journals of the Commissioners of the Indian Trade*, March 9, 1711, 6; May 30, 1711, 8, 9; July 28, 1711, 11, 12; August 3, 1711, 14–17; September 13, 1711, 18; March 21, 1712, 20; April 17, 1712, 22, 23; May 14, 1712, 24; July 9, 1712, 33; October 25, 1712, 38; March 26, 1713, 43; August 19, 1713, 49; September 25, 1713, 50, 51; May 5, 1714, 55; Crane, *Southern Frontier*, 116, 117. For a discussion of friendships that developed between South Carolina men and Indian warriors, see Hahn, "'Indians That Live about Pon Pon,'" 346, 347, and LeMaster, "War, Masculinity, and Alliances," 165, 166, 176; Gallay, *Indian Slave Trade*, 8, 9, 194.

7. Gallay, *Indian Slave Trade*, 8, 147, 148, 185, 187, 188, 297, 298, 301–5, 311, 312; A. Moore, *Nairne's Muskhogean Journals*, 47, 48; Hahn, *Invention of the Creek Nation*, 52, 53, 77; Worth, "Razing Florida," 299–307; Shuck-Hall, "Alabama and Coushatta Diaspora and Coalescence," 264.

8. Worth, "Razing Florida," 249, 305, 306; Gallay, *Indian Slave Trade*, 311, 312; Hewitt, "State in the Planters' Service," 56; McDowell, *Journals of the Commissioners of the Indian Trade*, December 18, 1712, 39; Le Jau to the Society, May 21, 1715, in Klingberg, *Chronicle of Le Jau*, 159; A. Moore, *Nairne's Muskhogean Journals*, 35, 75.

9. Gregorie, *Records of the Court of Chancery*, 245–47; Bossy, "Godin & Co.," 123–29; Le Jau to the Society, May 14, 1715, in Klingberg, *Chronicle of Le Jau*, 154, 155; McDowell, *Journals of the Commissioners of the Indian Trade*, March 21, 1712, 20; June 12, 1712, 26; June 20, 1712, 27; June 17, 1712; October 25, 1712, 38; March 25, 1713, 42; March 26, 1713, 43; April 16, 1713, 44; July 16, 1713, 47; August 17, 1713, 48; August 18, 1713, 49; August 19, 1713, 49; June 9, 1714, 58; November 12, 1714; letter of Corcoles, January 25, 1716; SCCHJ, August 24, 1715, 447; Hahn, *Invention of the Creek Nation*, 78; Gallay, *Indian Slave Trade*, 246–48.

10. Governor Johnson to the Council of Trade and Plantations, January 12, 1720, in *CSP, AWI*, 1719–20, 301, 302; Swanton, *Early History of the Creek Indians*, 100; Worth, "Razing Florida," 305.

11. Worth, "Razing Florida," 305; "Rodd to His Employer in London," 169; Charles Craven to Lord Townsend, May 23, 1715, in *CSP, AWI*, 1714–15, 227; Abel Kettleby and other planters and merchants . . . to the Council of Trade and Plantations, July 18, 1715, in *CSP, AWI*, 1714–15, 236; Hewitt, *Historical Account of the Rise and Progress*, 1:214, 215; TePaske, *Governorship of Spanish Florida*, 198, 199, 216, appendix 1.

12. Col. William Rhett to William Rhett Junr, April 28, 1719, in *CSP, AWI*, 1719–20, 80; John Barnwell to Governor Johnson, April 20, 1719, in *CSP, AWI*, 1719–20, 80; Worth, *Struggle for the Georgia Coast*, 125n48, 201. During 1734 sixty-year-old El Cacique Clospo, the Huspaw king, was the mico of the Yamasee town of Potalaca located near Saint Augustine. He would have been forty-one years old during 1715. Swanton, *Early History of the Creek Indians*, 84, 104, 105; McDowell, *Journals of the Commissioners of the Indian Trade*, May 30, 1711, 8; July 10, 1712, 35; SCCHJ, April 20, 1716, 74; May 3, 1716, 93, 94; May 8, 1716, 97; May 18, 1716, 110; November 22, 1716, 174.

13. Hudson, *Southeastern Indians*, 242–44; Swanton, *Indians of the Southeastern United States*, 694; TePaske, *Governorship of Spanish Florida*, 216.

14. Hudson, *Southeastern Indians*, 242–44; Swanton, *Indians of the Southeastern United States*, 694; "Rodd to His Employer in London," 167, 169; Charles Craven to Lord Townsend, May 23, 1715, in *CSP, AWI*, 1714–15, 228.

15. Hahn, *Invention of the Creek Nation*, 39, 40, 48–52, 71–73, 81; Governor Johnson to the Council of Trade and Plantations, January 12, 1720, in *CSP, AWI*, 1719–20, 301, 302. Coweta was also known as Caveta and Kawita; Crane, *Southern Frontier*, 36, 132, 133; letters of Corcoles, July 5, 1715; January 25, 1716.

16. Wright arrived in South Carolina thirty years earlier as an indentured servant to Robert Hull. Salley, *Warrants for Lands,* 395, 623; Gregorie, *Records of the Court of Chancery,* 45, 46, 49, 50; Bossy, "Godin & Co.," 124–29; David Crawley to Wm. Byrd, July 30, 1715, in *CSP, AWI,* 1714–15, 247, 248; McDowell, *Journals of the Commissioners of the Indian Trade,* March 25, 1713, 41; November 23, 1714, 63.

17. Letters of Corcoles, July 5, 1715; January 25, 1716; Boyd, "Diego Pena's Expedition," 11. See note 17 of chapter 5 in regard to the Palachacola towns; Swanton, *Early History of the Creek Indians,* 131. An excellent narrative of Emperor Brims's involvement with the beginning of the war is contained in Hahn, *Invention of the Creek Nation,* 81; Le Jau to the Society, May 14, 1715, in Klingberg, *Chronicle of Le Jau,* 155; Sweeney, *Archaeology of Indian Slavers,* fig. 11.

18. Hewett, *Historical Account of the Rise and Progress,* 1:215–17; McDowell, *Journals of the Commissioners of the Indian Trade,* June 20, 1712, 28; October 25, 1712, 39; March 26, 1713, 42, 43; Wright, "Petitioners to the Crown," 91.

19. McDowell, *Journals of the Commissioners of the Indian Trade,* April 12, 1715, 65; "Rodd to His Employer in London," 167; Swanton, *Indians of the Southeastern United States,* 262.

20. Huspaw King to Governor Craven, April 1715; Hudson, *Southeastern Indians,* 366–75; Worth, "Razing Florida," 305. Yamasee foraging parties surreptitiously returned to the Indian Land during the summer and early fall of 1715 to harvest their corn and vegetables. Samuel Eveleigh to Boone and Berresford, ca. July 1715, in *CSP, AWI,* 1714–15, 297; *CSP, AWI,* 1714–15, Council of Trade and Plantations to Mr. Secretary Stanhope, July 19, 1715, 299; *Boston News-Letter,* June 13, 1715; September 26, 1715; October 31, 1715; Sweeney, *Archaeology of Indian Slavers,* fig. 11; Barnwell to the Governor, March 12, 1712, in J. W. Barnwell, "Tuscarora Expedition," 43–46; Le Jau to the Society, May 14, 1715, in Klingberg, *Chronicle of Le Jau,* 155; SCCHJ, June 14, 1716, 126.

21. Mahon, "Anglo-American Methods of Indian Warfare," 257, 260, 261; SCCHJ, August 12, 1712, 98; Barnwell to the Governor, February 4, 1712, in J. W. Barnwell, "Tuscarora Expedition," 30, 31; Worth, "Razing Florida," 305; Crane, *Southern Frontier,* 75–77, 79–81.

22. McDowell, *Journals of the Commissioners of the Indian Trade,* July 10, 1712, 35. Burrows was in Pocotaligo and escaped when the massacre began on April 15. "Rodd to His Employer in London," 167; *Boston News-Letter,* June 13, 1715; Auditor General Memorial Books, 1:354; Langley, *South Carolina Deed Abstracts,* 57. Nairne owned more than eighteen hundred acres of land on Saint Helena Island. See note 46, chapter 2. The only reasonable location for a house and farmstead on Eddings Point Creek is on the south side of the second eastern bend of the creek near the junction of Highways 478 and 479; Cooper and McCord, *Statutes,* "Act for . . . Look-Outs . . . ," July 5, 1707, 2:301.

23. A. Moore, *Nairne's Muskhogean Journals,* 3–25, 75–77; McDowell, *Journals of the Commissioners of the Indian Trade,* July 10, 1712, 35; December 18, 1712, 39, 40;

March 19, 1713, 40; March 25, 1713, 41, 42; March 26, 1713, 42, 43; August 17, 1713, 48; March 25, 1714, 52; Salley, *Warrants for Lands*, 582; "Historical Notes," 117; Nairne, *Letter from South Carolina*, 34, 35.

24. "Rodd to His Employer in London," 167; SCCHJ, June 8, 1714, 272; November 17, 1714, 303, 304; November 18, 1714, 305, 306; November 19, 1714, 308. Two period accounts stated that Gov. Charles Craven ordered Nairne and Cochran to go to Pocotaligo and take action to placate the Yamasees. Both accounts may have been based on the letter of Capt. Jonathan St. Lo to Josiah Burchett, July 12, 1715, 1, and on the *Boston News-Letter*, June 13, 1715. The governor did not issue such an order. A message sent from Port Royal to the governor in Charles Town regarding the Yamasee unrest and the governor's reply sent from Charles Town to Port Royal would have taken a minimum of three days by horseback and more by water. Craven did not mention giving such an order to Nairne and Cochran in his report to the British secretary of state. Wright and Cochran were already in the town. Nairne went to Pocotaligo on his own volition as Indian agent; Governor Craven to Lord Townshend, May 23, 1715, in *CSP, AWI*, 1714–15, 227–29. On Nairne and Wright's mutual animosity, see Gallay, *Indian Slave Trade*, 315–19.

25. "Rodd to His Employer in London," 167; letter of Corcoles, January 25, 1716; Huspaw King to Governor Craven, April 1715; Worth, *Timucuan Chiefdoms of Spanish Florida*, 2:150, table 9-2. See note 16 of this chapter for Wright.

26. Huspaw King to Governor Craven, April 1715; "Rodd to His Employer in London," 167; *Boston News-Letter*, June 13, 1715; St. Lo to Burchett, July 12, 1715, 1; Governor Johnson to the Council of Trade and Plantations, January 12, 1720, in *CSP, AWI*, 1719–1720, 301, 302; letter of Corcoles, January 25, 1716.

CHAPTER 5: Easter Weekend, April 15–17, 1715

1. "Rodd to His Employer in London," 167. For Charles Rodd see Gregorie, *Records of the Court of Chancery*, 93; *Boston News-Letter*, June 13, 1715; Cooper and McCord, *Statutes*, "Act to Divide Saint Helen's Parish . . . ," May 25, 1745, 3:658. Barnwell's plantation was located about 3.25 miles northwest of present-day Beaufort, near Clarendon Plantation, at the western terminus of Highway 71 on the east bank of the Whale Branch. Auditor General Memorial Books, 1:74, 77, 366; Salley, *Warrants for Land*, 626, 627, 639, 645. It appears that Barnwell's daughter Elizabeth Deveaux received the plantation as a gift from her widowed mother. Desaussure, *Reports of Cases Argued*, 1:497, 498; The "Devaux" plantation is shown on Stuart, *Map of South Carolina and a Part of Georgia*.

2. "Rodd to His Employer in London," 167; *Boston News-Letter*, June 13, 1715.

3. Osborne to the Secretary, May 28, 1715, in Williams, ed. *Letters from the Clergy of the Anglican Church in South Carolina*.

4. "Rodd to His Employer in London," 167, 168.

5. Osborne to the Secretary, May 28, 1715, in Selected Papers Relating to South Carolina from Library of Congress, 100.

6. "Rodd to His Employer in London," 168; Governor Craven to Lord Townsend, May 23, 1715, in *CSP, AWI, 1714–15*, 228.

7. Hewett relates that Cochran's and Bray's families were put to death; however it is unlikely that the children were killed. Hewett, *Historical Account of the Rise and Progress*, 1:221; S. C. Williams, *Adair's History of the American Indians*, 278, 279. It has been suggested that Cochran's and Bray's wives may have been Yamasees, but that seems unlikely; McDowell, *Journals of the Commissioners of the Indian Trade*, March 21, 1712, 20.

8. McDowell, *Journals of the Commissioners of the Indian Trade*, September 21, 1710, 3, 4; May 30, 1711, 8, 9; July 27, 1711, 10; July 28, 1711, 11; August 1, 1711, 13; August 15, 1711, 16, 17; March 14, 1712, 19; June 20, 1712, 27, 28; October 25, 1712, 37, 38; March 25, 1713, 41, 42; March 26, 1713, 42, 43; April 16, 1713, 44; September 25, 1713, 50, 51; November 24, 1714, 52; May 20, 1714, 57, 58; June 9, 1714, 58; August 31, 1714, 59; April 12, 1715, 65; SCCHJ, May 3, 1716, 93; Gregorie, *Records of the Court of Chancery*, 245–47; Bossy, "Godin & Co.," 124–29.

9. McDowell, *Journals of the Commissioners of the Indian Trade*, July 11, 1711, 10; March 14, 1712, 19; January 28, 1718, 252; March 21, 1718, 262; Wright, "Petitioners to the Crown," 91. Callahan had a plantation on the north end of Port Royal Island; Auditor General Memorial Books, 4:482.

10. "Rodd to His Employer in London," 168; Le Jau to the Secretary, May 14, 1715, in Klingberg, *Chronicle of Le Jau*, 154, 155.

11. Le Jau to the Secretary, May 14, 1715, in Klingberg, *Chronicle of Le Jau*, 155; SCCHJ, August 24, 1715, 447.

12. "Rodd to His Employer in London," 167; SCCHJ, August 24, 1715, 447; Le Jau to the Society, May 14, 1715, in Klingberg, *Chronicle of Le Jau*, 154, 155.

13. "Rodd to His Employer in London, 167; Gallay, *Indian Slave Trade*, 186, 187; "Slavery in Province, Colony, and State," 567, 568; Cooper and McCord, *Statutes*, "Act for Settling the Island Called Palawanee, upon the Cusaboe Indians, Now Living in Granville County, and Upon Their Posterity for Ever," December 12, 1712, 2:599, 600; Hann, "St. Augustine's Fallout," 186, 188; Swanton, *Indians of the Southeastern United States*, 129.

14. De Brahm, *Map of South Carolina and a Part of Georgia;* William Guy to the Society, September 20, 1715, in Pennington, "South Carolina Indian War," 255, 256; Le Jau to the Society, May 14, 1715, in Klingberg, *Chronicle of Le Jau*, 154, 155; Jack Leland, interview with the author, Charleston, South Carolina, June 1971; William Bull to Council of Trade and Plantations, May 25, 1728 (citing affidavit of Joseph Parmenter, February 16, 1727), in *CSP, AWI, 1728–29*, February 104.

15. SCCHJ, August 2, 1716, 155; August 4, 1716, 161.

16. Selected Papers Relating to South Carolina from Library of Congress, Osborne to the Society, March 1, 1715, 93; May 28, 1715, 100; William Bull to the Society, August 10, 1715, in Klingberg, "Mystery of the Lost Yamasee Prince,"

23; Le Jau to the Society, August 22, 1715, in Klingberg, *Chronicle of Le Jau,* 162; Geiger, "St. Bartholomew's Parish," 176.

17. Governor Johnson to the Council of Trade and Plantations, January 12, 1720, in *CSP, AWI,* 1719–20, 302. Apalachicola (Apalachicalo, Apalachicoli, Apalachicolo) was also sometimes used by the Spanish to refer to all of the Lower Creek; letters of Corcoles, July 5, 1715; November 28, 1715; January 25, 1716; Swanton, *Early History of the Creek Indians,* 129–32; Swanton, "Distribution of Indian Tribes," places Palachacola on the west side of Savannah River. Another map, John A. Barnwell's of southeastern North America, also shows Palachacola on the west side of the Savannah River. Barnwell's depiction of Palachacola would place at least one of the towns a short distance northwest of the present-day Highway 119 bridge over the river in Effingham County. However a later map, Bowen, *New and Accurate Map of the Province,* places Palachacola on the east, or South Carolina, side of the river. As additional evidence for that site, archaeologists have found remains of a period Indian town, which they believe is Palachacola, in the James W. Webb Wildlife Center and Game Management Area on the east side of the river near the southwest corner of Hampton County. Thus the South Carolina site was probably the location of Palachacola. Caldwell, "Palachacolas Town," 321; Cobb, "First Season"; Cobb, "2011 Field School." The town on the Georgia side of the river was probably Tukassa (Tuckesaw, Cusa?) which is shown on De Brahm, *Map of South Carolina and a Part of Georgia,* as Tukassa King's Bluff. A dozen years later, the Tuckesaw King and his people occupied a town among the Lower Creeks. Hahn, *Life and Times of Mary Musgrove,* 58; Hahn, "'Indians That Live about Pon Pon,'" 360.

18. Patrick Mackay to James Oglethorpe, March 29, 1735, Colonial Records of the State of Georgia, 20:542.

19. Boyd, "Diego Pena's Expedition," 11; Fitch, "Tobias Fitch's Journal," 193, 210.

20. Osborne to the Society, May 28, 1715, in Selected Papers Relating to South Carolina from Library of Congress, 100; Le Jau to the Society, May 14, 1715, in Klingberg, *Chronicle of Le Jau,* 154; Le Jau to the Society, May 21, 1715, in Klingberg, *Chronicle of Le Jau,* 158; William Dry to Col. Barnwell, August 19, 1720, in *CSP, AWI,* 1720–21, 190. Many whites and blacks who were initially reported as killed were actually captured and later taken to Florida or to the Lower Creeks. War parties seized several black slaves from the Port Royal plantations of James Cochran, James Petterson, John Barnwell, William Ford, Daniel Dicks, Robert Graham, William Adams, and George Duckett; Deposition of George Duckett, ca. August 1716, in *CSP, AWI,* 1716–17, 225, 226. Five years later the Spanish ransomed several white captives from the Indians and returned them to South Carolina. The Spaniards refused to return the captured black slaves, who remained in Florida as free persons. The names of the few white prisoners that are known are Joseph Cooper, Hugh Bryan, a Mrs. Sisson, a Mrs. Macartey, and the wife of John Bull. Hugh Banks and Martha Hart were captured later by the Creeks. McDowell, *Journals of the Commissioners of the Indian Trade,* June 3, 1718, 280–82.

CHAPTER 6: Counterattack, April–May 1715

1. McDowell, *Journals of the Commissioners of the Indian Trade,* April 12, 1715, 65; Capt. Jonathan St. Lo to Josiah Burchett, July 12, 1715, 2; Governor Craven to Lord Townshend, May 23, 1715, in *CSP, AWI,* 1714–15, 228; Governor and Council of Carolina to the Council of Trade and Plantations, September 17, 1709, in *CSP, AWI,* 1708–9, 466; Cooper and McCord, *Statutes,* "Act for the Better Settling and Regulating the Militia," July 19, 1707, 9:630. The kettle drum, trumpets, and other accoutrements were purchased from England; SCCHJ, June 4, 1712, 67, 68.

2. Sirmans, *Colonial South Carolina,* 96, 100, 113, 114.

3. McDowell, *Journals of the Commissioners of the Indian Trade,* April 12, 1715, 65; Governor Craven to Lord Townsend, May 23, 1715, in *CSP, AWI,* 1714–15, 228; H. A. M. Smith, "Upper Ashley," 174–77, with accompanying map; Stuart, *Map of South Carolina and a Part of Georgia.*

4. William Bull to the Secretary, August 10, 1715, in Klingberg, "Mystery of the Lost Yamasee Prince," 23. Woodward's Fort was located in Saint Bartholomews Parish, at the head of Folly Creek and just east of Godfrey's Savannah, about four miles west-southwest of present-day Ritter in Colleton County. Woodward was about thirty-three years old. He married Elizabeth Stanyarne in 1702. He died in 1727. He was the son of Henry Woodward, the colony's first settler. Woodward's Fort was also known as the Horseshoe Fort in 1716. "Rodd to His Employer in London," 168; Le Jau to the Secretary, May 10, 1715, in Klingberg, *Chronicle of Le Jau,* 153; Le Jau to the Secretary, May 14, 1715, in Klingberg, *Chronicle of Le Jau,* 155; McDowell, *Journals of the Commissioners of the Indian Trade,* April 12, 1715, 65; J. W. Barnwell, "Dr. Henry Woodward," 32–34; SCCHJ, December 13, 1716, 203; J. A. Barnwell, Southeastern North America, shows a fort titled "Woodwards" on the upper Ashepoo River; Manuscript Plats (loose) for John and Richard Woodward, 1705, 1706, 1715, and 1733, and Records of the Secretary of the Province (Proprietary Grants), 39:14, show their lands near the heads of the Ashepoo River and Folly Creek; Salley, *Warrants for Land,* 234. The location of the site is described as being a short distance east of Godfrey's Savannah (which did not receive that name until after 1721), and the appearance of the fort's ruins as it looked in 1734 are described in "New Voyage to Georgia," 2:50. By 1734 the fort had been abandoned for at least fourteen years. The palisades and buildings would have badly deteriorated or have been destroyed by the weather and termite infestation, and the only clear evidence of a fort's ruins would probably have been an eroded ditch and earthen wall. The site was adjacent to the northwest corner of the Ashepoo Barony, which was located on the west side of the main crossing of the Ashepoo just below its junction with Horseshoe Creek. The Bellinger family owned the entire barony until about 1768, when they began selling parts of it; H. A. M. Smith, "Ashepoo Barony," 3–51, 66, 67, 71, with accompanying map.

The paths taken by Governor Culver and his troop are shown on De Brahm, *Map of South Carolina and a Part of Georgia,* and Boss and Brailsford, Map of South Carolina From the Savannah Sound to St. Helena's Sound, ca. 1750.

5. Heyward, "Heyward Family of South Carolina," 146; SCCHJ, April 28, 1709, 423; May 11, 1716, 104; June 20, 1716, 133; Cooper and McCord, *Statutes,* "Additional Act . . . for Appointing Ferries," November 10, 1711, 9:19.

6. Bull to the Society, August 10, 1715, in Klingberg, "Mystery of the Lost Yamasee Prince," 23; "Rodd to His Employer in London," 168; Le Jau to the Society, May 14, 1715, in Klingberg, *Chronicle of Le Jau,* Le Jau 155; J. W. Barnwell, "Tuscarora Expedition," 28–54; A message from the Governor & Council [of South Carolina] . . . relating to Col. John Barnwell, August 9, 1712, in Saunders, *Colonial Records of North Carolina,* 1:902–4; Gallay, *Indian Slave Trade,* 274–76, 282, 283.

7. St. Lo to Burchett, July 12, 1715, 2; *Boston News-Letter,* June 13, 1715; Salley, *Journal of His Majesty's Council,* June 1, 1721.

8. Letter of Corcoles, January 25, 1716; "Rodd to His Employer in London," 168; SCCHJ, May 8, 1715, 399. Harris's plantation was located southeast of the east branch of the Cooper River and northeast of Charles Town in Berkeley County; Cooper and McCord, *Statutes,* "Act to Continue the Currency of Thirty Thousand Pounds in Bills of Credit," June 30, 1716, 2:666. Lebas's plantation was located at or near present-day Moncks Corner; Smith, "Some Forgotten Towns in Lower South Carolina," 138.

9. Bull to the Society, August 10, 1715, in Klingberg, "Mystery of the Lost Yamasee Prince," 23; "Rodd to His Employer in London," 168; *Boston News-Letter,* June 13, 1715; St. Lo to Burchett, July 12, 1715, British Records Calendar, 2; Le Jau to the Society, May 21, 1715, in Klingberg, *Chronicle of Le Jau,* 158. The most likely location for Sadkeche (Salchiches, Salkehatchie) is about 4.25 miles east-southeast of present-day Yemassee. See note 21, chapter 3.

10. One of the dead militiamen was a man named John Snow; "Rodd to His Employer in London," 168; Governor Craven to Lord Townsend, May 23, 1715, in *CSP, AWI,* 1714–15, 227, 228; *Boston News-Letter,* June 13, 1715; St. Lo to Burchett, July 12, 1715, 2; Le Jau to the Society, May 14, 1715, in Klingberg, *Chronicle of Le Jau,* 155; A. Moore, *Nairne's Muskhogean Journals,* 43; Swanton, *Indians of the Southeastern United States,* 688; Hudson, *Southeastern Indians,* 249.

11. "Rodd to His Employer in London," 168; *Boston News-Letter,* June 13, 1715; St. Lo to Burchett, July 12, 1715, 1; Huspaw King to Governor Craven, April 1715; Cooper and McCord, *Statutes,* "Act for Mending and Keeping in Repair the Causway over the Marsh of Combee River," February 25, 1715, 2:37; Committee of the Assembly of Carolina to Boone and Berresford, August 6, 1716, in *CSP, AWI,* 1716–17, 219, 220; SCCHJ, May 3, 1716, 93. William L. Ramsey discovered the Huspaw King's letter in the North Carolina Archives while researching information for his book *The Yamasee War: A Study of Culture, Economy, and Conflict in the Colonial South.* The text of the letter reads as follows (Ramsey, *Yamasee War,* 227–28):

Mr. Wright said that the white men would come and [illegible] the Yamasees in one night and that they would hang four of their head men and take all the rest of them for Slaves, and that he would send them all off the County, for he said that the men of the Yamasees were like women, and shew'd his hands one to the other, and what he said vex'd the great Warrier's, and this made them begin the war, and the Indians have kill'd forty or fifty white persons, and the Indians are all comeing to take all the Country, they are three hundred, that are going to watch to take the Fort at Capt. Woodwards and that at Well Town for in short all the Indians upon the main are comeing and they say that the white People will not be a handful for them for they say they will fight Six year's but they will take the Country

Charles Craven may goe off himself, for the Indians love him, and they say that he and they are like Brothers.

The Indians say that they that will not fight of the White men, they will save alive, but they that do fight, they will kill, as for the Women and Children them they will save alive, this is all from the

Huspaw King

To Charles Craven King

att Charles Town

Note that Shewing hands one to the other is the Custom of the Indians, when they goe to warr, which Signifie, they intend to Sweep off all Clean ——·

12. Huspaw King to Governor Craven, April 1715; "Rodd to His Employer in London," 168.

13. "Rodd to His Employer in London," 168, 169; *Boston News-Letter,* June 13, 1715. The location of the Sadkiechee Fight is depicted on J. A. Barnwell, "Southeastern North America."

14. *Boston News-Letter,* June 13, 1715; "Rodd to His Employer in London," 168.

15. Salley, *Warrants for Lands,* 190, 608, 620, 623; Barnwell to the Governor, February 4, 1712, in J. W. Barnwell, "Tuscarora Expedition," 30; Barnwell to the Governor, April 20, 1712, , in J. W. Barnwell, "Tuscarora Expedition," 47; J. W. Barnwell, "Second Tuscarora Expedition," 33–48.

16. Salley, "Barnwell of South Carolina," 47–49; Fisher, "John Barnwell and British Western Policy," 23; Gallay, *Indian Slave Trade,* 261; Crane, *Southern Frontier,* 163. For the location of Barnwell's homestead, see note 1 of chapter 5.

17. Le Jau to the Society, May 14, 1715, in Klingberg, *Chronicle of Le Jau,* 155; *Boston News-Letter,* June 13, 1715; SCCHJ, June 14, 1716, 126.

18. Le Jau to the Society, May 14, 1715, in Klingberg, *Chronicle of Le Jau,* 155.

19. U.S. Geological Survey Map, Yemassee, South Carolina, 1943, Scale 1:62, 500. Among the other sites considered for the Yamasee fort is a location a short distance west of the Salkehatchie River. During the spring of 1734, a man

traveling southwest from the site of Woodward's Fort to the Salkehatchie River reported that "as soon as we crossed the river we came to a small savannah, where we had once a terrible battle with the Indians, and lost a great many of our men. There are several large pine trees now to be seen, full of bullets." The site is between present-day Yemassee and the west bank of the river. The traveler's informant was a ranger captain's servant who was helping him navigate the paths to the captain's nearby plantation. At that time a company of rangers was stationed about half a mile away. It appears that the servant was "pulling the leg" of the traveler. There is no contemporary evidence that a battle occurred there. More important, the site was not a favorable defensive location. Nor does the site fit any descriptions of the fort or the resulting skirmish. "New Voyage to Georgia," 2:51.

20. *Boston News-Letter,* June 13, 1715; Memorial Books, 4:314; Cooper and McCord, *Statutes,* "Act to Continue the Garrison at Savano Town and the Two Scout Boats . . . and to Discharge the Officers and Soldiers . . . in the Late Expedition to the Creek Indians . . . ," February 20, 1719, 3:72; Langley, *South Carolina Deed Abstracts,* 1:321, 322. Margaret Palmer was the daughter of Landgrave William Bellinger; H. A. M. Smith, "The Ashepoo Barony," 67. During the ensuing years, Palmer continued to fight the Yamasees successfully until his death in battle with Spaniards and Yamasees at Fort Mosa near Saint Augustine during the summer of 1740; Easterby, *Journal of the Commons House of Assembly,* 82, 114, 115, 215, 240.

21. The square, palisaded Yamasee town of Chechessee is depicted ca. 1700 on "Colored Plat of 1590 Acres Located between Two Branches of the Ashepoo River, Purchased by John Stanyarne," 1701; Barnwell to the Governor, February 4, 1712, in J. W. Barnwell, "Tuscarora Expedition," 32, 33; March 12, 1712, 43–46.

22. *Boston News-Letter,* June 13, 1715.

23. During the period 1711 to 1714, Cochran operated a "punch house," or tavern, without a license at his Cochran's Point plantation, where he sold rum to the Yamasees. The Indian Land was nearby to the north across the Whale Branch. The fort was probably constructed on Cochran's farmstead. This soon became the primary scout-boat base. McDowell, *Journals of the Commissioners of the Indian Trade,* May 20, 1714, 58; "Rodd to His Employer in London," 168; Osborne to the Society, May 28, 1715, in Williams, ed. *Letters from the Clergy of the Anglican Church in South Carolina*; William Guy to the Society, September 20, 1715, in Pennington, "South Carolina Indian War," 255; SCCHJ, March 5, 1716, 20; March 7, 1716, 27; March 10, 1716, 35; March 16, 1716, 43; March 17, 1716, 46; March 21, 1716, 52; August 2, 1716, 157; November 14, 1716, 166; November 23, 1716, 181; December 5, 1716, 190; December 6, 1716, 193; December 7, 1716, 195; February 20, 1717, 249; De Brahm, *Map of South Carolina and a Part of Georgia; Boston News-Letter,* June 13, 1715.

24. Letter of Corcoles, January 25, 1716.

CHAPTER 7: Preparations for Survival, May–July 1715

1. Letters of Corcoles, July 5, 1715; January 25, 1716. The letters are confusing regarding the Spanish identity of Brims's emissaries and the Lower Creek towns from which they came. Ystopojole's town, which the Spanish scribe listed as Nicunapa or Nicupana, was probably Cakinonpa, Kasinampo, or Casquinonpa, which were apparently synonyms for Tukabahchee. Brave Dog stated that he represented both Brims and Cherokeekiller. Swanton, *Early History of the Creek Indians* 131, 212–14, 279, "Territory of the States of Georgia and Alabama"; Hahn, *Invention of the Creek Nation*, 48, 52–79, 83, 84. For a more detailed discussion of the Palachacola towns, see note 17 of chapter 5.

2. Hahn, *Invention of the Creek Nation*, 84; Swanton, *Early History of the Creek Indians*, 105; letters of Corcoles, July 5, 1715; January 25, 1716.

3. Letters of Corcoles, July 5, 1715; January 25, 1716; Hahn, *Invention of the Creek Nation*, 84, 85.

4. Letters of Corcoles, July 5, 1715; January 25, 1716.

5. Letters of Corcoles, July 5, 1715; January 25, 1716; Worth, *Timucuan Chiefdoms of Spanish Florida*, 2:143, fig. 8-1, 144; Boyd, "Diego Pena's Expedition," 9.

6. Swanton, *Early History of the Creek Indians*, 100–102; J. A. Barnwell, "Northern B[ra]nch of Altamana River"; *Boston News-Letter,* October 31, 1715; Eveleigh to Boone and Berresford, October 7, 1715, in *CSP, AWI,* 1714–15, 297; Chicken, "Journal from Carolina in 1715," 336; Hann, "St. Augustine's Fallout," 185–87; Hahn, *Invention of the Creek Nation*, 85.

7. The South Carolina 1715 census listed the Yamasees' population as 413 men, 345 women, and 462 children, for a total of 1,220 people. During 1717 a Spanish census of the survivors listed approximately 232 men, 191 women, and 174 children, for a total of 597 people; Governor Johnson to the Council of Trade and Plantations, January 12, 1720, in *CSP, AWI,* 1719–20, 302; Hann, "St. Augustine's Fallout," 185–90.

8. Letter of Corcoles, November 28, 1715; Chatelain, *Defenses of Spanish Florida,* 79, 94; TePaske, *Governorship of Spanish Florida,* 72, 79, 82–87, 95, 198, 199.

9. SCCHJ, May 4, 1714, 245; June 9, 1714, 276; February 25, 1715, 385; May 6, 1715, 388; H. A. M. Smith, "Charleston and Charleston Neck," 24, 25 and accompanying map.

10. "Rodd to His Employer in London," 169; Governor Craven to Lord Townshend, May 23, 1715, in *CSP, AWI,* 1714–15, 228; Governor Johnson to the Council of Trade and Plantations, January 12, 1720, in *CSP, AWI,* 1719–20, 302; SCCHJ, May 8, 1715, 399.

11. "Rodd to His Employer in London," 169; Commons House to Boone and Berresford, March 15, 1716, in Salley, *Records in the British Public Record Office,* 6:159; Swanton, *Early History of the Creek Indians,* 33; Bull to the Secretary, August 10, 1715, in Klingberg, "Mystery of the Lost Yamasee Prince," 23; Crane, *Southern Frontier,* 169, 170; *Boston News-Letter,* June 13, 1715.

12. SCCHJ, May 6, 1715, 388, 389; May 8, 1715, 399; Chicken, "Journal from Carolina in 1715," 333, 334.

13. SCCHJ, May 10, 1715, 410; McDowell, *Journals of the Commissioners of the Indian Trade,* May 10, 1717, 179; June 14, 1717, 187, 188; June 17, 1717, 188.

14. SCCHJ, May 6, 1715, 389.

15. Ibid.

16. SCCHJ, May 7, 1715, 391; May 9, 1715, 404; May 10, 1715, 407; Samuel Eveleigh to Boone and Berresford, July 19, 1715, in *CSP, AWI,* 1714–15, 299.

17. SCCHJ, May 7, 1715, 391, 392; May 8, 1715, 399; August 19, 1715, 440; August 24, 1715, 448.

18. SCCHJ, May 7, 1715, 392; "Rodd to His Employer in London," 169. Snow's plantation was located about two miles south of the junction of Fosters Creek and the Back River, at the present-day U.S. Naval Ammunition Depot in Berkeley County. Heitzler, *Goose Creek,* 1:221, 222 (plate 7.17), 223 (plate 7.18); Le Jau to the Secretary, May 21, 1715, in Klingberg, *Chronicle of Le Jau,* 159; Le Jau to the Secretary, August 22, 1715, in Klingberg, *Chronicle of Le Jau,* 162; Le Jau to the Secretary, August 23, 1715, in Klingberg, *Chronicle of Le Jau,* 164.

19. Cooper and McCord, *Statutes,* "Act for the Better Settling and Regulating the Militia," July 19, 1707, 9:625–31; SCCHJ, May 7, 394, 397.

20. Governor and Council of Carolina to the Council of Trade and Plantations, September 17, 1709, in *CSP, AWI,* 1708–9, 466; SCCHJ, May 7, 1715, 395; May 10, 1715, 408.

21. SCCHJ, May 7, 1715, 392. See note 4 of chapter 6 for Woodward's Fort and note 23 of chapter 6 for Port Royal Fort. The fort sites that were designated but not fortified were Joseph Ford's plantation, Richard Godfrey's plantation, and Johns Island; Ford owned land on the west side of the Wando River, northeast of Charles Town. One of his plantations was located on the southwest side of French Quarter Creek, perhaps about two miles southeast of its junction with the east branch of the Cooper River in present-day Berkeley County; Smith, "Quenby and the Eastern Branch of Cooper River," 31. There is no indication that a fort was ever constructed on any of Ford's lands. Robert Fenwick's fort, located on the east side of the Wando River, was the only fortification maintained in that general area; Richard Godfrey's plantation was located near present-day Middleton Gardens, adjoining old Ashley Barony on the west bank of the Ashley River, about eight miles southwest of present-day Summerville. The plantation was later known as Middleton Place. Godfrey was deceased when the war began. A fort that was planned for that location was not mentioned again. H. A. M. Smith, "Ashley River," 115, 116, with accompanying map; De Brahm, *Map of South Carolina and Part of Georgia.* Peter Cattell's plantation, less than a mile downriver, was fortified and garrisoned. There is no record of a fort's being constructed on Johns Island. The fort at John Beamor's plantation at Stono Bridge on the north side of Stono River in present-day Charleston County may have served that purpose. There is the possibility, however, that a fort was built on Johns Island, on or near John

Fenwick's plantation south of Penny's Creek on the eastern end of Johns Island, near the junction of present-day Highways 54 and 700.

22. SCCHJ, May 7, 1715, 392; Bowen, *New and Accurate Map*. J. A. Barnwell, "Southeastern North America," shows Schenkingh's Fort on the east side of a creek, separating it from the "Dutche" (Dorchee) house; "Dauches House" is also shown on the Samuel Cordes plat, McGrady Plat Collection, which places it on the south bank of the Santee River above old Ferguson, which is shown on the Geological Survey map, Eutawville quadrangle, scale 1/62,500, 1942. Schenkingh was granted five hundred acres on a bluff below "dachee bluff" in 1703; Salley, *Warrants for Lands*, 608. That tract of land is shown on "Plan of Skinking Plantation." The plan shows the land located between Rocks Creek on the west, the Santee River on the north, and Greenland Swamp on the east. A north-south trail to the Santee River and a set of buildings on the trail are depicted. The plantation is shown as Schenkingh's on the "Map Showing Several Plantations," and on an Unnamed Plat of the south side of the Santee River and west of Greenland Swamp, It is also shown on "Plan of a Tract of Land Belonging to Thomas Eveleigh"; Salley, "Letters from the Schenckingh Smiths of South Carolina," 5, 6. Schenkingh was thirty-seven years old and was an experienced soldier, having commanded a company in the 1702 invasion of Saint Augustine. Cooper and McCord, *Statutes*, "Act . . . for Satisfying the Debts . . . of the Late Expedition against Saint Augustine," May 8, 1703, 2:207; "Rodd to Boone and Berresford"; Le Jau to the Society, August 22, 1715, in Klingberg, *Chronicle of Le Jau*, 161.

23. Wassamassaw Fort was located on the east side of the Cypress. The Great Cypress Swamp is the head of Ashley River. SCCHJ, May 7, 1715, 392; March 7, 1716, 27, 28; J. A. Barnwell, "Southeastern North America"; H. A. M. Smith, "Upper Ashley," 188, 189, and accompanying map; Cheves, "Izard of South Carolina," 208, 226; C. T. Moore, *Abstracts of Records of the Secretary*, 356. Walter Izard was twenty-three years old. He and his wife, Mary Turgis, had been married two years. They resided further south near the Ashley River.

24. Edisto Bluff Fort was located on the east bank of the Edisto River, below Four Hole Creek; SCCHJ, May 7, 1715, 392; August 5, 1715, 425; March 7, 1716, 27; Auditor General Memorial Books, 5:141; J. A. Barnwell, "Southeastern North America"; Bowen, *New and Accurate Map*.

25. SCCHJ, May 8, 1715, 399.

26. Fenwick owned at least two plantations in Christ Church Parish on the southeast side of the Wando River. Data plantation was located about 5 miles northeast of Mount Pleasant in Charleston County. Laurel Hill, the other plantation, was located about 2 miles further to the northeast, perhaps near present-day Highway 41 about 1.5 miles north of its junction with Highway 17. Salley, *Warrants for Lands*, 36, 466; D. E. H. Smith, "Account of the Tattnall and Fenwick Families," 4; SCCHJ, August 5, 1715, 425; Moore and Simons, *Abstracts of the Wills of the State of South Carolina*, 117; Gregorie, "Map of Christ Church Parish."

27. Richbourg's Fort was about three-quarters of a mile south of Santee River and about four miles southeast of present-day Leneuds Ferry Bridge on Highway 17A. The Huguenots were originally Calvinists, but many of them soon adhered to the Church of England. The parsonage was also used as an inn or tavern for the benefit of travelers. SCCHJ, March 7, 1716, 27, 28; Johnston to the Secretary, January 27, 1716, in Klingberg, *Carolina Chronicle*, 155; Hirsch, *Huguenots of Colonial South Carolina*, 61–63, 63n; Richbourgh to the Society, February 12, 1716, in Pennington, "South Carolina Indian War," February 263; De Brahm, *Map of South Carolina and a Part of Georgia;* Moll, *Map of the Improved Part of Carolina;* James Cook, *Map of the Province of South Carolina.*

28. Wantoot Fort was located at the head of the Cooper River. SCCHJ, August 5, 1715, 425; March 7, 1716, 27, 28; March 10, 1716, 35; March 14, 1716, 36; March 17, 1716, 47, 48; Moore and Simmons, *Abstracts of the Wills of South Carolina*, 60; "Pierre De St. Julien's Last Will and Testament"; J. A. Barnwell, "Southeastern North America"; Bowen, *New and Accurate Map;* "General Plan of the Canal and Its Environs"; Gaillard, "Map of Berkeley and Parts of Charleston and Dorchester Counties."

29. Cattell's Fort was located in Charleston County, about fifteen miles north-northwest of Charles Town, about two-tenths of a mile southeast of the present-day Charleston County line, and a short distance south of the Ashley River. Richard Godfrey's plantation, less than a mile upriver, was ordered fortified and garrisoned, but Cattell's Fort was apparently used instead. SCCHJ, August 5, 1715, 425; March 7, 1716, 27, 28; H. A. M. Smith, "Ashley River," 112, with accompanying map; Moll, *Map of the Improved Part of Carolina.*

30. SCCHJ, August 9, 1715, 429; Elliott's Fort was located about 12 miles west of Charles Town, about 1.3 miles northwest of the conflux of Rantowles Creek and the Wallace River, and about half a mile west of Rantowles Creek near the junction of present-day Highways 17 and 317 in Charleston County. Rantowles Creek is the east branch of the Wallace River, which is a branch of the Stono River. There was a bridge nearby over Rantowles Creek that served the roads from Colleton County to Charles Town. SCCHJ, August 5, 1715, 425; August 9, 1715, 429. Thomas Elliott owned at least two, and perhaps more, plantations on the Stono. The only one that can be pinpointed is the above site, which is shown on De Brahm's 1757 map. Another bridge, LaRoche's Bridge, probably about 1 mile to the west near the same road, spanned the west branch of the Wallace River and was also appointed a garrison. Elliott's fortified plantation probably became a government fort during August 1715. Elliott was a Quaker and had been in South Carolina since before 1696. He and his wife, Sarah, apparently resided a short distance north of Charles Town on "The Neck"; Webber, "Records from the Elliott-Rowland Bible," 57; Moore and Simmons, *Abstracts of the Wills of the State of South Carolina*, 168, 169; Cooper and McCord, *Statutes*, "Additional Act out from the Road on the North Side of Ashley River to the Town of Wiltown . . . ," November 10, 1711, 9:18–21; Cooper and McCord, *Statutes*, "Additional Act to the Several Acts for Making and Repairing

of Highways," June 7, 1712, 9:27; Cooper and McCord, *Statutes*, "Act to ... Keep in Repair the Road ... in Berkeley County ... ," April 28, 1735, 9:89; De Brahm, *Map of South Carolina and a Part of Georgia*.

31. LaRoche's Fort was located near present-day Rantowles and probably on the north side of present-day Highway 17 in Charleston County. It received a government garrison in August 1715. The bridge over the west branch of the Wallace that the fort protected served the roads from Colleton County to Charles Town. There was another bridge about one mile to the east near the same road on Elliott's plantation, spanning Rantowles Creek, which also had a fort and a government garrison. SCCHJ, August 5, 1715, 425; Moore and Simons, *Abstracts of the Wills of the State of South Carolina*, 67. LaRoche's 1701 plat shows the bridge and house site and depicts Wallace River as the "Middle Branch of Stono"; McCrady Plats, no. 4:49.

32. Beamor's Fort was situated about 12.5 miles west of Charles Town in present-day Charleston County. SCCHJ, August 5, 1715, 425; March 7, 1716, 27, 28; Moll, *Map of the Improved Part of Carolina;* "Colored Map of the Coast of South Carolina, Georgia, and Florida" shows the Stono Bridge site; Salley, "Governor Joseph Morton and Some of His Descendants," 114.

33. The Ponds fort was located east of the Great Cypress Swamp at the head of the Ashley River, south of Hurricane Branch, about a mile west of present-day Highway 17A and about six miles southwest of Summerville in Dorchester County. SCCHJ, August 5, 1715, 425; March 7, 1716, 27, 28; J. A. Barnwell, "Southeastern North America"; H. A. M. Smith, "Upper Ashley," 174, 175, and accompanying map; Moll, *Map of the Improved Part of Carolina;* Thornton and Morden, *This New Map*.

34. Nichols Fort may have been located about 6.5 miles north-northwest of present-day Ravenel, near the site where Highway 165 crosses Highway 317, the boundary between Dorchester County and Charleston County; SCCHJ, March 7, 1716, 27, 28; Auditor General Memorial Books, 5:2; Moore and Simons, *Abstracts of the Wills of the State of South Carolina*, 165; Langley, *South Carolina Deed Abstracts*, 1:212, 233, 296, 299, 315; 2:226, 286, 296, 348; 3:160. Stuart, *Map of South Carolina and a Part of Georgia*, shows nearby Drayton and Elliott plantations. The north-south path had been in use for at least twenty years; Thornton and Morden, *This New Map*. The east-west path had been used since about 1705; Cooper and McCord, *Statutes*, "Act for Making a New Road between the North and Middle Branch of Stono River," March 11, 1726, 9:66. Both paths and the crossroads are shown on Moll, *Map of the Improved Part of Carolina*, and James Cook, *Map of the Province of South Carolina*.

35. Willtown Fort was located on Willtown Bluff, about half a mile south of the terminus of the unnumbered western extension of present-day Highways 38 and 55 and about 4.75 miles southwest of Adams Run in Charleston County; SCCHJ, August 5, 1715, 425; March 7, 1716, 27, 28; March 20, 1716, 50; May 3, 1716, 93; May 11, 1716, 103; June 7, 1716, 118; December 8, 1716, 197; Smith, "Willtown or New London," 31, with accompanying map; Moore and Simons, *Abstracts of*

the *Wills of the State of South Carolina,* 128; J. A. Barnwell, "Southeastern North America"; Moll, *Map of the Improved Part of Carolina.*

36. Bennett's Point Fort was located on the north side of the junction of the Ashepoo River and Mosquito Creek, near the southern terminus of Highway 26 in Colleton County; SCCHJ, March 7, 1716, 27, 28; Auditor General Memorial Books, 5:330; Dickinson, *Jonathan Dickinson's Journal,* 75; William Rhett to Capt. Beamour, April 21, 1719, in *CSP, AWI,* 1719–20, 81; De Brahm, *Map of South Carolina and a Part of Georgia.*

37. SCCHJ, March 20, 1716, 51; March 22, 1716, 54. Screven's Fort was located at or near present-day Maryville, across the river from Georgetown in Georgetown County, where Screven initially owned one hundred acres and received an additional five hundred in 1710. Cooper and McCord, *Statutes,* "Act for Establishing Five Ferries . . . ," March 11, 1726, 9:69, 70; Cooper and McCord, *Statutes,* "Act or Laying out a Public Road . . . to Mr. Robert Scriven's Plantation, opposite Georgetown . . . ," September 22, 1733, 9:74; SCCHJ, March 20, 1716, 51; March 22, 1716, 54; Auditor General Memorial Books, 4:364, 366.

38. Hasell's Fort was located south of the Cooper River's junction with Quenby Creek, probably between Middleburg Plantation and Pompion Chapel about thirteen miles southeast of present-day Moncks Corner and about two miles southwest of Huger in Berkeley County. Johnston to the Society, January 27, 1716, in Klingberg, *Carolina Chronicle,* 155; Thomas Hasell to the Society, December 1, 1715, in Pennington, "South Carolina Indian War," 254; Smith, "Quenby and the Eastern Branch of Cooper River," 18, 19, and accompanying map.

39. Maule's Fort was located near the southeast bank of present-day Lake Moultrie, west of Highway 52, and about 3.75 miles north-northeast of Moncks Corner in Berkeley County. Johnston to the Society, January 27, 1716, in Klingberg, *Carolina Chronicle,* 155; Le Jau to the Society, May 21, 1715, in Klingberg, *Chronicle of Le Jau,* 160; "Sketch Map of the Site of St. Johns French Church"; "General Plan of the Canal and Its Environs" marks the site as "31" and as "Glebe Land."

40. Broughton's Mulberry fort was located near the site of the present-day Mulberry Plantation, four miles southeast of present-day Moncks Corner. SCCHJ, March 15, 1716, 38; Le Jau to the Secretary, May 21, 1715, in Klingberg, *Chronicle of Le Jau,* 158, 159; Moore and Simons, *Abstracts of the Wills of the State of South Carolina,* 242, 243; Smith, "Fairlawn Barony," 194–97 and accompanying map; Moll, *Map of the Improved Part of Carolina;* Gregorie, *Records of the Court of Chancery,* 207n, 208n.

41. Chicken's Fort was located about 5.5 miles north of the present-day city of Goose Creek, about a quarter mile west of present-day Highway 791, and about 1.5 miles southwest of the junction of Highway 791 (Old Highway 52) and Highway 9; Le Jau to the Society, May 10, 1715, in Klingberg, *Chronicle of Le Jau,* 153; Le Jau to the Society, May 21, 1715, in Klingberg, *Chronicle of Le Jau,* 159. Chicken's wife was the widow of Thomas Bellamy. Langley, *South Carolina Deed Abstracts,* 2:73; Moll, *Map of the Improved Part of Carolina,* shows the

Bellamy plantation; Chicken, "Journal from Carolina in 1715," 324n. Chicken's plantation was later known as Cedar Grove. The house site is shown on the Cedar Grove Plantation plat, 1799, McGrady Plat Collection. A copy of the plat was kindly provided by Michael J. Heitzler.

42. Moore and Simons, *Abstracts of the Wills of the State of South Carolina*, 102; Le Jau to the Society, May 21, 1715, in Klingberg, *Chronicle of Le Jau*, 158; "Historical Notes," *South Carolina Historical and Genealogical Magazine* 11 (1910):190; Smith, "Radnor, Edmundsbury and Jacksonborough," 46; J. A. Barnwell, "Southeastern North America," shows the fort labeled as "Jackson."

43. Muller, *Treatise Concerning the Elementary Part of Fortification;* Gallardo, "Spaniards and the English Settlement," 134–36; "Plan of King George's Fort at Allatamaha South Carolina."

44. "Plan of King George's Fort at Allatamaha"; J. W. Barnwell, "Fort King George," 197–200; Tunis, *Colonial Living,* 31, 32; SCCHJ, January 26, 1722; Salley, *SCCHJ*, November 5, 1725, 13, 17.

45. SCCHJ, May 7, 395; May 8, 1716, 399; May 10, 1715, 408.

46. SCCHJ, May 7, 1715, 392.

47. Crane, *Southern Frontier,* 95, 96, 124, 160; Samuel Eveleigh to Boone and Berresford, July 19, 1715, in *CSP, AWI,* 1714–15, 298; At a Council, May 25, 1715, in Saunders, *Colonial Records of North Carolina,* 2:180; SCCHJ, August 27, 1715, 452.

48. Webber, "First Governor Moore and His Children," 14, 15; At a Council, May 25, 1715, in Saunders, *Colonial Records of North Carolina,* 2:180.

49. Lt. Governor Spotswood to Secretary Stanhope, May 27, 1715, in *CSP, AWI,* 1714–15, 226, 227; Samuel Eveleigh to Boone and Berresford, October 7, 1715, in *CSP, AWI,* 1714–15, 298; Joseph Boone to Richard Berresford, December 5, 1716, in *CSP, AWI,* 1716–17, 215–17; Spotswood to the Lords Commissioners of Trade, July 15, 1715, in Brock, *Official Letters of Alexander Spotswood,* 119; At a Council, May 26, 1715, in McIlwaine, *Executive Journals of the Council of Colonial Virginia,* 3:399, 400; At a Council, June 20, 1715, in McIlwaine, *Executive Journals of the Council of Colonial Virginia,* 402–4; At a Council, December 7, 1715, in McIlwaine, *Executive Journals of the Council of Colonial Virginia,* 418; At a Council, October 26, 1715, in McIlwaine, *Executive Journals of the Council of Colonial Virginia,* 416; SCCHJ, August 17, 1715, 437.

50. SCCHJ, May 7, 1715, 393, 396; May 8, 1715, 398, 402; May 10, 1715, 408; May 11, 1715, 411; August 26, 1715, 451.

51. SCCHJ, May 8, 1715, 398, 400; May 10, 406, 407.

52. Cooper and McCord, *Statutes,* "Act to Confirm and Justify the Proceedings of the . . . Governor . . . the . . . Deputy Governor, and the Rest of the Members of the Council . . . in Defense of the Province," May 10, 1715, 2:623, 624; SCCHJ, May 10, 1715, 406; May 12, 1715, 413; May 13, 1715, 415.

53. "Rodd to His Employer in London," 169; Abel Kettleby and other planters and merchants trading in Carolina to the Council of Trade and Plantations, July 18, 1715, in *CSP, AWI,* 1714–15, 236.

CHAPTER 8: Northern Indians' Invasion, May–June 1715

1. SCCHJ, May 8, 1715, 399.

2. Le Jau to the Society, May 14, 1715, in Klingberg, *Chronicle of Le Jau,* 157; Le Jau to the Society, May 21, 1715, in Klingberg, *Chronicle of Le Jau,* 158; SCCHJ, May 7, 1715, 395; Bull to the Society, August 10, 1715, in Klingberg, "Mystery of the Lost Yamasee Prince," 23.

3. Webber, "First Governor Moore and His Children," 4–8. Moore's home was located about a quarter of a mile south of Highway 529 and about two miles east of Highway 52, not far from the previous junction of Liberty Hall Road and Old Back River Road; Moll, *Map of the Improved Part of Carolina;* Heitzler, "Boochawee," 36, 37, 42.

4. SCCHJ, May 7, 1715, 392; Le Jau to the Society, May 21, 1715, in Klingberg, *Chronicle of Le Jau,* 159. Hearn's plantation was located about 1.5 miles northeast of Santee in Orangeburg County. Langley, *South Carolina Deed Abstracts,* 3:50; J. A. Barnwell, "Southeastern North America"; Moll, *Map of the Province of Carolina;* Webber, "First Governor Moore and His Children," 21.

5. Barker was a young boy when he arrived in South Carolina with his family about 1695. Salley, *Warrants for Lands,* 486, 487; Edgar, *Biographical Directory of the South Carolina House of Representatives,* 39. The plantation home of Thomas and Rebecca Barker was located less than a quarter mile east of the junction of Highway 52 (Goose Creek Boulevard) and Central Avenue in present-day Goose Creek. The plantation, later known as Button Hall, was a gift to Rebecca from her father, James Moore Sr.; Heitzler, "Boochawee," 64, 65, 68; Le Jau to the Secretary, May 21, 1715, in Klingberg, *Chronicle of Le Jau,* 159; Bull to the Society, August 10, 1715, in Klingberg, "Mystery of the Lost Yamasee Prince," 24; Ramsay, *Ramsay's History of South Carolina,* 2:291.

6. Le Jau to the Society, May 21, 1715, in Klingberg, *Chronicle of Le Jau,* 158; Governor Johnson to the Council of Trade, January 12, 1720, in *CSP, AWI,* 1719–20, 301, 302; Fogelson, "Cherokee in the East," 337, 338, 346; "Rodd to Boone and Berresford," 320.

7. Governor Johnson to the Council of Trade, January 12, 1720, in *CSP, AWI,* 1719–20, 301, 302; Merrell, *Indians' New World,* 92–94, 109; Rudes, Blumer, and May, "Catawba and Neighboring Groups," 301, 302 (fig. 1), 303, 308–10, 315–18; Urban and Jackson, "Social Organization," 704; D. S. Brown, *Catawba Indians,* 98, 124. For a discussion regarding the distinction between Cheraw and Saraw, see Beck, *Chiefdoms, Collapse, and Coalescence,* 247–51. The stated locations of the northern Indian towns during May and June 1715 are approximate; J. A. Barnwell, "Southeastern North America"; Milling, *Red Carolinians,* 203, 209, 212–16, 219, 222.

8. Lefler, *New Voyage to Carolina,* 36, 39, 40, 197, 199, 201, 202; Bonnefoy, "Journal of Antoine Bonnefoy," 244; Gallay, *Indian Slave Trade,* 184, 185; A. Moore,

Nairne's Muskhogean Journals, 51–53; Fogelson, "Cherokee in the East," 339 (fig. 2); Rudes, Blumer, and May, "Catawba and Neighboring Groups," 304, 305 (fig. 5); DeMallie, "Tutelo and Neighboring Groups," 295; D. S. Brown, *Catawba Indians,* 16; Le Jau to the Secretary, August 22, 1715, in Klingberg, *Chronicle of Le Jau,* 160, 161; Hudson, *Southeastern Indians,* 244, 245, 260–62, 380; Milling, *Red Carolinians,* 5, 6, 26, 27, 216; Burke, "Eighteenth-Century English Trade Guns in the South," 6–11, 15.

9. Le Jau to the Society, May 21, 1715, in Klingberg, *Chronicle of Le Jau,* 158, 159.

10. Moll, *Map of the Improved Part of Carolina;* J. A. Barnwell, "Southeastern North America"; Stuart, *Map of South Carolina and a Part of Georgia;* James Cook, *Map of the Province of South Carolina;* Cooper and McCord, *Statutes,* "Acts Relating to Roads, Bridges and Ferries," June 7, 1712, 9:26–27.

11. Le Jau to the Society, May 21, 1715, in Klingberg, *Chronicle of Le Jau,* 159; Le Jau to the Society, August 22, 1715, in Klingberg, *Chronicle of Le Jau,* 160, 161.

12. J. A. Barnwell, "Southeastern North America," shows the general location of the battle site, southeast of Hearn's Plantation. The exact site of the battle is depicted on Mouzon et al., *Accurate Map of North and South Carolina;* Le Jau to the Society, May 21, 1715, in Klingberg, *Chronicle of Le Jau,* 159; Le Jau to the Society, August 22, 1715, in Klingberg, *Chronicle of Le Jau,* 160, 161; Le Jau to the Society, August 23, 1715, in Klingberg, *Chronicle of Le Jau,* 163; Samuel Eveleigh to Boone and Berresford, July 19, 1715, in *CSP, AWI,* 1714–15, 297; Bull to the Society, August 10, 1715, in Klingberg, "Mystery of the Lost Yamasee Prince," 23, 24; "Rodd to Boone and Berresford," 319. Young Goose Creek planters James Beard and William Rowsham Jr. were among those that were killed; Gregorie, *Records of the Court of Chancery,* 42, 204.

13. Bull to the Society, August 10, 1715, in Klingberg, "Mystery of the Lost Yamasee Prince," 23, 24; Le Jau to the Society, May 21, 1715, in Klingberg, *Chronicle of Le Jau,* 159; Le Jau to the Society, August 22, 1715, in Klingberg, *Chronicle of Le Jau,* 160, 161; Committee of the Assembly to Boone and Berresford, August 6, 1716, in *CSP, AWI,* 1716–17 221.

14. Le Jau to the Society, May 10, 1715, in Klingberg, *Chronicle of Le Jau,* 153; Le Jau to the Society, May 21, 1715, in Klingberg, *Chronicle of Le Jau,* 158, 159; Le Jau to the Society, August 23, 1715, in Klingberg, *Chronicle of Le Jau,* 163. For Snow's plantation see note 18, chapter 7.

15. Le Jau to the Society, May 21, 1715, in Klingberg, *Chronicle of Le Jau,* 159; Le Jau to the Society, May 10, 1715, in Klingberg, *Chronicle of Le Jau,* 154.

16. Le Jau to the Society, May 21, 1715, in Klingberg, *Chronicle of Le Jau,* 158, 159. For Wantoot plantation see note 28, Chapter 7; For Mulberry Plantation see note 40, chapter 7; Thomas Broughton to Nathaniel Broughton, November 1715, in D. E. H. Smith, "Broughton Letters," 173, 174; SCCHJ, December 11, 1717, 417. For Chicken's plantation see note 41, chapter 7.

17. Klingberg, Le Jau to the Society, August 22, 1715, in *Chronicle of Le Jau,* 161; "Rodd to Boone and Berresford," 319; Eveleigh to Boone and Berresford, July 19, 1715, in *CSP, AWI,* 1714–15, 297. For Schenkingh's Fort see note 22, chapter 7.

18. Le Jau to the Society, August 22, 1715, in Klingberg, *Chronicle of Le Jau*, 161; Le Jau to the Society, August 23, 1715, in Klingberg, *Chronicle of Le Jau*, 163; "Rodd to Boone and Berresford," 319; Lefler, *New Voyage to Carolina*, 53, 207–9; Mahon, "Anglo-American Methods of Indian Warfare," 257, 260, 261.

19. "Rodd to Boone and Berresford," 319; Le Jau to the Society, August 22, 1715, in Klingberg, *Chronicle of Le Jau*, 161; Le Jau to the Society, August 23, 1715, in Klingberg, *Chronicle of Le Jau*, 163; Bull to the Secretary, August 10, 1715, in Klingberg, "Mystery of the Lost Yamasee Prince," 24; SCCHJ, August 20, 1715, 442.

20. Langley, *South Carolina Deed Abstracts*, 2:73; *Yearbook of the City of Charleston 1894*, 315, 324n2; "Rodd to Boone and Berresford," 319; Edgar, *Biographical Directory of the South Carolina House of Representatives*, 31, 32, 34, 39; Poyas, *Olden Times of Carolina*, 110, 111; Eveleigh to Boone and Berresford, July 19, 1715, in *CSP, AWI*, 1714–15, 297. For the location of Woodward's Fort, see note 4 of Chapter 6; Le Jau to the Society, August 22, 1715, in Klingberg, *Chronicle of Le Jau*, 161; Le Jau to the Society, August 23, 1715, in Klingberg, *Chronicle of Le Jau*, 163; SCCHJ, May 8, 1715, 399.

21. The Cypress is now known as the Great Cypress Swamp. For the Ponds plantation fort, see note 33, chapter 7; for Izard's Wassamassaw cowpen fort, see note 23, chapter 7; for Edisto Bluff plantation fort, see note 24, chapter 7.

22. "Rodd to Boone and Berresford," 319; Eveleigh to Boone and Berresford, July 19, 1715, in *Calendar of State Papers, Colonial Office Series: America and the West Indies*, ed. W. Noel Sainsbury et al., 1714–15, 297; J. A. Barnwell, "Southeastern North America," depicts the battle site to the north of "Percivals" (Ponds) and labels it as "The Indians defeated in 1715"; H. A. M. Smith, "Upper Ashley," 179, 180, and accompanying map.

23. Le Jau to the Society, August 22, 1715, in Klingberg, *Chronicle of Le Jau*, 161; Le Jau to the Society, August 23, 1715, in Klingberg, *Chronicle of Le Jau*, 163; At a Council, October 18, 1715, in McIlwaine, *Executive Journals of the Council of Colonial Virginia*, 3:412; At a Council, February 22, 1716, 3: 421, 422; McDowell, *Journals of the Commissioners of the Indian Trade*, May 9, 1717, 177–79.

24. "Rodd to Boone and Berresford," 319, 320; Eveleigh to Boone and Berresford, July 19, 1715, in *CSP, AWI*, 1714–15, 297, 298.

25. Eveleigh to Boone and Berresford, July 19, 1715, *Calendar of State Papers, Colonial Office Series: America and the West Indies*, ed. W. Noel Sainsbury et al., 1714–1715; "Rodd to Boone and Berresford," 319, 320; Le Jau to the Society, August 22, 1715, in Klingberg, *Chronicle of Le Jau*, 161; Le Jau to the Society, August 23, 1715, in Klingberg, *Chronicle of Le Jau*, 163, 164.

26. Eveleigh to Boone and Berresford, July 19, 1715, in *CSP, AWI*, 1714–15, 298; "Rodd to Boone and Berresford," 320; Gallay, *Indian Slave Trade*, 185–89.

27. Le Jau to the Society, August 22, 1715, in Klingberg, *Chronicle of Le Jau*, 161; Eveleigh to Boone and Berresford, July 19, 1715, in *CSP, AWI*, 1714–15, 298; SCCHJ, December 11, 1717, 417; August 20, 1715, 441, 442; May 11, 1716, 103.

28. Lefler, *New Voyage to Carolina*, 53, 207–9; Hudson, *Southeastern Indians*, 240–44,

247, 249; Swanton, *Indians of the Southeastern United States,* 690, 691, 695; Fogelson, "Cherokee in the East," 346, 347.

29. Cooper and McCord, *Statutes,* "Act for the Better Settling and Regulating the Militia," July 19, 1707, 9:625–31; Peterson, *Arms and Armor in Colonial America,* 159, 160, 162.

30. SCCHJ, August 20, 1715, 441.

31. Le Jau to the Society, August 22, 1715, in Klingberg, *Chronicle of Le Jau,* 161; Le Jau to the Society, August 23, 1715, in Klingberg, *Chronicle of Le Jau,* 163, 164; Bull to the Secretary, August 10, 1715, in Klingberg, "Mystery of the Lost Yamasee Prince," 24; At a Council, July 18, 1715, in McIlwaine, *Executive Journals of the Council of Colonial Virginia,* 3:406; At a Council, October 18, 1715, in McIlwaine, *Executive Journals of the Council of Colonial Virginia,* 3:411, 412; At a Council, February 22, 1716, in McIlwaine, *Executive Journals of the Council of Colonial Virginia,* 3: 421, 422; Committee of the Assembly to Boone and Berresford, August 6, 1716, in *CSP, AWI,* 1716–17, 221, 222.

32. Le Jau to the Society, March 19, 1716, in Klingberg, *Chronicle of Le Jau,* 173.

CHAPTER 9: Western Indians' Raid, July 1715

1. Eveleigh to Boone and Berresford, July 19, 1715, in *CSP, AWI,* 1714–15, 298; Commissioners appointed by the Commons House to Boone and Berresford, August 25, 1715, in Salley, *Records in the British Public Record Office,* 6:130; At a Council, May 25, 1715, in Saunders, *Colonial Records of North Carolina,* 2:180; Le Jau to the Society, August 22, 1715, in Klingberg, *Chronicle of Le Jau,* 161; *Boston News-Letter,* September 5, 1715; "Rodd to Boone and Berresford," 321.

2. "Rodd to Boone and Berresford," 321; Eveleigh to Boone and Berresford, July 19, 1715, in *CSP, AWI,* 1714–15, 298; Le Jau to the Society, August 22, 1715, in Klingberg, *Chronicle of Le Jau,* 161, 162; Mosley, *New and Correct Map of the Province of North Carolina.*

3. Eveleigh to Boone and Berresford, July 19, 1715, in *CSP, AWI,* 1714–15, 298, 299. For Richbourg's fortified parsonage, see note 27 of Chapter 7; Cooper and McCord, *Statutes,* "Additional Act for the Making and Mending of Roads and Highways . . . ," November 28, 1709, 9:12; De Brahm, *Map of South Carolina and a Part of Georgia.*

4. Le Jau to the Society, August 23, 1715, in Klingberg, *Chronicle of Le Jau,* 164; Commissioners appointed by the Commons House to Boone and Berresford, August 25, 1715, in Salley, *Records in the British Public Record Office,* 6:131.

5. Commissioners appointed by the Commons House to Boone and Berresford, August 25, 1715, in Salley, *Records in the British Public Record Office,* 6:130, 131; Le Jau to the Society, August 23, 1715, in Klingberg, *Chronicle of Le Jau,* 164; Governor Johnson to the Council of Trade and Plantations, January 12, 1720, in *CSP, AWI,* 1719–20, 302; J. A. Barnwell, "Southeastern North America."

6. Memorial and Representation of Mary Bosomworth, August 10, 1747, Colonial

Records of the State of Georgia, 36:260; Walker, "Creek Confederacy before Removal," 388; Hahn, *Life and Times of Mary Musgrove*, 14, 53, 54.

7. SCCHJ, August 20, 1715, 441; Commissioners appointed by the Commons House to Boone and Berresford, August 25, 1715, in Salley, *Records in the British Public Record Office*, 6:129–31.

8. A. Moore, *Nairne's Muskhogean Journals*, 42; Le Jau to the Secretary, May 21, 1715, in Klingberg, *Chronicle of Le Jau*, 158. For Jackson's Pon Pon Fort, see note 42 of chapter 7.

9. Eveleigh to Boone and Berresford, July 19, 1715, in *CSP, AWI,* 1714–15, 299; Commissioners appointed by the Commons House to Boone and Berresford, August 25, 1715, in Salley, *Records in the British Public Record Office*, 6:129. Livingston's land abutted the south and east side of Willtown. Smith, "Willtown," accompanying map; Zierden, Linder, and Anthony, *Willtown*, 127 (fig. 61). For the Huspaw King's letter, see note 11 of chapter 6.

10. Eveleigh to Boone and Berresford, July 19, 1715, in *CSP, AWI,* 1714–15, 299; Commissioners appointed by the Commons House to Boone and Berresford, August 25, 1715, in Salley, *Records in the British Public Record Office*, 6:129; "Rodd to Boone and Berresford," 322nn1–2; Salley, "Governor Joseph Morton and Some of His Descendants," 110, 111; Langley, *South Carolina Deed Abstracts,* 2:82; Salley, *Warrants for Lands,* 571, 573, 600, 618. There is a possibility that Boone's ship was located on Boone's Barony, on the west side of the Edisto River, about four miles north of Pon Pon Bridge; Smith, "Boone's Barony," 74, 75, and accompanying map. The plantations of Blake, Boone, and Morton are shown on Moll, *Map of the Improved Part of Carolina.* Eve's plantation was on the south side of Toogoodoo Creek; Moore and Simmons, *Abstracts of the Wills of the State of South Carolina,* 84.

11. Commissioners appointed by the Commons House to Boone and Berresford, August 25, 1715, in Salley, *Records in the British Public Record Office*, 6:129. For Beamor's Fort see note 32 of chapter 7; Cooper and McCord, *Statutes,* "Act for Building a Bridge and Causeway . . . to the Land of Madame Elizabeth Blake," June 7, 1712, 9:24. The plantations of Farr and Beamor are shown on Moll, *Map of the Improved Part of Carolina.*

12. Lt. Governor Spotswood to [Secretary Stanhope?], October 24, 1715, in *CSP, AWI,* 1714–15, 316.

13. Samuel Eveleigh to Boone and Berresford, July 19, 1715, in *CSP, AWI,* 1714–15, 299; Johnston to the Society, January 27, 1716, in Klingberg, "Papers of Commissary Gideon Johnston," 155; Bull to the Society, August 10, 1715, in Klingberg, "Mystery of the Lost Prince," 24; Le Jau to the Society, August 23, 1715, in Klingberg, *Chronicle of Le Jau,* 164; "Rodd to Boone and Berresford," 322.

14. Eveleigh to Boone and Berresford, July 19, 1715, in *CSP, AWI,* 1714–15, 299.

15. Ibid.; Commissioners appointed by the Commons House to Boone and Berresford, August 25, 1715, in Salley, *Records in the British Public Record Office*, 6:131.

16. Swanton, *Early History of the Creek Indians,* 101.

CHAPTER 10: Scout Boatmen, July–October 1715

1. Letter of Corcoles, January 25, 1716; Commissioners appointed by the Commons House to Boone and Berresford, August 25, 1715, in *CSP, AWI,* 1714–15, 300; Governor Craven to Lord Townshend, May 23, 1715, in *CSP, AWI,* 1714–15, 228; Bull to the Society, August 10, 1715, in Klingberg, "Mystery of the Lost Yamasee Prince," 23, 24; Guy to the Society, September 20 1715, in Pennington, "South Carolina Indian War," 255; Le Jau to the Society, August 22, 1715, in Klingberg, *Chronicle of Le Jau,* 161; Le Jau to the Society, in Klingberg, *Chronicle of Le Jau,* October 3, 1715, 167.

2. Fenwick's plantation was located on the northeastern side of Johns Island near the junction of present-day Highways 54 and 700; Salley, *SCCHJ,* August 15, 1701, 6; August 21, 1702, 68; April 30, 1703, 80; June 17, 1707, 36; SCCHJ, December 15, 1713, 219; Cooper and McCord, *Statutes,* "Act . . . Look-Outs . . . ," July 5, 1707, 2:300, 301; Cooper and McCord, *Statutes,* "Act for Appointing Two Scout Canoes, and Providing Necessities for the Same," December 18, 1713, 2:607–9.

3. Dampier, *New Voyage Round the World,* 1:29, 214, 215; Lefler, *New Voyage to Carolina,* 16, 17, 103; Chandler and Knight, *Colonial Records of the State of Georgia,* 1:219, 2:109, 3:124; *South Carolina Gazette,* May 17, 1740. Canoes are depicted in Gordon, *View of Savannah;* Public Treasurer, fols. 32, 77, 78, 113; Chapelle, *American Small Sailing Craft,* 14.

4. Chapelle, *American Small Sailing Craft,* 21. *Piragua* was commonly written as *pettyager, pirogue, periagoe,* etc.; Dampier, *New Voyage Round the World* 1:29; F. Moore, "Voyage to Georgia," 1:112; Lefler, *New Voyage to Carolina,* 16, 17, 103. Periguas are depicted on *A View of the Town of Savannah.* In Hvidt, *Von Reck's Voyage,* a period drawing of a cargo piragua with sails is shown on page 71 and a piragua without sails being rowed by four men upstream on the Savannah River is shown as figure B on page 85. Salley, *SCCHJ,* August 21, 1702, 69; May 5, 1703, 85; May 7, 1703, 89.

5. Jones, "John Martin Boltzius' Trip to Charleston," 92, 93, 96, 97; Cooper and McCord, *Statutes,* "Additional Act . . . for Making and Repairing of Highways," June 7, 1712, 9:26; Cooper and McCord, *Statutes,* "Act for Continuing a Road to Edisto Island . . . ," June 12, 1714, 9:35; J. W. Barnwell, "Fort King George," 195–97; V. S. Wood, "Georgia Navy's Dramatic Victory," 176n22, 179n31, 184n37, 185n41, 188n51; Public Treasurer, fol. 77.

6. Eveleigh to Boone and Berresford, July 19, 1715, in *CSP, AWI,* 1714–15, 296, 297; Fischer, *Champlain's Dream,* 111, 658n17; Chapelle, *American Small Sailing Craft,* 14, 22, 23, 41, 42 (fig. 15); SCCHJ, March 7, 1716, 27. An original early whaleboat is on display at the Interpretation Center, Red Bay National Historic Site, Labrador, Canada. A copy of a period painting of a two-masted whaleboat built for military use, ca. 1778, is shown on Franklin and Malo, "Rediscovering Fort Haldimand."

7. Letter of Corcoles, November 28, 1715; Eveleigh to Boone and Berresford, ca. July 1715, in *CSP, AWI,* 1714–15, 297; Eveleigh to Boone and Berresford, July 19, 1715, in *CSP, AWI,* 1714–15, 299; *Boston News-Letter,* October 31, 1715; Le Jau to the Secretary, October 3, 1715, in Klingberg, *Chronicle of Le Jau,* 167.

8. SCCHJ, August 5, 1715, 424; Eveleigh to Boone and Berresford, July 19, 1715, in *CSP, AWI,* 1714–15, 299.

9. Eveleigh to Boone and Berresford, July 19, 1715, in *CSP, AWI,* 1714–15, 299; SCCHJ, October 31, 1709, 460; Salley, *Warrants for Lands,* 601, 604.

10. Eveleigh to Boone and Berresford, October 7, 1715, in *CSP, AWI,* 1714–15, 296, 297; Bull to the Society, October 31, 1715, in Pennington, "South Carolina Indian War," 260.

11. Bull to the Society, October 31, 1715, in Pennington, "South Carolina Indian War," 260; *Boston News-Letter,* September 26, 1715; Eveleigh to Boone and Berresford, October 7, 1715, in *CSP, AWI,* 1714–15, 296, 297.

12. Le Jau to the Society, October 3, 1715, in Klingberg, *Chronicle of Le Jau,* 167; Eveleigh to Boone and Berresford, October 7, 1715, in *CSP, AWI,* 1714–15, 297; *Boston News-Letter,* October 31, 1715.

13. *Boston News-Letter,* October 31, 1715; Eveleigh to Boone and Berresford, October 7, 1715, in *CSP, AWI,* 1714–15, 297.

CHAPTER 11: Reorganization, Late Summer 1715

1. Representation of inhabitants of South Carolina to the King, April 30, 1717, in *CSP, AWI,* 1716–17, 291; Governor Johnson to the Council of Trade and Plantation, January 12, 1720, in *CSP, AWI,* 1719–29, 300, 301; Commissioners appointed by the Commons House to Boone and Berresford, August 25, 1715, in *CSP, AWI,* 1714–15, 301; SCCHJ, August 5, 1715, 425; December 11, 1716, 198; Cooper and McCord, *Statutes,* "Act for the Better Relief of the Poor of the Province," December 12, 1712, 2:593–98; Le Jau et al. to the Society, October 13, 1715, in Klingberg, *Carolina Chronicle,* 147; Johnston to the Society, November 19, 1714, in Klingberg, *Carolina Chronicle,* 143, 144; December 19, 1715, 150, 151; January 27, 1716, 155; Halsey, *Historical Charleston on a Map.*

2. Johnston to the Society, January 27, 1716, in Klingberg, *Carolina Chronicle,* 155; Gregorie, *Records of the Court of Chancery,* 136–39; *Boston News-Letter,* September 26, 1715; Le Jau to the Society, August 23, 1715, in Klingberg, *Chronicle of Le Jau,* 166; Guy to the Society, September 20, 1715, in Pennington, "South Carolina Indian War," 255.

3. "Rodd to His Employer," 169; Webber, "Records of the Quakers in Charles Town," 30; Merrens and Terry, "Dying in Paradise," 540.

4. Le Jau to the Society, August 23, 1715, in Klingberg, *Chronicle of Le Jau,* 164; Merrens and Terry, "Dying in Paradise," 534, 540–46, 549, 550; Waring, "Colonial Medicine in Georgia and South Carolina," 143, 145.

5. Waring, "Colonial Medicine in Georgia and South Carolina," 143, 145; Le Jau to the Society, August 23, 1715, in Klingberg, *Chronicle of Le Jau,* 164.

6. Johnston to the Society, January 27, 1716, in Klingberg, *Carolina Chronicle*, 155; Le Jau to the Society, May 21, 1715, in Klingberg, *Chronicle of Le Jau*, 159, 160.

7. Hasell to the Secretary, May 26, 1715, 242, in Williams, ed. *Letters from the Clergy of the Anglican Church in South Carolina*; Johnston to the Society, January 27, 1716, in Klingberg, *Carolina Chronicle*, 155; Hasell to the Society, December 1, 1715, in Pennington, "South Carolina Indian War," 254; Bull to the Society, August 10, 1715, in Klingberg, "Mystery of the Lost Yamasee Prince," 24, 25.

8. Le Jau to the Society, October 3, 1715, in Klingberg, *Chronicle of Le Jau*, 167; Le November 28, 1715, 169; Bull to the Society, October 31, 1715, in Pennington, "South Carolina Indian War," 260; Cooper and McCord, *Statutes*, "Act . . . to Sell and Convey the Old Glebe Land at Chehaw . . . ," July 25, 1761, 4:152; Commissioners appointed by the Commons House to Boone and Berresford, August 25, 1715, in *CSP, AWI*, 1714–15, 302.

9. SCCHJ, August 2, 1715, 419, 420; August 9, 1715, 430, 431.

10. SCCHJ, February 24, 1715, 372, 373; May 13, 1715, 414; Governor Craven to Lord Townsend, May 23, 1715, in *CSP, AWI*, 1714–15, 227–29; Abel Kettleby and other planters and merchants to the Council of Trade and Plantations, July 18, 1715, in *CSP, AWI*, 1714–15, 236–38; Eveleigh to Boone and Berresford, July 19, 1715, in *CSP, AWI*, 1714–15, 298; Council of Trade and Plantations to Secretary Stanhope, July 19, 1715, in *CSP, AWI*, 1714–15, 239; Commissioners appointed by the Commons House to Boone and Berresford, August 25, 1715, in *CSP, AWI*, 1714–15, 299–302; Council of Trade and Plantations to the Proprietors, July 14, 1715, in *CSP, AWI*, 1714–15, 231.

11. Lords Proprietors of Carolina to the Council of Trade and Plantations, July 15, 1715, in *CSP, AWI*, 1714–15, 231, 232; Assembly of South Carolina to Boone and Berresford, June 29, 1716, in *CSP, AWI*, 1716–17, 135; SCCHJ, April 20, 1716, 71.

12. Council of Trade and Plantations to Secretary Stanhope, July 19, 1715, in *CSP, AWI*, 1714–15, 238.

13. *CSP, AWI*, 1714–15, 238, 239; Council of Trade and Plantations to Secretary Stanhope, July 15, 1715, in *CSP, AWI*, 1714–15, 232; Address of the Representatives of South Carolina to the King, June 12, 1716, in *CSP, AWI*, 1716–17, 259; Assembly of South Carolina to [Boone and Berresford?], June [29?], 1716, in *CSP, AWI*, 1716–17, 135–38.

14. SCCHJ, August 6, 1715, 427; August 20, 1715, 442; March 7, 1716, 26; June 11, 1716, 124; Boone and Berresford to the Council of Trade and Plantations, December 5, 1716, in *CSP, AWI*, 1716–17, 215–17; Extract of a letter from South Carolina, August 30, 1715, in *CSP, AWI*, 1714–15, 222; Spotswood to Secretary Stanhope, October 24, 1715, in Brock, *Official Letters of Alexander Spotswood*, 131, 132; Spotswood to the Lords of Trade, October 24, 1715, in Brock, *Official Letters of Alexander Spotswood*, 135, 136.

15. SCCHJ, August 5, 1715, 424, 425; August 27, 1715, 456; Le Jau to the Society, August 23, 1715, in Klingberg, *Chronicle of Le Jau*, 164; Eveleigh to Boone and Berresford, July 19, 1715, in *CSP, AWI*, 1714–15, 299; Jno. Tate to John

Duddleston, September 16, 1715, in *CSP, AWI,* 1714–15, 351; Commissioners appointed by the Commons House to Boone and Berresford, August 25, 1715, in Salley, *Records in the British Public Record Office,* 6:132; Cooper and McCord, *Statutes,* "Act to Raise Forces to Prosecute the War against Our Indian Enemies . . . ," August 27, 1715, 2:627. That statute cannot now be found, and the Commons House Journals are used to reconstruct it.

16. SCCHJ, August 5, 1715, 424, 425; August 20, 1715, 441; April 27, 1716, 88; May 3, 1716, 93; Eveleigh to Boone and Berresford, October 7, 1715, in *CSP, AWI,* 1714–15, 299; Chicken, "Journal from Carolina in 1715," 324–26; Gregorie, *Records of the Court of Chancery,* 273n; Bull to the Society, May 16, 1716, in Pennington, "South Carolina Indian War," 265.

17. SCCHJ, August 5, 1715, 424, 425; Commissioners Appointed by the Commons House to Boone and Berresford, in *CSP, AWI,* 1714–15, August 25, 1715, 301; Tate to Duddleston, September 16, 1715, in *CSP, AWI,* 1714–15, 351. For Fenwick's Fort see note 26 of chapter 7; for Wantoot Fort see note 28 of chapter 7.

18. SCCHJ, August 5, 1715, 424, 425.

19. Ibid. For the Ponds Fort, see note 33 of chapter 7; for the Edisto Bluff Fort, see note 24 of Chapter 7; for Cattell's Fort see note 29 of chapter 7; for Elliott's Fort see note 30 of chapter 7; for LaRoche's Bridge Fort, see note 31 of chapter 7; for Beamor's Stono Bridge Fort, see note 32 of chapter 7; for Willtown Fort, see note 35 of chapter 7.

20. For Port Royal Fort, see note 23 of chapter 6; for De Richbourg's Fort see note 27 of chapter 7; for Wassamassaw Fort see note 23 of chapter 7; for Bennett's Point Fort, see note 36 of chapter 7; for Nichols's Fort see note 34 of chapter 7. For the private forts—Screven's, Hasell's, Maule's, Broughton's Mulberry, Chicken's, and Jackson's Pon Pon—see notes 37–42, chapter 7.

21. SCCHJ, August 5, 1715, 425, 426; Le Jau to the Society, November 28, 1715, in Klingberg, *Chronicle of Le Jau,* 169.

22. SCCHJ, August 9, 1715, 430, 431; August 10, 1715, 432; August 12, 1715, 434; August 20, 1715, 441; December 5, 1717, 392; receipt signed by Edmund Bellinger, June 29, 1717, in Wills, Inventories and Miscellaneous Records, vol. 56.

23. SCCHJ, August 24, 1715, 448.

24. SCCHJ, August 20, 1715, 441; Cooper and McCord, *Statutes,* "Act for Raising Forces to Prosecute the War against Our Indian Enemies . . . ," March 24, 1716, 2:636, 637.

25. SCCHJ, August 5, 1715, 425; Cooper and McCord, *Statutes,* "Act to Raise the Sum of Thirty Thousand Pounds . . . ," August 27, 1715, 2:627–33.

26. SCCHJ, August 9, 1715, 431; *Boston News-Letter,* September 5, 1715; September 26, 1715; October 31, 1715; Jno. Tate to John Duddleston, September 16, 1715, in *CSP, AWI,* 1714–15, 351; Le Jau to the Society, November 28, 1715, in Klingberg, *Chronicle of Le Jau,* 169.

27. SCCHJ, August 9, 1715, 431; Ames, "Cantey Family," 210, 211; Gregorie, *Records of the Court of Chancery,* 239n; Eveleigh to Boone and Berresford, October 7, 1715, in *CSP, AWI,* 1714–15, 296; Jervey and FitzSimons, "Items Relating to

Charles Town, S.C., ," 75–78. Fenwick's wife was Elizabeth Gibbs; D. E. H. Smith, "Account of the Tattnall and Fenwick Families," 13–16.

28. SCCHJ, August 9, 1715, 431; Eveleigh to Boone and Berresford, October 7, 1715, in *CSP, AWI,* 1714–15, 296; Cooper and McCord, *Statutes,* "Act . . . to Sell and Convey the Old Glebe Land at Chehaw . . . ," July 25, 1761, 4:152.

29. SCCHJ, August 9, 1715, 431; Eveleigh to Boone and Berresford, October 7, 1715, in *CSP, AWI,* 1714–15, 296; Cooper and McCord, *Statutes,* "Act for . . . Continuing the Road Port Royal . . . ," June 12, 1714, 9:34; Cooper and McCord, *Statutes,* "Act for Establishing a Ferry . . . over Combahee River . . . ," September 22, 1733, 9:81, explains that in 1733 John Barton owned Jackson's old plantation. De Brahm, *Map of South Carolina and a Part of Georgia,* shows the site (tract marked 87) of Barton's plantation.

30. Kettleby and other planters and merchants . . . to the Council of Trade and Plantations, July 18, 1715, in *CSP, AWI,* 1714–15, 236.

CHAPTER 12: Cherokee Expedition, November 1715–February 1716

1. SCCHJ, May 7, 1715, 391; May 9, 1715, 404; May 10, 1715, 407; August 6, 1715, 426; Tate to Duddleston, September 16, 1715, in *CSP, AWI,* 1714–15, 351; Committee of the Assembly of Carolina to Boone and Berresford, August 6, 1716, in *CSP, AWI,* 1716–17, 219. For the Cherokees' participation in the invasion of South Carolina, see chapter 8.

2. SCCHJ, August 6, 1715, 426; Eveleigh to Boone and Berresford, July 19, 1715, in *CSP, AWI,* 1714–15, 299; "Rodd to Boone and Berresford," 322; Governor Johnson to the Council of Trade and Plantations, January 12, 1720, in *CSP, AWI,* 1719–20, 302; Fogelson, "Cherokee in the East," 337–39; Bull, "Southeastern North America"; Hunter, "Cherokee Nation and the Traders' Path"; Woolley, "Cherokee Country prior to 1776"; Herbert, "New Mapp of His Majestys Flourishing Province"; Mouzon et al., *Accurate Map of North and South Carolina.*

3. Fogelson, "Cherokee in the East," 338, 341, 346, 347; Chicken, "Journal from Carolina in 1715," 330, 331, 334, 335, 344; Assembly of S. Carolina to [Boone and Berresford?], March 15, 1716, in *CSP, AWI,* 1716–17, 50.

4. Le Jau to the Society, November 28, 1715, in Klingberg, *Chronicle of Le Jau,* 169; Commons House to Boone and Berresford, March 15, 1716, in Salley, *Records in the British Public Record Office,* 6:156, 157; Crane, *Southern Frontier,* 179; McDowell, *Journals of the Commissioners of the Indian Trade,* May 14, 1713, 45; November 7, 1716, 123; January 14, 1717, 146; January 26, 1717, 153; January 29, 1717, 154; January 30, 1717, 155, 156; February 5, 1717, 158; May 9, 1717, 178; Chicken, "Journal from Carolina in 1715," 337; Fogelson, "Cherokee in the East," 338, 341.

5. Cooper and McCord, *Statutes,* "Act to Raise Forces to Prosecute the War against Our Indian Enemies . . . ," August 27, 1715, 2:627. That statute may have provided for an expedition to be organized to invade the Lower and Upper Creek towns, but it cannot now be found; Crane, *Southern Frontier,* 180; Le Jau to

the Society, November 28, 1715, in Klingberg, *Chronicle of Le Jau*, 169; Chicken, "Journal from Carolina in 1715," 324–27, 326n4, 348; SCCHJ, April 27, 1716, 87; B. J. Wood, "'Constant Attendance on God's Alter,'" 206; Edgar, *Biographical Directory of the South Carolina House of Representatives*, 50, 53; Salley, "Bull Family of South Carolina," 77–79; Sirmans, *Colonial South Carolina*, 81, 169, 191, 198, 199, 287.

6. Chicken, "Journal from Carolina in 1715," 324–26.

7. The northern route of the Savannah Path generally followed the present-day route of S.C. Highway 61, to the general vicinity of U.S. Highway 78. It then paralleled the route of Highway 78 west-northwest to the vicinity of U.S. Highway 278. The path then generally followed 278 to Savannah Town. Barnwell, "Southeastern North America"; Nairne, *Map of South Carolina*. The southern route of the Savannah Path generally followed present U.S. Highway 17 westward from Charles Town to Jackson's plantation at Pon Pon on the Edisto River. It continued to follow generally Highway 17 southwest to the Combahee River, across into the Indian Land, and then northwest, generally paralleling S.C. Highway 68 between the Salkehatchie and Coosawhatchie Rivers. At the head of the Coosawatchie River, it began generally following S.C. Highway 125 northwest to Savannah Town. Mouzon et al., *Accurate Map of North and South Carolina*; Stuart, *Map of South Carolina and a Part of Georgia*.

8. Chicken, "Journal from Carolina in 1715," 327, 328; Lawson, *History of the Uniforms of the British Army*, 1:43.

9. A large unit that was living off the land and traveling with packhorses would have had difficulty maintaining two miles per hour during a nine-hour day. Chicken, "Colonel Chicken's Journal to the Cherokees," 100, 101; Campbell, "Sketch of the Northern Frontiers of Georgia," 1780; Crane, *Southern Frontier*, 44, 187.

10. Chicken, "Colonel Chicken's Journal to the Cherokees," 166–68. By 1746 Fort Moore was nearly a ruin, despite having been repaired and rebuilt several times. It was rebuilt again. The height of the board walls was raised. Easterby, *SCCHJ*, March 6, 1750, 434, 435; Milligen-Johnston, "Short Description of the Province of South Carolina," 152; Gerard Monger to Governor Nicholson, September 22, 1723, in Original Papers, Letters, etc. from the Governors, fol. 63; SCCHJ, November 14, 1717, 366. For information regarding archaeological excavations at the site, see Groover, "Exploring Fort Moore"; Robertson and Robertson, "Town and Fort of Augusta," 64, 65.

11. Assembly of S. Carolina to Boone and Berresford, March 15, 1716, in *CSP, AWI*, 1716–17, 50.

12. Ibid.; Chicken, "Journal from Carolina in 1715," 327, 330, 331, 336, 339; Commons House to Boone and Berresford, March 15, 1716, in Salley, *Records in the British Public Record Office*, 6:157.

13. Chicken, "Journal from Carolina in 1715," 351.

14. Ibid., 326, 327, 329, 331, 333, 336, 339, 345, 347, 348; Commons House to Boone and Berresford, March 15, 1716, in Salley, *Records in the British Public Record Office*,

6:157; Statement by [John Savy?], September 18, 1728, in *CSP, AWI,* 1728–29, 209, 210; J. A. Barnwell, "Southeastern North America"; McDowell, *Journals of the Commissioners of the Indian Trade,* May 14, 1713, 45.

15. Chicken, "Journal from Carolina in 1715," 327, 328.

16. Ibid., 328, 329.

17. Ibid., 329n4. Locations of the Cherokee towns are approximate, based on period descriptions and maps. Tossee, or Tussee, was located on the west, or south, side of the Savannah River and south of Toccoa Creek about six miles east of present-day Toccoa in Stephens County, Georgia. Barnwell, "Southeastern North America"; Kitchin, *New Map of the Cherokee Nation;* Stuart, "Part of the Purcell Map"; Mouzon et al., *Accurate Map of North and South Carolina.*

18. Keowee was the principal town of the Lower Cherokees, but the regiment's officers apparently did not visit it. It was located on the Keowee River in present-day Oconee County about fifteen miles northwest of present-day Walhalla. Tugaloo, or Toogoola, was also a prominent Lower Cherokee town. It was located on the west, or south, side of Savannah River about a half mile northwest of present-day Highway 123, between the conflux of Toccoa Creek and the Savannah River, and about five miles northeast of present-day Toccoa in Franklin County, Georgia. After 1716 the town moved east across the river into South Carolina; Chicken, "Colonel Chicken's Journal to the Cherokees," 101n2, 104n1; Chicken, "Journal from Carolina in 1715," 329, 330; Stuart, Part of the Purcell Map; Bull, "Southeastern North America"; Hunter, "Cherokee Nation and the Traders' Path"; Woolley, "Cherokee Country prior to 1776"; Kitchin, *New Map of the Cherokee Nation;* Mouzon et al., *Accurate Map of North and South Carolina.* For additional maps showing the locations of Cherokee towns, see notes 2 and 17 in this chapter.

19. Chicken, "Journal from Carolina in 1715," 330; Fogelson, "Cherokee in the East," 340, 341, 346.

20. Chicken, "Journal from Carolina in 1715," 330, 331, 345.

21. Ibid., 330, 331, 343.

22. Ibid., 331.

23. Ibid., 331, 332, 339, 340, 347. Chota (Chote, Echote, Echota) was located in the Nacoochee Valley probably near present-day Sautee-Nachoochee, an unincorporated community in Habersham County, Georgia. It was northwest of, and close to, Nacoochee. Toccoa (Taccoa, Tawcoe) was probably located in the vicinity of present-day Toccoa in Franklin County, Georgia. Soquee (Soque) was probably located near the Soque River perhaps about five miles north of present-day Clarkesville in Habersham County, Georgia. Nacoochee (Nacouchee, Nocochee, Nagochee, Naguchee) was located probably near present-day Sautee-Nachoochee.

24. Chicken, "Journal from Carolina in 1715," 332; Swanton, *Indians of the Southeastern United States,* 402.

25. Chicken, "Journal from Carolina in 1715," 332, 333, 335; Governor Johnson to the Council of Trade and Plantations, January 12, 1720, in *CSP, AWI,* 1719–20,

302; SCCHJ, December 11, 1717, 413; Chicken, "Colonel Chicken's Journal to the Cherokees," 168, 169.

26. Chicken, "Journal from Carolina in 1715," 334.

27. Ibid., 336–38.

28. Ibid., 338, 339. The first intertown ball game was at Tehoee, which may have been located on the west side of the Seneca River near present-day Seneca in Oconee County, South Carolina. The next day a game was played at Estatohe between the men of that town and the men of Tugaloo. Estatohe was located on the west side of the Savannah River, perhaps about ten miles northwest of the conflux of where the Tallulah and Chattooga Rivers join to form the Tugallo River, on the border of Rabun and Habersham Counties, Georgia.

29. Chicken, "Colonel Chicken's Journal to the Cherokees," 131, 131n2; Chicken, "Journal from Carolina in 1715," 339–41, 345. Chauga (Chagey, Chagee, Chuge) was located on the east side of the Savannah River, near the mouth of the Chauga River, southwest of present-day Westminster in Oconee County, South Carolina.

30. Chicken, "Journal from Carolina in 1715," 340, 345, 348.

31. Ibid., 340, 341. Quanassee (Quanusee) was a town of the Overhill Cherokee. It was located to the west of most of the Overhill Cherokee towns and was probably near present-day Hayesville in Clay County, North Carolina.

32. Chicken, "Journal from Carolina in 1715," 342, 343.

33. Ibid., 343, 344.

34. Ibid., 344, 345. Cuttacochi was located to the south and not far from Sukeacha in present-day Towns County, Georgia.

35. Chicken, "Journal from Carolina in 1715," 343–45; Assembly of S. Carolina to Boone and Berresford, March 15, 1716, in *CSP, AWI*, 1716–17, 50; Statement by [John Savy?], September 18, 1728, in *CSP, AWI*, 1728–29, 209, 210.

36. Chicken, "Journal from Carolina in 1715," 345, 346. Kasihta was also known as Cussita.

37. Ibid., 346, 347.

38. Ibid., 347–49.

39. Ibid., 349–51. Noyowee (Noyouwee, Noyoee) was located on the east side of the Savannah River, probably near present-day Yonah Dam, west-northwest of Westminster in Oconee County, South Carolina. The Saluda River was formerly known as the Congaree River. The Little Saluda River was formerly known as the Saluda River.

40. Chicken, "Journal from Carolina in 1715," 351; Assembly of South Carolina to Boone and Berresford, June 29, 1716, in *CSP, AWI*, 1716–17, 137.

41. Assembly of South Carolina to Boone and Berresford, June 29, 1716, in *CSP, AWI*, 1716–17, 137; Boyd, "Diego Pena's Expedition," 25; Swanton, *Early History of the Creek Indians*, 221, 222, 226; Hahn, *Invention of the Creek Nation*, 90.

42. McDowell, *Journals of the Commissioners of the Indian Trade*, December 21, 1716, 141; May 9, 1717, 178; June 11, 1717, 186; October 23, 1717, 219; October 24, 1717, 220, 221. During the ensuing war with the Creeks, the town of Chagey was

fortified. The town of Estotoe was also fortified with a palisade wall, a ditch on the outside, wooden spikes in the ditch, and flankers at the corners of the wall. The Estotoe townhouse was also fortified. Chicken, "Colonel Chicken's Journal to the Cherokees," 149, 150; Statement by [John Savy?], September 18, 1728, in *CSP, AWI*, 1728–29, 209, 210.

CHAPTER 13: Stalemate, 1716

1. SCCHJ, February 28, 1716, 5; June 7, 1716, 117; Edgar, *Biographical Directory of the South Carolina House of Representatives*, 40; *Boston News-Letter*, September 26, 1715; Le Jau to the Secretary, August 23, 1715, in Klingberg, *Chronicle of Le Jau*, 166; Cooper and McCord, *Statutes*, "Act . . . to Sell and Convey the Old Glebe Land at Chehaw . . . ," July 25, 1761, 4:152; Cooper and McCord, *Statutes*, "Act to . . . Appoint Who Shall Be . . . Chosen Members of the Commons House . . . ," December 15, 1716, 2:686; Tate to Duddleston, September 16, 1715, in *CSP, AWI*, 1714–15, 351.
2. SCCHJ, February 29, 1716, 6–8.
3. Cooper and McCord, *Statutes*, "Act for Raising Forces to Prosecute the War against Our Indian Enemies . . . ," March 24, 1716, 2:634–41.
4. SCCHJ, August 5, 1715, 424, 425; April 20, 1716, 71; June 30, 1716, 150; January 26, 1724, 143; February 9, 1724, 171, 172; February 12, 1724, 184; Cooper and McCord, *Statutes*, "Act for Raising Forces to Prosecute the War against Our Indian Enemies . . . ," March 24, 1716, 2:634–41. The new army strength of 267 in March 1716 probably included the captain, lieutenant, and four men who garrisoned Johnson's Fort at Windmill Point on James Island, covering the Charles Town harbor. Cooper and McCord, *Statutes*, "Act to Settle a Guard in Johnson's Fort on Windmill Point," December 18, 1713, 2:613–15.
5. SCCH, August 20, 1715, 442; February 29, 1716, 10–11; March 1, 1716, 12; May 3, 1716, 94; June 7, 1716, 118; December 14, 1716, 204; December 11, 1717, 417; July 14, 1720, 455; Le Jau to the Secretary, August 23, 1715, in Klingberg, *Chronicle of Le Jau*, 165; Cooper and McCord, *Statutes*, "Act for the Better Ordering and Governing of Negroes and Other Slaves," February 23, 1722, 7:371–73, 382–84.
6. Cooper and McCord, *Statutes*, "Further Additional Act . . . for the Better Ordering and Governing of Negroes and Other Slaves . . . ," December 11, 1717, 7:368–70; Cooper and McCord, *Statutes*, "Act for the Better Ordering and Governing of Negroes and Other Slaves," February 23, 1722, 7:371, 373, 382–84; Cooper and McCord, *Statutes*, "Act for the Better Ordering and Governing of Negroes and Other Slaves," May 10, 1740, 7:397, 410, 411, 413; Sirmans, *Colonial South Carolina*, 208.
7. Cooper and McCord, *Statutes*, "Act for the Better Regulating of the Militia . . . ," June 13, 1747, 9:658.
8. Cooper and McCord, *Statutes*, "Act for Raising Forces to Prosecute the War against Our Indian Enemies . . . ," March 24, 1716, 2:635; SCCHJ, March 7, 1716, 27, 28; March 10, 1716, 35.

9. SCCHJ, March 7, 1716, 27; March 10, 1716, 35; March 14, 1716, 36; Salley, *Warrants for Lands*, 641.

10. Cooper and McCord, *Statutes*, "Act for Raising Forces to Prosecute the War against Our Indian Enemies . . . ," March 24, 1716, 2:635; SCCHJ, March 7, 1716, 27; May 18, 1716, 111; June 15, 128, 129; June 30, 1716, 151. For the location of Hearn's plantation, see note 4 of chapter 8.

11. Cooper and McCord, *Statutes*, "Act for Raising Forces to Prosecute the War against Our Indian Enemies . . . ," March 24, 1716, 2:635; SCCHJ, March 7, 1716, 27; May 5, 1716, 96. For Edisto Bluff Fort, see note 24 of chapter 7.

12. Cooper and McCord, *Statutes*, "Act for Raising Forces to Prosecute the War against Our Indian Enemies . . . ," March 24, 1716, 2:635; SCCHJ, March 7, 1716, 27; Salley, *SCCHJ*, June 16, 1724, 49. For Woodward's Fort see note 4 of chapter 6.

13. Cooper and McCord, *Statutes*, "Act for Raising Forces to Prosecute the War against Our Indian Enemies . . . ," March 24, 1716, 2:635; SCCHJ, March 7, 1716, 27; April 25, 1716, 83; April 27, 1716, 86, 88; May 12, 1716, 105, 106. Jackson had two Colleton County plantations that were fortified during the war. The plantation on which this fort was placed was located on the east side of the Combahee River. See note 29 of chapter 11. The other plantation was the Pon Pon plantation on the west side of the Edisto River. The fort on the Pon Pon plantation was abandoned early in the war. See note 42 of chapter 7; Barker, "Pryce Hughes," 305, 306, 312. Evans inherited his Combahee River plantation by Hughes's last will and testament; Withington, "South Carolina Gleanings in England," 221.

14. Cooper and McCord, *Statutes*, "Act for Raising Forces to Prosecute the War against Our Indian Enemies . . . ," March 24, 1716, 2:635; SCCHJ, March 7, 1716, 27; March 24, 1716, 59; April 17, 1716, 64; April 20, 1716, 72, 74; April 25, 1716, 83, 85; December 28, 1716, 214, 215. Major Blakewey's wife, Sarah, was the daughter of Deputy Governor Robert Daniel; Gregorie, *Records of the Court of Chancery*, 178n. For Fort Moore see note 10 of chapter 12.

15. Cooper and McCord, *Statutes*, "Act for Raising Forces to Prosecute the War against Our Indian Enemies . . . ," March 24, 1716, 2:635, 636; SCCHJ, March 7, 1716, 25, 27; March 16, 1716, 43; March 21, 1716, 52; August 2, 1716, 157; December 11, 1716, 199; December 13, 1716, 204; December 29, 1716, 218; Hewitt, *Historical Account of the Rise and Progress*, 1:223.

16. Cooper and McCord, *Statutes*, "Act to Appropriate the Yamasee Lands to the Use of Such Persons as Shall Come into and Settle Themselves in This Province . . . ," June 13, 1716, 2:641–46; Cooper and McCord, *Statutes*, ". . . Lords and Proprietors of the Province of Carolina, in America to the Governor and Council of South Carolina . . . ," July 22, 1718, 3:30, 31; SCCHJ, January 25, 1717, 230, 231; January 26, 1717, 231; April 18, 1717, 263; Petition of the Council and Assembly of the Settlements in South Carolina to the King, February 3, 1720, in *CSP, AWI*, 1719–20, 340, 341. For Port Royal Fort, see note 23 of chapter 6.

17. SCCHJ, February 29, 1716, 9–11; March 2, 1716, 14, 15, 17; April 20, 1716, 75; January 24, 1717, 228; January 26, 1717, 234; Cooper and McCord, *Statutes*, "Act for Raising Forces to Prosecute the War against Our Indian Enemies . . . ," March 24, 1716, 2:634, 635, 640; Committee of the Assembly of Carolina to Boone and Berresford, August 6, 1716, in *CSP, AWI*, 1716–17, 221.

18. SCCHJ, March 7, 1716, 25; March 9, 1716, 32; March 17, 1716, 47, 48; April 17, 1716, 63.

19. Klingberg, "Mystery of the Lost Yamasee Prince," 18. For Euhaw Town see note 20 of chapter 3.

20. Klingberg, "Mystery of the Lost Yamasee Prince," 20–23.

21. Ibid., 27; Le Jau to the Secretary, August 23, 1715, in Klingberg, *Chronicle of Le Jau*, 165; October 3, 1715, 167; March 19, 1716, 175; Governor of Saint Augustine to Lt. Governor Spotswood, May 30, 1716, in *CSP, AWI*, 1716–17, 293.

22. Klingberg, "Mystery of the Lost Yamasee Prince," 27, 28.

23. Ibid., 27–29, 32; Le Jau to the Society, March 19, 1716, in Klingberg, *Chronicle of Le Jau*, 175; SCCHJ, March 24, 1716, 62; Commons House to Boone and Berresford, March 15, 1715, in Salley, *Records in the British Public Record Office*, 6:159, 160; Hann, "St. Augustine's Fallout," 186.

24. SCCHJ, April 18, 1716, 65–67; April 25, 1716, 78; Gregorie, *Records of the Court of Chancery*, 144n47; Sirmans, *Colonial South Carolina*, 118, 119.

25. Governor Craven's Speech to the Assembly of South Carolina, March 24, 1716, in *CSP, AWI*, 1716–17, 138; Reply of the Assembly of South Carolina to Governor Craven's Speech, March 24, 1716, in *CSP, AWI*, 1716–17, 138, 139; Marquis de Monteleon to [Secretary Stanhope?], February 3, 1716, in *CSP, AWI*, 1716–17, February 11; [?] to [Marques de Monteleon?], [June?] 1715, in *CSP, AWI*, 1716–17, 11; Proprietors to Craven, February 23, 1716, in *CSP, AWI*, 1716–17, February 26, 27; Paul Methvan to the Proprietors, August 8, 1716, in *CSP, AWI*, 1716–17, 162; In the Case of the Marquis of Navarres, 1719, in *CSP, AWI*, 1719–20, 292; Estimate of arrears due to the Proprietors, March [25?], 1728, in *CSP, AWI*, 1728–29, 72; Inventory of Jewels, etc., June 2, 1715, in Salley, *Records in the British Public Record Office*, 6:4, 5.

26. SCCHJ, March 6, 1716, 23; March 7, 1716, 26; March 16, 1716, 41, 42; June 6, 1716, 115; June 11, 1716, 124; June 22, 1716, 137; June 28, 1716, 143; Commons House to Boone and Berresford, March 15, 1716, in Salley, *Records in the British Public Record Office*, 6:161; Boone and Berresford to the Council of Trade and Plantations, December 5, 1716, in *CSP, AWI*, 1716–17, 215–17; Agents of Carolina and merchants trading thither to the Council of Trade and Plantations, September 16, 1715, in *CSP, AWI*, 1714–15, 287; Council of Trade and Plantations to Secretary Stanhope, September 16, 1715, in *CSP, AWI*, 1714–15, 288; Popple to Lt. Governor Spotswood, September 22, 1715, in *CSP, AWI*, 1714–15, 288; Spotswood to the Council of Trade and Plantations, April 16, 1717, in Brock, *Official Letters of Alexander Spotswood*, 238–41.

27. SCCHJ, March 7, 1716, 27; January 17, 1717, 222; Cooper and McCord, *Statutes*, "Act for the Better Regulation of the Indian Trade . . . ," June 30, 1716,

2:677–80; Cooper and McCord, *Statutes,* "Additional Act to an Act for the Better Regulation of the Indian Trade . . . ," 2:691–94; McDowell, *Journals of the Commissioners of the Indian Trade,* August 11, 1716, 104; October 2, 1716, 115, 116; November 7, 1716, 123; November 29, 1716, 134; December 5, 1716, 136, 137; February 12, 1717, 160; February 14, 1717, 161; February 20, 1717, 162; February 27, 1717, 167; March 6, 1717, 168; June 11, 1717, 186; June 17, 1717, 188; September 10, 1717, 205; September 20, 1717, 212.

28. SCCHJ, August 1, 1716, 153; August 2, 1716, 154, 156; November 22, 1716, 175; December 7, 1716, 196; Committee of the Assembly of Carolina to Boone, March 8, 1718, in *CSP, AWI,* 1717–18, 207; McDowell, *Journals of the Commissioners of the Indian Trade,* June 24, 1718, 295; W. B. Smith, *White Servitude,* 29, 32.

29. Assembly of South Carolina to Boone and Berresford, [April?] 1716, in *CSP, AWI,* 1716–17, 135.

30. Assembly of South Carolina to Boone and Berresford, March 15, 1716, in *CSP, AWI,* 1716–17, 50; Address of the Representative of South Carolina to the King, March 1716, in *CSP, AWI,* 1716–17, 51; Assembly of South Carolina to [Boone and Berresford?], [April?] 1716, in *CSP, AWI,* 1716–17, 135–38; Committee of Correspondence of the Assembly of South Carolina to Boone and Berresford, November 30, 1716, in *CSP, AWI,* 1716–17, 208, 209; Address of the Assembly of South Carolina to the King, November 30, 1716, in *CSP, AWI,* 1716–17, 209.

31. Committee of the Assembly of Carolina to Boone and Berresford, November 30, 1716, in *CSP, AWI,* 1716–17, 208, 209; Committee of the Assembly of Carolina to Boone and Berresford, August 6, 1716, in *CSP, AWI,* 1716–17, 219; Le Jau to the Society, July 1, 1716, in Klingberg, *Chronicle of Le Jau,* 180; Le Jau to the Society, November 16, 1716, in Klingberg, *Chronicle of Le Jau,* 188; Boyd, "Diego Pena's Expedition," 9; SCCHJ, November 20, 1716, 173; February 12, 1723, 185; Salley, *SCCHJ,* April 26, 1726, 91; Salley and Webber, *Death Notices in the South Carolina Gazette,* 3; Salley, *Warrants for Lands,* 172, 185; Ivers, "Rangers, Scouts, and Tythingmen," 155, 156.

32. SCCHJ, December 15, 165.

33. SCCHJ, November 20, 1716, 173; November 30, 1716, 187; May 29, 1717, 290; June 29, 1717, 334; South Carolina Council Journals, September 3, 1717, 117.

34. SCCHJ, November 14, 1716, 166; November 23, 1716, 177; December 6, 1716, 193; December 7, 1716, 195, 196; Cooper and McCord, *Statutes,* "Act for Appointing Rangers to Guard the Frontiers of This Province . . . and for Making a Further Provision for the Garrisons of Port Royal and Savano Town," December 15, 1716, 2:691. This statute is lost and has to be reconstructed from the Commons House journals; McDowell, *Journals of the Commissioners of the Indian Trade,* November 23, 1716, 130; October 10, 1717, 218.

35. SCCHJ, November 30, 1716, 186, 187; December 7, 1716, 194; December 11, 1716, 199; December 12, 1716, 200; Cooper and McCord, *Statutes,* "Act for Appointing Rangers to Guard the Frontiers of This Province . . . and for Making a Further Provision for the Garrisons of Port Royal and Savano Town," December 15, 1716, 2:691; Cooper and McCord, *Statutes,* "Act to Appropriate . . . Moneys . . .

for Appointing Rangers . . . and Soldiers Belonging to Port Royal, and Savano Town Garrisons . . . ," June 29, 1717, 3:7, 8; South Carolina Council Journals, September 3, 1717, 118.

36. Cooper and McCord, *Statutes,* "Act . . . for Appointing a Scout at Pon Pon . . . ," 9:61, 62.

37. SCCHJ, November 30, 1716, 187; December 13, 1716, 203; December 29, 1716, 218; January 26, 1717, 231, 234; Salley, *SCCHJ,* June 16, 1724, 49. For Hearn's Fort see note 4 of chapter 8; for Woodward's Fort see note 4 of chapter 6; for Combahee Fort see note 13 of this chapter; McDowell, *Journals of the Commissioners of the Indian Trade,* November 23, 1716, 130; November 29, 1716, 134.

CHAPTER 14: South Carolinians, 1717–20

1. Governor Johnson to the Council of Trade and Plantation, June 12, 1720, in *CSP, AWI,* 1719–20, 300. For South Carolina's 1715 population, see note 2 of chapter 2; McDowell, *Journals of the Commissioners of the Indian Trade,* May 9, 1718, 273.

2. Committee of the Assembly of Carolina to Boone and Berresford, August 6, 1716, in *CSP, AWI,* 1716–17, 221; Certificate of Robert Daniel, August 13, 1716, in *CSP, AWI,* 1716–17, 225; Deposition of George Duckett, [August?] 1716, in *CSP, AWI,* 1716–17, 226; [?] to Boone, June 24, 1720, in *CSP, AWI,* 1720–21, 57; William Dry to Col. Barnwell, August 19, 1720, in *CSP, AWI,* 1720–21, 190; Chatelain, *Defenses of Spanish Florida,* 79, 160, 161; SCCHJ, August 2, 1716, 155; December 4, 1716, 204; June 10, 1720, 446; June 11, 1720, 447; July 15, 1720, 455; August 15, 1721, 534, 535; June 21, 1722, 39; February 20, 1828, 386.

3. Agents of South Carolina and London merchants . . . to the Council of Trade and Plantations, February 22, 1717, in *CSP, AWI,* 1716–17, 258, 259; Address of the Representatives of South Carolina to the King, February 22, 1717, in *CSP, AWI,* 1716–17, 259.

4. Extract of a Letter from S. Carolina to [Berresford?], April 8, 1717, in *CSP, AWI,* 1716–17, 232; Extracts of a Letter from South Carolina, March 30, 1717, in *CSP, AWI,* 1716–17, 280; Extract of a Letter from South Carolina, April 24, 1717, in *CSP, AWI,* 1716–17, 290; Extract of letter from South Carolina to Joseph Boone, June 8, 1717, in *CSP, AWI,* 1716–17, 325; SCCHJ, November 28, 1716, 180, 181; November 29, 1716, 183; December 4, 1716, 188; December 7, 1716, 196; December 12, 1716, 201; December 13, 1716, 201–3; January 25, 1717, 229, 230; December 5, 1717, 392; Cooper and McCord, *Statutes,* "Act for Cutting and Clearing . . . Biggon Creek," March 11, 1726, 7:481; Auditor General Memorial Books, 5:166; McDowell, *Journals of the Commissioners of the Indian Trade,* December 10, 1716, 138; August 7, 1718, 317.

5. McDowell, *Journals of the Commissioners of the Indian Trade,* December 31, 1716, 143; April 11, 1717, 173; May 1, 1717, 176; May 24, 1717, 183; Extracts of Letters from South Carolina, March 29 and March 30, 1717, in *CSP, AWI,* 1716–17, 280; Extract of a Letter from S. Carolina, April 8, 1717, in *CSP, AWI,* 1716–17, 232;

Extract of a Letter from South Carolina to Boone, June 8, 1717, in *CSP, AWI,* 1716–17, 325.

6. Your Enee (Youre Hene and Uauenea) is shown on De Brahm, *Map of South Carolina and a Part of Georgia.* Collins may have been a squatter, for there appears to be no plat or grant for his Black River site. McDowell, *Journals of the Commissioners of the Indian Trade,* April 16, 1717, 174; June 14, 1717, 187, 188; August 10, 1717, 202; September 10, 1717, 206; September 11, 1717, 206; September 12, 1717, 209; November 25, 1717, 232; January 30, 1718, 253; February 27, 1718, 258, 259.

7. McDowell, *Journals of the Commissioners of the Indian Trade,* October 23, 1717, 219; October 24, 1717, 220–22; November 2, 1717, 223; December 2, 1717, 236, 237; May 8, 1718, 272; May 9, 1718, 272; May 29, 1718, 278, 279; June 14, 1718, 290; July 19, 1718, 310, 311; Crane, *Southern Frontier,* 127, 128, 165, 166.

8. McDowell, *Journals of the Commissioners of the Indian Trade,* May 1, 1717, 175; June 18, 1717, 192; September 12, 1717, 207; November 28, 1717, 233; Cooper and McCord, *Statutes,* "Act to Impower the . . . Governor to . . . Enlist Soldiers . . . and to Provide a Fund . . . ," December 11, 1717, 3:27–29; Extracts of Letters from South Carolina, March 29 – April 27, 1717, in *CSP, AWI,* 1716–17, 280; M. Woods, "Culture of Credit," 359–63.

9. P. M. Brown, "Early Indian Trade," 122, 123; Clowse, *Economic Beginnings in Colonial South Carolina,* 207; McDowell, *Journals of the Commissioners of the Indian Trade,* July 19, 1718, 306; Cooper and McCord, *Statutes,* ". . . Lords and Proprietors of the Province of Carolina, in America to the Governor and Council of South Carolina . . . ," July 22, 1718, 3:31.

10. Otto, "Origins of Cattle-Ranching," 118, 122, 123; Clowse, *Economic Beginnings in Colonial South Carolina,* 222, 223.

11. Clowse, *Economic Beginnings in Colonial South Carolina,* 171, 173, 177, 208.

12. Ibid., 128, 129, 217–20; Menard, "Slave Demography in the Lowcountry," 282, 283.

13. Cooper and McCord, *Statutes,* "Act to Revive and Continue an Act for Appointing Rangers . . . and . . . for the Garrisons of Port Royal and Savano Town," June 29, 1717, 3:9; that statute has been lost, but it can be reconstructed from the Commons House journals. Cooper and McCord, *Statutes,* "Act to Impower the . . . Governor, to Raise Forces for the Defense of This Province . . . ," December 11, 1717, 3:23–27; Gregorie, *Records of the Court of Chancery,* 144n46; SCCHJ, June 29, 1717, 336.

14. Cooper and McCord, *Statutes,* "Act to Impower the . . . Governor, to Raise Forces for the Defense of This Province . . . ," December 11, 1717, 3:24; SCCHJ, June 30, 1716, 151; McDowell, *Journals of the Commissioners of the Indian Trade,* December 21, 1717, 245; January 28, 1718, 253; May 22, 1718, 275; August 7, 1718, 316, 318; August 22, 1718, 320; August 29, 1718, 320. Congaree Fort is shown on "Sketch Map of the Rivers" and on De Brahm, *Map of South Carolina and a Part of Georgia;* Michie, "Discovery of Old Fort Congaree," 10–13, 18–25, 42–57.

15. Cooper and McCord, *Statutes,* "Act to Impower the . . . Governor, to Raise Forces for the Defense of This Province . . . ," December 11, 1717, 3:23, 24;

SCCHJ, December 11, 1717, 420; September 2, 1720, 460; December 15, 1720, 480; August 12, 1721, 530; January 26, 1724, 143; McDowell, *Journals of the Commissioners of the Indian Trade,* September 13, 1717, 209; March 21, 1718, 262; August 7, 1718, 317. Pinckney Island has also been known as Espalamga Island, Watch Island, Lookout Island, and Mackays Island.

16. Cooper and McCord, *Statutes,* "Act to Impower the . . . Governor, to Raise Forces for the Defense of This Province . . . ," December 11, 1717, 3:24, 25; Salley, *SCCHJ,* June 16, 1724, 49; SCCHJ, November 9, 1717, 364; McDowell, *Journals of the Commissioners of the Indian Trade,* July 9, 1717, 194, 196, 197; August 7, 1717, 201.

17. Cooper and McCord, *Statutes,* "Act . . . for Part of the Land Belonging to Beaufort . . . ," December 11, 1717, 3:14; H. A. M. Smith, "Beaufort," 141–43, and accompanying map; Salley, *Warrants for Land,* 585; SCCHJ, May 23, 1717, 270; May 24, 1717, 277, 278; June 15, 1717, 323. The South Carolina government reported to the British government that Beaufort Fort was garrisoned with thirty men under pay, suggesting that they were provincial regulars, but they were probably militiamen; Council and Assembly of South Carolina to the Council of Trade and Plantations (with Answers to Queries by the Board of Trade), January 29, 1720, in *CSP, AWI,* 1719–20, 320. The site of the fort is shown on "Mapp of Beaufort in South Carolina," 1721.

18. SCCHJ, November 1, 1717, 347, 348; Cooper and McCord, *Statutes,* "Act to Continue the Garrison at Savano Town and the Two Scout Boats Appointed to Be Placed to the Southward and to Discharge the Officers and Soldiers Who Were Employed in the Late Expedition to the Creek Indians . . . ," July 5, 1718, 3:84. The original of this statute was in poor condition and could not be copied. Its title indicates that it made no provision for rangers; Cooper and McCord, *Statutes,* "Act to Impower . . . the Governor to Raise Forces to Be Sent to the Assistance of the Cherokee against Their Enemies . . . ," July 5, 1718, 3:39–41; McDowell, *Journals of the Commissioners of the Indian Trade,* July 20, 1718, 309.

19. Cooper and McCord, *Statutes,* "Act to Settle and Regulate the Indian Trade," March 20, 1719, 3:86–96; Cooper and McCord, *Statutes,* "Act for the Better Regulation of the Indian Trade . . . ," September 19, 1721, 3:141–46; McDowell, *Journals of the Commissioners of the Indian Trade,* August 7, 1718, 317, 318; Salley, *SCCHJ,* June 16, 1724, 49; Clowse, *Economic Beginnings in Colonial South Carolina,* 199, 207.

20. Agents of South Carolina and London merchants to the Council of Trade and Plantations, February 22, 1717, in *CSP, AWI,* 1716–17, 258, 259; Address of the Representatives of South Carolina to the King, June 12, 1716, in *CSP, AWI,* 1716–17, 259; Extract of Letters from South Carolina, April 24 and 25, 1717, in *CSP, AWI,* 1716–17, 290; Extract of a letter from South Carolina to Joseph Boone, April 25, 1717, in *CSP, AWI,* 1716–17, 290, 291; Representatives of inhabitants of South Carolina to the King, April 30, 1717, in *CSP, AWI,* 1716–17, 291, 292; Governor and Council of South Carolina to the Council of Trade and Plantations, November 6, 1719, in *CSP, AWI,* 1719–20, 259–63; Petition of the

Council and Assembly of the Settlements in South Carolina to the King, February 3, 1720, in *CSP, AWI*, 1719–20, 332–43; Act for supporting the present Government under the administration of the Honble. James Moore Esq. or any succeeding Governor, August 16, 1720, in *CSP, AWI*, 1719–20, 102, 103; SCCHJ, October 29, 1717, 339, 340; October 31, 1717, 342–44; November 28, 1717, 381; Gregorie, *Records of the Court of Chancery*, 207n; Cooper and McCord, *Statutes*, ". . . Lords and Proprietors of the Province of Carolina, in America to the Governor and Council of South Carolina . . . ," July 22, 1718, 3:30, 31; Clowse, *Economic Beginnings in Colonial South Carolina*, 184, 188–95; Sirmans, *Colonial South Carolina*, 129–63; Stumpf, "Edward Randolph's Attack"; Douglas, "Impeaching the Impeachment," 112–16; Scheerer, "Proprietors Can't Undertake," 273–87; A. Moore, "Marooned," 256.

21. Governor Johnson to the Council of Trade and Plantations, January 12, 1720, in *CSP, AWI*, 1719–20, 300, 301.

22. [?] to Boone, June 24, 1720, in *CSP, AWI*, 1720–21, 58.

23. Hahn, "'Indians That Live about Pon Pon,'" 351, 352; Rowland, Moore, and Rogers, *History of Beaufort County*, 1:101.

CHAPTER 15: Southeastern Indians, 1717–20

1. Le Jau to the Society, May 14, 1715, in Klingberg, *Chronicle of Le Jau*, 155; Perdue, "American Indian Survival," 215–18; SCCHJ, August 9, 1715, 430, 431; August 10, 1715, 432; August 12, 1715, 434; August 20, 1715, 441; August 24, 1715, 448; December 5, 1717, 392; Receipt signed by Edmund Bellinger, June 29, 1717, Wills, Inventories and Miscellaneous Records, vol. 56.

2. Le Jau to the Society, July 1, 1716, in Klingberg, *Chronicle of Le Jau*, 180, 181; At a Council, July 18, 1715, in McIlwaine, *Executive Journals of the Council of Colonial Virginia*, 3:406; At a Council, October 18, 1715, in McIlwaine, *Executive Journals of the Council of Colonial Virginia*, 3:411, 412; At a Council, February 22, 1716, in McIlwaine, *Executive Journals of the Council of Colonial Virginia*, 3: 421, 422; Committee of the Assembly to Boone and Berresford, August 6, 1716, in *CSP, AWI*, 1716–17, 221, 222; Extract of a letter from South Carolina, August 6, 1716, in *CSP, AWI*, 1716–17, 225; SCCHJ, April 18, 1717, 261; McDowell, *Journals of the Commissioners of the Indian Trade*, September 11, 1717, 206; September 12, 1717, 209; April 11, 1718, 264, 265; Lerch, "Indians of the Carolinas since 1900," 329 (fig. 1), 333 (table 1), 335, 336; Perdue, "American Indian Survival," 216, 217, 224–34.

3. See note 35 of chapter 12 for the Cherokees' declaration of war against the Creeks; McDowell, *Journals of the Commissioners of the Indian Trade*, December 21, 1716, 141; May 9, 1717, 178; June 11, 1717, 186; October 23, 1717, 219; October 24, 1717, 220–22; Chicken, "Colonel Chicken's Journal to the Cherokees," 149, 150; Crane, *Southern Frontier*, 269, 270.

4. Assembly of South Carolina to Boone and Berresford, June 29, 1716, in *CSP, AWI*, 1716–17, 137; Extract of a letter from S. Carolina, March 22 and April 8,

1717, in *CSP, AWI,* 1716–17, 232; Extract of a letter from South Carolina, March 30, 1717, in *CSP, AWI,* 1716–17, 280; Extract of a letter from South Carolina to Joseph Boone, June 8, 1717, in *CSP, AWI,* 1716–17, 325; Boyd, "Diego Pena's Expedition," 4, 9, 25; Hahn, *Invention of the Creek Nation,* 90.

5. Hahn, *Invention of the Creek Nation,* 85–87, 94–97, 102–19.

6. Ibid., 94, 95; Extract of a Letter from S. Carolina to [Berresford?], March 22, 1717, in *CSP, AWI,* 1716–17, 232; Extract of a Letter from South Carolina to [Boone?], April 25, 1717, in *CSP, AWI,* 1716–17, 290; Extract of a Letter from South Carolina, April 27, 1717, in *CSP, AWI,* 1716–17, 280; SCCHJ, May 24, 1717, 275; November 15, 1717, 367.

7. SCCHJ, May 24, 1717, 275; June 12, 1717, 311; Crane, *Southern Frontier,* 257.

8. SCCHJ, June 15, 1717, 325; Extract of a letter from South Carolina to Joseph Boone, June 8, 1717, in *CSP, AWI,* 1716–17, 324, 325.

9. McDowell, *Journals of the Commissioners of the Indian Trade,* June 17, 1717, 188, 189; SCCHJ, November 9, 1717, 361, 362; Committee of the Assembly of Carolina to Boone, March 8, 1718, in *CSP, AWI,* 1716–17, 206; Hudson, *Southeastern Indians,* 310; Pena to the Governor of Florida, September 20, 1717, in Boyd, "Documents Describing the Second and Third Expeditions," 115, 116, 118; Crane, *Southern Frontier,* 134, 256, 257.

10. Swanton, *Early History of the Creek Indians,* 125; Boyd, "Diego Pena's Expedition," 5, 6, 8–12; Hahn, *Invention of the Creek Nation,* 86, 97; TePaske, *Governorship of Spanish Florida,* 199–201.

11. Boyd, "Diego Pena's Expedition," 6, 9; Hahn, *Invention of the Creek Nation,* 39–51, 87; Crane, *Southern Frontier,* 34–36.

12. Boyd, "Documents Describing the Second and Third Expeditions," 110–13; Pena to the Governor of Florida, September 20, 1717, in Boyd, "Documents Describing the Second and Third Expeditions," 115, 116.

13. Pena to the Governor of Florida, September 20, 1717, in Boyd, "Documents Describing the Second and Third Expeditions," 117–22, 124, 126; Hahn, *Invention of the Creek Nation,* 105.

14. Pena to the Governor of Florida, September 20, 1717, in Boyd, "Documents Describing the Second and Third Expeditions," 118; Hahn, *Life and Times of Mary Musgrove,* 3, 57, 58, 61–63.

15. Committee of the Assembly of Carolina to Boone, March 8, 1718, in *CSP, AWI,* 1717–18, 206, 207; SCCHJ, November 1, 1717, 349; November 12, 1717, 363; November 14, 1717, 366; November 15, 1717, 367; Salley, *SCCHJ,* December 13, 1726, 34, 35; December 21, 1726, 45, 46; Hahn, *Invention of the Creek Nation* 100, 107; Crane, *Southern Frontier,* 259, 260; McDowell, *Journals of the Commissioners of the Indian Trade,* November 9, 1717, 224, 225; December 12, 1717, 240, 241; June 3, 1718, 280–82; July 16, 1718, 303, 304.

16. McDowell, *Journals of the Commissioners of the Indian Trade,* December 12, 1717, 240; December 13, 1717, 241; June 3, 1718, 280–82; July 16, 1718, 303; SCCHJ, November 15, 1717, 367; Hahn, *Invention of the Creek Nation,* 113–15.

17. Hahn, *Invention of the Creek Nation,* 115–19; Governor of Pensacola to the

Governor of Florida, September 9, 1717, in Boyd, "Documents Describing the Second and Third Expeditions," 130.

18. Klingberg, "Mystery of the Lost Yamasee Prince," 28, 29; SCCHJ, March 24, 1716, 62; December 15, 209; McDowell, *Journals of the Commissioners of the Indian Trade,* November 29, 1716, 134; February 12, 1717, 160; February 14, 1717, 161; February 20, 1717, 162; February 27, 1717, 167; March 6, 1717, 168; April 16, 1717, 175; May 14, 1717, 182; June 11, 1717, 186; June 18, 1717, 192; November 23, 1717, 231; November 30, 1717, 235; May 8, 1718, 272. Of the initial 309 Indian captives that were sold into slavery, at least 50 of them were probably Cape Fear Indians that Maurice Moore captured in July 1715; Governor Johnson to the Council of Trade and Plantations, January 12, 1720, in *CSP, AWI,* 1719–20, 302. There were ten Indian towns near Saint Augustine, but only six of them contained Yamasees and Guales; Hann, "St. Augustine's Fallout," 184–86; Worth, *Struggle for the Georgia Coast,* 50; SCCHJ, December 15, 1716, 209.

19. Hann, "St. Augustine's Fallout," 184–86; Worth, *Timucuan Chiefdoms of Spanish Florida,* 2:149.

20. Hann, "St. Augustine's Fallout," 184–86, 190–99.

21. Eveleigh to Boone and Berresford, October 7, 1715, in *CSP, AWI,* 1714–15, 297; William Rhett to William Rhett, junr., April 28, 1719, in *CSP, AWI,* 1719–20, 80.

22. SCCHJ, April 18, 1716, 65; April 20, 1716, 74; May 3, 1716, 93, 94. Hugh Bryan later owned a plantation abutting Huspah Neck to the west, near the former site of Huspaw Town; De Brahm, *Map of South Carolina and a Part of Georgia;* Cooper and McCord, *Statutes,* "Act for Mending and Keeping in Repair the Causway over the Marsh of Combee River," February 25, 1715, 9:37; Cooper and McCord, *Statutes,* "Act for the Payment of . . . Five Hundred Pounds Current Money unto Maria, the Wife of John Charlton, Late of This Province, Vintner, in Case She Procures the Huspaw King, Now at Saint Augustine and His People, to Return . . . ," December 15, 1716, 4:695; Committee of the Assembly of Carolina to Boone and Berresford, August 6, 1716, in *CSP, AWI,* 1716–17, 219, 220; Chatelain, *Defenses of Spanish Florida,* 77, 80; Crane, *Southern Frontier,* 264–66n26; Oatis, *Colonial Complex,* 268, 269.

23. Hann, "St. Augustine's Fallout," 184, 185; Worth, "Yamasee," 248, table 2; Extract of a letter from Col. William Rhett to William Rhett, junr., April 28, 1719, in *CSP, AWI,* 1719–20, 80; Hahn, "'Indians That Live about Pon Pon'"; Oatis, *Colonial Complex,* 269–72.

24. Extract of a letter from Barnwell to Governor Johnson, April 20, 1719, in *CSP, AWI,* 1719–20, 80, 81; Governor and Council of South Carolina to the Council of Trade and Plantations, November 6, 1719, in *CSP, AWI,* 1719–20, 259–61; John Parris to [Governor Johnson?], July 18, 1719, in *CSP, AWI,* 1719–20, 261–63.

25. Barnwell to Gov. Johnson, October[?] 1719, in *CSP, AWI,* 1719–20, 306–8.

26. Ibid.; Public Treasurer, fol. 104. Men named Thomas Melvin and Alexander Melvin later participated in the 1728 Yamasee Expedition into Florida. Muster Roll of Captain Peters' Company, *Records in the British Public Record Office,* 13:196; Hicks, *South Carolina Indians,* 118, 127; Crane, *Southern Frontier,* 265–69.

Steven C. Hahn suggests that Melvin may have been either William or John Melvin, both of whom lived near the Musgroves; Hahn, "'Indians That Live about Pon Pon,'" 350, 352, 353; Oatis, *Colonial Complex*, 269–72. It is unlikely that Wettly, or Whitle Mico, was actually a Creek mico. South Carolinians probably called him by that name either as an honor or in jest.

27. Barnwell to Gov. Johnson, October[?] 1719, in *CSP, AWI*, 1719–20, 306, 307.
28. Ibid., 307, 308.
29. Committee of the Assembly of Carolina to Boone and Berresford, August 6, 1716, in *CSP, AWI*, 1716–17, 221; William Dry to Col. Barnwell, August 19, 1720, in *CSP, AWI*, 1720–21, 190; Boyd, "Diego Pena's Expedition," 10; Fitch, "Tobias Fitch's Journal," 193, 210.

CHAPTER 16: Raids and Counterraids, 1721–27

1. Crane, *Southern Frontier*, 218–34, 256, 261–63.
2. Ibid.; SCCHJ, July 29, 1720, 504; Sirmans, *Colonial South Carolina*, 134.
3. Crane, *Southern Frontier*, 219, 220, 229; Sirmans, *Colonial South Carolina*, 135.
4. Crane, *Southern Frontier*, 219–20, 228, 229; Sirmans, *Colonial South Carolina*, 131.
5. Crane, *Southern Frontier*, 229–35; Jeannine Cook, *Fort King George*, 16, 17, 21. Cook has written one of the better accounts of the construction of Fort King George. Sirmans, *Colonial South Carolina*, 135.
6. Jeannine Cook, *Fort King George*, 18–22; R. W. Smith, *South Carolina as a Royal Province*, 192; Barnwell to Governor Nicholson, June 3, 1721, in *CSP, AWI*, 1720–21, 366; Col. Barnwell's Commission, Col. Barnwell's Instructions, Blank Commission [to Barnwell] for a Commander of a Garrison to Southward, June 8, 1721, in *CSP, AWI*, 1720–21, 367; Contract . . . for the sloop *Jonathan and Sarah*, Warrant to Lt. Joseph Lambert of the Independent Company at Port Royal to deliver stores required by Col. Barnwell, Warrant to Col. Brewton to deliver powder to Col. Barnwell, Warrant to Thomas Lloyd to deliver 4 field pieces to Col. Barnwell, June 9, 1721, in *CSP, AWI*, 1720–21, 367.
7. Barnwell to Nicholson, July 3, 1721, in *CSP, AWI*, 1720–21, 367, 368; J. W. Barnwell, "Fort King George," 189–94; Public Treasurer, fol. 5.
8. J. W. Barnwell, "Fort King George," 195, 196, 202; SCCHJ, August 5, 1721, 517; Jeannine Cook, *Fort King George*, xv–xxii, 23–25, 31, 50, 52.
9. J. W. Barnwell, "Fort King George," 194, 196–200; Jeannine Cook, *Fort King George*, 24–26, 29, 32, 33; Salley, *SCCHJ*, June 9, 1724, 17.
10. J. W. Barnwell, "Fort King George," 198, 200; "Plan of King George's Fort at Alltamaha." A reconstructed fort is located at the Fort King George State Historical Site, Darien, Georgia. R. W. Smith, *South Carolina as a Royal Province*, 192; Jeannine Cook, *Fort King George*, frontispiece, 26, 27, 31, 34, 36, 37, 39, 40, 48, 50, 52, 62, 68.
11. SCCHJ, August 5, 1721, 517–20; February 23, 1723, 214.
12. SCCHJ, August 5, 1721, 519; August 11, 1721, 524, 527; August 12, 1721, 529, 530; August 15, 1721, 534; January 26, 1722, 7.

13. J. W. Barnwell, "Fort King George," 199; SCCHJ, August 11, 1721, 527; Jeannine Cook, *Fort King George*, 27, 33; R. W. Smith, *South Carolina as a Royal Province*, 192.

14. Crane, *Southern Frontier*, 238–45; TePaske, *Governorship of Spanish Florida*, 125–30; Worth, *Struggle for the Georgia Coast*, 11 (fig. 1), 29 (fig. 2), 44 (fig. 4).

15. Crane, *Southern Frontier*, 238–45, 239; SCCHJ, June 14, 1722, 10; February 22, 1723, 212, 213.

16. Cooper and McCord, *Statutes*, "Act for Regulating the Guard at Johnson's Fort, and . . . in the Several Forts and Garrisons . . . ," February 15, 1723, 3:234–36.

17. Cooper and McCord, *Statutes*, "Act for the Better Strengthening and Securing the Frontiers . . . ," February 23, 1723, 3:179–83; Public Treasurer, fol. 5; SCCHJ, March 10, 1722, 4; June 23, 1722, 46; February 16, 1723, 207; May 16, 1723, 248; January 29, 1724, 149; March 17, 1725, 47; Salley, *SCCHJ*, June 12, 1724, 34; June 16, 1724, 51, 52; March 12, 1725, 39; April 7, 1725, 73; April 30, 1726, 103; Hahn, "'Indians That Live about Pon Pon,'" 353–55; Monger to Governor Nicholson, September 22, 1723, in Original Papers, Letters, etc. from the Governors, fol. 63.

18. Cooper and McCord, *Statutes*, "Act for the Better Strengthening and Securing the Frontiers . . . ," February 23, 1723, 3:180; Bellinger to Governor Nicholson, August 31, 1723, in Original Papers, Letters, etc. from the Governors, fol. 65; SCCHJ, June 14, 1722, 13. Congaree Fort is shown on Sketch Map of the Rivers."

19. Hahn, *Invention of the Creek Nation*, 133, 134; Sirmans, *Colonial South Carolina*, 150, 151; Swanton, *Early History of the Creek Indians*, 103; Fitch, "Tobias Fitch's Journal," 204.

20. Hann, "Saint Augustine's Fallout," 184–86, 194; Swanton, *Early History of the Creek Indians*, 103; Chatelain, *Defenses of Spanish Florida*, 78, 166, 167.

21. Swanton, *Early History of the Creek Indians*, 103.

22. Ibid.; Hann, "Saint Augustine's Fallout," 192.

23. Swanton, *Early History of the Creek Indians*, 103; Fitch, "Tobias Fitch's Journal," 205–9; Hann, "Saint Augustine's Fallout," 192.

24. Fitch, "Tobias Fitch's Journal," 208, 209.

25. Hann, "Saint Augustine's Fallout," 192, 193, 196; Worth, *Timucuan Chiefdoms of Spanish Florida*, 2:152 (table 9-4); Oatis, *Colonial Complex*, 269–71; Hahn, *Invention of the Creek Nation*, 127, 130, 132, 135–37.

26. Salley, *SCCHJ*, February 2, 1726, 77; April 29, 1726, 99, 102; Cooper and McCord, *Statutes*, "Ordinance of the General Assembly," February 4, 1726, 3:246, 247; Jeannine Cook, *Fort King George*, 29, 30, 49, 56–61; Crane, *Southern Frontier*, 245, 246.

27. Crane, *Southern Frontier*, 268–70.

28. Middleton to the Duke of Newcastle, June 13, 1728, in *CSP, AWI*, 1728–29, 132; TePaske, *Governorship of Spanish Florida*, 130.

29. Public Treasurer, fol. 86; SCCHJ, January 18, 1724, 136; January 19, 1724, 136; October 7, 1726, 9, 10; October 8, 1726, 12, 33, 71; September 23, 1727, 53; February 1, 1728, 349; Salley and Webber, *Death Notices in the South Carolina Gazette*, 16; Salley, *SCCHJ*, February 23, 1727, 139. James McPherson's homestead and

his grants are depicted on Stuart, *Map of South Carolina and a Part of Georgia.* McPherson and his rangers supported the new colony of Georgia beginning in 1733. The company was placed under Georgia's provincial establishment in 1737 and served until late 1738. Ivers, *British Drums,* 11–23, 27, 29, 52, 71.

30. Salley, *SCCHJ,* January 13, 1727, 69; February 8, 1727, 101; Public Treasurer, fols. 2, 4, 5, 19, 27, 28, 29, 30, 72–75, 78; South Carolina Council Journals, July 6, 1727, 25; July 8, 1727; Cooper and McCord, *Statutes,* "Act for Appropriating . . . Pounds . . . towards the Payment of Public Debts," August 20, 1731, 3:334–41.

31. Middleton to the Duke of Newcastle, June 13, 1728, in *CSP, AWI,* 1728–29, 132, 133.

32. Jeannine Cook, *Fort King George,* 61–67; South Carolina Council Journals, June 16, 1727, 8; March 15, 1728, 173.

33. TePaske, *Governorship of Spanish Florida,* 130; Crane, *Southern Frontier,* 248; Middleton to the Duke of Newcastle, June 13, 1728, in *CSP, AWI,* 1728–29, 132, 133; SCCHJ, March 6, 1728, 433; March 22, 1728, 467; Salley, "Bull Family of South Carolina," 76, 77, 85, 86.

34. Chatelain, *Defenses of Spanish Florida,* 79, 160, 161; Middleton to the Duke of Newcastle, June 13, 1728, in *CSP, AWI,* 1728–29, 133.

35. SCCHJ, February 1, 1728, 349; Salley, *SCCHJ,* December 9, 1726, 31.

CHAPTER 17: Florida Expedition, 1728

1. McDowell, *Journals of the Commissioners of the Indian Trade,* November 12, 1714, 60; September 6, 1716, 108; Salley, *SCCHJ,* June 5, 1724, 10, 11; March 5, 1725, 32. A fortified storehouse at that site is shown on Barnwell, "Southeastern North America."

2. Middleton to the Duke of Newcastle, June 13, 1728, in *CSP, AWI,* 1728–29, 132, 133; SCCHJ, August 2, 1727, 558, 560; July 16, 1728, 538, 541; South Carolina Council Journal, September 21, 1727, 90; Hahn, *Invention of the Creek Nation,* 139; Crane, *Southern Frontier,* 248.

3. Crane, *Southern Frontier,* 249, 270; Cooper and McCord, *Statutes,* "Act for Carrying on Several Expeditions against Our Indians and Other Enemies . . . ," September 30, 1727, 3:273; South Carolina Council Journal, September 1, 1727, 70–71; SCCHJ, February 8, 1728, 366; Public Treasurer, fols. 102–4; President Middleton's Commission and Instructions to Col. John Palmer, September 1727, in *CSP, AWI,* 1728–29, 135. Palmer was commissioned as a colonel of militia in June 1724. Salley, *SCCHJ,* June 5, 1724, 11; December 9, 1726, 31; January 20, 1727, 74, 81.

4. Easterby, *SCCHJ,* July 1, 1741, 82; South Carolina Council Journal, February 9, 1728, 128; April 12, 1728, 187; Cooper and McCord, *Statutes,* "Act for Appropriating . . . Pounds . . . towards the Payment of Public Debts," August 20, 1731, 3:338, 339.

5. Alexander Parris to Wargent Nicholson, March 27, 1728, in Salley, *Records in the British Public Record Office,* 13:187.

6. A partial muster roll for the expedition is contained in Public Treasurer, fols. 104–5. A complete muster roll is contained in Salley, *Records in the British Public Record Office,* 13:194–96; Middleton to the Duke of Newcastle, June 13, 1728, in *CSP, AWI,* 1728–29, 134; SCCHJ, August 2, 1727, 559; May 3, 1728, 501, 502.

7. Middleton to the Duke of Newcastle, June 13, 1728, in *CSP, AWI,* 1728–29, 134; Swanton, *Early History of the Creek Indians,* 104, 105. The ford was later protected by two forts. Fort Picolata was on the east bank of the Saint Johns River in present-day Picolata near Highway 13, a short distance north of its junction with Highway 208. Fort Pupo was on the west bank about three miles south of present-day Green Cove Springs near the end of Bayard Point.

8. Chatelain, *Defenses of Spanish Florida,* 82, 84–87.

9. Hann, "St. Augustine's Fallout," 192, 193; Worth, *Timucuan Chiefdoms of Spanish Florida,* 2:152 (table 9-4), 227.

10. The Palmer Map is cited as "Draft of ye town and Harbour of St Augustine and Coast of Florida . . .", 1730. A copy is in the Saint Augustine Historical Society Library, Saint Augustine. The framed title reads, "To/The Honble/ Sr Charles Wager/A draft of ye town and Harbour/of St Augustine upon ye Coast of Florida/with all its fortifications/Latt. 30° Humbly/Dedicated being taken/1730/AT." The identity of AT is unknown; Worth, *Timucuan Chiefdoms of Spanish Florida,* 2:152 (table 9-4).

11. Within six years San Juan del Puertyo de Palica was relocated not far north of Pocotalaca, and a town known as Nuestra Señora del Rosario de la Punta was located on Palica's old site. Arrendondo, "Plan de la Ciudad de St Agustin"; Worth, *Timucuan Chiefdoms of Spanish Florida,* 2:152 (table 9-4); TePaske, *Governorship of Spanish Florida,* 182, 188; Swanton, *Early History of the Creek Indians,* 104, 105; Hann, "St. Augustine's Fallout," 184–86, 190–92, 194. Maria Sanchez Creek and its marsh have long since been tiled and covered.

12. "Draft of ye town and Harbour of St Augustine"; Hann, "St. Augustine's Fallout," 195–98; Worth, *Timucuan Chiefdoms of Spanish Florida,* 2:152 (table 9-4).

13. Worth, *Timucuan Chiefdoms of Spanish Florida,* 2:149, 152 (table 9-4); Nombre de Dios Amacarisa was also known later as Nombre De Dios Marcaris, Macaris, or Macariz. That name was probably used because the town was located near Macaris Creek, which the British later designated as Hospital Creek; TePaske, *Governorship of Spanish Florida,* 208; Swanton, *Early History of the Creek Indians,* 96, 104; Chatelain, *Defenses of Spanish Florida,* 84, 85; Hann, "St. Augustine's Fallout," 196; Arnade, *Siege of St. Augustine,* 48, 49; "Draft of ye town and Harbour of St Augustine," 1730.

14. "Draft of ye town and Harbour of St Augustine," 1730; Worth, *Timucuan Chiefdoms of Spanish Florida,* 2:152 (table 9-4); Hann, "St. Augustine's Fallout," 186, 195. Tolomato was probably located at a site known as Ayachin, southwest of Moze. After Palmer's 1728 raid, Tolomato was moved to a site near the northwest corner of Saint Augustine's wall and south of the Cubo Line. Chatelain, *Defenses of Spanish Florida,* 91, 92, 93, 167. Several years later Moze (Mosa, Mossy) was given to South Carolina's runaway slaves as their village. Fort

Mosa was constructed there for their protection. Fort Mosa is shown on a number of eighteenth-century maps, including Castello, "Plano del Presidio de Sn. Agustin" and "Plan of the Land between Fort Mossy and St Augustine."

15. "Draft of ye town and Harbour of St Augustine"; Hann, "St. Augustine's Fallout," 195, 196; Middleton to the Duke of Newcastle, June 13, 1728, in *CSP, AWI,* 1728–29, 134; Swanton, *Early History of the Creek Indians,* 104; Parris to Nicholson, March 27, 1728, in Salley, *Records in the British Public Record Office,* 13:188, 189; TePaske, *Governorship of Spanish Florida,* 209n44.

16. "Draft of ye town and Harbour of St Augustine"; Middleton to the Duke of Newcastle, June 13, 1728, in *CSP, AWI,* 1728–29, 134; Swanton, *Early History of the Creek Indians,* 104; Parris to Nicholson, March 27, 1728, in Salley, *Records in the British Public Record Office,* 13:188. The name of Chiquito's mico, Francisco Iospogue, suggests that he and some of his followers may have been related in some manner to the Huspaw King. During the late seventeenth century, Ospogue (Azpogue, Jospo, Ospo) was a town in the Spanish province of Guale. The townspeople may have divided, some migrating north to the Yamasees in South Carolina, where they became the town of Huspaw, and the remainder staying in Guale as part of the mission town of San Phelipe on present-day Cumberland Island, Georgia. During 1701 a man named Francisco was the mico of the town of Jospo in the Spanish mission system; TePaske, *Governorship of Spanish Florida,* 209n44, appendix 2; Worth, *Struggle for the Georgia Coast,* 25, 106, 125n48, 201.

17. Middleton to the Duke of Newcastle, June 13, 1728, in *CSP, AWI,* 1728–29, 134; "Draft of ye town and Harbour of St Augustine"; Swanton, *Early History of the Creek Indians,* 104; Hann, "St. Augustine's Fallout," 196, 197.

18. Although it is not clear, "Draft of ye town and Harbour of St Augustine" may depict a fort at Pocotalaca. Arrendondo, "Plan de la Ciudad de St Agustin," definitely shows a later fort in the town of Pocotalaca; Middleton to the Duke of Newcastle, June 13, 1728, in *CSP, AWI,* 1728–29, 135.

19. Middleton to the Duke of Newcastle, June 13, 1728, in *CSP, AWI,* 1728–29, 134; Parris to Nicholson, March 27, 1728, in Salley, *Records in the British Public Record Office,* 13:188; SCCHJ, March 23, 1728, 470; Chatelain, *Defenses of Spanish Florida,* 88; Crane, *Southern Frontier,* 130, 250.

20. Middleton to the Duke of Newcastle, June 13, 1728, in *CSP, AWI,* 1728–29, 134; Parris to Nicholson, March 27, 1728, in Salley, *Records in the British Public Record Office,* 13:188.

21. Puente, "Saint Augustine and Vicinity"; Worth, *Timucuan Chiefdoms of Spanish Florida,* 2:154 (fig. 9-1); Swanton, *Early History of the Creek Indians,* 105; Hann, "St. Augustine's Fallout," 194, 195.

22. SCCHJ, March 23, 1728, 471; April 4, 1728, 476; April 6, 1728, 481, 482; South Carolina Council Journal, March 23, 1728, 177, 178; April 4, 1728, 179; April 5, 1728, 181, 182; April 6, 1728, 183. Palmer's personal journal has apparently been lost.

23. Parris to Middleton, June 1, 1728, in Salley, *Records in the British Public Record Office,* 13:191; 95th Article of his Majtys Royll Instructions to the Govr of South Carolina, September 20, 1728, in Salley, *Records in the British Public Record Office,* 13:193; Middleton to the Duke of Newcastle, June 13, 1728, in *CSP, AWI,* 1728–29, 131–35.

24. South Carolina's provincial military units for the period 1727–31 are listed in Cooper and McCord, *Statutes,* "Act for Appropriating . . . Pounds . . . towards the Payment of Public Debts," August 20, 1731, 3:335. After Palmer's raid Nombre de Dios was moved south across the creek just inside the Hornwork. The people of Nuestra Señora del Rosario at Moze probably moved to a location just south of Saint Augustine where Palica was formerly located. The new town became known as La Punta. The town of Tolomato was moved just inside the Cubo Line, near the northwest bastion of Saint Augustine's wall. Palica was moved to a location not far west of and near the middle of Saint Augustine's western wall. The towns are shown on Puente, "Saint Augustine and Vicinity," and in Worth, *Timucuan Chiefdoms of Spanish Florida,* 2:154 (fig. 9-1); Crane, *Southern Frontier,* 250, 251, 272; Hahn, *Invention of the Creek Nation,* 139–44.

Conclusion

1. Le Jau to the Society, May 10, 1715, in Klingberg, *Chronicle of Le Jau,* 153; Bull to the Society, August 10, 1715, in Klingberg, "Mystery of the Lost Yamasee Prince," 23; Johnston to the Society, December 19, 1715, in Pennington, "South Carolina Indian War," 262; Maule to the Society, February 16, 1716, in Pennington, "South Carolina Indian War," February 263, 264.

2. Sirmans, *Colonial South Carolina,* 108–11, 145–67.

3. Cooper and McCord, *Statutes,* "Act for Appropriating . . . Pounds . . . towards the Payment of Public Debts," August 20, 1731, 3:334–41; Cooper and McCord, *Statutes,* "Schedule, or Estimate, to Which the Act Annexed Refers," April 9, 1734, 3:390–92; Sirmans, *Colonial South Carolina,* 167, 168; Meriwether, *Expansion of South Carolina,* 32–109; Ivers, *British Drums,* 9–30.

4. Ivers, *British Drums,* 9–30, 194, 195.

5. Worth, "Yamasee," 252; Swanton, *Myths and Tales of the Southeastern Indians,* 83.

Bibliography ———

Manuscript Sources

Auditor General Memorial Books, vols. 1–12, microfilm, South Carolina Department of Archives and History, Columbia.

"Colonial Records of Georgia," vols. 20, 27–39. Typescript. Georgia Archives, Atlanta.

Corcoles y Martinez, Francisco de. Letters, July 5, 1715; November 28, 1715; January 25, 1716 (which includes copies of letters dated May 28 and May 29, 1715). Archivo General de las Indias, Seville, and Biblioteca Nacionale, Madrid. These letters were kindly provided to me by Dr. John Worth from his research materials and were translated by Nathan Gordon.

Huspaw King to Governor Craven, April 1715, British Records, 1715, PRO ADM 1/2451, 72, 1410.1, North Carolina Archives, Raleigh.

Original papers, Letters, etc., from the Governors, Colonial Office 5/359. Microfilm. South Carolina Archives, Columbia.

Public Treasurer. Ledger A, 1725–30. South Carolina Archives, Columbia.

Records of the Secretary of the Province, Land Grants, Colonial Series of Royal Grants (Proprietary Grants). South Carolina Archives, Columbia.

St. Lo, Capt. Jonathan, to Josiah Burchett, July 12, 1715, British Public Record Office, Admiralty Office, 1:2451:1–4; photocopy in British Public Records Calendar, 1712–16, 72.1409:1–4. North Carolina Archives, Raleigh.

South Carolina Commons House Journals. See Charles E. Lee and Ruth S. Green, "A Guide to the Commons House Journals of the South Carolina General Assembly, 1692–1721," *South Carolina Historical Magazine* 68 (1967):85–96, 165–83 ("1721–75").

South Carolina Council Journals. See Charles E. Lee and Ruth S. Green, "A Guide to South Carolina Council Journals, 1671–1775," *South Carolina Historical Magazine* 68 (1967):1–13.

South Carolina Upper House Journals. See Charles E. Lee and Ruth S. Green, "A Guide to the Upper House Journals of the South Carolina General Assembly, 1721–75," *South Carolina Historical Magazine* 67 (1966):187–202.

Wills, Inventories and Miscellaneous Records, vol. 56, 1714–17; vol. 58, 1722–24; vol. 59, 1722–26; vol. 60, 1724–25; vols. 61A–61B, 1726–27. Microfilm. South Carolina Archives, Columbia.

Printed Sources

Barnwell, Joseph W., ed. "Fort King George—Journal of Col. John Barnwell." *South Carolina Historical and Genealogical Magazine* 27 (1926):189–203.

———, ed. "The Tuscarora Expedition: Letters of Colonel John Barnwell." *South Carolina Historical and Genealogical Magazine* 9 (1908):28–54.

Bonnefoy, Antoine. "Journal of Antoine Bonnefoy, 1741–1742." In *Travels in the American Colonies,* edited by Newton D. Mereness, 241–55. New York: Antiquarian Press, 1961.

Boston News-Letter. Microfilm. University of Iowa Library, Iowa City.

Boyd, Mark, ed. "Diego Pena's Expedition to Apalachee and Apalachicolo in 1716." *Florida Historical Quarterly* 28 (1949):1–27.

———, ed. "Documents Describing the Second and Third Expeditions of Lieutenant Diego Pena to Apalachee and Apalachicolo in 1717 and 1718." *Florida Historical Quarterly* 31 (1952):109–39.

Brock, R. A. ed. *The Official Letters of Alexander Spotswood: Lieutenant-Governor of the Colony of Virginia, 1710–1722.* 2 vols. Richmond: Virginia Historical Society, 1935.

Chandler, Allen D., and Lucian L. Knight, eds. *The Colonial Records of the State of Georgia.* 39 vols. Atlanta: Franklin, 1904–16.

Chicken, George. "Colonel Chicken's Journal to the Cherokees, 1725." In *Travels in the American Colonies,* edited by Newton Mereness, 93–172. New York: Antiquarian Press, 1916.

———. "A Journal from Carolina in 1715." In *Yearbook of the City of Charleston,* edited by Langdon Cheves, 324–54. Charleston, S.C.: Walker, Erono & Cogswell, 1894.

Cooper, Thomas, and David J. McCord, eds. *The Statutes at Large of South Carolina.* 10 vols. Columbia: Johnson, 1836–41.

Dampier, William. *A New Voyage round the World.* 3 vols. London, 1717.

Desaussure, Henry W. ed., *Reports of Cases Argued and Determined in the Court of Chancery of the State of South Carolina.* 4 vols. Philadelphia: Small, 1854.

Dickinson, Jonathan. *Jonathan Dickinson's Journal: or, God's Protecting Providence.* Port Salerno: Florida Classics Library, 1985.

Easterby, J. H., ed. *The Journal of the Commons House of Assembly,* May 18, 1741–July 10, 1742. Columbia: Historical Commission of South Carolina, 1953.

Edgar, Walter B., ed. *Biographical Directory of the South Carolina House of Representatives: Session Lists, 1692–1973.* Columbia: University of South Carolina Press, 1974.

Fitch, Tobias. "Tobias Fitch's Journal to the Creeks." In *Travels in the American Colonies,* edited by Newton D Mereness, 176–212. New York: Antiquarian Press, 1961.

Friedlander, Amy, ed. "Commissary Johnston's Report, 1713." *South Carolina Historical Magazine* 83 (1982):259–71.

Gallardo, Jose M., ed. "The Spaniards and the English Settlement in Charles Town." *South Carolina Historical and Genealogical Magazine* 37 (1936):131–41.

Geiger, Florence G., ed. "St. Bartholomew's Parish as Seen by Its Rectors." *South Carolina Historical Magazine* 50 (1949):173–203.

Glen, James, and George Milligen-Johnston. *Colonial South Carolina: Two Contemporary Descriptions*. Columbia: University of South Carolina Press, 1951.

Gregorie, Anne King, ed. *Records of the Court of Chancery of South Carolina, 1671–1779*. Washington, D.C.: American Historical Association, 1950.

"Historical Notes: Inscriptions from St. Andrews Church Yard." *South Carolina Historical and Genealogical Magazine* 13 (1912):113–18.

Hvidt, Kristian, ed. *Von Reck's Voyage: Drawings and Journal of Philip Georg Friedrich von Reck*. Savannah: Beehive, 1980.

Jervey, Theo. D., and Mrs. Waveland FitzSimons, eds. "Items Relating to Charles Town, S.C., from the *Boston News-Letter:* From Monday October 7 to Monday October 14, 1706." *South Carolina Historical and Genealogical Magazine* 40 (1939):73–78.

Jones, George F, ed. "John Martin Boltzius' Trip to Charleston, October 1742." *South Carolina Historical Magazine* 82 (1981):87–110.

Jones, George F., Renate Wilson, and Don Savelle. *Detailed Reports on the Salzburger Emigrants Who Settled in America, 1733–1734*. Athens: University of Georgia Press, 1968.

Klingberg, Frank J., ed. *The Carolina Chronicle of Dr. Francis Le Jau, 1706–1717*. Berkeley: University of California Press, 1956.

———, ed. *Carolina Chronicle: The Papers of Commissary Gideon Johnston, 1707–1716*. Berkeley: University of California Press, 1946.

Langley, Clara A. ed. *South Carolina Deed Abstracts,* 3 vols. Easley, S.C.: Southern Historical Press, 1983.

Lefler, Hugh T., ed. *A New Voyage to Carolina by John Lawton*. Chapel Hill: University of North Carolina Press, 1967.

McDowell, W. L., ed. *Journals of the Commissioners of the Indian Trade, 1710–1718*. Columbia: State Commercial Printing Company, 1955.

McIlwaine, H. R., ed. *Executive Journals of the Council of Colonial Virginia*. 6 vols. Richmond: Superintendent of Public Printing, 1906–78.

Moore, Alexander, ed. *Nairne's Muskhogean Journals: The 1708 Expedition to the Mississippi River*. Jackson: University Press of Mississippi, 1988.

Moore, Caroline T., ed. *Abstracts of Records of the Secretary of the Province of South Carolina, 1692–1721*. Columbia: Bryan, 1978.

Moore, Caroline T., and Agatha A. Simons, eds. *Abstracts of the Wills of the State of South Carolina, 1670–1740*. Columbia: Bryan, 1960.

Moore, Francis. "A Voyage to Georgia Begun in the Year 1735." *Collections of the Georgia Historical Society,* vol. 1, 80–152. Savannah: Georgia Historical Society, 1840.

Muller, John. *A Treatise Concerning the Elementary Part of Fortification.* London: Wingrave, 1746.

Nairne, Thomas. *A Letter from South Carolina: Giving an Account of the Soil, Air, Product, Trade, Government, Laws, Religion, People, Military Strength, & of That Province.* London: Baldwin, 1710.

"A New Voyage to Georgia." *Collections of the Georgia Historical Society,* vol. 2, 39–60. Savannah: Georgia Historical Society, 1842.

Pennington, Edgar Legare, ed. "The South Carolina Indian War of 1715, as Seen by the Clergymen." *South Carolina Historical and Genealogical Magazine* 32 (1931): 251–69.

"Pierre De St. Julien's Last Will and Testament, June 2, 1718." *Transactions of the Huguenot Society of South Carolina* 11 (1904):39.

"Rodd to His Employer in London, 8 May 1715 [Rodd's Relation]." In *Calendar of State Papers, Colonial Series, America and the West Indies,* vol. 28:166–69. London, 1928. The original letter, written in French, is in Original Correspondence and Papers from the Governors of South Carolina (CO 5/387), 1715–29, 15, 16. Microfilm. South Carolina Department of Archives and History, Columbia.

"Rodd, George to Joseph Boone and Richard Berresford, 19 July 1715." In *Yearbook of the City of Charleston,* ed. Langdon Cheves, 319–23. Charleston: Walker, Erono, & Cogswell, 1894.

Sainsbury, W. Noel, et al., eds. *Calendar of State Papers, Colonial Office Series: America and the West Indies.* 45 vols. London: Her Majesty's Stationary Office, 1860–1994.

Salley, A. S., Jr. *Journal of His Majesty's Council for South Carolina, May 29, 1721–June 10, 1721.* Atlanta: Foote & Davis Company, 1930.

———. "Letters from the Schenckingh Smiths of South Carolina to the Boylston Smiths of Massachusetts." *South Carolina Historical and Genealogical Magazine* 35 (1934):1–12.

———, ed. *Records in the British Public Record Office Relating to South Carolina, 1663–1710.* Transcribed by W. Noel Sainsbury. 5 vols. Columbia: Historical Commission of South Carolina, 1947.

———, ed. *Warrants for Lands in South Carolina, 1692–1711.* Columbia: University of South Carolina Press, 1973.

Salley, Alexander, and Mable L. Webber, eds. *Death Notices in the South Carolina Gazette, 1732–1775.* Columbia: Crowson-Stone, 1954.

Saunders, William L. ed. *Colonial Records of North Carolina.* 10 vols. Raleigh: Hale, 1886–90.

Smith, D. E. Huger, ed. "Broughton Letters." *South Carolina Historical and Genealogical Magazine* 15 (1914):171–96.

South Carolina Gazette.

Swanton, John R., ed. *Myths and Tales of the Southeastern Indians.* Norman: University of Oklahoma Press, 1995.

Webber, Mabel L., ed. "Records from the Elliott-Rowland Bible." *South Carolina Historical and Genealogical Magazine* 11 (1910):57–71.

——, ed. "Records of the Quakers in Charles Town." *South Carolina Historical and Genealogical Magazine* 28 (1927):22–43, 94–107, 176–97.

Williams, George W., ed. *Letters from the Clergy of the Anglican Church in South Carolina, c. 1696–1775.* http://speccoll.cofc.edu/pdf/SPGSeriesABC.pdf (accessed January 20, 2015).

Williams, Samuel Cole, ed. *Adair's History of the American Indians.* New York: Promontory, 1930.

Withington, Lothrop, ed. "South Carolina Gleanings in England." *South Carolina Historical and Genealogical Magazine* 5 (1904):100–107.

Wright, David McCord, ed. "Petitioners to the Crown against the Proprietors, 1716–1717." *South Carolina Historical Magazine* 62 (1961):88–95.

Maps

For detailed information regarding most of the following maps, see William P. Cummings, ed., *The Southeast in Early Maps.* 3rd ed. Chapel Hill: University of North Carolina Press, 2014.

Arredondo, Antonio de. "Plan de la Ciudad de St Agustin de la Florida, Havana, 1737." In *The Defenses of Spanish Florida, 1565–1763,* by Verne E. Chatelain, end piece. Washington, D.C.: Carnegie Institution of Washington, 1941.

Barnwell, John A. "The Northern B[ra]nch of Altamana River which joynes ye main River 3 miles higher up." 1721. South Carolina Department of Archives and History, Columbia.

——. "Southeastern North America." Ca. 1721–24. Original in the British Public Record Office. Tracing in the South Carolina Department of Archives and History, Columbia.

Bonar, William. "A Draught of the Creek Nation". 1757. EMAS Collections, North America, CO 700. Public Record Office, London.

Boss and Brailsford. "A Map of South Carolina from the Savannah Sound to the St. Helena's Sound." ca. 1750 and 1771. South Carolina Department of Archives and History, Columbia.

Bowen, Emanuel. *A New and Accurate Map of the Province of North and South Carolina, Georgia, &c.* London, 1747.

Bull, William. "Southeastern North America." 1738. Manuscript in British Public Record Office, London. Basically, a copy of Barnwell's map.

Campbell, Archibald. "Sketch of the Northern Frontiers of Georgia," 1780. Copy in Georgia Surveyor General Office, Atlanta.

Castello, Pablo. "Plano del Presidio de Sn. Agustin, 1764." In *The Defenses of Spanish Florida, 1565–1763,* by Vern E. Chatelain. Washington, D.C.: Carnegie Institution of Washington, 1941.

"Chart of Parts of the Coast of South Carolina, from Port Royall to Charlestown," ca. 1700. In *Crown Collection of Photographs of American Maps,* edited by Archer Butler Hulbert. Series I, vol. 5, no. 31. Cleveland: Clark, 1907. This map depicts the Yamasee near the Ashepoo and Combahee Rivers ca. 1685–1700 and shows the original names of the islands at Port Royal.

"A Colored Map of the Coast of South Carolina, Georgia, and Florida," ca. 1770. In *Crown Collection of Photographs of American Maps,* edited by Archer Butler Hulbert. 1st series, vol. 5, nos. 32, 33. Cleveland: Clark, 1907.

"Colored Plat of 1590 Acres Located between Two Branches of the Ashepoo River, Purchased by John Stanyarne," 1701. Pringle-Garden Family Papers. South Carolina Historical Society Library, Charleston. Also, see the James Stanyarne Plat, 1700. Auditor Memorial Books 4:183, South Carolina Department of Archives and History, Columbia, S.C. This is another version, perhaps the surveyor's field sketch and notes. It appears that between the making of this preliminary plat in February 1700 and the completion of the final plat the following year, ownership was transferred from James Stanyarne to his brother, John.

Cook, James. *A Map of the Province of South Carolina.* London, 1773.

De Brahm, William. *A Map of South Carolina and a Part of Georgia.* London, 1757.

"A Draft of Town and Harbour of St Augustine and Coast of Florida . . . ," 1730. It is sometimes known as the Palmer Map. Copy in the Saint Augustine Historical Society Library, Saint Augustine.

Gaillard, J. P. "Map of Berkeley and Parts of Charleston and Dorchester Counties." South Carolina Historical Society, Charleston.

General Highway Maps, South Carolina. South Carolina State Highway Department (now the South Carolina Department of Transportation), 1969, 2005.

"General Plan of the Canal and Its Environs between Santee and Cooper Rivers." Undated Manuscript. South Carolina Department of Archives and History, Columbia.

Gordon, Peter. *A View of Savannah as it Stood on the 29th of March 1734.* London, 1734.

Gregorie, Anne King. "Map of Christ Church Parish." South Carolina Historical Society Library, Charleston.

Halsey, Alfred O. *Historical Charleston on a Map.* 1949. South Carolina Historical Society.

Harris, John. *A Compleat Description of the Province of Carolina in 3 Parts.* London: Edward Crisp, 1711. South Caroliniana Library, University of South Carolina, Columbia. Contains Nairne's 1711 map of the Southeast and an inset of Charles Town and vicinity.

Herbert, John. "A New Mapp of His Maiestys Flourishing Province of South Carolina: Showing ye Settlements of y[e] English, French and Indian Nation," 1725. Certified as correct by George Hunter, 1744.

Hunter, George. "Cherokee Nation and the Traders' Path from Charles Town via Congaree. 1730." In *Bulletins of the Historical Commission of South Carolina,* vol. 4. Columbia, 1917.

———. Survey Plat for Robert Johnson, 1732. Shows village sites of Altamaha,

Okatie, & Chechessee. John McGrady Plat Collection. Charleston County Courthouse, Charleston, and microfilm in South Carolina Department of Archives and History, Columbia, S.C.

Kitchin, T. *A New Map of the Cherokee Nation with the Names of the Towns and Rivers. They are Situated On.* London, 1760.

McGrady, John. Plat Collection, 1680–1929. Charleston County Courthouse, Charleston, and microfilm in South Carolina Department of Archives and History, Columbia.

Manuscript Plats (loose). South Carolina Department of Archives and History, Columbia.

Map of Pinckney's Island, 1710. South Carolina Department of Archives and History, Columbia.

"Mapp of Beaufort in South Carolina," 1721. Newberry Library, Chicago.

"Map Showing Several Plantations Situate in St. John's Parish Berkeley County, S.C.," October 10, 1949. South Carolina Historical Society, Charleston.

Moll, Herman. Carolina. ca. 1736. MS 1361-MP 238. Georgia Historical Society, Savannah.

———. *A Map of the Improved Part of Carolina with the Settlements etc.* London, 1711, 1715.

———. *A Map of the Province of Carolina, Divided into Its Parishes &c. According to the Latest Accounts.* London, 1730.

Mosley, Edward. *A New and Correct Map of the Province of North Carolina.* London, 1733.

Mouzon, Henry, et al. *An Accurate Map of North and South Carolina with Their Indian Frontiers.* London, 1775. This map shows Barker's 1715 defeat near Santee River. It is a good one for showing the most-used trails. It depicts the Cherokee towns of Tossee, Tugaloo, Tawcoe (Taruraw?), Tehoee (Tetohe?), Estatohe (Estatoe), Chauga (Chagee), Noyowee.

Nairne, Thomas. *A Map of South Carolina, 1711.* An insert on John Harris. *A Compleat Description of the Province of Carolina in 3 Parts.* London, 1711.

Palmer Map. See "A Draft of Town and Harbour of St Augustine and Coast of Florida . . . ," 1730.

"A Plan of King George's Fort at Allatamaha, South Carolina," ca. 1722. In *Crown Collection of Photographs of American Maps,* edited by Archer Butler Hulbert, 3rd Series, sheet 132, no. 7. Cleveland: Clark, 1915.

"Plan of the Land between Fort Mossy and St Augustine, East Florida, 1765." In *The Defenses of Spanish Florida, 1565–1763,* Vern E. Chatelain. Washington, D.C.: Carnegie Institution of Washington, 1941.

"A Plan of Skinking Plantation Belonging to Ralph Izard Esquire," 1795 (loose). South Carolina Historical Society, Charleston.

"Plan of a Tract of Land Belonging to Thomas Eveleigh," January 14, 1817. South Carolina Historical Society, Charleston.

Plat of the south side of the Santee River and west of Greenland Swamp. South Carolina Historical Society, Charleston.

Puente, Juan Jose Eligio de la. "Saint Augustine and Vicinity, 1764." In Vern E. Chatelain. *The Defenses of Spanish Florida, 1565–1763*. Washington: Carnegie Institution of Washington, 1941.

"A Sketch Map of the Rivers Santee, Congaree, Wateree, Saludee, etc., with the Road to the Cuttauboes," ca. 1750. In *Crown Collection of Photographs of American Maps*, edited by Archer Butler Hulbert, 3rd series, sheet 25, no. 25. Cleveland: Clark, 1915. This map depicts Congaree Fort.

"Sketch Map of the Site of St. Johns French Church." *Transactions of the Huguenot Society of South Carolina* 71 (1966):44.

Stuart, John. *A Map of South Carolina and a Part of Georgia*. London, 1780. This is a later, expanded edition of De Brahm's 1757 map.

———. "Part of the Purcell Map Compiled Not Later than 1770 in the Interest of British Indian Trade." Edward E. Ayer Collection, Newberry Library, Chicago.

Swanton, John R. "The Distribution of Indian tribes in the southeast at different periods." In *The Early History of the Creek Indians and Their Neighbors*, by John R. Swanton, plate 3. Washington: Government Printing Office, 1922.

———. "Locations of Indian tribes in the Southeast at different periods." In *Indians of the Southeastern United States*, by John R. Swanton, 34. Washington: Government Printing Office, 1946.

———. "Territory of the States of Georgia and Alabama Illustrating the Geographical Distribution and Movements of the Tribes and Twons of the Creek Confederacy, 1919." In *The Early History of the Creek Indians and Their Neighbors*, by John R. Swanton, plate 2. Washington: Government Printing Office, 1922.

Thornton, John, and Robert Morden. *This New Map of the Chief Rivers, Bayhes, Creeks, Harbours, and Settlements, in South Carolina*. London, ca. 1695.

U.S. Department of the Interior, Geological Survey, maps of varying scales and dates for locations in Florida, Georgia, and South Carolina.

A View of the Town of Savannah, in the Colony of Georgia, in South Carolina. London, 1741.

Woolley, "Cherokee Country prior to 1776." University of Georgia Library, Special Collections Division.

Secondary Sources

Ames, Joseph S. "Cantey Family." *South Carolina Historical and Genealogical Magazine* 11 (1910):203–58.

Arnade, Charles. *The Siege of St. Augustine in 1702*. Gainesville: University Press of Florida, 1958.

Barker, Eirlys M. "Pryce Hughes, Colony Planner of Charles Town and Wales." *South Carolina Historical Magazine* 95 (1994):302–13.

Barnwell, Joseph W. "Dr. Henry Woodward, the First English Settler in South Carolina, and Some of His Descendants." *South Carolina Historical and Genealogical Magazine* 8 (1907):29–41.

———. "The Second Tuscarora Expedition." *South Carolina Historical and Genealogical Magazine* 10 (1909):33–48.

Beck, Robin A., Jr. *Chiefdoms, Collapse, and Coalescence in the Early American South.* New York: Cambridge University Press, 2013.

Bossy, Denise I. "Godin & Co.: Charleston Merchants and the Indian Trade, 1674–1715." *South Carolina Historical Magazine* 114 (2013):96–131.

Bowne, Eric R. "'Caryinge awaye Their Corne and Children': The Effects of Westo Slave Raids on the Indians of the Lower South." In *Mapping the Mississippian Shatter Zone: The Colonial Slave Trade and Regional Instability in the American South,* edited by Robbie Etheridge and Sheri M. Shuck-Hall, 104–14. Lincoln: University of Nebraska Press, 2009.

Braund, Kathryn Holland. *Deerskins and Duffels: The Creek Indian Trade with Anglo-America, 1685–1815.* Lincoln: University of Nebraska Press, 1993.

Brightman, Robert A., and Pamela S. Wallace. "Chickasaw." In *Southeast,* edited by Raymond D. Fogelson, 478–495. Vol. 14 of *Handbook of North American Indians,* edited by William C. Sturtevant. Washington, D.C.: Smithsonian Institution, 2004.

Brown, Douglas S. *The Catawba Indians: The People of the River.* Columbia: University of South Carolina Press, 1966.

Brown, Philip M. "Early Indian Trade in the Development of South Carolina: Politics, Economics, and Social Mobility during the Proprietary Period, 1670–1719." *South Carolina Historical Magazine* 76 (1975):118–28.

Buckland, Kristie. "The Monmouth Cap." *Costume: The Journal of the Costume Society* 13 (1979):23–37.

Burke, Lee. "Eighteenth-Century Trade Guns in the South: or, The Carolina Gun, Its Time and Place in History." *American Society of Arms Collectors Bulletin* 65 (1991):3–16.

Caldwell, Joseph R. "Palachacolas Town, Hampton County, South Carolina." *Journal of the Washington Academy of Sciences* 38 (1948):321–24.

Catesby, Mark. *The Natural History of Carolina, Florida and the Bahama Islands.* 2 vols. London: Marsh, 1754.

Chapelle, Howard I. *American Small Sailing Craft: Their Design, Development, and Construction.* New York: Norton, 1951.

Chatelain, Vern E. *The Defenses of Spanish Florida, 1565–1763.* Washington, D.C.: Carnegie Institution of Washington, 1941.

Cheves, Langdon. "Izard of South Carolina." *South Carolina Historical and Genealogical Magazine* 2 (1901):203–40.

Clowse, Converse D. *Economic Beginnings in Colonial South Carolina, 1670–1730.* Columbia: University of South Carolina Press, 1971.

Cobb, Charles R. "First Season at Palachacolas Town." *Legacy* 13, no. 2 (2009):10, 11.

———. "2011 Field School at Palachacolas Town." *Legacy* 15, no. 2 (2011):10–12.

Coclanis, Peter A. "Death in Early Charleston: An Estimate of the Crude Death Rate for the White Population of Charleston, 1722–1731." *South Carolina Historical Magazine* 85 (1984):280–91.

Cook, Jeannine. *Fort King George: Step One to Statehood.* Darien, Ga.: Darien News, 1990.

Covington, James W. "Apalachee Indians, 1704–1763." *Florida Historical Quarterly* 50 (1972):366–84.

——. "The Yamasee Indians in Florida." *Florida Anthropologist* 23 (1970):119–28.

Crane, Verner W. *The Southern Frontier, 1670–1732.* Ann Arbor: University of Michigan Press, 1959.

DeMallie, Raymond J. "Tutelo and Neighboring Groups." In *Southeast,* edited by Raymond D. Fogelson, 286–300. Vol. 14 of *Handbook of North American Indians,* edited by William C. Sturtevant. Washington, D.C.: Smithsonian Institution, 2004.

Douglas, John E. "Impeaching the Impeachment: The Case of Chief Justice Nicholas Trott of South Carolina." *South Carolina Historical Magazine* 94 (1993): 102–16.

Duff, Meaghan N. "Creating a Plantation Province: Proprietary Land Policies and Early Settlement Patters." In *Money, Trade, and Power: The Evolution of Colonial South Carolina's Plantation Society,* edited by Jack P. Greene, Rosemary Brana-Shute, and Randy J. Sparks, 108–41. Columbia: University of South Carolina Press, 2001.

Fischer, David Hackett. *Champlain's Dream.* New York: Simon & Schuster, 2008.

Fisher, Mrs. George. "John Barnwell and British Western Policy." *Proceedings of the South Carolina Historical Association* (1957).

Fogelson, Raymond D. "Cherokee in the East." In *Southeast,* edited by Raymond D. Fogelson, 337–53. Vol. 14 of *Handbook of North American Indians,* edited by William C. Sturtevant. Washington, D.C.: Smithsonian Institution, 2004.

Franklin, Mike, and Paul Malo. "Rediscovering Fort Haldimand." *Thousand Islands Life Magazine,* April 15, 2008, http://www.thousandislandslife .com/BackIssues/Archive/tabid/393/articleType/ArticleView/articleId/86/ Rediscovering-Fort-Haldimand-compiled-by-Mike-Franklin-and-Paul -Malo.aspx (accessed June 10, 2013).

Gallay, Alan. *The Indian Slave Trade: The Rise of the English Empire in the American South, 1670–1717.* New Haven: Yale University Press, 2002.

Galloway, Patrick. "Confederacy as a Solution to Chiefdom Dissolution." In *The Forgotten Centuries: Indians and Europeans in the American South,* edited by Charles Hudson and Carmen Chaves Tesser, 319–23. Athens: University of Georgia Press, 1994.

Green, William G. "The Search for Altamaha: The Archaeology and Ethnohistory of an Early Eighteenth-Century Yamasee Indian Town." MA thesis, University of South Carolina, 1991.

Green, William G., Chester B. DePratter, and Bobby Southerlin. "The Yamasee in South Carolina: Native American Adaption and Interaction along the Carolina Frontier." In *Another's Country: Archaeological and Historical Perspectives on Cultural Interactions in the Southern Colonies,* edited by J. W. Joseph and Martha Zierden, 12–29. Tuscaloosa: University of Alabama Press, 2002.

Groover, Mark. "Exploring Fort Moore." Mark Groover's Archaeological Publications and Research Projects, http://mdgroover.iweb.bsu.edu/GPR%20Ft.%20Moore.htm (accessed in September 2012).

Hahn, Steven C. "'The Indians That Live about Pon Pon': John and Mary Musgrove and the Making of a Creek Indian Community in South Carolina, 1717–1732." In *Creating and Contesting Carolina: Proprietary Era Histories,* edited by Michelle LeMaster and Bradford J. Wood, 343–66. Columbia: University of South Carolina Press, 2013.

———. *The Invention of the Creek Nation, 1670–1763.* Lincoln: University of Nebraska Press, 2004.

———. *The Life and Times of Mary Musgrove.* Gainesville: University Press of Florida, 2012.

Hann, John H. "St. Augustine's Fallout from the Yamasee War." *Florida Historical Quarterly* 68 (1989–90):180–200.

Hanover House. National Register Properties in South Carolina. Pickens County (Clemson University). www.nationalregistersc.gov/pickens/S10817739012. Accessed 30 August 2014.

Heitzler, Michael J. "Boochawee: Plantation Land and Legacy in Goose Creek." *South Carolina Historical Magazine* 111 (2010):34–69.

———. *Goose Creek: A Definitive History: Planters, Politicians and Patriots.* 2 vols. Charleston, S.C.: History Press, 2005.

Henning, Cohen. *The South Carolina Gazette.* Columbia: University of South Carolina Press, 1953.

Hewett, Alexander. *An Historical Account of the Rise and Progress of the Colonies of South Carolina and Georgia.* 2 vols. London: Donaldson, 1779.

Hewitt, Gary L. "The State in the Planters' Service." *In Money, Trade, and Power,* edited by Jack P. Greene, Rosemary Brana-Shute, and Randy J. Sparks, 49–73. Columbia: University of South Carolina Press, 2001.

Heyward, James B., "The Heyward Family of South Carolina." *South Carolina Historical and Genealogical Magazine* 59 (1958):143–58.

Hicks, Theresa M., ed. *South Carolina Indians, Indian Traders, and Other Ethnic Connections Beginning in 1670.* Spartanburg, S.C.: Reprint Company, 1997.

Hirsch, Arthur H. *The Huguenots of Colonial South Carolina.* Durham, N.C.: Duke University Press, 1928.

Hudson, Charles. *Southeastern Indians.* Knoxville: University of Tennessee Press, 1976.

Inscoe, John C. "Carolina Slave Names: An Index to Acculturation." *Journal of Southern History* 49 (1983):527–54.

Ivers, Larry E. *British Drums on the Southern Frontier: The Military Colonization of Georgia, 1733–1749.* Chapel Hill: University of North Carolina Press, 1974.

———. "Rangers, Scouts, and Tythingmen." In *Forty Years of Diversity: Essays on Colonial Georgia,* edited by Harvey H. Jackson and Phinizy Spalding, 152–62. Athens: University of Georgia Press, 1984.

———. "Scouting the Inland Passage, 1685–1737." *South Carolina Historical Magazine* 73 (1972):117–29.

Jackson, Jason Baird. "Yuchi." In *Southeast*, edited by Raymond D. Fogelson, 415–28. Vol. 14 of *Handbook of North American Indians*, edited by William C. Sturtevant. Washington, D.C.: Smithsonian Institution, 2004.

Klingberg, Frank J. "The Mystery of the Lost Yamasee Prince." *South Carolina Historical Magazine* 63 (1962):18–32.

Lawson, Cecil C. P. *A History of the Uniforms of the British Army: From the Beginnings to 1760.* 3 vols. London: Norman Military Publications, 1940–61.

LeMaster, Michelle, "War, Masculinity, and Alliances on the Carolina Frontiers." In *Creating and Contesting Carolina: Proprietary Era Histories*, edited by Michelle LeMaster and Bradford J. Wood, 164–185. Columbia: University of South Carolina Press, 2013.

Lerch, Patricia B. "Indians of the Carolinas since 1900." In *Southeast*, edited by Raymond D. Fogelson, 328–36. Vol. 14 of *Handbook of North American Indians*, edited by William C. Sturtevant. Washington, S.C.: Smithsonian Institution, 2004.

Levine, Victoria Lindsay. "Music." In *Mapping the Mississippian Shatter Zone: The Colonial Indian Slave Trade and Regional Instability in the American South*, edited by Robbie Etheridge and Sheri M. Shuck-Hall, 720–33. Lincoln: University of Nebraska Press, 2009.

Luzader, John. *Saratoga: A Military History of the Decisive Campaign of the American Revolution.* New York: Savas Batie, 2010.

McEwan, Bonnie G. "Apalachee and Neighboring Groups." In *Southeast*, edited by Raymond D. Fogelson, 669–76. Vol. 14 of *Handbook of North American Indians*, edited by William C. Sturtevant. Washington, D.C.: Smithsonian Institution, 2004.

McKivergan, Andrew. "Migration and Settlement among the Yamasee in South Carolina." M.A. thesis, University of South Carolina, 1991.

Mahon, John K. "Anglo-American Methods of Indian Warfare, 1676–1794." *Mississippi Valley Historical Review* 45 (1958):254–75.

Martin, Jack B. "Languages." In *Southeast*, edited by Raymond D. Fogelson, 68–86. Vol. 14 of *Handbook of North American Indians*, edited by William C. Sturtevant. Washington, D.C.: Smithsonian Institution, 2004.

Menard, Russell R. "Financing the Lowcountry Export Boom: Capital and Growth in Early Carolina." *William and Mary Quarterly* 51 (1994):659–76.

———. "Slave Demography in the Lowcountry, 1670–1740: From Frontier Society to Plantation Regime." *South Carolina Historical Magazine* 96 (1995):280–303.

Meriwether, Robert. *The Expansion of South Carolina, 1729–1765.* Kingsport, Tenn.: Southern Publishers, 1941.

Merrell, James. *The Indians' New World: Catawbas and Their Neighbors from European Contact through the Era of Removal.* Chapel Hill: University of North Carolina Press, 1989.

Merrens, H. Roy, and George D. Terry. "Dying in Paradise: Malaria, Mortality, and the Perceptual Environment in Colonial South Carolina." *Journal of Southern History* 50 (1984):553–50.

Michie, James L. "The Discovery of Old Fort Congaree." Research Manuscript Series, Scholar Commons, University of South Carolina, no. 193. Columbia: University of South Carolina, http://scholarcommons.sc.edu/cgi/viewcontent.cgi?article=1192&context=archanth_books (accessed July 3, 2013).

Milling, Chapman J. *Red Carolinians.* Chapel Hill: University of North Carolina Press, 1940.

Moore, Alexander. "Daniel Axtell's Account Book and the Economy of Early South Carolina." *South Carolina Historical Magazine* 95 (1994):280–301.

——. "Marooned: Politics and Revolution in the Bahamas Islands and Carolina." In *Creating and Contesting Carolina: Proprietary Era Histories,* edited by Michelle LeMaster and Bradford J. Wood, 256–72. Columbia: University of South Carolina Press, 2013.

Mustard, Harry S. "On the Building of Fort Johnson." *South Carolina Historical Magazine* 64 (1963):129–35.

Oatis, Steven James. *A Colonial Complex: South Carolina's Frontiers in the Era of the Yamasee War, 1680–1730.* Lincoln: University of Nebraska Press, 2004.

Otto, John S. "The Origins of Cattle Ranching in Colonial South Carolina." *South Carolina Historical Magazine* 87 (1986):117–24.

Pennington, Edgar Legare. "The South Carolina Indian War of 1715 as Seen by the Colonial Missionaries." *South Carolina Historical and Genealogical Magazine* 32 (1931):251–99.

Perdue, Theda. "American Indian Survival in South Carolina." *South Carolina Historical Magazine* 108 (2007):215–34.

Peterson, Harold L. *Arms and Armor in Colonial America, 1526–1783.* Mineola, N.Y.: Dover, 2000.

Poyas, Elizabeth. *The Olden Times of Carolina.* Charleston, S.C.: Courtenay, 1855.

Pruden, Elizabeth M. "Investing Widows: Autonomy in a Nascent Capitalist Society." In *Money, Trade, and Power,* edited by Jack P. Greene, Rosemary Brana-Shute, and Randy J. Sparks, 344–62. Columbia: University of South Carolina Press, 2001.

Quarles, Benjamin. "The Colonial Militia and Negro Manpower." *Mississippi Valley Historical Review* 45 (1959):117–33.

Ramsay, David. *Ramsay's History of South Carolina from Its First Settlement in 1670 to the Year 1808.* 2 vols. Charleston, S.C.: Duffie, 1858.

Ramsey, William. *The Yamasee War: A Study of Culture, Economy, and Conflict in the Colonial South.* Lincoln: University of Nebraska Press, 2008.

Robertson, Heard, and Thomas H. Robertson. "The Town and Fort of Augusta." In *Colonial Augusta: Key of the Indian Country,* edited by Edward J. Cashin, 59–75. Macon, Ga.: Mercer University Press, 1986.

Rowland, Lawrence Sanders, Alexander Moore, and George Rogers Jr. *The*

History of Beaufort County, South Carolina. 2 vols. Columbia: University of South Carolina Press, 1996, 2006.

Rudes, Blair A., Thomas J. Blumer, and J. Alan May. "Catawba and Neighboring Groups." In *Southeast,* edited by Raymond D. Fogelson, 301–18. Vol. 14 of *Handbook of North American Indians,* edited by William C. Sturtevant. Washington, D.C.: Smithsonian Institution, 2004.

Salley, A. S., Jr. "Barnwell of South Carolina." *South Carolina Historical and Genealogical Magazine* 2 (1901):46–88.

———. "The Bull Family of South Carolina." *South Carolina Historical and Genealogical Magazine* 1 (1900):76–90.

———. "Governor Joseph Morton and Some of His Descendants." *South Carolina Historical and Genealogical Magazine* 5 (1904):108–16.

Salo, Edward. "The Development of the Combahee Ferry: An Ethnohistory of Ferry Transportation in the South Carolina Lowcountry." Paper presented at the North American Society for Oceanic History–Council of American Maritime Museums Conference, Pensacola, Florida, May 2008.

Scheerer, Hanno E. "The Proprietors Can't Undertake for What They Will Do: A Political Interpretation of the South Carolina Revolution of 1719." In *Creating and Contesting Carolina: Proprietary Era Histories,* edited by Michelle LeMaster and Brandford J. Wood, 273–94. Columbia: University of South Carolina Press, 2013.

Shuck-Hall, Sheri M. "Alabama and Coushatta Diaspora and Coalescence in the Mississippian Shatter Zone." In *Mapping the Mississippian Shatter Zone: The Colonial Slave Trade and Regional Instability in the American South,* edited by Robbie Etheridge and Sheri M. Shuck-Hall, 250–71. Lincoln: University of Nebraska Press, 2009.

Sirmans, Marion Eugene. *Colonial South Carolina: A Political History.* Chapel Hill: University of North Carolina Press, 1966.

"Slavery in Province, Colony, and State." In *Yearbook of the City of Charleston,* vol. 2, 527–40. Charleston, S.C.: News and Courier Book Presses, 1883.

Smith, D. E. Huger. "An Account of the Tattnall and Fenwick Families in South Carolina." *South Carolina Historical and Genealogical Magazine* 14 (1913):3–19.

Smith, Henry A. M. "Ashepoo Barony." *South Carolina Historical and Genealogical Magazine* 15 (1914):63–72.

———. "The Ashley River: Its Seats and Settlements." *South Carolina Historical and Genealogical Magazine* 20 (1919):3–57, 75–122.

———. "Beaufort: The Original Plan and the Earliest Settlers." *South Carolina Historical and Genealogical Magazine* 9 (1908):141–60.

———. "Boone's Barony." *South Carolina Historical and Genealogical Magazine* 13 (1912):71–83.

———. "Charleston and Charleston Neck." *South Carolina Historical and Genealogical Magazine* 19 (1918):3–76.

———. "The Fairlawn Barony." *South Carolina Historical and Genealogical Magazine* 11 (1910):193–202.

——. "Quenby and the Eastern Branch of Cooper River." *South Carolina Historical and Genealogical Magazine* 18 (1917):3–36.

——. "Radnor, Edmundsbury and Jacksonborough." *South Carolina Historical and Genealogical Magazine* 11 (1910):39–49.

——. "Some Forgotten Towns in Lower South Carolina." *South Carolina Historical and Genealogical Magazine* 14 (1913):132–46.

——. "Tomotley Barony." *South Carolina Historical and Genealogical Magazine* 15 (1914):9–12.

——. "The Upper Ashley and the Mutations of Families." *South Carolina Historical and Genealogical Magazine* 20 (1919):151–98.

——. "Willtown or New London." *South Carolina Historical and Genealogical Magazine* 10 (1909):20–32.

Smith, Roy W. *South Carolina as a Royal Province, 1719–1776.* New York: Macmillan Company, 1903.

Smith, Warren B. *White Servitude in Colonial South Carolina.* Columbia: University of South Carolina Press, 1961.

Stern, Jessica. "The Economic Philosophies of Indian Trade Regulation Policy in Early South Carolina." In *Creating and Contesting Carolina: Proprietary Era Histories,* edited by Michelle LeMaster and Bradford J. Wood, 97–117. Columbia: University of South Carolina Press, 2013.

Stumpf, Stuart O. "Edward Randolph's Attack on Proprietary Government in South Carolina." *South Carolina Historical Magazine* 79 (1978): 6–18.

Swanton, John R. *The Early History of the Creek Indians and Their Neighbors.* Gainesville: University Press of Florida, 1998.

——. *Indians of the Southeastern United States.* Washington, D.C.: Smithsonian Institution, 1946.

Sweeney, Alex. *The Archaeology of Indian Slavers and Colonial Allies: Excavations at the Yamasee Capital of Altamaha Town.* Atlanta: Brockington, 2009.

TePaske, John Jay. *The Governorship of Spanish Florida, 1700–1763.* Durham, N.C.: Duke University Press, 1964.

Tunis, Edwin. *Colonial Living.* Cleveland: World, 1957.

Urban, Greg, and Jason Baird Jackson. "Social Organization." In *Southeast,* edited by Raymond D. Fogelson, 697–706. Vol. 14 of *Handbook of North American Indians,* edited by William C. Sturtevant. Washington, D.C.: Smithsonian Institution, 2004.

Van Ruymbeke, Bertrand. "The Huguenots of Proprietary South Carolina: Patters on Migration and Integration," In *Money, Trade, and Power: The Evolution of Colonial South Carolina's Plantation Society,* edited by Jack P. Greene, Rosemary Brana-Shute, and Randy J. Sparks, 26–42. Columbia: University of South Carolina Press, 2001.

Waddell, Gene. *Indians of the South Carolina Lowcountry, 1562–1751.* Columbia: University of South Carolina Press, 1980.

Walker, Willard B. "Creek Confederacy before Removal." In *Southeast,* edited by Raymond D. Fogelson, 373–92. Vol. 14 of *Handbook of North American Indians,* edited by William C. Sturtevant. Washington, D.C.: Smithsonian Institution, 2004.

Waring, Joseph I. "Colonial Medicine in Georgia and South Carolina." *Georgia Historical Quarterly* 69 (1975): S141–S53.

Webber, Mabel L. "Colonel Alexander Parris, and Parris Island." *South Carolina Historical and Genealogical Magazine* 26 (1925):137–45.

———. "The First Governor Moore and His Children." *South Carolina Historical and Genealogical Magazine* 37 (1936):1–23.

Williams, Justin. "English Mercantilism and Carolina Naval Stores, 1705–1776." *Journal of Southern History* 1 (1935):169–85.

Winston, Lane, Jr. "Economic Power among Eighteenth-Century Women of the Carolina Lowcountry: Four Generations of Middleton Women, 1678–1800." In *Money, Trade, and Power,* edited by Jack P. Greene, Rosemary Brana-Shute, and Randy J. Sparks, 322–43. Columbia: University of South Carolina Press, 2001.

Wood, Bradford J., "'A Constant Attendance on God's Alter': Death, Disease, and the Anglican Church in Colonial South Carolina, 1706–1750." *South Carolina Historical Magazine* 100 (1999):204–20.

Wood, Virginia Steele. "The Georgia Navy's Dramatic Victory of April 19, 1778." *Georgia Historical Quarterly* 90 (2006):165–95.

Woods, Michael. "The Culture of Credit in Colonial Charleston." *South Carolina Historical Magazine* 99 (1998):358–80.

Worth, John E. "Guale." In *Southeast,* edited by Raymond D. Fogelson, 238–44. Vol. 14 of *Handbook of North American Indians,* edited by William C. Sturtevant. Washington, D.C.: Smithsonian Institution, 2004.

———. "Razing Florida: The Indian Slave Trade and the Devastation of Spanish Florida, 1659–1715." In *Mapping the Mississippian Shatter Zone: The Colonial Indian Slave Trade and Regional Instability in the American South,* edited by Robbie Etheridge and Sheri M. Shuck-Hall, 295–311. Lincoln: University of Nebraska Press, 2009.

———. *The Struggle for the Georgia Coast: An Eighteenth-Century Spanish Retrospective of Guale and Mocama.* New York: American Museum of Natural History, 1995.

———. *The Timucuan Chiefdoms of Spanish Florida.* 2 vols. Gainesville: University Press of Florida, 1998.

———. "Yamasee." In *Southeast,* edited by Raymond D. Fogelson, 245–53. Vol. 14 of *Handbook of North American Indians,* edited by William C. Sturtevant. Washington, D.C.: Smithsonian Institution, 2004.

Zierden, Martha, Suzanne Linder, and Ronald Anthony. *Willtown: An Archaeological and Historical Perspective.* Charleston: South Carolina Department of Archives and History, 1999.

Index ———